THE RELIGIOUS PHILOSOPHY
OF TANABE HAJIME

NANZAN STUDIES IN RELIGION AND CULTURE
James W. Heisig, General Editor

Heinrich Dumoulin, *Zen Buddhism: A History. Vol. 1, India and China*. Trans. by J. Heisig and Paul Knitter (New York: Macmillan, 1988).

Heinrich Dumoulin, *Zen Buddhism: A History. Vol. 2, Japan*. Trans. by J. Heisig and Paul Knitter (New York: Macmillan, 1989).

Frederick Franck, ed., *The Buddha Eye: An Anthology of the Kyoto School* (New York: Crossroad, 1982).

Winston L. King, *Death Was His Kōan: The Samurai-Zen of Suzuki Shōsan*, with a Foreword by Nakamura Hajime (Berkeley: Asian Humanities Press, 1986).

Robert E. Morrell, *Early Kamakura Buddhism: A Minority Report* (Berkeley: Asian Humanities Press, 1987).

Nagao Gadjin, *The Foundational Standpoint of Mādhyamika Philosophy*. Trans. by John Keenan (Albany, SUNY Press, 1989).

Nishitani Keiji, *Religion and Nothingness*. Trans. by Jan Van Bragt with an Introduction by Winston L. King (Berkeley: University of California Press, 1982).

Nishitani Keiji, *Nishida Kitarō*. Trans. by Yamamoto Seisaku and J. Heisig (Berkeley: University of California Press, forthcoming).

Nishitani Keiji, *The Self-Overcoming of Nihilism*. Trans. by G. Parkes and S. Aihara (Albany: SUNY Press, 1990).

Nishida Kitarō, *Intuition and Reflection in Self-Consciousness*. Trans. by Valdo Viglielmo et al., with an Introduction by Joseph O'Leary (Albany: SUNY Press, 1987).

Paul Swanson, *Foundations of T'ien-T'ai Philosophy: The Flowering of the Two Truths Theory in Chinese Buddhism* (Berkeley: Asian Humanities Press, 1989).

Takeuchi Yoshinori, *The Heart of Buddhism: In Search of the Timeless Spirit of Primitive Buddhism*. Trans. with Introduction by J. Heisig and a Foreword by Hans Küng (New York: Crossroad, 1983).

Tanabe Hajime, *Philosophy as Metanoetics*. Trans. by Takeuchi Yoshinori et al., with an Introduction by J. Heisig (Berkeley: University of California Press, 1987).

Taitetsu Unno, ed., *The Religious Philosophy of Nishitani Keiji: Encounter with Emptiness* (Berkeley: Asian Humanities Press, 1990).

Hans Waldenfels, *Absolute Nothingness: Foundations for a Buddhist-Christian Dialogue*. Trans. by J. Heisig (Ramsey, NJ: Paulist Press, 1980).

THE RELIGIOUS PHILOSOPHY
OF TANABE HAJIME

THE METANOETIC IMPERATIVE

EDITED BY

Taitetsu Unno

&

James W. Heisig

ASIAN HUMANITIES PRESS
Berkeley, California

ASIAN HUMANITIES PRESS

Asian Humanities Press offers to the specialist and the general reader alike the best in new translations of major works and significant original contributions to our understanding of Asian religions, cultures, and thought.

Library of Congress Cataloging-in-Publication Data

The Religious philosophy of Tanabe Hajime: the metanoetic imperative / edited by Taitetsu Unno & James W. Heisig
(Nanzan studies in religion and culture)
  Papers presented at an International Symposium on Metanoetics, held at Smith College, Fall 1989.
  Includes bibliographical references and index
  ISBN 0-89581-872-8 (cloth), — ISBN 0-89581-873-6 (paper)
  1. Tanabe, Hajime, 1885 — Congresses. 2. Religion-Philosophy—Congresses. 3. Philosophy, Buddhist—Congresses. I. Unno, Taitetsu, 1929– .
II. Heisig, James W., 1944– . III. International Symposium on Metanoetics (1989: Smith College). IV. Title: Metanoetics. V. Series.
B5244.T34R45 1990
  200'.56—dc20   90-41500
                                                                           CIP

CONTENTS

PART THREE: PHILOSOPHY

PART FOUR: SOCIETY

Editors' Introduction

The essays brought together in this volume are offered as an interdisciplinary, intercultural response to *Philosophy as Metanoetics,* a pivotal work in the religious philosophy of Tanabe Hajime (1885-1962). Most of the contributions were first presented at an "International Symposium on Metanoetics" held at Smith College in the fall of 1989.

As the successor of Nishida Kitarō, who is generally credited with being the first modern philosopher of Japan, Tanabe shared the vision of applying the rigors of the Western philosophical tradition to the intellectual tradition of Japan and at the same time cultivating a more Oriental expression to philosophical questions. As with Nishida, this led Tanabe away from the separation of philosophy and religion that has characterized philosophy in the West and towards a standpoint in which the two work symbiotically, distinguishable but inseparable.

It is hardly surprising that a thinker as saturated with the philosophical spirit as Tanabe would eventually apply his critical mind to the work of his teacher and set off in a new direction of his own. Whereas Nishida had laid the greatest accent on the "Zen experience" and only later in life made an effort to incorporate the insights of Pure Land Buddhism, *Philosophy as Metanoetics* sets itself squarely in the Pure Land tradition of Shinran, relegating Zen to a secondary position. Behind this difference in religious perspective lay a decade and more of a growing impatience on Tanabe's part with some of the key concepts of Nishida. More immediately, the work stands against the backdrop of Japan's aggressive failure in the Pacific War. All of this is woven, subtly but unmistakably, into Tanabe's argument for a philosophy of metanoia, a "philosophy that is not a philosophy."

As the essays in this volume should make plain, the particular history surrounding the composition of Tanabe's work is far from rendering it an esoteric text of interest only to Japanologists. Experience in adopting *Philosophy as Metanoetics* for seminars on Buddhism has demonstrated the appeal of its rigorous intellectual analysis, radical self-criticism, powerful integrity of feeling, and confessional tone bordering on religious faith. More importantly, it has spawned questions about the relationship between philosophy and religion, Shin Buddhism and Christianity, and personal and social transformation, as well as about the impact of historical events on philosophical thought.

If the English translation—painstakingly prepared under the direction of Tanabe's most illustrious living disciple and a ranking philosopher in his own right, Takeuchi Yoshinori—has made Tanabe's thought accessible to a wider Western readership, it must be seen as no more than a *partial* translation. Only the ongoing translation of its content into modes of thinking and questioning different from Tanabe's own can truly "carry it over" from Tanabe's world to our own. It was with this in mind that fifteen scholars from the United States, Japan, Germany, and Canada gathered at Smith College in the first week of October of 1989 for three intense days of discussion.

The contents of the present volume reflect the design of the symposium itself. Opening recollections of Professor Tanabe by Takeuchi Yoshinori, public lectures by James Heisig on the Kyoto School in general and by Langdon Gilkey on Tanabe's philosophy of religion in particular, and a detailed analysis of *Philosophy as Metanoetics* by James Fredericks set the stage for the four panels on the meaning of metanoetics for Shin Buddhism, Christianity, Philosophy, and Society. Among the many questions that came up for discussion in the course of the four panels, the matter of the role of Tanabe and the Kyoto school in fostering Japanese nationalism and the spirit of military expansionism during World War II found the least agreement among participants. The variety of information and perspectives brought to bear on this difficult question, now a half century later, only served to highlight the need for more careful attention to the use and abuse of intellectual conscience under imperialist, colonialist, or militaristic regimes.

The success of the Symposium and the publication of this volume was the result of much hard work by more persons than space allows us to acknowledge. We are especially grateful to Mary Maples Dunn, President of Smith College, and Robert Merrit, Dean of the Faculty, for their support and participation in the project; to all the colleagues in religious studies who played an active role in the proceedings, whether by chairing the panels

(Elizabeth Carr, Karl Donfried, Dennis Hudson, and Janet Gyatso) or preparing responses for discussion (Jean Higgins, Quentin Quesnell, Carol Zaleski, and Jamie Hubbard); to research assistants Caroline Butterworth and Susan Olson, who worked selflessly behind the scenes; to the administrative assistant of the religion department, Donna Gunn, whose organizational talents behind the scenes made everything immeasurably easier for all; and to the generous financial support provided by the Japan Foundation, the Ada Howe Kent Fund, and the Jacob Ziskind Fund of Smith College.

The editors join together with the contributors in hoping that this small volume may serve as one more stepping stone on the path that leads religious and philosophical traditions of the world into dialogue with each other.

CONTRIBUTORS

JAMES FREDERICKS currently teaches systematic theology at St. Patrick's Seminary in Menlo Park, California. His area of research is the Kyoto school of philosophy, especially the contributions of Tanabe Hajime, and he has published articles in the *Horizon* and *The Eastern Buddhist.*

LANGDON GILKEY is Shailer Mathews Professor Emeritus of Theology at the Divinity School, University of Chicago. His numerous writings in the field of philosophical and religious discourse include *Naming the Whirlwind: The Renewal of God-Language.*

HASE SHŌTŌ 長谷正当 recently assumed the Chair of Philosophy and Religion at Kyoto University. A specialist in French philosophy of religion, he has edited several philosophical collections in the field and is the author of *Symbol and Imagination* (in Japanese).

JAMES W. HEISIG is a Permanent Fellow of the Nanzan Institute for Religion and Culture in Nagoya, Japan. In addition to numerous books, articles, and translations in the philosophy and psychology of religion, he was part of the team responsible for the translation of Tanabe's *Philosophy as Metanoetics.*

JEAN HIGGINS is Professor of Religion and Biblical Literature at Smith College. Specializing in Christian theology and religion and literature, East and West, her publications include studies on the Japanese novelist, Endō Shūsaku, and comparative analyses of Shinran and Luther.

HIMI KIYOSHI 氷見 潔 studied philosophy at Kyoto University before taking up his current post as Associate Professor of Philosophy at Nara Prefectural College, Japan. He has published widely in Japanese journals on the thought of Tanabe and on the philosophy of religion.

JAMIE B. HUBBARD is Numata Lecturer in Buddhist Studies at Smith College. His research deals with the relationship between Buddhist doctrine and institution, focusing on Chinese economic and social welfare organizations. He is editor of the Buddhist section of the American Academy of Religion newsletter and producer of the BBC film, "The Yamaguchi Story: Buddhism and the Family in Contemporary Japan."

KAWAMURA EIKO 川村永子 did doctoral studies in systematic theology at Hamburg University, and is currently Professor of Religion at Hanazono University, Kyoto. Her many publications on the Kyoto school include a recent work on *Christianity and Nishida Philosophy.*

WHALEN LAI is Professor of Religious Studies and Chairman of the Department at the University of California, Davis. In addition to numerous articles on Chinese Buddhism and philosophy, he is co-editor of *Early Ch'an in China and Tibet.*

JOHANNES LAUBE is Professor of Japanology at the University of München. His publications focus on religion and philosophy of modern Japan, and include a study of Tanabe's philosophy of religion, *Dialektick der absoluten Vermittlung.*

JOHN MARALDO is Professor of Philosophy at the University of North Florida. In addition to many essays on the thought of Dōgen and Nishida, he is co-author of *Piety of Thinking: Martin Heidegger* and co-editor of *Buddhism in the Modern World.*

DONALD MITCHELL is Associate Professor of Philosophy at Purdue University. Along with his own research and publications in the area of comparative philosophy and spirituality, he is editor of the Newsletter of the Society for Buddhist-Christian Studies and a member of the steering committee of the International Buddhist-Christian Theological Encounter Group.

QUENTIN QUESNELL is Rowe/Straut Professor in the Humanities and Chairman of the Department of Religion at Smith College. He works in both New Testament exegesis and philosophical theology. His principal publications include *The Mind of Mark* and *The Authority of Authority.*

TAKEUCHI YOSHINORI 武内義範 is Professor Emeritus of Philosphy and Religion at Kyoto University, where he had succeeded Tanabe Hajime. A representative sampling of his many works has been published in English under the title *The Heart of Buddhism*.

UEDA YOSHIFUMI 上田義文 is Professor Emeritus of Indian Philosophy and Buddhist Studies at Nagoya University, Japan. Besides many works on Buddhist philosophy in Japanese, he serves as general editor of the Shin Buddhism Translation Series in which the complete works of Shinran are being published. He is co-author of *Shinran: An Introduction to His Thought*.

TAITETSU UNNO is Jill Ker Conway Professor of Religion and East Asian Studies at Smith College. In addition to numerous publications in the area of East Asian Buddhist thought, he serves on the board of directors of the Society for Buddhist-Christian Studies and is the editor of *The Religious Philosophy of Nishitani Keiji: Encounter with Emptiness*.

YAMASHITA TADANORI 山下忠規 is Professor of Religion at Mt. Holyoke College. His teaching and research center on ancient Near East and Japanese religion and culture. He is the author of *Goddess Asherah*.

JEFFREY WATTLES, formerly with the Centre for Religious Studies at the University of Toronto, is currently Assistant Professor of Philosophy at Kent State University. Specializing in the field of religious philosophy, a work dealing with the concepts of truth, beauty, and goodness as they relate to the philosophy of living is forthcoming.

CAROL ZALESKY is Assistant Professor in the Department of Religion and Biblical Literature at Smith College. Her chief interest is in the interpretation of religious experience from the standpoint of the philosophy and comparative history of religion. She is the author of *Other World Journeys: Accounts of Near-Death Experience in Medieval and Modern Times*.

ABBREVIATIONS USED IN THIS WORK

MN   *Monumenta Nipponica.*

NKZ   西田幾多郎全集 *[Collected Works of Nishida Kitarō].* Tokyo: Iwanami, 1978. 19 vols.

PM   Tanabe Hajime, *Philosophy as Metanoetics.* Berkeley: University of California Press, 1986. Translated by Takeuchi Yoshinori with a Foreword by James W. Heisig.

RN   Nishitani Keiji, *Religion and Nothingness.* Berkeley: University of California Press, 1982. Translated by Jan Van Bragt with a Foreword by Winston L. King.

THZ   田辺元全集 *[Collected Works of Tanabe Hajime]* (Tokyo: Chikuma Shobō, 1964), 15 vols.

ZMK   絶対無と神 — 西田・田辺哲学の伝統とキリスト教 *[Absolute Nothingness and God: The Nishida-Tanabe Philosophical Tradition and Christianity],* ed. by the Nanzan Institute for Religion and Culture. Tokyo: Shunjūsha, 1981.

Recollections of Professor Tanabe

TAKEUCHI Yoshinori

ON the occasion of this International Symposium which has as one of the focal points of East-West exchange the philosophy of Tanabe Sensei I am filled with the greatest joy. I had really looked forward to it as a learning experience for myself, but unfortunately bad health has forced me to change my plans. The brief paper I have prepared for the Symposium is a kind of snapshot of Tanabe Sensei. Sensei disliked being photographed. As a result very few pictures of him remain, and those that do are amateur. What I have described in the following pages falls in the same class.

I

I first received instruction from Dr. Tanabe in 1933, the year after he had published his *Hegel's Philosophy and Dialectics*.[1] I distinctly remember the day I saw it in the "New Books" section of the Maruzen Book Store in Sendai. Although I was able to understand almost nothing of the work as I was still a student in upper school (equivalent to a college sophomore today), the last few lines of the Preface left a deep impression upon me:

> I must confess that I have greater hopes and expectations of those who are now just beginning the adventure of thought than thinkers who have already established their own views.

Moved by these words I read the two essays at the beginning of this volume over and over, and finally made up my mind to become his student.

I can still recall the excitement the first time I heard him lecture on the introduction to philosophy. Dr. Tanabe arrived

---

[1] ヘーゲル哲学と弁証法 THZ 3:73-369.

right on schedule and entered the room, which was filled with students from several faculties of Kyoto University, as well as numerous older auditors. His noticeably white hair was cropped close to his head. At first I could not believe that this rustic old man with his squared face was the "Professor Tanabe" of my dreams. (My views were no doubt biased by my rural background, leaving me quite out of touch with the conservative fashions that were in vogue in Tokyo at the time.) For a moment I thought that a professor of Buddhist Studies, Indian Philosophy, or Asian Studies had wandered in by mistake. But all such thoughts vanished as soon as he took the podium and began to speak.

As I recall, he used to give the lectures for both his regular philosophy courses and his seminar on "Topics in Philosophy" in Lecture Hall 1. Not even a trace remains today of this hall, which used to be the largest of its kind in the Faculty of Letters; for those of us who were there, all that exists are the ghosts of old memories. Even in its prime, however, it had a sort of ghoulish appearance as it stood enormous and isolated from the rest of the campus in the midst of some pine woods. Still, students from all over the Kyoto-Osaka-Kobe region, many of them already well-known scholars in their own right, filled the hall from wall to wall, and a singular atmosphere of tension permeated the room.

Dr. Tanabe would appear, take the podium, look slightly to the side, and greet the students in his own unique manner. He would pick up a piece of chalk and concentrate his thoughts in stillness. One could almost see the light of his intellectual activity radiating from between his brows. There was a sense of painful and suffocating intensity which had probably been building up in him since the previous night, a night of little sleep. We would catch our breaths. When he finally began to speak, it was in a slow whisper, so that not even those in the front who strained their ears could hear him very well. But this was only the beginning, like the quiet mists of an incipient storm. Eventually the powerful flow of his thought filled the room. For nearly one hour and forty minutes we were blown about by the gales of his cogitations, until we were literally left breathless at the end.

Speaking of his lectures as a project in progress, he would say, "I am going to invite you into my workshop." His workshop was always in spotless order. (I was once allowed into his private study, and it was the same.) Twenty minutes before the end of the lecture, always precisely at eleven-thirty, he would take his watch out of his fob. The train of his thought proceeded exactly on schedule, thoroughly organized; and yet at the same time it was also en route, in the making. This had not changed in the least in his later writings in Kita-Karuizawa, which were eventually published as *Introduction to Philosophy*.[2] Even his attire remained the same. But I do feel that the earlier period before *Philosophy as Metanoetics*, the period in which he formulated his "logic of species," best reflects the unique rigor of his thought, which was simultaneously in process and complete at each moment.

Hearing that he received visitors on Saturdays, I went to his home immediately after the first lecture. I wrote about this in the postscript to the publication of Yasuda Jirō's posthumous work where I recount my memories of the author. It captures some of the atmosphere of Dr. Tanabe's home, since I had no intention of writing about him directly:

> I will never forget that day when I first met Yasuda Jirō. It was a Saturday in the latter part of April, 1933. I visited Dr. Tanabe shortly after enrolling at Kyoto University. There were already a number of guests present engaged in vigorous discussion, with him at the center of the lively exchanges. As the conversation progressed I came to learn that the others were mostly up and coming thinkers who had already made a name for themselves in philosophical circles. I had just begun to tread the path of philosophy, and the high-level discourse taking place around me seemed almost miraculous.
>
> When it grew dark and everyone was about to go home, Dr. Tanabe stopped a few of us new students and spoke to us with great gentleness: "Since there were many older people here it was probably difficult for you to talk. Please take the time now to ask about anything you like." Thus encouraged, each of us explained why we wanted to study philosophy, asked what books we should read, and so on.
>
> As we left his home, the setting sun was casting its last brilliant rays upon the boulevard of Yoshida. By coincidence I found myself together with Yasuda and Andō Takayuki. We

---

[2] The several volumes have been collected in vol. 11 of Tanabe's *Collected Works*.

introduced ourselves to each other, as our shadows fell on the orange-hued earthen walls along the road.[3]

No doubt this was a common experience among those of us who gathered at Dr. Tanabe's home and developed close friendships.

Many students formed small reading circles to discuss philosophical texts of thinkers like Hegel or Kant, and we would often go together to visit Dr. Tanabe. He never engaged in small talk. Whenever we called on him, we knew he would greet us with the words, "Why have you come?", and hence always came prepared with a couple of questions we had put together the day before. Often they would be about the text from our reading groups or a difficult point regarding his lectures. He would often respond with his own difficult questions, as though putting us through an oral examination.

Professor Tanabe's personality evoked great fear in us. When I visited him on Saturdays, it felt as though I were walking on thin ice. By the time I went home my neck and shoulders were completely stiff, and I could hardly sleep that night. Yet I always felt as though I had gained more than if I had stayed up two or three nights studying. I put up with the pain because of the sense of satisfaction it gave me. Senior professors like Kōsaka, Nishitani, Shimomura, and Kōyama would often arrive around three in the afternoon, and form a circle of heated discussion. Sometimes the same problems we younger students had raised would be repeated in different form. Dr. Tanabe's attitude was always the same, whether he was speaking with professors or students. The nature of his philosophical dialogue may be compared to a lion concentrating all its energies on its prey, even if it is only a rabbit. At times we novices would be struck a painful blow, but we knew that it was motivated by our teacher's love of philosophy, waiting for us to recover before he would attack again.

II

Dr. Tanabe Hajime retired from his position as Professor of Philosophy in the Philosophy Department of the Faculty of Letters,

---

[3] 安田二郎 , 中国近世思想研究 *[Studies in Modern Chinese Thought]* (Tokyo, Kōbundō, 1948), 211.

Kyoto University, in March of 1945. It was just around that time that I had a chance to meet with Dr. Takahashi Satomi, Professor of Philosophy at Tōhoku University. I was deeply influenced by the unique thought of both of these thinkers who were regarded as the two great pillars of philosophy in Japan at the time.

At our meeting Dr. Takahashi expressed his gratitude for the fact that a figure such as Tanabe had been able to carry out the full duties of his academic post right up to his retirement. It was rare, he said, for a philosopher to fulfill his duties to the end without any major disruptions. The kind of persecution which befell Kant and Fichte is the more common fate of the philosopher. Those who were surrounded by favorable circumstances or able to overcome the contradictions facing them by the sheer power of practical wisdom are the exceptions to the rule. Others were able to avoid crises only by acquiescing to historical trends and settling for mediocrity.

Dr. Tanabe was not entirely free of the inner turmoil brought about by historical circumstance; in fact, his later years were filled with pain and struggle. At one point he seriously considered re-signing—and to this day it is my belief that had he done so he would have ended up committing suicide—but neither Dr. Taka-hashi nor I, who had been visiting Dr. Tanabe frequently during his period of illness, had the slightest intimation of this fact. We only conversed about philosophical matters, Buddhist thought (especially that of Shinran), and such religious poets as Rilke. I occasionally caught a glimpse of joy in his clear, serene eyes, as though the blue sky was breaking through the clouds—at such times I felt that Dr. Tanabe was truly at peace.

I had no inkling of the depth of anguish and the gravity of his inner state that resulted from his personal confrontation with the situation at large. As a man who demanded of himself the integrity to actualize his philosophical standpoint in his own life, Dr. Tanabe stood squarely in the midst of the tension and opposition between individual and societal concerns as Japan continued to tread the path of self-destruction. In my own case faith had been solely an inner, personal problem, and my thought had not yet developed to the point of integrating, paradoxically, faith with historical and social concerns. It shames me now to think that I had not realized this crucial aspect of Dr. Tanabe's thought when I had had the opportunity to study so closely with him—it was as though I had been sitting back to back with him in the same room, unable to appreciate his total presence.

1985 marked the hundredth anniversary of Dr. Tanabe's birth. That year Mrs. Hannah Tillich wrote to me that it was also the hundredth anniversary of Dr. Paul Tillich's birth. I had greatly admired Dr. Tillich, and called to mind an event indelibly branded in my memory. It was after a lecture that I heard him give at the University of Hamburg over twenty years ago. We were walking along a beautiful avenue near city hall on the way to his hotel. He suddenly stopped and asked me to wait for a while. After a brief silence he confessed to me:

> When I have the thought that someone who is walking in back of me might be going in the same direction, I am suddenly overcome with anxiety. When that happens, I wait for the person to pass me by before going on my way.

At that moment I shared his pain, thinking that he must still be harboring the wounds that he received when he was persecuted by the Nazis and fled to the United States. His systematic theology was a model of lucidity and his analysis of human *Angst* was penetrating. But in the depths of his own being there was an emotional turbulence, a discordant spirit crying out to the future. This, I thought, must be what the existentialist philosophers called "the outsider," the depth of a strong personality seen in the very weakness of being human. Perhaps it is only through the opening of these wounds that the contradictions and fissures at the depths of humanity and society are revealed.

As for myself there is no such profundity. To borrow Dr. Takahashi's words, I am nothing but one of those fortunate professors who has completed his academic career without any major incidents due to an excess of mediocrity.

III

In an essay entitled "The Limits of Existentialism,"[4] Dr. Tanabe focused on two of Jaspers's latest published works, *Vernunft und Existenz* (1935) and *Existenzphilosophie* (1938), noting that they differed from his earlier works by opening up to a new dimension,

---

[4] 実存哲学の限界 , THZ 7:1-24.

particularly evident in the second of the volumes. He showed how Jaspers's thought and experience had deepened and how his concepts had become clearer and more concise, thus giving new meaning to such notions as *Existenz, das Umgreifende,* and *Transcendenz.*

Dr. Tanabe developed these views in greater detail in a course entitled, "Existentialism vs. Phenomenology." In it Jaspers's new *Existenz Philosophie* was brought into confrontation with his own "logic of species," which was just taking shape. These investigations were published in October and December of 1941 under the title "The Development of Existential Concepts,"[5] but the publication of this journal was interrupted by the escalation of the war before Dr. Tanabe could bring his latest ideas to completion.

The publication of his work was thus brought temporarily to a halt, but he continued on his own, publishing the fruit of his labors over the next several years as "The Practical Structure of the Logic of Species."[6] There he dealt with the problem of reason and *Existenz* primarily from the perspective of modern philosophy, trying to elucidate the question on the basis of social existence and the development of the true significance of Hegelian dialectics. The two pivotal ideas around which his work revolved were (1) the activity of absolute nothingness as the middle term of a syllogism, taking the standpoint of what Hegel calls the "concrete universal"; and (2) the definition of genus, species, and individual as the deductive terms of the syllogism.

This train of thought was further developed in a book entitled *Philosophy, Poetry, and Religion,*[7] which focused on post-Hegelian philosophy, and on Heidegger in particular, but also encompassed ancient Greek philosophy and medieval philosophy as well. Dr. Tanabe clarified the relation between genus, species, and individual by examining Scotus's idea of *haecceitas* and dealing with the concept of the individual as it appears in the thought of such figures as Aquinas and Scotus. This line of thought is based on the view developed there that the idea of *Existenz* is originally rooted in *haecceitas*[8] and involves the problem of the universality

---

[5] 実存概念の発展 , THZ 7:211-50.

[6] THZ 7:253-372. The title in the collected works is 種の論理の弁証法 ["The Dialectic of the Logic of Species"].

[7] 哲学と詩と宗教 , THZ 13:307-520. See also his special Kita-Karuizawa lectures in THZ 15:287-417.

of love vis-à-vis the individual who turns his back on this love through sin.

In this stage of his thought we have yet to see the lines of development which would mature into the views as formulated in his final years. At this point, however, I would like to examine in greater detail the period in which his logic of species took shape.

IV

The "logic of species" may be seen as the driving principle behind the dynamism of deepening self-awareness linking the stage of Dr. Tanabe's thought represented by *Hegel's Philosophy and Dialectics* with the next stage, marked by his *Philosophy as Metanoetics*. In fact, the developments that took place in his thought after his metanoetics may broadly be regarded as a continuation of a train of thought already present in *The Dialectics of the Logic of Species*. This is not to deny the originality of his metanoetics, a new and unexpected principle of self-awareness, a new synthesis based on a breakthrough or leap beyond reason. In it we see the relation of a "discontinuous continuity and continuous discontinuity," that unique correspondence of double-exposure so characteristic of Tanabe's philosophy.

"Species" refers to the middle term of the logical sequence, type-species-individual. We may consider this in three steps.

First, in formal logic the universality of genus is determined by differences in species, thus establishing the concept of species. When the concept of species is successively determined in a similar manner, the concept of the individual will ultimately be attained. The syllogism performs a logical deduction on these three terms: genus, species, and individual. Take, for example, the classical syllogism:

> All men must die.
> Socrates is a man.
> Therefore, Socrates must die.

On this scheme, a logical deduction is set up that moves from possibility (genus) → man (species) → Socrates (individual). If the

---

[8] See THZ 7:213ff.

major premise that all men must die and the minor premise that Socrates is a man are correct, then the conclusion that Socrates must die becomes a necessary truth.

Second, we have just seen how a syllogism is deduced in the order genus→species→individual, but that it may also begin with the individual and be developed in the direction of greater universality in the order individual→species→genus. That is, the individuality of the individual is understood as "that which becomes the subject but does not become a predicate," grasping this fact through wisdom-intuition, or tracing it back in the direction of genus through experiential intuition. In most cases, however, we humans can neither perform the necessary induction with perfect precision nor exercise a wisdom-intuition untainted by sensuous intuition.

Whether we speak of the concept of the individual or the genus, we cannot but fall into contradiction when we attempt to grasp a perfectly concrete individual or a perfectly universal genus concept. Logic as formal syllogism cannot serve as a means of grasping the concrete truth or the necessity of this truth. If a syllogism is to be effective and concrete, the middle term must function in a manner similar to Hegel's "concrete universal."

In order to bring this about, genus (G) and individual (I) must be dialectically unified through species (S). Then, G and I, while standing in complete mutual contradiction, are lifted above *(aufgehoben)* the contradiction through S and enter into a concrete unified form, or synthesis. For this to take place, S must undergo self-negation in the midst of the mutual opposition and contradiction of G and I, identify itself with these two, and raise them to the level of the concrete manifestation of the truth. Hegel has depicted the mediatory function of the species as a concrete development of the middle term in the following three syllogisms:

$$G \to S \to I$$
$$S \to I \to G$$
$$I \to G \to S$$

That is, genus, species, and individual must each serve as the middle term and form a kind of circular relation wherein they are fused to become one through the three syllogisms. In other words, mediation as the absolute mediation, and the unique synthetic nature of species are both realized for the first time through the absolute mediation of genus, species, and individual.

This absolute mediation is the outstanding characteristic of the logic of species as a philosophy which realizes a unique self-awareness transcending Hegelian dialectics. Hegel's logic does contain a similar syllogism but in incomplete form and fails to attain the practical self-awareness realized by Tanabe.

In Tanabe's philosophy individuals confronting each other, consciously or unconsciously, express the societal power of contradiction, conflict, and opposition, but the individual also sacrifices itself and creates harmony and unity by abandonment to love, thus bringing the synthesis of I and Thou to completion and leading the opposing powers of society into harmony.

The foregoing has singled out a few aspects of the logic of species and the process of its formation that have been etched on my mind. In sum, this logic attains a greater degree of practical self-awareness through action than Hegel's dialectical logic; it is achieved through the development of a unique syllogism parallel to Hegel's use of the syllogistic form which was also the model for systematic self-understanding. Consequently the logic of species takes the form of an absolute mediation and begins to approach the Buddhist notion of 円融三諦 or "fusion of the three truths" which involves the three terms of 空 *emptiness,* 仮 *provisional truth,* and 中 *the middle.* As in Hegel's dialectic, the logic of species endeavors to elucidate the nature of such things as the nation-state, *Gesellschaft,* and *Gemeinschaft.* This in turn elevates existence to the standpoint of social praxis and has the effect of emphasizing what Jaspers calls the "battle of love."

Jaspers's notion of the Encompassing (*das Umgreifende*) of the Encompassing (spatiality), together with Hegel's syllogism, provides us with the locus for this "battle of love." This locus of love is also the eternal locus of communion. Supported by the bodhisattva's compassion-in-action realized in the two phases of going to and returning from the Pure Land, Jaspers's "communion of saints" is elevated to Emptiness as absolute negation.

V

As mentioned, Dr. Tanabe took up Jaspers's thought again in his courses from around 1938. Our interest in Jaspers was stimulated through these lectures. Later I heard from Ōshima Yasumasa that Dr. Tanabe tried to use the Cultural Exchange Agreement between Japan and Germany to assist Jaspers, who was being persecuted by the Nazis. The high acclaim that Jaspers was receiving in Japan may have had some positive influence in his resistance of the Nazis. Ultimately, of course, he was forced into a long exile from his homeland. I was deeply moved when, one spring evening in 1961, Jaspers told me in his study in Basel: "It was a great solace for me to know that I had good friends in the distant lands of East Asia. I will never forget the kindness that Dr. Tanabe extended to me during my most difficult days." When I told him then that Dr. Tanabe was ill, he joined me in thoughts of my teacher, his face clearly revealing his deep concern.

In one of his last works, *Die Grossen Philosophen* (1957), Jaspers probed the thought of such figures as Plato, Augustine, Kant, as well as Śākyamuni, Nāgārjuna, and Confucius. He told me that it was a great comfort for him during the painful war years to study the thought of these Eastern sages. As I listened to him, I could not help wondering if Dr. Tanabe might not have blended with and become part of Jaspers's image of these Eastern sages.

When it came time for me to leave, he gave me a copy of his recent work, *Schelling*, and signed it with the inscription, "In memory of the marvelous conversation with my friend, in gratitude, Basel, March 27, 1961, Karl Jaspers."[9] There was an irrepressible stirring in my heart when I later learned that he had personally corrected all of the proofs for this book. I accepted his tremendous generosity as the reflection of his feelings intended for Dr. Tanabe. I thought about the events of that day over and over as I walked back towards my inn in Basel along a quiet road lined with magnolia trees in blossom.

[Translated by Mark Unno]

---

[9] I would like to thank Professors Jan Van Bragt and Karl Neumann of Nanzan University for helping me decipher Jaspers's handwriting.

The Religious Philosophy
of the Kyoto School

James W. HEISIG

WHILE it seems clear enough that the thought of the "Kyoto School" belongs to the history of philosophy, indeed to the *world* history of philosophy, there is some difficulty defining its membership and placing it historically. In the West, the term is now broadly taken to refer to the intellectual tradition centered on the figure of Nishida Kitarō 西田幾多郎 , Japan's first original philosopher, who died in 1945 at the age of 75. Nishida was succeeded at Kyoto University by his disciple Tanabe Hajime, who died in 1962 at age 77. The "School" thus formed was carried on by another of Nishida's disciples, Nishitani Keiji 西谷啓治, who will be 90 next February.[1] These are the three pivotal personalities, and it is through a sort of "triangulation" of their respective positions that one can be said to operate within the tradition of the Kyoto school.[2]

Among the living figures federated to their circle, perhaps the best known in philosophical circles are Tanabe's principle disciple and a successor to Nishitani, Takeuchi Yoshinori 武内義範, and Ueda Shizuteru 上田閑照, a disciple of Nishitani who held the chair of Religion at Kyoto until just this year, conceding it to Professor Hase Shōtō 長谷正当 .

In Japan, one is more likely to hear in philosophical circles of "Nishida Philosophy" (where we may place Nishitani and Ueda) and "Tanabe Philosophy" (which Takeuchi is more closely affiliated with). These lines are not tightly drawn, and the term "Kyoto School" would really be more suitable, were it not for certain

---

[1] While Nishida and Tanabe held chairs in the department of philosophy, with Nishitani the chair moved to the department of religion.

[2] The term is Takeuchi's, 田辺哲学と絶対無 ["Absolute Nothingness and the Philosophy of Tanabe"], ZMK, 198.

unpleasant connotations that the term has come to bear because of post-war criticisms of the role of the Kyoto philosophers in supporting Japanese nationalism.

As nearly as I can determine, the term *Kyōto-gakuha* 京都学派 was introduced in 1932 by Tosaka Jun 戸坂　潤(1900–1945), the year after the Manchurian incident, which soon became a symbol for Japan's incipient policy of expansionism in Asia. For Tosaka the term pointed to a "hermeneutical, transhistorical, formalistic, romantic, phenomenological philosophy"—in short, a bourgeois ideology.[3] The number of thinkers he associated with the school was restricted to Nishida, Tanabe, and their immediate disciples,[4] and the political ideology he wished to attach to the name was one of "racial philosophy" and the "philosophy of total war." In time, the list of thinkers associated with the school by pro-Marxist, anti-nationalist thinkers like Tosaka grew. In any event, the appellation stuck, fairly well flattening out philosophical differences. Even Tanabe's eleventh hour call for a "metanoetics" to purge philosophy of its tainted innocence was viewed as courageous only in the sense that a dive from a burning ship can still be an act of courage for one who cannot swim. Only in later years would a serious attempt be made by those of the same persuasion to tell the story in fairer detail, albeit without departing the initial judgment.[5]

After the war the major figures of the Kyoto School survived with only minor bruises the furious attacks against all remnants of "imperialist philosophy" by Japan's strong emerging left, to resurrect and clear their name in the mainstream of philosophical

---

[3] 山田宗睦 Yamada Munemutsu, 昭和の精神史—京都学派の哲学 *[The Intellectual History of the Shōwa Period: The Philosophy of the Kyoto School]* (Kyoto, 1975) 280-81.

[4] These latter included Miki Kiyoshi 三木　清 (1897–1945), Kōsaka Masaaki 高坂正顕 (1900–1969), Kōyama Iwao 高山岩男 (1905–), and Nishitani Keiji (1900–).

[5] Yamada thus distinguishes in his book between figures on the "right" like Tanabe and Kōsaka, figures in the "center" like Nishida and Nishitani, and figures on the "left" like Miki, noting, however, that everything left and center gradually turned more and more to the right (38-106). The account of Ienaga Saburō 家永三郎, which centers its attention on Tanabe but also looks at the other key figures in the Kyoto School, is much more sensible and free of animus. See his 田辺元の思想史的研究 *[An Intellectual History of Tanabe Hajime]* (Tokyo, 1974), 1-176.

and religious academia. While something of the stigma remains, the role that Western interest in the religious philosophy of Nishida, Tanabe, and Nishitani has played to minimize it is not insignificant. Still, as more and more details of Japan's disastrous flirtation with nationalist expansionism are known and more and more study is undertaken into the diffusion of ideology and the role of Japan's intelligentsia in the process, there are those among Western historians who resent what they see as a camouflage of retreat into religious questions.[6]

This is not the place to untangle the threads of what can only look from the outside like a hopeless face-off between sideswipers and side-steppers, the one trying to apportion blame, the other resisting the effort. One longs for good debate and discussion of the issue, but so much is still so fresh to living memory, and so much resistant to a simple policing of history in the light of current events.

Permit me recourse to a story from the Chinese classic, *Zhan guo ce* 戰國策, to illustrate the choice I have made and then move on. It seems that a certain Ji-liang who, hearing that his master, the Lord of Wei, intended to launch an attack against the capital city of Handan, interrupted his journey and rushed back to the palace. Dusty and disheveled, he threw himself at the feet of the Lord of Wei, and eager to convince him that he would not become a true leader by trying to enlarge his kingdom at the expense of others, told his lord this story:

> I met a man in Daxing Mountains. His chariot was facing north and he told me that he was going to Chu. "But if you want to go to Chu," I asked him, "why are you headed north?"
>
> "I have a good horse," he told me.
>
> "Your horse may be good, but that does not make this the road to Chu," I replied.
>
> "I have plenty of provisions," he retorted.
>
> "However great your provisions, this is still not the way to Chu," I insisted.
>
> "Ah," but he replied, "my charioteer is first-rate."

---

[6] One of the most strongly-worded and uncompromising, if amply documented, statements written in this vein is an article (translated from the French) by Pierre Lavelle entitled "The Political Thought of Nishida Kitarō" which recently came to my attention in advance of publication.

"The stronger your horse, the better equipped you are, the more skillful your driver," I told him, "the further you will end up away from where you want to go."[7]

Read as a parable about the failure of the Kyoto School, the meaning is transparent. However respectable their research, however deep their philosophical reflections, it is to no avail if it is headed in the direction of a warring ideology. What purpose can it serve to look the horse in the mouth, examine the provisions, and test the driver? If the direction is wrong, what can be right?

There is a second, more sympathetic reading that I would invite you to consider. Careful study of the works of Nishida, Tanabe, and Nishitani is as rewarding as can be for those eager to lay the foundations for a world philosophical forum and point the way to a self-conscious religious pluralism. But that requires a sense of where these thinkers were headed—which is clearly *not* in the direction of a philosophy of war or nationalism or imperialist expansionism. Simply by being equipped with the tools to see how even noble philosophic and religious aims and disciplined thought can be perverted at their weakest point (in the present case, Japan's inexperience at assuming a role in the modern world after two centuries of isolation) is no guarantee that one has grasped their fundamental orientation. I do not mean to claim that the Kyoto philosophers are as innocent as, say, Nietzsche was, of the way his thought was twisted to the ends of patriotic nationalism; but only that what guilt there is does not belong among the fundamental inspirations of these three thinkers. Familiarity with the texts cannot, I think, yield any other conclusion. The irony is that in a sense, the failure of Japan's nationalist aims was a victory for the true aims of the Kyoto philosophers, calling them less to a laundering of their image than to a return to their fundamental inspirations.

There are other ironies in the fire, but to pull them out would distract us from the task that still remains to be done. For without some rudimentary poetic sense of what the adventure of philosophy is all about for the Kyoto philosophers, there is much that invites misunderstanding or trivialization. Unfortunately, such

---

[7] The story appears in Vol. 7/2 of the *Anli Wang* 安釐王 . The translation is my own.

insight is not as close to the surface of the texts as one might expect. More often than not it hides in the empty spaces between the lines, which the Japanese—who came rather late to writing, about a millennium after Western philosophy—value as ultimately a more reliable way of "loving wisdom" than the written word. I do not mean to say that there is anything more exotic or mysterious about the Kyoto philosophers than there is about, say, a Plato or a Boehme or a Heidegger. I only mean that their surface language and allusions to sources can be deceptive in the sense of hiding what is distinctive about their starting point.

Biographical outlines of the lives of Nishida, Tanabe, and Nishitani are available in introductions to translations of their work, or in standard philosophical references works, and need not detain us here. Our task is rather to try to put ourselves in a position to acquire a "knack" for what they were doing, which is precisely the way Nishida counseled his students to study Western philosophy in order to make it their own.[8] It begins with a recognition of the relative novelty of the philosophical disciplines in Japan when compared with the West.

To say that philosophy is new to Japan—in fact, it is only just over a century old—does not mean that it enjoyed a normal infancy. It was denied the natural aging process that produced Western philosophy as we know it. Fully twenty-three centuries earlier, the Greeks on the coast of Asia Minor, pressured by the advance of surrounding civilizations, had sought to break free of the confines of a mythical world-view and describe the world and its origins in natural, realistic terms. Within a century there emerged metaphysical principles which crystallized the critique of mythical anthropomorphism into conceptual terms and widening the way to an objective study of nature. This confrontation between the world beyond of the gods and the world of nature here below set an agenda to philosophy that continues to inform vast areas of Western culture.

---

[8] See Nishitani Keiji, 西田幾多郎—その人と思想 (Tokyo, 1984), 97-98. An English translation of this work by Yamamoto Seisaku and myself has been completed under the title *Nishida Kitarō*, and should be published in the near future.

The Japanese, in contrast, entered the world of modern philosophy standing on the shoulders of post-Kantian preoccupations with epistemology, scientific methodology, and the overcoming of metaphysics. Despite the remarkable advances that the study of philosophy made in Japan's institutions of higher learning, and the more remarkable fact that it took them only one generation to produce their first original philosopher in the person of Nishida Kitarō, they did not inherit the problem of where to locate literal truth and where the symbolic, or of how to deal with the progressive the triumph of reason over myth and science over religion. There was little symbolic theory or rationalist demythifying in their past to lend such a concern any of the emotional surplus it had in the West. One might say that in Japanese Buddhism—especially in the Zen form with which Nishida was most familiar—there is a spontaneous sense that in matters of the heart, literalness is pathological. It was this very failure to be moved by one of the major motive forces of received philosophical tradition that laid the ground for his own fresh and original contribution.

Another element not to be overlooked is the considerable machinations that the Japanese had to go through to translate philosophical works into their own language. In assimilating new ideas, they often preferred not to draw on terms from their own intellectual history and thus force assimilation, but to learn a foreign vocabulary and let it seep into the culture naturally. As ponderous and unattractive as this new vocabulary was, the etymological transparency lent to it by the Chinese characters made it more immediately suggestive than the Greek and Latin terms which philosophy has tended to adopt for its technical terminology have been to the West.

When borrowing words from Western languages, the Japanese typically take their flat, surface meaning only. They have no way to turn inside and unlock the door to associations of feeling or history through literature. One is disappointed, if hardly astonished, to see how little feeling Nishida had for the prose and allusions of the philosophers he read in French, English, and German.[9] But once the thought received Japanese expression, how-

---

[9] Nishida's German was best, followed by English and French. This predilection for reading Western philosophy in modern European langauges was shared by Tanabe and Nishitani and impressed strongly on their disciples, so

ever formidable the terminology, new doors are opened. Well before Heidegger's works were translated into English, and even
while the battles over how to render his wordplays into acceptable
idiom were waging, the Japanese proved their natural affinity for
his attempts to disclose the wonderful world within worlds of language. Among the Kyoto philosophers, Nishitani's writings stand
out for his ability to do the same thing. Still, even Nishida's and
Tanabe's heavy prose show at every turn the working of linguistic
associations peculiar to Japan and its intellectual history.

All of that by way of introduction. I would now like to single
out a number of ideas central to the Kyoto School, most of which
have their origins in Nishida's work.

SELF-AWARENESS

If there is one notion that seems to run like a golden thread
throughout the entire, rich tapestry that Kyoto philosophers have
woven, it is that of *jikaku* 自覚 or self-awareness.[10] Indeed, it served
Nishida as a critical tool for resisting the self-understanding being
urged on Japan from the outside world: the understanding of self
and world in terms of scientific theories of knowledge or philosophical ontology. It strikes me as a stroke of great originality on
Nishida's part that he did not simply seek to *preserve* Japan's
traditional self-understanding in the face of the onslaught of foreign ideas and ideals, but to submit it to the rigorous critique of
philosophy. The idea of self-awareness gave him a foothold from

---

much so that Miki once wrote an essay against the slighting of reading in translation. See his 読書と人生 *[Reading and Life]* (Tokyo, 1974), 117-20.

[10] Sueki Takehiro 末木剛博 has gone to great pains to show how Nishida's
philosophy can be read as a "system of self-awareness" in his elaborate four-vol-
ume study, 西田幾多郎—その哲学体系 *[The Philosophical System of Nishida Kitarō]*
(Tokyo, 1983-88). There are those, like Kōsaka Masaaki, who have seen Nishida's concern with *jikaku* as no more than one stage in his development. See his
西田幾多郎先生の生涯と思想 *[The Life and Thought of Nishida Kitarō]* (Tokyo,
1965), 62-64. More to the point is Ueda Shizuteru's attempt to see the notion of
jikaku as a fundamental inspiration informing all of Nishida's work, a notion that
found its depth in the Zen of pure experience (as *kaku*) and its breadth in the
reasons of philosophy (the dialectical unity of self and world). For a simplified
account, see his essay 西田哲学における宗教理解について ["The Understand-
ing of Religion in Nishida's Philosophy"], ZMK, 78-79.

which he might straddle two previously alien worlds to this purpose.[11]

In his lectures, Nishida is said time and again to have described his aim more concretely as seeking a rational foundation
for Zen.[12] For East and West alike, the project was counter-cul-
tural. On the one hand, the idea of using religious belief or
practice as a foundation for philosophy is something the West has
resisted vigorously, or at least tried to relegate to the realms of
theology. On the other, protagonists of Zen in the East had bran-
dished their irrationalities and paradoxes around like a sword that
cut through the presumption of rationalism and protected them
from outside criticism. Nishida set out to give a rational foundation
to Zen from outside of Zen, and in the process to put philosophy
to work when it was still no more than an infant on all fours.

In philosophical circles, *jikaku*—a not uncommon· word in
modern Japanese—was already being used to translate the Western
notion of self-consciousness. But for Nishida, it also served as a
fitting philosophical equivalent for Buddhist "enlightenment."[13] Its

---

[11] It is in this sense that I am inclined to understand many of Nishida's statements supposedly showing him up as a right-wing nationalist. For example, we
read in the Foreword to his book 働くものから見るものへ *[From Working to See-
ing]* (NCW 4:6):

> There is obviously a great deal to be admired and learned from the splendid
> developments in Western cultures that have found being and goodness in the
> form of things, but is there not something latent in the ground of Oriental
> cultures that our predecessors have nurtured for thousands of years, some-
> thing which sees the form of the formless and hears the voice of the voiceless?
> It is not enough that our hearts seek such things out; I wish also to give phil-
> osophical moorings to this desire.

[12] See Noda Matao 野田又夫 , 哲学の三つの伝統 *[Three Philosophical Tradi-
tions]* (Tokyo, 1984), 101-102. Nishida himself practiced *zazen* for ten years in his
30's. In his writings, however, Zen does not appear with anything like the reg-
ularity one might expect; overall, references to Zen hardly outnumber those to
other Buddhist traditions or even Christianity.

[13] *Jikoishiki* 自己意識 is also used by Nishida in early writings when he means
to draw attention to what he considers the limitations of the classical understanding of self-consciousness, or its variations in Kant's transcendental ego or
Husserl's eidetic consciousness. There is, of course, no question of confusing
such a Buddhist term for "enlightenment" with the meaning of the European
enlightenment. Indeed, it is the precise opposite of this latter. For it is not a matter of waking up to the symbolic nature of religious belief (both in theology and
philosophy) and letting the scientific spirit go ahead untrammeled, but of trans-

meaning is contained in a rather subtle double-entendre, both of whose meanings fly in the face of the usual meaning of self-consciousness—which is why it is best translated as *self-awareness*. It does not refer to awareness of oneself as a conscious being in the midst of the world, as a subject that exists in a realm of objects. Rather, it begins precisely where such self-consciousness exhausts itself.[14]

In its first meaning, *jikaku* refers to an awareness of a self other than the everyday self, a "true self" that *is* and yet needs to be *realized* by being awakened to.[15] Awakening to this self means that consciousness "sees" itself as an event in reality even as it "sees through" any attempt to set itself over against the incessant change and interdependence of all things that are in the world of being. It is not ordinary consciousness, which sets itself up as a knower of the world to be known and hence puts itself in a position to change it, but a sort of consciousness of being conscious in the world. In this sense, as Nishitani points out, self-awareness is not the awareness of a self set up in opposition to another, but of a true self in which self and other are no longer two.[16] The transformation of ordinary consciousness into self-awareness— an overtly religious event—is the primary fact that Nishida seeks to ground rationally through the discipline of philosophy.

The more Nishida learned of the history of philosophy, of

---

cending the dichotomies of such thinking.

Rorty's complaints about the captivity of Western philosophy by epistemology in *The Mirror of Nature* would have sounded self-evident to the Kyoto philosophers, even though they chose to work their way through the philosophy after the Kantian revolution.

[14] I now consider it a mistake to have gone along with "self-consciousness" as a translation in some earlier works of the Kyoto thinkers, because the connotations of this term in Western thought are too strong. For example, I think *Intuition and Reflection in Self-Awareness* to be more in the spirit of the meaning of Nishida's 自覚に於ける直観と反省 .

[15] Nakamura Yūjirō 中村雄二郎 finds a cognate here in Jung's distinction between "ego" and "self," the former referring to mere self-consciousness, the latter to self-awareness. See his 西田幾多郎 *[Nishida Kitarō]* (Tokyo, 1984), 66-71. The comparison is only superficially correct, and breaks down as he carries it further into its psychological ramifications. It would seem more accurate, and useful, to trace the idea in the West directly to Nietzsche, beginning with the third of his *Untimely Meditations*.

[16] See his *Nishida Kitarō*, 146-48.

course, and the deeper he threw himself into its stream, the more he realized that there were cognates to be found in the West for the notion of a self that loses itself in being aware of itself, and hence that there was no need to assume its strictly Buddhist quality. His task gradually came to take the shape of making the knowing, feeling, experiencing self of ordinary consciousness the maidservant of self-awareness—hence inverting Western philosophy as he met it.

The second meaning of the double-entendre of self-awareness can be stated simply: it is an awareness that unfolds itself spontaneously and out of itself, not the result of conscious technique. It is a *self*-awareness, not an achieved one. Its attainment is not the result of a disciplined attempt to mirror the things of life objectively in "reflection," and hence to *lead* awareness to the world, so much as an attempt to *follow* awareness to a point where self and world are one.

Compared with Nishida, Tanabe's understanding of *jikaku* developed slowly through his early writings on Kant and Hegel. In his later writings, he used the notion deliberately to stress his differences from Nishida, but the basic meaning, and the fact that it had to do with the goal of philosophical thought, were never questioned.[17] In contrast, Nishitani's most explicit treatment of the notion of *jikaku* as such is contained in his positive assessment of his debt to Nishida, even though it is in his own writings that the association of philosophy with the rational grounding of enlightenment is the clearest.

PURE EXPERIENCE

If the notion of self-awareness carries Nishida's search for a rational approach to religious enlightenment, it is the notion of "pure experience"—namely, experience prior to the distinction of subject and object—that carries his esteem for the Zen experience into the world of logic.

Given the aim of putting Western philosophy to work in the

---

[17] I take up this question in a later contribution to the present volume. Johannes Laube finds the notion of *jikaku* (which he distinguished from *Selbstbewusstsein* by writing it *SELBST-Bewusstsein*) "one of the Tanabe's most difficult terms." See his *Dialektik der absoluten Vermittlung* (Freiburg, 1984), 27-28.

quest for a rational grounding to Eastern enlightenment, it was obvious to Nishida from the start that a logic of substantial subjects and accidental predicates was not up to the task. A different set of forms for thinking, one that would reflect the "spontaneous self-unfolding of reality *in self-awareness*" and not be tied down to the subject-object dichotomy, was called for. In order for things to be related to one another in any form, one needs some sense of *where* separation and unification take place. Since Nishida was predisposed to see separation as the work of conscious discrimination, any appeal to a "universal" of thought to provide a principle of unification would have been like Baron von Munchausen pulling himself out of the swamp by his own pigtail. It seems to me that his whole philosophy was the search for a concrete logical universal that would escape this dilemma. I would distinguish five elements that combine—more or less like ascending "stages of thought"—in his philosophy to resolve this problem.[18]

In the first place, we have Nishida's idea of *pure experience*— that is, immediate experience in which the subject-object dichotomy has been overcome, and with it the primacy of the word over silence. To put the matter somewhat crudely: in contrast to Western philosophy after Kant, which seeks to draw unreflected language out of its initial naivete by uncovering its tacit presuppositions, only then to restore that language as the higher and purer *logos* of a post-reflective naivete, Nishida would see the role of disciplined reflection as recovering and enhancing the silence of experience for a higher self-awareness, at which point the tools of reflection and language drop away like crutches whose purpose has been served. Pure experience is not in any sense a naive realism, nor even the radical empiricism it was for William James, but a way of describing philosophically the cultivated achievement of self-awareness.

As a logical universal, pure experience makes unified consciousness the norm and relegates discrimination and distinction

---

[18] Japanese historians of philosophy have subjected Nishida's development to a dizzying array of schemes. Sueki lists several of the more important ones in the opening chapter to his *Nishida Kitarō*. Less important than sorting them out is the fact that Nishida himself viewed his work as a series of transitions from one standpoint to another, each adding new shifts of new vocabulary without departing from earlier insights. In this sense, the genealogy of his ideas is more transparent than that of Tanabe or Nishitani.

to an ancillary role. That is, it is both a universal category of thought that encompasses all other modes of thought and also a continued and very real achievement of mind. In Hegel's terms, which Nishida does not hesitate to use, it is a "concrete universal."

Pure experience is the best known idea of Nishida's best known work, *An Inquiry into the Good,* his first major study. It is not for that reason the best understood. As Nishitani points out in a brilliant study on that work which is as much a statement of his own mature thought as it is a careful reading in the hindsight of Nishida's later work, the adoption of the concept as a logical universal is difficult on two counts. As pure *experience*, it sets aside the traditional assumption that objectivity in truth is a function of reason; and as *pure* experience, its sees the truth as a function of cultivated "appropriation."[19] If reality and self-awareness are one, and if that one is rational, then the rational principle is one of a unity attained in consciousness. This is the experiment in thought that the term *pure experience* was meant to represent.

ACTING INTUITION

Now an idea of pure experience as a unifying principle of the universe (bringing together the objective world and the subjective world), and one that contains its own inbuilt moral imperative (the search for true self), looks suspiciously like a psychologistic reductionism. Not unaware of the criticism, Nishida had two ways to go.

The first was to look more closely at the dynamism that moves reality before it gets carved up into matter and consciousness. He was attracted to the vitalism of his time in general and to Bergson's idea of an *élan vital* in particular, but chose himself to speak of "need" (or perhaps better, the "desire") that reaches its culmination in self-awareness. This, he felt, would help make it clear that pure experience and the true self are not the exclusive property of the human world, even though human consciousness provides the analogy for talk about the universe in general. Unlike European philosophy, Nishida did not draw directly on evolutionary theory for his insight, perhaps because unlike the Christian West, Japan's religious mythologies were not directly threatened

---

[19] See *Nishida Kitarō*, ch. 6.

by the findings of science. There was no opposition, indeed something of a Buddhist sense of *déjà vu* about the idea that when a scientist looks through a microscope at an atom, what has actually happened is that the atom has finally reached the point that it can look at itself.

The second tack open to him was to look more closely at the way in which the mind actually sets itself up on an Archimedean point outside of the world, imagining that its knowledge gives it objective truth, and hence outlining the process by which this can be reversed. Particularly attractive for this latter direction was Fichte's idea of the *Tathandlung* (that all *data* about the objective world are ultimately the *capta* of consciousness). There was promise, Nishida felt, in the attempt to see the ground rules of logic as actually a projection of the ego's consciousness of itself. On Fichte's model, the principle of identity is based on the ego's positing of its own existence (*A* is *A*), and the principle of the excluded middle on its positing of the world of the not-ego (*A* is not *B*). Fittingly, Fichte had also seen that only in the moral insight that there was a single dynamism behind the world could this split be healed in true self-awareness.

Although Nishida's very earliest writings are full of hints about the former approach, many of which found there way into *An Inquiry into the Good*, he chose the latter course, landing himself in a dark tunnel of epistemological conundrums that he escaped from only with considerable difficulty.[20] The positive outcome of his tortured reflections was to provide a larger context to the two orientations by means of the idea of acting intuition, the second of his universal principles of logic.

If we may gloss over the course of the argument and look at the results, acting intuition is a conceptualization of the conversion in a *jikaku* way of looking at the relation between the self and the world.[21] On the face of it, acting and intuiting seem to represent two distinct but equally human ways of relating oneself to the world. Nishida's aim was to show their correlation in con-

---

[20] This was the tortured book *Intuition and Reflection in Self-Consciousness*. I originally sanctioned the title, but would now prefer to call it "Self-Awareness," for reasons described above.

[21] I am drawing here on the helpful account of Yuasa Yasuo in his book, *The Body* (New York, 1987), 50-52, 65-72.

sciousness and then to suggest that self-awareness is cultivated by inverting that relationship.

As a subject, I relate myself to the world—indeed I posit myself there—by acting on it, whether bodily or mentally. As mental action, this is reflection in which *(pace* Fichte's *Tathandlung)* the ego seeks to mirror the world, including itself, in itself.

Meantime, as an object in the world among other objects, I am acted upon passively by a dynamic that transcends me. This is what I experience as need or desire, and what in the mental realm Nishida refers to here as intuition. If reflective action invents the dichotomy of self and world, intuition discovers a unity there. It is part and parcel of all thinking, from everyday perceptions to artistic imagination and religious awakening.

Action and intuition are thus not opposite modes of being there for the choosing, but correlative components of consciousness. In all knowing, there is not only an active, reflective grasp of things but a passive intuition in which one is grasped by things. But for their synthesis to function as a logical universal of self-awareness, a conversion must take place. It must not be a matter of allowing mental intuition completely to overwhelm mental action, but of cultivating a new relationship in which intuition becomes active and action becomes passive. In other words, intuition has to be deliberately *cultivated* as a way of acting on the world, participating in the world's dynamic by expressing it in creative form, without interposing the subject-object dichotomy on it. Acting intuition thus amounts to purging the self of its Fichtean ego; as Nishida says, it is like a "seeing without a seer."

Nishida describes this conversion of self-awareness as "knowing a thing by becoming it" where one "becomes a thing by running up against it."[22] In acting intuition we know not by allowing ourselves to be a passive object before that which is to be known, but by actively casting ourselves out of our subjectivity, identifying with things.

Put in terms of will, we might say that acting intuition represents a purging of subjective wishes in order to become at one with the will (the universal need or desire) of reality. In a word, it is a conversion from the everyday self to the true self.

---

[22] The English translators of Yuasa's *The Body* miss the point here by rendering this as "becoming a thing and exhausting it" (70).

If this is a provisional answer to the self-enclosed psychologism of the universal of pure experience, the tendency towards a contemplative distancing of the self from concrete action in the world and human society remains. Nishida would try to set this right in his later works, but not until Tanabe had launched a frontal attack on the notion.

Nishitani, meantime, was persuaded that Nishida had corrected his tendency to psychologism with his logic of place,[23] to which we shall turn presently. While he does not often use the term *acting intuition* himself except when speaking directly of Nishida, he has made the idea of "knowing a thing by becoming it" a central theme in his mature work. Already from his early philosophical work, he was preoccupied with an analysis of subjectivity (a multivalent term in English which Japanese does a much better job of distinguishing) aimed at breaking through the Western notion of the ego that knows a world of objects.

In a later study on European nihilism, Nishitani reads the history of modern Western philosophy as a series of struggles to set up and knock down the idea of two worlds, the sensory and the suprasensory. In his now classic work, *Religion and Nothingness*, these same echoes of Nishida's acting intuition reverberate on all sides as he struggles to delineate a conversion to the world in its "true suchness," a world that is neither subjective nor substantial.[24]

Though you would not know it from my paraphrase, Nishitani's work shows a buoyancy of expression, an unabashed use of the Zen tradition, and a gift for concrete examples that make it stylistically Nishida's and Tanabe's superior. This is the sort of originality that shows up less in major innovations of thought than in a making intelligible and tangible much of what his predecessors had left in the abstract. Without Nishitani's genuine feel for the heart of the philosophical problems that Nishida and Tanabe were dealing with, I have no hesitation in saying that the term "Kyoto School" would have little of the currency it now enjoys.

---

[23] *Nishida Kitarō*, 91.
[24] For a brief statement, see RN, 125-28.

ABSOLUTE NOTHINGNESS

If the cultivation of acting intuition is a way of engaging oneself with things in such a way as to forfeit one's status as the mere passive subject of intuition and to deny the world its status as the mere object of intuition, it is clear that the "action" involved is not a manipulation of matter but a transformation of perspective towards reality. Until Nishida could come up with a universal that would include reality, the psychologism of his earlier writings was not fully overcome. It is here, I think that we have to see his reasons for introducing into philosophy the idea of Oriental nothing to replace the universal of being.

Nothing is not as alien a notion to our traditional Western modes of thought as we might think. Obviously, we know what it means that things that *are* pass away into things that *are not*. We have all at one time or another felt the reality of absence or loss, where there was once presence and meaning. Who among us does now know the enchantment of imaginary worlds? Or again, do we not commonly speak of the potential of things to be something other than what they are as "real"? And where would philosophy be without the ideals of the so-called "intelligible world" — ideas like freedom and love? Indeed, in one form or another, the reality of nothing is a necessary counterpart to our idea of being. If things could not *become*, if they could not *not be*, how could we talk about them *being*?

What the Kyoto philosophers have done, under Nishida's initial inspiration, is to draw the insight into nonbeing out of the realm of the privative and restore it to the level of being as the notion of *nothingness*, and then to elevate it above being as *absolute nothingness*. In a late work, Tanabe makes the point clearly:

> All science needs takes some entity or other as its object of study. The point of contact is always in being, not in nothing. The discipline that has to do with nothingness is philosophy. Religion encounters nothingness and overcomes it in faith, art in feeling; but it is only philosophy that deals with nothingness in *knowing* from the academic standpoint. Since Aristotle metaphysics has been defined as the study of existence as such, of being itself; but if being is something that can only be known concretely through the mediation of nothingness, it is

more fitting that we should define philosophy in terms of nothingness, paradoxical as this may look at first.[25]

Once given philosophical status, of course, the idea of absolute nothingness soon took on a role in philosophical thought altogether unfamiliar to the West, and it was only natural that its cognates in the Buddhist tradition would guide the course of speculation for Nishida, Tanabe, and Nishitani.

The place of absolute nothingness in Nishida's overall scheme is best left for a consideration of his logic of place. Here I would only add a comment on the peculiar designation of nothingness as an *absolute*.

On the one hand, of course, to make nothingness an absolute is to see it as a logical universal that embraces all of reality much as being has done in classical metaphysics. Moreover, if we follow Heidegger in seeing ontology as basically *ontotheology*, and if we further recall that the introduction of the idea of the *Absolute* into philosophy came with Schelling and Hegel, it is clear that absolute nothingness is being suggested as an Oriental cognate for the Western notion of God.[26]

On the other hand, absolute nothingness is not primarily an ontological principle, since that would make it subsidiary to the realm of being, but a principle of self-awareness.[27] As such, it is not a state of being or the absence of such a state, but a transcending of the perspective of being. This does not make it powerless or inactive. Quite the contrary, it is the dynamic ground of being. To see how this functions, we have to look at the logic that Nishida devised as a context for this notion.

---

[25] 実存と愛と実践 *[Existenz, Love, and Praxis]* THZ 9:5. The section in which these sentences appear (14-30) read almost like a paraphrase of the central argument of Nishitani's *Religion and Nothingness*, which was actually published before Tanabe's book and which I shall treat briefly here under the rubric of "The Standpoint of Emptiness." Although I have no proof of the fact, Tanabe's whole work seems to owe a great if unacknowledged debt to Nishitani.

[26] Incidentally, Schelling saw the Absolute as revealed to intuition as the identity of the knower and the known. As a young scholar, Nishitani translated Schelling's *Essence of Human Freedom* into Japanese.

[27] See the paper by Hase Shōtō below, 75-102.

PLACE

The logic of place, the most disputed of all of Nishida's ideas, represents a fourth logic aimed at providing self-awareness with a universal. In fact, it is his first deliberately devised "logic," one in which he sought to relativize the self not only to the world of objects and thought, but also to an ultimate absolute nothingness. In short, it was Nishida's mature attempt at a grand-scale system of the unfolding of the true self.[28]

The *place* of this logic refers as much to where one is coming from as to where one is going. It is not a matter simply of bodily location, though it is meant to include the idea of the body in self-awareness. In its relation to mental activities, it is not simply a kind of spatial metaphor, like the container imagery used to describe consciousness and its contents, but is a kind of symbolic space indicating one's orientation or values, a space that can be sacred or profane. Finally, it has to do with the "positing" of a standpoint; it is the shadow side of the standpoint from which one argues, the repository of tacit assumptions. In short, Nishida's idea of place is a multivalent metaphor aimed at a search for the "locus of self-awareness."[29]

Earlier I suggested that for Nishida's idea of acting intuition, all transformation must be seen as a transformation of perspective, and this is what I see conceptualized in the logic of place. Nishida himself—his students tell us[30]—liked to depict his idea of the tri-partite logic of place by drawing a number of small circles on a board, surrounding them with a single larger circle, and then adding a final all-embracing circle drawn with a broken line, to indicate his idea of place. The movement from the innermost cluster of small circles to the outermost one, whose circumference is nowhere,[31] describes three phases.

---

[28] The fascination with system-building is not something inherited from Western thought only. It also had something to do with the pressures of the Meiji period in which Japan found itself asking new questions of itself, among them the demand for giving an account of its intellectual history.

[29] I have drawn here on the exposition of Nakamura Yūjiro, *Nishida Kitarō*, 78-85.

[30] See Kōsaka Masaaki, *Nishida Kitarō*, 98.

[31] Nishida grew fond in his late years of this saying, a Gnostic idea of the soul that he discovered in Nicolas of Cusa as "a sphere whose center is everywhere

In the first phase, the subject-predicate model of Aristotelian logic, which Nishida assumed to be foundational for all Western logic,[32] is inverted. Classical logic puts the weight of its judgments on the substantial individual, the "subject that cannot become a predicate." Nishida turned this on its head, putting the weight on the universal which, as a predicate that transcends the grammatical subject, relativizes the existence of the individual. If the judgment, "The flower is red," is put in the service of a philosophy of objective being, it is the flower that is central. But if it is adapted to a philosophy aimed at heightening self-awareness by breaking through the dichotomy of the seeing subject and its seen objects, then it is the redness that is of greater moment. Redness relates to flowers as the nothingness of judgment that relativizes objective being. This is the first circle, where the self "locates" itself after the manner of acting intuition: not apart from things but in the mode in which it becomes things by its perceptual judgments.

The second phase begins when we try to locate our predicative judgments, to ask *where* universals like redness are, against what horizon they become present. The answer, of course, is that they exist only in the nothingness of consciousness. For the being that was taken away from the objects in the world survives as the being of conscious contents, indicated by the larger closed circle. The move from universal predicates to consciousness is thus a further transition from being to nothingness. But while the *contents* of consciousness look to us to be real, pure consciousness without them does not, since there is no way it can become an object to itself. In fact, at this locus, we see that the propositional subject, redness, of which we predicate consciousness, exists only because of the consciousness and could not exist without it. This is the second circle, where predicates turn out to be subjects of consciousness, and consciousness the universal predicate.

---

and whose circumference, nowhere".

[32] Western languages tend to conflate the subject who does the knowing or perceiving of objects with the subject of predicative judgments, which is actually the object in the former sense. Japanese is clear on this point.

We should note that Nishida did not take advantage of conditional, let alone symbolic logic. Even though he was alert to modern scientific quantum theory, and even wrote about it, he never ventured to make use of its logic for his own purposes. In this sense, the contortions Sueki goes through to eke a logic out of Nishida's development are somewhat out of place. See note 10.

The final transition is to the locus that grounds consciousness, the universal of all universals. At first glance, it might seem that the nothingness of consciousness is ultimately real and everything beyond it mere image and fantasy, a reality predicated as universal and embracing the plurality of consciousness. But consciousness itself is only a relative nothingness (one which needs its contents in order to be real). It cannot be grounded on being in any experiential sense, Nishida's argument runs, since that would undo the labors of the first two perspectives and would assume that it could "see" its own ground as a subject seeing an object. The only possible ground that can serve as a locus for consciousness is a final overcoming of the world of being. The logical subject, consciousness, then turns out to be the predicate of a higher reality than being, *absolute* nothingness. It is "in" this insight that the true self is "located."[33] It is here that reality ultimately "takes place," that it works as one, spontaneously unfolding itself.

Though Nishida does not explicitly speak of this progression to absolute nothingness as stages in a spiritual process, it is clearly set up that way. The logic of place enabled him to organize the whole of the efforts of philosophy—perceptual judgment, phenomenology of consciousness, enlightenment—into a single systematic whole. It should also be clear that the adoption of Western notions of God to help describe absolute nothingness, or to reinterpret the divine in the light of this category, are intended neither to argue for the existence nor the nonexistence of God in the classical Western sense.

Tanabe and Nishitani reacted differently to this logic of place. Tanabe rejected it, as much out of a growing aggravation with Nishida himself as with his own attachment to a "logic of species" that he had been developing around the same time. Nishitani embraced the final stage as a "standpoint of emptiness," apparently finding the logical apparatus itself of little service. We will have a chance to look at their respective views after a brief consideration of Nishida's final logic.

---

[33] The word-play is Nishida's own, and indeed seems to have been lost initially on some of his disciples. See Kōsaka, *Nishida Kitarō*, 99.

DIALECTICAL WORLD

The use of dialectic runs throughout the writings of the Kyoto School, surfacing most self-consciously in Nishida's late writings and remaining close to the surface through most of Tanabe's thought. If it was because of Hegel that Nishida came to the dialectic, it was because of its resonances in Buddhist thought that he stayed with it. The same can be said of Tanabe. Only Nishitani took Buddhist tradition—in particular Zen—as his primary model.

From Hegel, Nishida's dialectical thinking picked up three main traits. First, the dialectic provided a convenient method of searching for deeper insight into things by confronting one's conceptualizations with their logical opposites and then trying to find a unity between the two (as, for example, in his idea of pure experience as a conscious unity of the opposites of subject and object). Second, it provided the theoretical supposition about a single world order which logic only mirrors (as in his idea that there is a basic need or desire behind the functions of consciousness that entails a clash of opposites in will and judgment). Third, it installed a permanent critique of reason into philosophical speculation in the sense that formal logic works in contradictories because reality does not cater to our ideas of it except we phrase them as paradox (as in his final turn to the identity of contradictories).

Basically there are two carriers of the dialectic in his writings. The first is the Chinese copula *soku* 即, which appears often in Buddhist texts and furnished him with a handy device for demonstrating the "Oriental character" of his philosophy,[34] namely to remove it from the ontology of Hegel and put it at the service of a theory of absolute nothingness.

---

[34] Honda Masaaki has gone to considerable trouble over these past many years to clarify the Oriental religious meaning of *soku* and suggest its usefulness for Christian theology. A résumé of his efforts can be found in the talks and discussions recorded in 大乗禅 [*Mahāyāna Buddhism*] 5-6 (1989).

There are numerous translations for the term. Van Bragt chose *sive*; in the Tanabe translation we used *qua*. I now prefer the English term *in* because it seems to capture the sense best. Happily, the Japanese term for being *an-sich* (the essential nature of a thing) is *sokuji* 即自, literally, in (or as)-itself; the term of the *für-sich* 対自 (the freedom of a thing vis-à-vis other things) is *taiji*, literally, against itself.

Second is his idea of the "self-identity of absolute contradictories," the formal term he used in his late writings to introduce a dialectical universal that would draw the logic of place out of its apparent confinement to the individual self and into the world. Under pressure from his critics,[35] Nishida returned to his earlier Hegelian inspiration to view self-awareness as an awakening to the correlative relationship of the self and the historical world, each of which affirms itself by negating the other. Not content, however, simply with the assertion that without the self there is no world, and without the world no self, he was concerned with an insight into the higher unity of the two. In one sense, there is no easier assurance that one has reached an ultimately universal concept than by taking care to include everything and its opposite. Nishida clearly wanted more than a logical category. He wanted to describe it as an insight that participates in, or converts itself to, the "inverse correlation" at the ground of the order of things. The point is to achieve a self-identity (a unity of the true self that takes place by itself) by seeing the negation-in-affirmation and the affirmation-in-negation.

It may be argued that this did not draw his thought any closer to the demands of concrete praxis in history. Ironically, given its full consistency, indeed its culmination of his former thought,[36] it served to highlight what is perhaps the most fundamental shortcoming of his philosophical system — its systematic tendency to distance philosophy from its role in shaping concrete moral consciousness.

LOGIC OF SPECIES

For his part, Nishitani has used the dialectic as a tool without developing his own theory of it — and indeed, he has not spent

---

[35] Principal among them are the critiques of Tosaka Jun and later of Tanabe (which Nishida initially acknowledged and then dismissed as a misunderstanding). See Nishida, NCW Supplement 5:410, 460.

[36] Dilworth has argued this in his important work, *Last Writings: Nothingness and the Religious Worldview* (Honolulu, 1987). The opening and concluding essays represent a condensation of the ideas of the one Western scholar who more than any other has struggled to appropriate the uniqueness of Nishida's thought critically into the Western philosophical tradition.

much time on logic at all. Tanabe's mathematical background and interest in scientific method, in contrast, made him especially alert to logical questions. From his most technical writing to his more popular works, he was not only content to think dialectically but to continually remind the reader that this is what he is doing. On the face of it, Tanabe's differences with Nishida over the meaning and use of dialectic are minor, and Nishida's closest disciples have tended to side with their teacher in the view that these differences were in fact based on Tanabe's misunderstanding of Nishida's ideas.[37]

In general, Tanabe's critique centers on two points. First, he resisted the idea of a final locus for self-awareness that would not set the self squarely in the realms of practical judgment. Second, Tanabe stressed the dynamic quality of absolute nothingness in the world of being, whereas Nishida had put the stress on sub-jective insight into absolute nothingness. As we saw above, Nishida tried to remedy this—at least in formal logical terms—in his final writings. Be that as it may, each of these critiques is attached to one of the two key philosophical ideas associated with Tanabe's name, namely the logic of species and metanoetics.

Tanabe's attempt to find a logic for absolute nothingness was more modest, in a sense, than Nishida's. He had grown weary of the heights of abstraction and longed for something closer to what he perceived as the soil of existential experience. Even so, this

---

[37] Nishitani is a case in point. See the final two chapters of his *Nishida Kitarō*. I would only note here that so vehement was the division that when the first edition of Nishida's *Collected Works* was published, Nishida's correspondence with Tanabe (over 100 letters in all) were omitted! Pressures from the academic community had them instated in a later edition.

Whatever the personal and theoretical clashes, the texts themselves seem to support Nishitani's conclusion:

> Indeed it is my impression that a close examination of Nishida's philosophy at the points criticized by Tanabe reveals in many cases that Nishida's views are surprisingly similar to Tanabe's own. In particular, their philosophies share a distinctive and common basis that sets them apart from traditional Western philosophy as a whole: "absolute nothingness.". . . . For all the noteworthy dif-ferences of terminology and logical system that separated them, when one looks closely at the core of what each was trying to say, the gap that may at first have looked like a vast chasm gradually narrows and in many instances even gives the impression of having been bridged by identical views (*Nishida Kitarō*, 210-11).

has to be understood in terms of the subject matter, since Tanabe's style quite roundly betrays such purpose. It is not only every bit as abstract as Nishida's, but its almost arithmetical rigor walks one step at a time where Nishida is forever taking imaginative leaps. In any case, Tanabe's aim was to return from the airy realms of the contemplative to the real world, and he grew short of temper with relegating it to a minor circle enveloped in the all-embracing circle of absolute nothingness. He wanted to see absolute nothingness at work everywhere and in all things.

The logic of species, which Tanabe described from the outset as a dialectical method, was a first step in this direction.[38] Just as Hegel's notion of "objective spirit" had filled out the notion of a concrete universal for the realm of being, Tanabe's logic of species would do the same for the realm of absolute nothingness.[39]

Fundamentally, the project is cut of the same cloth as the Neo-Kantian concern with locating the conditions for the possibility of knowing (or in Tanabe's case, of self-awareness) as lying not only in the transcendental structure of consciousness but also in the variable structures of social convention. It is society, the culture created by particular races, that filters humanity to the individual and brings the individual in touch with the absolute (call it God or absolute nothingness). Race and culture introduce a radical, ineluctable irrationality into every attempt at pure contemplative reason. Tanabe argued that classical logic—by which he meant classical logic as Nishida had used it in his logic of place—had focused on universals and individuals, failing to give sufficient weight to the role of the category of species that falls in between them and prevents absolute knowledge of the one through the other.[40] The principal reason he felt obliged to correct

---

[38] The central ideas of his project are laid out in a late essay translated by David Dilworth and Satō Taira as "The Species as Dialectics," MN 24 (1969):273-88. The translation is not a particularly good one, but in fairness to the efforts of the translators, the article itself is more recondite than the ideas presented there deserve. The work was never completed.

[39] See Takeuchi, "Absolute Nothingness and the Philosophy of Tanabe," 208-209.

[40] There are shades of this not only in Hegel's philosophy of religion, but already in the Platonic method of *diaresis* (as found, for instance, in *Phaedrus* and *Sophist*) where the definition of a thing is sought by a moving continually from genus to species, stopping short only when one meets the concrete individual.

this oversight was to help critical social praxis find a way into a philosophy of nothingness. An added motive, as he writes in hindsight, was to provide a rational context for reflecting on the nationalism emerging in Japan in the late 1930s. By setting up a dialectical relationship between the subjective individual and the race, he hoped to argue the case against a simple, unreflected totalitarianism.[41]

In any case, by stressing mediation, Tanabe means to stress the intermediary steps to self-awareness. There is, he tells us, more than merely universals that bring together a one and a many in intuition; there are real mediating forces in the world that bring together the human individual and the human race, or the religious subject and the power of absolute nothingness. "God does not act directly on the individual," he wrote. "The salvation of the individual is accomplished through the mediation of nation and society which already exist as communities of individuals."[42] These "communities of individuals" are precisely what he wishes to circumscribe by the notion of species.

Now in order to return from this excursus into the theory of praxis back to the theory of absolute nothingness required the additional step of what Tanabe called "absolute mediation," namely the idea that absolutely everything in existence is mediated, that at bottom it is mediated by absolute nothingness, and that the mediation consists in an absolute negation that opens up into an absolute affirmation. This brings us to the notion of metanoesis.

METANOETICS

In trying to bring the subject in search of its true self closer to interaction with the historical world, Tanabe had also to show how this relationship was grounded in absolute nothingness. While Nishida's logic of place had shown how the forces of history *take place* in the universal of absolute nothingness, Tanabe was more concerned with showing how absolute nothingness *takes time* in the concreteness of history. For the logic of species also to be a true "logic of self-awareness,"[43] it could not be self-enclosed in the

---

[41] See the preface to "The Species as Dialectics," 272, note 2.

[42] "The Species as Dialectics," 287.

[43] According to Yamada (*Intellectual History of the Shōwa Period*, 99), this was

correlative identity of self and world, but neither could the absolute nothingness that encompassed it be merely a logical category. It had to be dynamic, at work as much in the world as in consciousness seeking awareness. This provided the central idea for his idea of philosophy as metanoetics.

One might say that Tanabe's aim in all of this was to reinstate the primacy of religious experience by distinguishing it more clearly from philosophical reflection than Nishida had done. For if philosophy was to reach its terminus in religious insight (self-awareness), then it could not begin from pure experience but only from the radical impurity of insight and experience. The rational hubris that he found in Nishida's philosophy would have to be replaced by a conversion of reason. The conceptualization of this process was metanoetics, a "philosophy that was not a philosophy."

Where Nishida had used Zen as his primary source of Oriental inspiration, Tanabe took up the True Pure Land (Shin) Buddhist tradition which was based on reliance on Other-power and for which Zen was a religion of self-power. In other words, self-awareness would no longer be the work of a self that cultivates itself through acting intuition, whose primary symbol is the Buddha-nature that all beings possess and need to realize, but rather the work of letting go of the self before the power of absolute nothingness, whose primary symbol is the saving grace of Amida Buddha. Since it is the subject of our conference to look at this idea more closely, there is no need to do into further detail here. I would rather like to pull out what seems to me a tacit structure underlying Tanabe's philosophy of religion and hence to draw it out of the frame of a debate between the relative merits of Zen and Shin Buddhism.

There are three elements to the attainment of religious self-awareness, all of which show up in *Philosophy as Metanoetics* and still more clearly in his next work, *Existenz, Love, and Praxis*. First, there is the self-negating dynamic of a recognition of the radical limits of the world that we can know and control.[44] This appears

---

in fact the title of a series of special lectures whose contents were woven into the lectures that would become *Philosophy as Metanoetics*.

[44] It is interesting that in the closing chapter of *Existenz, Love, and Praxis*, Tanabe makes considerable use of vol. 2 of Jaspers's *Philosophie*, where the idea of the *Grenzsituationen* is posed.

in the use of the self-power of reason to advance by tearing reason to pieces (the metanoia of *ōsō*), or what Tanabe call's "absolute critique." Second, there is the Other-affirming dynamic of a recognition of forces unknown and uncontrollable that transcend the power of the self and yet are encountered in human experience (the metanoia of *gensō*). Third, there is the world of the uniting symbols generated in the true self of self-awareness, where the first two dynamics are related to each other dialectically (the metanoetics of *ōsō*-in-*gensō*, or of negation-in-affirmation) in religious praxis. There are two kinds of symbols Tanabe uses in this regard. For symbols of personal repentance and metanoia (the logic of self-awareness), he draws on the myth of the bodhisattva Dharmākara and later on the myth of Jesus. For a symbols of praxis in the world (the logic of species), he draws on the image from the *Lotus Sūtra* of a mutual correspondence among the Buddhas, and later on the Christian notion of the *communio sanctorum*.

STANDPOINT OF EMPTINESS

Like Tanabe, Nishitani took up the challenge of Nishida's logic of place and forged his own creative response. Unlike Tanabe, however, Nishitani has not put great stock in differentiating his position from that of his teacher or provoking a confrontation. His concern was rather to relocate Nishida's locus of absolute nothingness squarely in the existential struggles of contemporary consciousness through what he has called a "standpoint of emptiness."

If Nishida and Tanabe shared a common philosophical background in Hegel and Kant, Nishitani's major influence has no doubt been Nietzsche. As a young man grappling with the problems of life and unsure where to turn, he once told me, he used to carry *Thus Spoke Zarathustra* around with him "like my bible." Philosophical tutoring in Nishida's circle and the inspiration of Suzuki Daisetsu that turned him to Zen never undid his early affections for Nietzsche. Quite the contrary, they matured into a profound understanding more or less contemporary with the rediscovery of Nietzsche in the West.[45]

---

[45] Walter Kaufmann's *Nietzsche* was published in 1950. In the spring of that same year, Nishitani was delivering the lectures on Nietzsche that form the cen-

Where Nishida had tried to frame an idea of the locus of consciousness from Leibnitz's monadology, Nishitani was closer to Nietzsche's "perspectivism,"[46] understanding the logic of place as a process of conversion from one standpoint to the next. The stages in this process as he lays them out amount to a critique and reinterpretation of Nietzsche in the light of Zen Buddhism.

The basic pattern is laid out most clearly in Nishitani's major work, *Religion and Nothingness*. In outline form, the argument runs like this: The ordinary, pre-awakened self is the ego of self-consciousness that sets itself up outside the world of things as a knowing subject. This is the standpoint of *egoity*. Driven by death and an awareness of the impermanence of all things to see the empty abyss that yawns underfoot of ordinary egoity, one awakens to an initial sense of the vanity of self and world. This is what Nishitani calls the standpoint of *nihility*. It represents a conversion to a standpoint of nothingness, but only a relative nothingness. By facing this abyss of nihility squarely and yet not clinging to it as ultimate, a final standpoint is opened up, the standpoint of *emptiness* in which things appear just as they are, in their "suchness," and in which the true self is seen to reside not in the workings of egoity but in a letting go of ego. The awareness of the relative nothingness of nihility is converted spontaneously and of its own to an awareness of absolute nothingness.[47]

Using this model of religious conversion, Nishitani considers key notions of self and self-nature in Zen Buddhism, as well as their conceptual counterparts in Western philosophy and theology. The logic of the critique he levels against the doctrines of a wholly personal God, the kenōsis of God in Jesus, and even the immaculate conception of the Virgin Mary,[48] appeals regularly to the

---

tral section of his book ニヒリズム *[Nihilism]* (an English translation of which by Graham Parkes and Aihara Setsuko is scheduled for publication with SUNY Press in 1989 under the title *The Self-Overcoming of Nihilism*).

[46] Nietzsche speaks of perspectivism as an approach "by virtue of which every force center — and not only man — construes the whole rest of the world from its own viewpoint." See *The Will to Power*, trans. by W. Kaufmann and R. J. Hollingdale (New York, 1968), sec. 636.

[47] For a fuller account, see Sasaki Tōru 佐々木 徹, 西谷啓治―その思索への道標 *[Nishitani Keiji: Guideposts to His Thought]* (Kyoto, 1988), 161-86.

[48] In an important essay composed in 1955, at the same time as *Religion and Nothingness*, 仏教とキリスト教 ["Buddhism and Christianity"], Nishitani sug-

Western mystical tradition, but in the end rests on his Buddhist strategy of emptying language into self-awareness of the true self.

CONCLUSION

Current intellectual pressures in Japan make it almost obligatory to add a word about the "uniqueness" of the Kyoto philosophers. To use the term in its weak sense in which every cultural achievement is unique would be to say nothing very much at all. To use it in the strong sense that it now in certain circles of contemporary Japanese intelligentsia—the quest for an arcana of culturally and genetically bound traits, the argument for whose existence and nature must rely entirely on the intuition of those who possess them—would be to beg all the important questions.

I am inclined to recall how Nietzsche warned his fellow Germans in the third of his *Untimely Meditations* that uniqueness is not something one seeks out by rummaging through what one has been given, but something that one makes from it. We are born raw and ordinary; uniqueness is the judgment that others make about what our efforts have wrought. For my part, I am content to try to locate their achievement in the context of a world intellectual history in the making, of which the current exchange of philosophies and religions East and West is the coping stone.

The point is not as self-evident as it might seem. In theory, there seems everything to recommend such interchange and little to discourage it. The practice is another matter. To those who occupy as professional fields of study the traditions the Kyoto philosophers straddle, they must look like cuckoo birds hatching their brood in someone else's nest. Are they carrying Eastern eggs to Western nests? Or are they bringing Western eggs to Eastern nests? Whichever the case, there is something kooky about it all.

In the spirit in which they worked, however, I think we must resist either the judgment that the Kyoto philosophers have reduced philosophy to Buddhism or conversely that they have simply

---

gests that the doctrine of *theotokos* (mother of God) and the virgin birth should be extended to describe religious consciousness in general and not restricted to one historical personality. For a résumé of the argument, a critique by Mutō Kazuo, and a discussion of it with Nishitani, see ZMK, 114-20, 146-48.

reupholstered Buddhist thought in Western terminology,[49] doing disservice to both. One can no more approach Nishida or Tanabe or Nishitani as Buddhist scholars than as Christian theologians. Their primary context is the philosophical tradition that goes back to the early Greeks and now belongs also to the Orient. To deprive that context of its access to religious thought simply because the religious frame of reference has widened to include Buddhism would be to cut off its legs

Each in his own way, the philosophers of the Kyoto School have tried to introduce *into their philosophical thought* their own inner struggles with religious "affiliation" in a religiously plural world. Tanabe described his situation as one of both belief and unbelief, clearly in debt to both Buddhism and Christianity, and yet ultimately only able to claim: "I am no more a believer in Shin Buddhism than I am a Christian. I remain a student of philosophy."[50]

Nishitani explicitly acknowledges Tanabe's dilemma, but goes on to word his own position somewhat differently. Although he speaks out of the Buddhist framework, he says, he cannot bring himself to identify entirely with Buddhism, but neither can he reject Christianity out of hand. He describes his position as one a "Buddhist made but in-the-making" and at the same time as a "not made but Christian in-the-making."[51] These are not private statements made outside of the philosophical framework; they are a fundamental inspiration for the Kyoto philosophers.

This does not, of course, do much to answer the question of whether their use of Western philosophy has done any lasting, positive service to Buddhist self-understanding, and vice-versa. This is a rather too large question to pronounce on summarily. On the one hand, we want to know how this philosophical excursus has fared compared to Buddhism's own rich intellectual history, what lacunae, if any, it has filled and what its major oversights have been. On the other, we have to see what the distinctively

---

[49] See, for example, Yamada's claim that Nishida's philosophy is simply a further subjectification of already subjective Zen intuition (*Intellectual History of the Shōwa Period*, 18).

[50] *Existenz, Love, and Praxis*, 5. Chapter 1 of his 哲学入門 *[Introduction to Philosphy]* spells this out in further detail.

[51] Cited in Jan Van Bragt, "Nishitani on Japanese Religiosity," J. Spae, *Japanese Religiosity*, 280-81.

Oriental inspirations of their thought does to illuminate neglected corners of Western thought—whether through misunderstanding or superior insight—and what it does to obfuscate matters of little moment. On all these counts, there is much to be said. Happily, one hears more and more voices joining forum to say it.

Philosophy as Metanoetics:
An Analysis

James FREDERICKS

TO paraphrase a Javanese proverb, a first reading of *Philosophy as Metanoetics* is somewhat akin to a water buffalo listening to a gamelon. Even after several readings, the contrapuntal play of themes and recurrent problems only seems to deepen in its complexity and interest, its originality and its demand on the reader. Any attempt to summarize this complexity of course risks losing some of the nuance and effect of the original. In the case at hand, however, the price to be paid is yet greater. Given the existential richness of the original, to summarize unfortunately is to caricature. What survives is mere torso.

This is partly the case because identifying Tanabe's text as a genre familiar to us is itself a challenge and a danger. Is this a philosophy of religion? Is it a pseudo-religious philosophy? Certainly the multiple problems of interpretation presented by the text stem in part from the rich existential meaning of Tanabe's effort. With this in mind, I have tried to interpret the thrust and direction of the text cognizant of the fact that its author had undergone a significant religious conversion and that this conversion comprised not only the topic of the text, but also the existential standpoint from which the text was written. *Philosophy as Metanoetics* is a philosophy of religion written from an intensely existential point of view. To lose track of this is fundamentally to misinterpret the text. In his metanoetic philosophy, Tanabe believed that he had identified the "Archimedean point outside the world of philosophical tradition from which to dislodge that world and set it spinning in a new orbit."[1] With Kierkegaard and Shinran as guides, he seems to have made a "leap" to a perspective in which the essential problems of metaphysics, ethics, social and

---

[1] James Heisig, "Foreword," in PM, xiv.

historical life, rationality and religious experience could come into radical new self-awareness by means of a genuine religious subjectivity. Comparison with Augustine of Hippo comes easily enough. *Philosophy as Metanoetics* is certainly a kind of *Confessions.* It is the account of a soul converting from a philosophical conviction no longer existentially sustaining to a religious perspective not yet fully articulated nor completely understood but deeply transforming. But the comparison with Augustine stops when it is realized that Tanabe, keeping apart from any particular religious tradition although a student of several of them, is not a theologian. Tanabe wrote from the point where philosophy and religion engage one another in the tumult of the existential transformation of the individual. He offers us a genuinely philosophical faith, created from philosophy yet claiming to go beyond it in order to fulfill its own philosophical promise.

Thus my analysis of Tanabe's views reflects several compromises. No analysis of Tanabe's intricate critique of Heidegger's notion of temporality, Nietzsche's understanding of nihilism, or Eckhart's notion of *Gottheit* are included, for each would be a study in itself. Neither will any account of Tanabe's controversial interpretation of Shinran and the *Kyōgyōshinshō* be attempted. This must be left to competent exegetes of the Pure Land tradition. Instead, this analysis (1) begins with Tanabe's own account of his religious transformation, (2) sketches his views in general regarding the "way of metanoia," (3) summarizes his views on the "absolute critique" as the logic of metanoetic philosophy, (4) and closes with an account of the "absolute mediation" as a way of better understanding the controversy between Tanabe and Nishida Kitarō regarding the meaning of absolute nothingness.

A PERSONAL CRISIS

Tanabe Hajime was born in Tokyo on 3 February 1885 (Meiji 18) and eventually entered Tokyo Imperial University to study mathematics. Before completing his undergraduate studies, however, he transferred to the Department of Philosophy (somewhat discouraged with the status of theoretical mathematics at the university), graduating in 1908 with an impressive academic record. His first published contribution to philosophy, "On Thetical Judgment," appeared in the *Journal of Philosophy* two years after his graduation.[2] After a time spent teaching English, he moved to Sendai in 1915 to take up a post as lecturer in the philosophy of science at Tōhoku Imperial University. In Sendai, Tanabe published in rapid succession a book on the philosophy of science in Japan, a series of articles, and a second book on scientific logic. During this period, Tanabe was greatly interested in the Marburg branch of neo-Kantianism (especially the work of Cohen and Natorp), which coincided with his interest in the re-creation of Kantian transcendentalism through phenomenology, Bergsonian vitalism and also the concepts of "pure experience" and "absolute will" being advanced by the young Nishida Kitarō in Kyoto.[3]

Tanabe had attracted the attention of Nishida as early as 1913,[4] and in 1919 was brought by Nishida to Kyoto as an assistant professor in the Faculty of Arts and Letters. Tanabe and Nishida were in agreement on the importance of exploring the epistemological limitations of the Marburg School, and worked together on an extended experiment with neo-Kantianism which led eventually to their abandoning of interest in it.[5]

Tanabe left Japan for studies in Germany in 1922. In Freiburg, he made a favorable impression on Husserl, who hoped his young Japanese student would carry on the phenomenological movement in Japan. Such was not to be the case. Tanabe's gradual disenchantment with the phenomenological movement as envisioned by Husserl led him eventually to the ideas of his tutor, Martin Heidegger.

---

[2] Takeuchi Yoshinori, "Translator's Introduction," PM, xxxi.

[3] James Heisig, "Foreword," PM, x-xi.

[4] It is not exactly clear when Tanabe began his collaboration with Nishida. Although Nishida's first monograph, *An Inquiry into the Good*, was published in 1911, a year after Tanabe's first essay, it had appeared piecemeal in the pages of *Tetsugaku kenkyū* 哲学研究 *[Journal of Philosophy]* between 1907 and 1909. Nishida had also given a lecture regarding "pure experience" in Tokyo in November of 1909. Tanabe's third essay, "The Limits of Rationalism in Epistemology" (1914), was cited by Nishida in print. Tanabe's name appears in Nishida's diary for the first time in the entry of Sunday, 6 April, 1913. It has been alleged that Tanabe wrote a letter directly to Nishida asking for advice before this date, but this can not be confirmed. See Takeuchi Yoshinori, "Translator's Introduction," PM, xxxiii-iv.

[5] The results of this experiment were published by Nishida in 1917 under the title, *Intuition and Reflection in Self-Consciousness*, trans. V. Viglielmo, Takeuchi Yoshinori, and Joseph O'Leary (Albany: SUNY Press, 1987).

Tanabe returned to Kyoto in 1924 excited about Heidegger, only to find that he was expected to lecture on Kant. A detailed study of Kant's teleology convinced Tanabe that Kantian criticism must be carried out to its ultimate conclusion in a metaphysics free of the dogmatism of German Idealism and the epistemological inadequacies of neo-Kantianism. He began to envision a teleological metaphysics grounded in a religious standpoint which would give existential priority to practical reason over pure reason and be capable of distinguishing the pure possibility of moral action from its concrete realization by the acting subject.[6] These early lectures on Kant are noteworthy not only in that they serve to highlight Tanabe's characteristic interest in the relationship between religious consciousness and social, historical and ethical questions, but also in that they led Tanabe to a lengthy investigation of Hegel and thence to a confrontation with Marx and (as will be examined in some detail) Nishida.[7]

Tanabe's public break with Nishida dates from an essay entitled, innocently enough, "Looking to the Teachings of Nishida" (1930). This initial departure from the position established by his mentor, visibly painful for the high-strung Tanabe, marked the beginning of his commitment to developing a "logic of species," which eventually would be recognized as an alternative to Nishida's "logic of place" and a lasting legacy to the Kyoto School.

However, after the publication of *Essays on the Logic of the Species* in 1941, Tanabe refrained from publishing another monograph until the appearance of *Philosophy as Metanoetics* in 1946. The intervening years marked a time of crisis for both the man and his nation. *Philosophy as Metanoetics* is based on lectures delivered in Kyoto during this crisis. The lectures included such

---

[6] Tanabe Hajime, カントの目的論 *[On Kant's Teleology]* (1924), THZ, 3:1-71.

[7] Tanabe lectured on Hegel's *Phenomenology* for thirteen years. Besides his encounter with Hegel, the social thought of Miki Kiyoshi (1897-1945) and Tosaka Jun (1900-1945) forced Tanabe to recognize the challenge posed by Marx's material dialectic to Japanese intellectuals. These deliberations led him to the "logic of species" *(shu no ronri* 種の論理 *)* a philosophical standpoint more attentive to the social, economic and political realities of modern Japan. Tanabe returned to the problem of "species" after the publication of *Philosophy as Metanoetics*. See for instance Tanabe Hajime, "The Logic of Species as Dialectics," trans. David Dilworth and Satō Taira, MN 24/3 (1969): 273-88.

topics as "Absolute Knowledge" (October 1942-March 1943), "The Logic of Self-Consciousness" (1943) and "Metanoetics" (1944).

The "Preface" to *Philosophy as Metanoetics* is uncharacteristically self-revealing for this private, intense, and at times somewhat unapproachable man. After calling to mind the plight of the Japanese people as the war effort began to collapse, Tanabe wrote of his own personal moral and professional dilemma as a professor of philosophy at an imperial university, caught as he was between the conflicting alternatives of a confrontation with the government over its war policies and the need for social cooperation in time of national disaster.

> My own indecision, it seemed to me, disqualified me as a philosopher and university professor. I spent my days wrestling with questions and doubts like this from within and without, until I had been quite driven to the point of exhaustion and in my despair concluded that I was not fit to engage in the sublime task of philosophy.
>
> At that moment something astonishing happened. In the midst of my distress I let go and surrendered myself humbly to my own inability. I was suddenly brought to new insight! My penitent confession — metanoesis — unexpectedly threw me back on my own interiority and away from things external. There was no longer any question of my teaching and correcting others under the circumstances — I who could not deliver myself to do the correct thing. The only thing for me to do in the situation was to resign myself honestly to my weakness, to examine my own inner self with humility, and to explore the depths of my powerlessness and lack of freedom. Would not this mean a new task to take the place of the philosophical task that had previously engaged me? Little matter whether it be called "philosophy" or not: I had already come to realize my own incompetence as a philosopher. What mattered was that I was being confronted at the moment with an intellectual task and ought to do my best to pursue it (1).

Tanabe's experience of emotional turmoil and professional confusion, his sense of "incompetence as a philosopher" as well as deliverance from his personal crisis form the biographical context of his reflections about metanoetic philosophy. Any adequate reading of *Philosophy as Metanoetics* must be mindful of this biographical context. Tanabe left Kyoto in July of 1945 for his mountain retreat in Kita-Karuizawa, bringing his lecture notes with him. *Philosophy as Metanoetics* was published the following year.

THE WAY OF METANOIA

Tanabe began his reflections by introducing his neologism "metanoetics" *(zange-dō* 懺悔道). Metanoetics designates for Tanabe true philosophical inquiry, indeed "the only possible philosophy" (1). It is the path *(dō)* of metanoia *(zange).* "Metanoetics" is not meant to suggest merely a philosophical reflection on the theme of repentance. It is not a philosophy "of" metanoia, in the sense of a critically directed inquiry into the phenomenon of repentance, nor is it one branch of philosophy among others. Metanoetics is the discourse that begins only when all prior philosophical methods have been negated in their entirety, a philosophy of "destruction" even more radical than the Cartesian *dubito*. Tanabe's concern, therefore, is with philosophy "as" *(toshite)* metanoetics, the only possible philosophy, which arises after the "death and resurrection of philosophy" (lv).

This qualification reflects Tanabe's fascination with a paradox whose tension is felt throughout the text, viz. that metanoetics is "a philosophy that is not a philosophy."

> I call it a philosophy that is not a philosophy because, on the one hand, it has arisen from the vestiges of a philosophy I had cast away in despair, and on the other, it maintains the purpose of functioning as a reflection on what is ultimate and as a radical self-awareness, which are the goals proper to philosophy (1).

Seemingly, Tanabe was trying to locate the point where, after the failure of philosophical inquiry, a new discourse arises in the break-through to true self-awareness which is both philosophical and religious. Tanabe was not envisioning yet another philosophy founded on the autonomous power of reason to know the truth, but rather a philosophy which takes as its basis the existential transformation of self-awareness and also the "death and resurrection" of rational discourse itself in the experience of metanoia.

Central to Tanabe's understanding of metanoetics as a "philosophy that is not a philosophy" is the nature of the transformation of subjectivity which gives rise to metanoetic cognition. Three points are outstanding.

First of all, the existential fact of transformation distinguishes metanoia from the merely psychological experience of remorse. Metanoetics begins only when self-consciousness, that hitherto had clung to the logic of non-contradiction, "breaks through" itself to a radical self-awareness. As long as the subject clings to its self-affirmation through the innate power of reason to grasp the real, metanoetics is not yet a possibility for it. Only in the act of existential self-surrender does metanoetic consciousness arise. Therefore this transformation has a peculiar structure: even though as repentance it is an act of the self, it is at the same time an overcoming of the standpoint of finite subjectivity. For this reason it is an action that is no longer simply attributable to the self. Logically speaking, metanoetics is not a philosophy that can be pursued by reason's pretense to "self-power" (*jiriki* 自力), i.e. a philosophy that presumes the subject's innate capacity to know the truth through the inferences of a logic based on the principles of non-contradiction and self-identity. Instead, the original existential transformation and the metanoetic cognition that accompanies this transformation arise through the grace of that which is not the self, "Other-power (*tariki* 他力) (4).

Second, the experience of transformation carries with it a social and ethical dimension and for this reason metanoetic philosophy implies a doctrine of evil. Tanabe relies mainly on Kant's notion of "radical evil" which he apparently believed was a philosophical expression of the Christian doctrine of original sin (4). Evil is not an accidental phenomenon, but rather lies constitutively at the root of human existence as its negative determination. *Existenz* is established by the self's spontaneous self-determination. This is the foundation of the free will, but also the root of the subject's tendency to absolutize itself by substituting for the analogous relationship between relative being and the absolute, a relationship of simple identity. In Tanabe's view, this is to lose track of the mediatory role that relative being plays in making the absolute present in the world. In place of a mediation of the absolute by the relative through analogy which is their authentic relationship, there is the "radical evil" of the finite which is rooted (1) in the attempt to establish the absolute freedom of the self apart from its proper grounding in the absolute, and (2) in re-

maining oblivious of the existential fact that true freedom is established only in the experience of transformation realized through
the self-negation *(zange)* that results from the subject standing in
contradictory confrontation with the world. "Human freedom in
the true sense is rooted solely in the grace of the absolute" which
negates our being only in order to transform us into a new being
by first awakening within us a consciousness of our finitude, but
also a consciousness that true freedom is realized only within that
finitude (4). Metanoetics is the social and ethical philosophy that
springs from this "death and resurrection" of the self.

Third, the transformation of subjectivity that is the source of
this "philosophy that is not a philosophy" must be understood as
the event that gives rise to a metanoetic self-awareness which
Tanabe recognizes as "faith." The resurrection of the self through
Other-power is not made automatic with the act of repentant
self-surrender. The transformation by Other-power is neither pre-
dictable nor reducible to a logic of self-identity and non-contradiction. It remains a grace. Accordingly, Tanabe's "philosophy that
is not a philosophy" is rooted in an existence determined by the
ongoing death and resurrection of the subject in Other-power
where the transformation of existence from without *(tariki)* is always in correlation with the action of faith within *(jiriki)*.

THE ABSOLUTE CRITIQUE

Although Tanabe was unwilling to speak of metanoetics as a
"logic" in the Aristotelian tradition of rational inference which
takes non-contradiction and self-identity as its principles, he did
insist that there is a "logic" *(ronri)*[8] at work throughout metanoetics. The logic which governs metanoetic philosophy is the "absolute
criticism" (lv-lvi).

Any philosophy based on the autonomous power of reason
for criticism is a "self-power" *(jiriki)* philosophy. In Tanabe's view,
the pure reason presupposed as the basis of such a philosophy is

---

[8] Tanabe's use of the term *ronri* 論理 is in keeping with Nishida's understanding of it as a "form of discourse." David Dilworth explains *ronri* as "a pre-
dominating tissue of relations between the intellectual variables which it
articulates." See Dilworth, "Nishida Kitarō [1870-1945]: The Development of
His Thought," 166.

destined to fall into the dilemma of self-contradiction in any encounter with the ultimate irrationality of reality. Immanuel Kant
confronted the same problem in his discussion of the antinomies
of pure reason.[9] Since all reason is driven by the desire for absolute knowledge, Kant's recognition of the finite character of
reason brought with it the requirement of acknowledging its inherent inability to attain this goal. When pushed beyond its limits
in the pursuit of absolute knowledge, reason inevitably falls into
self-contradiction. Kant's solution to the problem of absolute
knowledge and finite reason was to limit carefully the province
of certain knowledge in order to make room for morality, aesthetics and religion beyond the pale of pure reason. This solution,
however, not only required distinguishing the realm of knowledge
(Wissen) from that of belief *(Glauben)* but also led Kant to the
epistemological dualism of the phenomena and the noumena. In
effect, Kant tried to evade the problem of the antinomies (which
Tanabe faced squarely as reason's inherent self-contradiction in
the face of the fundamental irrationality of reality) by insisting
that pure reason keep within carefully observed limits. The price
paid for this compromise is the elimination of speculative metaphysics and theology from the realm of certain knowledge and
the necessity of what is at best a pious agnosticism regarding the
absolute.[10]

Tanabe's desire to call Kant's critical philosophy into question
shaped his understanding of the "absolute critique." In fine, Tanabe argued that Kant's critique of reason is not radical enough
because Kant never considered the philosophical import of cri-
tiquing the critique of reason itself. Kant's position was (1) that
criticism is the proper task of philosophy, (2) that philosophy as
such becomes possible only when the possibility of criticism is
presupposed, and (3) that the possibility of criticism itself cannot
be called into doubt without abandoning philosophy. On the other
hand, Tanabe contended (1) that the hallmark of philosophy is

---

[9] Immanuel Kant, *The Critique of Pure Reason*, trans. F. Max Müller (Garden
City: Doubleday, 1966), 295-384, [A405-565; B430-593].

[10] PM, 32-35, 38, 42. For an analysis of Tanabe's understanding of Kant's
critical philosophy, see Johannes Laube, "Zur religionsphilosophischen Be-
deutung der 'Metanoetik' des japanischen Philosophen Hajime Tanabe," *Zeitschrift für Missionswissenschaft und Religionswissenschaft* 65/2 (1981): 124-29.

self-awakening, not criticism as such, (2) that philosophy becomes possible only when the metanoia of criticism is presupposed, and (3) that metanoetic philosophy ("the only possible philosophy") arises when the critical autonomy of reason is abandoned and reason undergoes a "death and resurrection." At the center of Tanabe's criticism of Kant is his conviction that critical philosophy failed to address radically the problem of the origin and destiny of criticism. In a real sense, Tanabe believed that the philosophical project begun in Kant's First Critique reaches its logical conclusion in metanoetic philosophy (38).

The many years Tanabe spent lecturing on Kant led him to the conviction that the critique of pure reason cannot provide the ultimate standpoint for philosophy as Kant claimed for it. The separation of the phenomenal and the noumenal is a "mere compromise incapable of bringing reason to its ultimate state of peace" (43). In place of this compromise, Tanabe worked out what he considered to be the "absolute critique" of reason. The absolute critique recognizes profoundly reason's innate self-contradiction which arises in its encounter with the actual world. When reason is driven to its limit, it inevitably is "torn to shreds" in the antinomies. Pure reason, crippled by the irrationality of the real, is no longer of any use in the subject's quest to know the absolute. Absolute criticism means that reason, faced with the dilemma of its "death" or "absolute disruption" in the antinomies, must surrender to this inherent self-contradiction of its own accord. In Tanabe's personal crisis of 1941-45, the meaning of this "surrender" became existential: subjectivity itself "dies" in the "absolute disruption" of reason.

> When reason criticizes reason, does the reason doing the criticizing stand outside of the critique as a criticizing subject, without becoming an object of criticism? If this is the case, the critique of reason cannot be a thorough critique of reason in its entirety.... Just as self-awareness must break through itself by awakening to a consciousness of nothingness, so must the self-criticism of reason run aground on the impassable antinomies of the one and the many, the whole and the individual, infinity and finitude, determinacy and spontaneity, necessity and freedom (38).

In reason's quest to know the absolute, subjectivity is not immune to the negation of the antinomies. It becomes instead completely entangled in its own self-contradiction. Subjectivity, like pure reason itself, must surrender to its own "dismemberment" in self-contradiction.

Absolute critique is achieved only by pushing the critique of reason to its radical conclusion. Using this as a basis, Tanabe was able to offer a reading of Western thought's arrested development toward the absolute critique. The unresolved problems of Kant's critical philosophy were eventually addressed by Hegel in *The Phenomenology of Mind,* where the transcendental logic of the former was developed into the historical dialectic of the latter. Tanabe singled out Hegel as the best example in the Western philosophical tradition of the recognition of reason's disruption by contradiction. Nevertheless, he criticized Hegel for maintaining that the disruption of reason (and therefore the death of the subject) can be overcome in the dialectical restoration of the original unity of reason in a synthetic *Begriff.* For Tanabe, this meant that negation could not be carried out to its fullest in the absolute disruption of reason. For instance, in the final chapter of the *Phenomenology of Mind,* Hegel speaks of absolute knowledge as that which is attained by means of historical dialectics with reason alone. Hegel never reached the absolute critique of reason because of his refusal to admit the radical and abiding character of reason's self-contradiction and the ultimately irrational character of the real. The aphorism, "the rational is the real" confirms that Hegelian dialectic is a self-power philosophy that does not take seriously enough the absolute disruption of reason (37, 51).

In contrast to the Hegelian *Aufhebung,* Tanabe's absolute critique looks to the resurrection of reason by Other-power. Unlike the synthesis of *Begriff,* Tanabe's "resurrection" is not a restoration of reason to its former self-identity and power of criticism. Taking the standpoint of a "self-power" philosophy, Hegel was led ineluctably to understand religious self-consciousness in terms of a restoration to a former unity, from which subjectivity has become separated. Guided by Kierkegaard, Tanabe rejected the idea of the restoration of reason in Hegel's *Begriff* because of its inability to cope with the absolute paradox of religious experience (44-45, 52). In genuine religious self-awakening, the absolute disruption of reason is itself a "unity" even as it remains a disruption and unresolvable contradiction. The contradiction that is unresolvable so long as it clings to the self-reliance of self-power becomes resolvable without ceasing to be a contradiction when the subject decides to "die its own death" and voluntarily abandons itself to its self-contradiction. Guided by Shinran as well,[11] Tanabe observed that this disruption-*qua*-unity is akin to Shinran's belief that "We participate in *nirvāṇa* during life, without cutting ourselves off entirely from our lusts."[12] Hegel, however, by maintaining that self-consciousness is the ultimate subject of religious action, cannot comprehend the paradox of religious awakening. Reflecting Buddhist religious insights, Tanabe saw that in religious awakening there is no "self" of which we come to be conscious, for the ephemeral ego is annihilated in the absolute disruption.

The transformation of the self into nothingness in all genuine religious action required Tanabe to return to his earlier criticisms of the *Nishida tetsugaku* and especially to the problem of "absolute nothingness" as a metaphysical category for interpreting genuine religious awakening in terms of the action of Other-power (45).

THE ABSOLUTE MEDIATION

A detailed analysis of the controversy between Nishida Kitarō and Tanabe Hajime regarding the meaning of absolute nothingness would go far beyond the confines of this summary.[13] To complicate matters, despite the fact that Nishida's ideas were repeatedly brought up for criticism, Tanabe never introduced Nishida's name explicitly into the text. All the same, I believe that in *Philosophy*

---

[11] Shinran is one of the major figures in the Pure Land movement in Japan. Tanabe was significantly influenced by the writings of Shinran, especially the *Kyōgyōshinshō* 教行信証 . For a discussion of Tanabe's use of Shinran, and his complex debt to Pure Land Buddhist thought in general, see Johannes Laube, "Die Interpretation des *Kyōgyōshinshō* Shinrans durch Hajime Tanabe," *Zeitschrift für Missionswissenschaft und Religionswissenschaft* 65/4 (1981): 227-93.

[12] PM, 45. For the source of the passage under discussion, see Shinran's *Shō-shin-ge* 正信偈 *[The Gatha of True Faith in the Nembutsu]* (Kyoto: Ryukoku Translation Series edition, 1961) 23, line 26.

[13] For a particularly clear and insightful presentation of Tanabe's and Nishida's disagreements regarding absolute nothingness, see Kōsaka Masaaki 高坂正顕 , 西田哲学と田辺哲学 *[The Philosophies of Nishida and Tanabe]*, reprinted in 高坂正顕著作集 *[The Collected Writings of Kōsaka Masaaki]*, Vol. 8 (Tokyo: Risōsha, 1965), 235-372.

as Metanoetics Tanabe's views of *Nishida tetsugaku* entered a new stage of development[14] and for this reason must be recognized as an important, if not always explicit, theme within the text.[15]

Some commentators have contended that Tanabe greatly overestimated his differences with Nishida while others take pains to note their precise points of disagreement.[16] Given the intricacies of both men, and the manifold of issues that unite and distinguish their positions, I am going to suggest the philosophical issues of monism and dualism as a useful way to bring some order to this tangled skein of problems. While Tanabe and Nishida are in agreement with one another on the non-dualistic character of absolute nothingness, Tanabe believed Nishida's "logic of place" leads inevitably to a monistic interpretation of absolute nothingness. In *Philosophy as Metanoetics*, Tanabe offered the "absolute mediation" as a more relatively adequate interpretation.

Tanabe is in agreement with Nishida's aphorism that "the true absolute does not negate the relative." Any absolute that can be thought of in opposition to relative being (as its negation) is by that very fact merely another form of relative being and not the true absolute. Only true nothingness, i.e. the absolute nothingness that can be opposed neither to being nor to non-being, can rightfully be acknowledged as the absolute. Since it cannot be opposed to the relative as its negation, absolute nothingness is experienced as its absolute affirmation.

---

[14] Tanabe turned from the "logic of species" as a basis for criticizing Nishida's notion of absolute nothingness to his theory of absolute mediation.

[15] The summary of Tanabe's dissent which follows should in no way obscure the fact that, to a certain extent, Nishida's final essay, "The Logic of the Place of Nothingness and the Religious Worldview" (see *Last Writings*, trans. David Dilworth, Honolulu: University of Hawaii Press, 1987, 47-123) can be read as a response to the criticisms leveled against his views on religious realization and absolute nothingness in Tanabe's lectures on metanoetics in Kyoto. Untangling the lines of these two colliding brigantines is rendered all the more difficult given the fact that not only was Nishida acquainted with Tanabe's fundamental position regarding metanoetics because of the lectures of 1941-1945, but also Tanabe was familiar with Nishida's final essay (which appeared the year previous to the publication of *Philosophy as Metanoetics*).

[16] For the former, see James Heisig's views on the Tanabe-Nishida controversy in his "Foreword" to the English translation of *Philosophy as Metanoetics*, xviii. For the latter, see Kōsaka Masaaki's carefully drawn comparison of Tanabe and Nishida in *The Philosophies of Nishida and Tanabe*.

To this extent, Tanabe's interpretation of absolute nothingness is fundamentally in keeping with that of Nishida (158). The
disagreement between the two, at least in Tanabe's estimation,
regards the way absolute nothingness is realized in the acting
subject. Tanabe insisted repeatedly that absolute nothingness cannot be realized by means of an aesthetic intuition into an experiential immediacy prior to the opposition of subject and object.
It arises mediately among relative beings in the transforming event
of Other-power. Were the absolute to "exist" immediately, it would
be being, not true nothingness. In order for it to be true nothingness, on the one hand, it cannot be understood apart from
religious self-awakening, while on the other hand, it is present
only in being mediated by the self-negation of the relative, having
no unmediated existence of its own. Since absolute nothingness
has no reality apart from the mediation of relative being, instead
of Nishida's notion of "place" (*basho*) as a metaphysical model for
absolute nothingness, Tanabe turned instead to the notion of "absolute mediation" (165).

Tanabe's preference for "mediation" (*baikai* 媒介) over "place"
(*basho* 場所) was required by his disagreement with Nishida regarding the manner in which true nothingness is realized in the
acting subject. Since for Tanabe absolute nothingness arises not
in an intuition but in the transformation of subjectivity by Other-
power, Tanabe's commitment to non-duality becomes a problem
for him in a way that it is not a problem for Nishida. If the
"otherness" of Other-power opposes it to the relative, it would be
experienced as the negation of the relative and not its absolute
affirmation as absolute nothingness. But since this was not the
case in Tanabe's experience of metanoia, his own religious experience led him to speak of the "mediation" of absolute nothingness
between relative being and relative being, instead of its *basho*.

Tanabe was required to argue the merits of mediation as a
non-dualism. In the absolute mediation that constitutes the relationship between the relative and the absolute, that which is mediated cannot be opposed to that which mediates. Tanabe offered
two reasons in which his fundamental affinity with Nishida becomes evident once again. First, since self-consciousness arises only
through the mediation of absolute nothingness as being-*qua*-noth-
ingness, the self is not a substance which can be opposed to the
absolute. Second, since absolute nothingness itself does not "exist"

as an object of intellectual experience, but is present as transformative power only in the mediation of relative being, it does not exist as an object which can be opposed to the relative. In other words, the self is not a substance, the absolute is not a thing. In the dialectics of mutual mediation of true self and absolute nothingness, the absolute mediation overcomes dualism.

The non-dualism of absolute mediation is inextricably related to the phenomenon of metanoia. All subjects, to the extent that they affirm themselves directly as non-contradictory self-identities (substances), must eventually experience their mutual relativity in the historical world and inevitably fall into the "radical evil" of reciprocal negation. However, in religious awakening, the negation of the finite subject is itself negated by means of the reciprocal mediation of the subject's self-negation (*zange*) and the affirming grace of Other-power *(tariki)*.

> Here we see the true nature of *tariki*. Although *zange* is an act of the self, it does not belong to the self but is an act of self-surrender and must be an act of absolute nothingness. Thus *zange*, as distinguished from the despair of arrogance, includes the despair of submission in which no self-assertion of the ego performing *zange* remains (7).

In this sense, the experience of metanoia and the metanoetic "philosophy that is not a philosophy" that arises from it must be understood in terms of "action without an acting self" *(musa-no-sa* 無作の作).

At the same time, absolute nothingness, even when understood as the transformative activity of *tariki* as Tanabe argued, does not negate the relative because it has no reality apart from being mediated by the relative in the action of self-surrender. That which can be affirmed directly or intuited immediately is "being," not true nothingness. Only true nothingness is free of all negation and for this reason the absolute affirmation of relative being. Therefore, absolute nothingness is present in the social and historical world "only by affirming relative beings, negating the immediacy of its own absolute power vis-à-vis relative beings in order to give them life" (158).

> Since the true absolute always entails an absolute mediation, it can never dispense with relative beings but brings about

their cooperation in this mediation in order to make its own nothingness real (158).

Paradoxically, therefore, absolute nothingness is "absolute" only through the self-negation *(zange)* of relative beings (157-59).

Tanabe's concern for a non-dualistic mediation of absolute nothingness led him to his own application of the Buddhist logic of *soku* 即.[17] *Zange*, like its Greek equivalent *metanoesis*, implies conversion as well as repentance. Conversion is the "transformed negativity" experienced in the "event" of the absolute affirmation of subjectivity by Other-power. Negativity is converted into absolute affirmation in two "directions" simultaneously: on the one hand, the self realizes through its religious "action" that it is the mediation of absolute nothingness; while on the other hand, the absolute negates itself in order to be mediated among relative beings as the true absolute (absolute nothingness). In the experience of religious transformation, *zange* as self-power *(jiriki*=the subject's innate capacity to surrender itself in repentance), and *zange* as Other-power *(tariki*=the transformation of subjectivity by the absolute), cannot be understood dualistically. *Jiriki* is possible only through the grace of *tariki*, while *tariki* is realized in the social and historical world only through the mediatory power of *jiriki* (6). If *tariki* were to act immediately on the subject, apart from its mediation in the self-surrender of the subject, it would form an opposition to the relative as its simple negation (acting extrinsically from without) and not its absolute affirmation. In keeping with the non-dualism implied in Nishida's aphorism, "the true absolute does not negate the relative," absolute nothingness,

---

[17] While the influence of German Idealism on the thought of the Kyoto School is not to be denied, the real source of the School's dialectical thinking is that of Mahāyāna Buddhism. In this regard, attention must be given to the conjunctive *soku* (which might be rendered with the Latin conjunction *sive*). Jan Van Bragt comments:

> Put between two contradictory concepts (for instance in the formula "emptiness-*sive*-form, form-*sive*-emptiness"), it is meant to draw off the total reality of the two poles into itself as their constitutive and ontological prior unity. It indicates the only point or "place" at which the opposites are realized and display their true reality. In order more clearly to show the "inverse correspondence" or "identity through negation" at work here, this has at times been referred to as the logic of *soku/hi (sive/non)* ["Translator's Introduction," RN, xxx].

realized in the transformation of subjectivity by Other-power, takes the logical form, *jiriki*-soku-*tariki*. For Tanabe, this can be the case only if the absolute and relative mediate one another absolutely.

TANABE'S CRITIQUE OF MONISM

Tanabe's mediation model of absolute nothingness precludes any dualistic interpretation of the absolute. In this respect at least, his views on absolute nothingness do not seem to differ significantly from the position espoused by Nishida. The problem of a monistic interpretation, however, remains to be addressed. I contend that Tanabe's dissatisfaction with a monistic interpretation of the absolute lies at the center of his criticism of the *Nishida tetsugaku*. In seeking to sustain a thoroughgoing non-dualism, the model of absolute nothingness as the "place" *(basho)* of absolutely contradictory self-identity *(zettai mujunteki jikodōitsu* 絶対矛盾的自己同一) inevitably led Nishida to the problem of a metaphysical monism, which (in Tanabe's estimation) the "logic of place" is unable to solve successfully. Using categories first used by Kierkegaard against Hegel, Tanabe maintained that the "logic of place" leads to "the aesthetic," not "the religious," and in so doing is unable ultimately to sustain "the ethical." Therefore I would like to suggest the principle "neither monism nor dualism" as a heuristic device useful in understanding Tanabe's dispute with Nishida.

Given the fact that the saving action of Other-power is his starting point, Tanabe is required to take great care in avoiding a dualistic interpretation of absolute nothingness. Did Tanabe's solution, the logic of absolute mediation, in fact lead him to a monistic alternative? Thus it would seem, of course, if Tanabe were claiming that in the "action without an acting self" there obtains a relationship of simple identity between the absolute and the relative. This however is not the case. Other-power has no unmediated existence apart from the metanoia of relative beings. It cannot be intuited immediately as a "pure experience" (the *junsui keiken* 純粋経験 of Nishida's *An Inquiry into the Good)*. Its reality is not that of an original totality prior to the differentiations of subject-object consciousness. Therefore, Tanabe became convinced that the religious event of conversion which overcomes all duality cannot be fully fathomed with Nishida's logic of the self-identity of absolute contradictories. In overcoming the dualism of absolute nothingness, *Nishida tetsugaku* also overcomes the alterity of the true religious absolute and thereby falls prey to a metaphysical monism.

> Instead of having its ground in "the self-identity of absolute contradictories," absolute nothingness must be grounded in the absolute mediatory activity of one's religious existence through "death and resurrection." Hence, absolute nothingness can also be called *tariki*, since it is experienced through faith-witness (*shin-shō* 信証) as the principle of the negation and transformation of the self. In this sense, *tariki* inevitably depends on *jiriki* as its mediatory "other" (8).

Tanabe remained committed to his interpretation of the absolute as the power which transforms subjectivity without thereby entering into opposition with it (non-dualism), while at the same time remaining its "other" (non-monism). Apart from the experience of transformation in the death and resurrection of the subject through the grace of Other-power, the concept of absolute nothingness decays into the idealism of an unmediated transcendent which in fact connotes being, not nothingness. When understood as a self-identity of absolute contradiction beyond all discrimination, absolute nothingness forms an immediacy of undifferentiated totality which is apprehended noetically as the content of a contemplative intuition. The logic of the self-identity of absolute contradictories secures the non-dualism of absolute nothingness but cannot affirm its "otherness." Thus Tanabe became convinced that only if the religious absolute is understood in terms of the absolute mediation of the transformative power of nothingness can the metaphysical critique of dualism avoid the complementary problem of monism with its attendant religious and ethical implications.[18]

ORDINARY MYSTICISM

Tanabe's position carries within it a rejection of what he called "ordinary mysticism" in the religious heritages of both the East and the West. In Plotinian mysticism, for instance, the twofold movement of transcendence (the *ek-stasis* of the soul into the One)

---

[18] For Tanabe's views on the ethical implications of metanoetics, see PM, 154-56.

and emanation (the descent of the One into the many) is based on the principles of self-identity and immediacy with no real religious transformation of subjectivity in the grace-event of Other-power.

> True self-consciousness of the absolute cannot come about through one continuous medium joining God or the absolute with the relative. The real awakening of self-consciousness in its religious or existential dimension comes only through the "death and resurrection" of a negative transformation that takes place between the absolute and the relative (12).

Without the death and resurrection of the subject (its "absolute disruption" logically speaking), which is mediated in the "action" of Other-power, there is merely the "ordinary mysticism" of contemplative union. Tanabe's complaint against neo-Platonic monism, interestingly, closely approximates Christian theological arguments against it: first, it presumes a relationship of simple identity between the absolute and the relative which can be realized apart from the death and resurrection of the subject, and second, this realization of primordial unity is accomplished contemplatively through the innate power of subjectivity without any need for grace *(tariki)*. Concurring with the Christian critique of neo-Platonism, Tanabe wrote that "the death on the cross and resurrection lose their significance, and yield the ascendancy to the aesthetic standpoint of pantheism."[19]

In criticizing Plotinian mysticism, Tanabe most certainly had Nishida in mind as well.

> [The self-identity of absolute contradictories] reverts back to the aesthetic contemplation involved in producing a work of art, after the manner of Plotinus who treats action only in terms of its relation to contemplation (80).

However, to contend that Tanabe "traced the philosophical pedigree of Nishida's position to the emanational logic of Plotinus and the Neoplatonists"[20] overlooks, I think, Tanabe's own ambivalence on the question. For instance, in one passage he clearly

---

[19] PM, 167. Once again it should be noted that Tanabe's personal crisis of the war years in Japan provides the biographical context which should not be separated from the text.

draws a distinction between Plotinus and Nishida without lessening his criticism of either.

> Some may imagine a self-identical totality directly accessible to the grasp of intellectual intuition, but the nothingness we are speaking of here cannot be intuited at all. In the case of "action-intuition" — intuition for the sake of action, into the content of one's formative (creative) activity, in contradistinction to Plotinus's concept of intuition — action is understood as the function of self-power that is at work in aesthetic expression-and-formation. It has nothing at all to do with action based on the Other-power of absolute nothingness (45).

Given these difficulties with the text, what can be said assuredly is that Tanabe associated to some degree Nishida's notion of intuition with the Plotinian metaphysics of totality. In each case, the monistic tendencies which result are unable to account for the mediation of the absolute in the transformation of the subject.

The problem of "ordinary mysticism," however, is not restricted to the Western tradition. Monistic tendencies in Buddhism are criticized as well. Tanabe's discussion of the Zen doctrine of "seeing into one's nature" *(kenshō 見性)* offers a good example. On the one hand, Zen's use of the *kōan* constitutes a way of absolute negation that corresponds, in Tanabe's estimation, to the absolute critique in metanoetics. The seeker of absolute truth, driving reason to its limit, inevitably runs into the wall of absolute contradiction where the resurrection of thought is captured in the Zen aphorism,

> Hanging from the edge of a precipice, one lets go and is immediately brought back to life (168).

But on the other hand, Zen remains a self-power *(jiriki)* philosophy. At the heart of Zen practice lies the subject's self-realization of its original Buddha-nature.

> Buddha and sentient beings relate to one another as water to ice. At first glance, sentient beings seem to stand in diametrical opposition to the Buddha, but in fact both share the same na-

---

[20] James Heisig, "Foreword" in PM, xviii.

ture. Death as a sentient being is none other than life as Buddha (169).

The diametrical opposition of Buddha and self is transcended through *jiriki* into the realm of total non-differentiation. However, Zen's insistence on the radical non-duality of the absolute and the relative, despite its recognition of the transformation of subjectivity, is not the same as the realization of absolute nothingness in absolute mediation. *Kenshō* based on self-power presumes the self-identity of Buddha and sentient beings. When Zen proclaims that "Mind, just as it is, is identical with the Buddha" (171), it risks decaying into an "ordinary mysticism" of unmediated self-identity. In this case, Tanabe claimed (using Kierkegaard's distinction) that Zen substitutes "the aesthetic" for "the religious" with the result that "religious action fails to be mediated by the rational seriousness of ethics" (171).

As with his association of Nishida with Plotinus, Tanabe's implicit criticism of Nishida by means of a criticism of Zen carries with it a tangle of subsidiary problems. For instance, Tanabe's assertion that Zen does not sufficiently negate the ego has not found a widely sympathetic audience among other members of the Kyoto School. Likewise, his claim that the *Nishida tetsugaku* is a philosophy of self-power with no true sense of the death and resurrection of subjectivity is problematic at best.[21]

Implicit in Tanabe's discussion of "ordinary mysticism" is an important criticism of Nishida's understanding of authentic religious "action" and the interpretation of absolute nothingness.

ACTION-FAITH AND ACTION-INTUITION

In agreement with Nishida Kitarō, Tanabe recognized neither the ultimate irrationality of the subject nor its absolute rationality. The former would effectively eliminate the possibility of freedom while the latter results in an unacceptably dehistoricized subject.

---

[21] Partially in response to Tanabe's lectures on metanoetics, Nishida specifically addressed the problem of self-power and Other-power as well as the centrality of self-negation in his philosophy of religious action. For a helpful treatment of Nishida's position vis-à-vis that of Tanabe, see Christopher Ives, "Non-dualism and Soteriology in Whitehead," EB 22/1 (Spring, 1989): 128-38, esp. 134.

However, unlike Nishida, he did not believe that the metaphysical ground of individual self-consciousness could be intuited. Instead of an intuition into the self-identity of absolute contradiction, Tanabe turned instead to the religious notion of faith as a model of authentic subjectivity (159-60). "Faith" is the metanoetic awareness that arises only after the death of subjectivity. Thus Nishida's "action-intuition" is to be contrasted with Tanabe's "action-faith." Once again, in Tanabe's estimation, the issue of existential transformation in the death and resurrection of subjectivity marks the critical element of difference between the two.

What does it mean for Tanabe to insist that "death" is a necessary moment in authentic religious action? First, Tanabe was not interested in death as an event "outside of the self." Such a death is no more than a scientific or social phenomenon. For it to become a true philosophical problem, the death in question must be the death of the self. Furthermore, this "death of the self" cannot be merely a future anticipation of non-being; rather it must be a "self-consciousness of death" as a present reality which determines the mode of subjectivity (161). In effect, death as "religious action" is something that is "practiced," not as suicide (the inauthentic death of self-assertion) but as Buddhism's "Great Death." For Tanabe, this "Great Death" is not something simply willed by the self as self-assertion (*jiriki*) but rather something mediated by absolute nothingness in the radical submission of the self to that which is not the self (*tariki*). Only such a "Great Death" is absolutely free from the ego. And so, in keeping with the non-dualistic principle of *jiriki-soku-tariki*, the self practices the "Great Death" by surrendering even its will to die.

> Briefly put, the terms "activity" and "passivity," or "initiation and promotion" and "voluntary submission," are complementary despite the dichotomy they suggest, because all of them refer to a state of transforming mediation. But in this transformation, which is one of reciprocal penetration, self-consciousness of death as a "living as one dead" or as "dying as one alive" is possible. It is the self living in the present that prepares itself for death in the future, but such a self-consciousness of death is possible only when the self is already dying to itself (162-63).

In the "religious action" of "acting as one who has died," the acting subject is confronted with the paradox of "living only through dying," a contradiction which can be neither denied nor transcended, only mediated by the authentic action of faith.

Tanabe's preference for "action-faith" over "action-intuition" returns us to the problem of dialectics. True "religious action" is a dialectic of "neither/nor." Not surprisingly given his views regarding "ordinary mysticism," Tanabe rejected Hegel's dialectical strategy of "both/and." The religious action of "death-in-life" (action-faith) cannot be sustained by a self-consciousness based on the logic of self-identity operating as the universal principle that unites both life and death into a greater synthesis. Hegel's twofold affirmation does not fully confront the "radical evil" of the irrational. More surprisingly, Tanabe finds Kierkegaard's dialectic of "either/or" (in which either the contradiction or the self can be affirmed) unsuitable because it distorts faith into a one-sided negation of the self, lacking the absolute affirmation of the self that is the hallmark of authentic "religious action." Tanabe's position seems to be that whereas with Hegel there is no cross, with Kierkegaard there is no resurrection. In place of the dialectics of Kierkegaard and Hegel, Tanabe articulated what he considered a Mahāyāna Buddhist dialectic of "neither/nor,"

> in which the self does not stand opposed to the contradiction nor the contradiction to the self, but negates the self by means of the contradiction, so that at the same time that the self is extinguished in the negation, the confrontation is also extinguished as that which opposes the self (164).

Only in the dialectical mediation of neither/nor is the dualistic opposition of life and death overcome in the self-awakening of authentic religious consciousness. But the alternative advanced by Tanabe to Hegelian and Kierkegaardian dialectics does not succumb to the danger of an unmediated monism in which both life and death, relative and absolute are reduced to undifferentiated unity. Contrary to Nishida, the nothingness that is the ground of this neither/nor cannot be intuited even as a self-contradictory identity. It is realized instead only in the mediating subjectivity of "action-faith." It is a self-awareness established not in the ultimate identity of the self and the absolute, but in the on-going passing away of the self as the self that lives only through dying (163-67, 176, 233).

Accordingly, it seems that Tanabe's notion of "action-faith" is consistent with his interpretation of absolute nothingness as absolute mediation. The absolute is not "known" noetically in an intuition. This is what Kierkegaard called "the aesthetic" in contrast to "the religious." Instead the absolute is "known" metanoetically in the transformation of subjectivity by Other-power that is at the same time an act of faith. Thus, in contrast to Nishida's concept of "action-intuition," Tanabe advances "action-faith" as a non-monistic alternative (163-64, 166).

The non-monistic character of authentic "religious action" carries with it a critique of Nishida's notion of "place" (*basho*) as a metaphor for absolute nothingness.

THE CRITIQUE OF THE "LOGIC OF PLACE"

Tanabe's first objection to "place" as a model for absolute nothingness was that nothingness is neither "something to which immediate experience can attest" (118) nor something that can be "intuited as a ground, or locus" (165). Since whatever can be experienced immediately belongs to the realm of being, not nothingness, Tanabe called into question the possibility of "pure experience" as the "field" (*basho*) of absolute nothingness. Any claim to know absolute nothingness noetically is misguided. In lieu of absolute nothingness as *basho*, Tanabe offered his model of absolute mediation.

> From the standpoint of dialectical mediation, knowledge or self-consciousness of nothingness is possible because there is no object that is known nor any self that knows, no self to be self-conscious or to become the object of self-consciousness (119).

Since the true absolute has no "existence" apart from the relative, there is no need to postulate an unmediated universal beyond all differentiation. Such a universal would be the totality of being, not true nothingness.

Tanabe's second objection to Nishida's notion of *basho* is that in confusing "the aesthetic" for "the religious," Nishida is unable to give an adequate accounting for "the ethical." It is not possible to determine the concrete social and historical meaning of religious transformation with the "logic of place." The self-identity of absolute contradictories belongs to the realm of noetics, not meta-noetics. In this respect (and in the face of Nishida's own explicit claim to the contrary), the *basho* of absolute nothingness is merely an abstract universal (an ideal), not the concrete universal, because it has yet to attain the concreteness of absolute mediation (10). In the authentic religious action of *zange*, there is no need to postulate a "place" of absolute nothingness. This standpoint fails to illuminate true religious action in that it is incapable of sustaining an ethical response to the historical world because it "neglects the deeper significance of the role of the axis in absolute transformation" (11). The specific ethical meaning of religious self-awareness cannot be determined with a "mere topological deduction" because the absolute arises historically and socially only in the reciprocal mediation of Other-power and the subject's *zange*. Relying on terminology drawn from the Pure Land tradition, Tanabe criticized Nishida's "logic of place" for clinging to *ōsō* 往相 (transcending this world in search of the Pure Land) and neglecting *gensō* 還相 (leaving the Pure Land and returning to this world, in the tradition of the Bodhisattva, with the ethics of the "Great Compassion") (11).

A third major objection Tanabe advances against Nishida's model of the *basho* of the self-identity of absolute contradictories recapitulates his critique of the Hegelian dialectic of "both/and." The religious action envisioned by Tanabe is not the realization of unity that brings contradictions into synthesis by way of negation and sublation, but a realization that leaves contradiction intact. Dialectical synthesis implies the removal of opposition between thesis and antithesis, and therefore does not go beyond the purview of self-identical reason and the principle of non-contradiction. In the absolute affirmation of true religious action, however, contradiction is never abrogated. Instead, "because the subject dies in the depths of the contradiction, the opposition ceases to be an opposition, but the contradictories are left as they are" (133).

Absolute nothingness as the negation of negation must not be misunderstood as the achievement of synthesis and the extinguishing of negation in the restoration of a former unity. This would be the establishment of a "unity of being": what Tanabe called the "all-encompassing." Instead of the "unity of being," Tanabe wrote, with some misgivings, of the "unity of nothingness." To the extent that this phrase can be used at all, the "unity of nothingness" cannot be construed as an all-encompassing *topos* capable of rendering contradictories into a greater synthesis of contradictory self-identity. The only "unity of nothingness" is that of transformation in absolute mediation where relative beings realize their true emptiness in their transformation by Other-power, even as their mutual contradiction remains. If this religious action cannot be realized with the Hegelian dialectic of "both/and," neither can it be understood with Nishida's concept of "place." It requires instead the Mahāyāna dialectic of "neither/nor" and Tanabe's notion of absolute mediation (132-33).

THE PHILOSOPHY THAT IS NOT A PHILOSOPHY

In keeping with Takeuchi's observations which began these reflections on *Philosophy as Metanoetics*, it must not be forgotten that for Tanabe, the existential significance of the absolute critique of reason held within it a deeply religious meaning. In the midst of the death of the subject and the "absolute disruption" of reason, the power of contradiction itself is contradicted, negation itself is negated. Tanabe believed that herein lay the logical form of what existentially was his religious metanoia and transformation through Other-power. Tanabe recognized the resurrection of subjectivity and the restoration of reason, but even more importantly, he argued that the discourse which arises from this transformation is no longer a philosophy that clings futilely to the power of reason to secure a knowledge of the absolute, but rather the "philosophy that is not a philosophy," a discourse that transcends the noetic without abandoning it. Tanabe was clearly not envisioning a problem for an analytical or even a transcendental logic: the absolute critique does not envision the elimination of reason's self-contradiction by yet another application of the law of identity and non-contradiction (39). Instead of pure reason, Tanabe's position was shaped by the religious experience of his existential transformation.

Metanoetic philosophy consists in submitting to this transformation obediently "in ceaseless joy and gratitude." Reason is resurrected from its death through the action of a "transcendent grace" such that, in reason's repentance, it becomes aware of its sinful pretense to absolute knowledge, the futility of its self-reliance and its innate finitude. It is not an action that the subject performs by itself, but paradoxically is "action based entirely on Other-power in spite of being our own power." In effect, Tanabe's argument is that the subject's metanoia is itself the mediation of "the religious" as the transformative event of "the other" (44).

In this religious transformation, the "philosophy that is not a philosophy" arises as a metanoetic (and meta-rational) cognition. Since reason has been shattered in the experience of "breaking through" itself without being formally aware of this fact in criticism, Tanabe speaks of "genuine action" (*gyōteki-ji* 行的事) as the concrete social and historical fact (*ji* 事) that arises in the resurrection of "new being" from relative nothingness by the power of absolute nothingness. The world (including the subject) is transformed into "being as *upāya*"[22] through the transformative power of absolute nothingness in which Tanabe recognizes the authentic "action of no-action" or "action without an acting self." In Buddhist terms, the illusion of the substantial ego is overcome in the realization of the "non-self" (*anātman*) since "action" is no longer rooted in the autonomy of the subject (as a *substantia*) or the autonomy of reason (as a tool of criticism).

The "genuine action" of Other-power brings with it the metanoetic awareness that the human predicament cannot be solved by reason alone and that "genuine action" is not only metanoetic, but meta-rational and meta-subjective as well. Since it is this "genuine action" arising in the transformative power of "the other" which makes it possible to establish the rational in spite of the negation and transcendence of the rational, the dynamic structure of being-*qua*-nothingness, or emptied being, forms the ground out of which reason is resurrected by breaking through itself.

While addressing the problem of the absolute critique of reason in its quest for absolute knowledge, Tanabe once again turned his attention to the problem of finite reason entering into an ultimate crisis in reaching its limits.

> It is both a matter of destiny and ultimate truth that in the pursuit of full autonomy, reason finally breaks down. But where can reason, shattered and sunk into sheer nothingness, find a

---

[22] The Sanskrit term *upāya* refers to the pragmatic and soteriological use finite realities serve after the illusion of substantial being has been overcome with wisdom (*prajñā*). It is often rendered in English with the expression "expedient means."

> foothold from which to break out of its crisis by breaking
> through itself from which to be transformed and resurrected
> from nothingness into new being? (39)

In answering his own question, Tanabe was led, like Nishida before him, to the notion of absolute nothingness. Yet unlike Nishida, instead of the metaphor "place" (basho), Tanabe looked to the
experience of existential transformation by Other-power.

> . . . the depths of reality as a whole can be fathomed only when
> we are convinced that the absolute consists solely in the trans-
> formative power of absolute nothingness (39).

Tanabe's concept of absolute mediation forms the metaphysical basis for his metanoetic philosophy as well. In keeping with
his concept of absolute criticism, philosophy begins in a consciousness of the self rooted in the autonomy of reason and from there
extends through the antinomies of reason to an awareness of the
fact that the self exists only through the mediation of absolute
nothingness, and conversely, that the absolute (i.e. absolute nothingness) has no reality apart from the mediation of relative beings.
Accordingly, philosophy itself is constituted by a religious self-
awakening to this reciprocal mediation: first, that the self is always
being-qua-nothingness, i.e. being as a mediation of emptiness (śūnyatā); and second, that absolute nothingness is realized in the
"genuine action" of self-consciousness. In this way, philosophy as
metanoetics begins in the death and resurrection of the acting
self to a new level of existence and self-awareness which is beyond
the dualities of life and death, immanence and transcendence,
subject and object. The action in which this reciprocal or "absolute" mediation arises is metanoesis. As I interpret Tanabe, its
logical form is neither a monism nor a dualism (17-18).

Thus the principle "neither monism nor dualism" also helps
to illuminate Tanabe's somewhat vague notion of the "philosophy
that is not a philosophy." The non-dualism/non-monism of absolute mediation is realized only in the event of transformation by
Other-power. The expression of this experience in philosophical
discourse is possible through the resurrected "self-consciousness of
reason" that results from this logic of mediation. The authentic
philosophical task, therefore, is to participate in this "wondrous
transformation" and thus fulfill its task of bringing concrete reli-

gious experience to speech through the abstract and critical mediation of concepts. True philosophy, philosophy as metanoetics, arises only in the "genuine action" of absolute nothingness which has no reality apart from the metanoia of the subject. The proper task of philosophy, i.e., the logical mediation of "being-*qua*-emptiness," is carried out by explaining how absolute knowledge and the finite concepts neither belong to an original identity (monism) nor simply oppose each other (dualism), but rather exist in a dialectical relation of "neither-one-nor-two", "neither-identity-nor-difference" (13). In Tanabe's view, this logical and linguistic cohabitation of the relative and absolute is only possible by means of the logic and language of absolute mediation in which the two never collapse into an immediate identity and yet remain "flowing into one another without duality" (15). The conjunction of absolute knowledge and finite language is dynamic by virtue of the dialectical tension of non-identity and non-difference which characterizes their reciprocal mediation. Once again, the principle of "neither monism nor dualism" is at work in Tanabe's metanoetic philosophy.

Tanabe and the Philosophy of Religion

Langdon GILKEY

OUR subject is Tanabe Hajime and the philosophy of religion. This is, let us note, a paradoxical subject, as Tanabe
well knew. On the one hand, Tanabe was to the end a
philosopher and saw himself in that role. It was as a philosopher,
not primarily as a Buddhist, that he experienced his intellectual
and moral breakdown when he thought he dared not speak out
in Imperial Japan. This silence, he said, was a betrayal of philosophy and of his own role as a teacher of philosophy. After his
experience of renewal, he saw his subsequent task in life as that
of philosopher (PM, 1). And his epitaph appropriately read: "My
search is for truth and for it alone" (2).

On the other hand, as we shall see, his creative thought is
consequent on the breakdown and death of autonomous philosophy (3); it is, he tells us, "a philosophy that is not a philosophy"
(4)—and most important, it is a mode of thinking issuing from
and so utterly dependent on a deeply religious experience, a union
with "Other-power," and thus a thinking directed entirely by the
requirements of that experience of religious "mediation." In effect,
philosophy is now "knowledge through self-abandonment, the self-
consciousness of *zange* (repentance)" (5). If philosophy of religion
means the critical survey and interpretation of religion by autonomous and thus objective reason, Tanabe is no philosopher of
religion. If philosophy of religion can mean—perhaps philosophical theology or religious philosophy are better labels—the intellectual articulation of existence from the perspective of a religious
mode of thinking, an articulation directed by the contours of
religious experience, then Tanabe is a philosopher of religion—but
he represents a very special breed.

This is not to say that there have not been other members
of this species—though many philosophers would be loath to recognize them as "rational" enough to be called philosophers. We

must include those who are generally called "mystical philosophers," thinkers of every great tradition who articulate conceptually the spiritual path of religious enlightenment they have
followed, philosophers of Religion A, to borrow Kierkegaard's term.
Nevertheless, Tanabe distinguished himself sharply from such philosophers in his own tradition, notably from his own mentor,
Nishida Kitarō—and by implication as well from Nishitani Keiji
and Abe Masao—since to him the "death" of thinking they referred
to was not real death, and the renewal of self they proclaimed
was not a genuine renewal. As ordinary philosophers of religion
assumed, even in criticism, the continued autonomy and self-suf-
ficiency of reason, so these mystical philosophers assumed a continuing identity of self with the Absolute that Tanabe's experience
would deny. His is then a special breed within a special breed.

He is, however, by no means alone. Also, in each of the great
traditions: Hindu, Buddhist, Islamic, Judaic and Christian, there
are "twice-born" thinkers, thinkers who, like Tanabe, have experienced their reason not only as broken and in disarray but even
more as renewed and redirected by Other-power—though interestingly, except for his references to Kierkegaard, Tanabe shows
virtually no dependence on (nor even much consciousness of)
these many important figures in the history of religious reflection.
Certainly in Christianity this has been a major, if not dominant,
tradition. Beginning with Paul, it finds its perennial ancestral
source in Augustine (as Tanabe was aware), moves on possibly to
Anselm, certainly to the great Reformers, and reappears again as
if from an underground spring in Kierkegaard and his epigones,
the twentieth century dialectical or *Krisis* theologians: Barth, Brun-
ner, Bultmann, Nygren, the Niebuhrs, and especially Tillich. Although these latter were all contemporaries of Tanabe, he was
apparently quite unaware of them—as they surely were of him!

There are, of course, several good reasons for this mutual
non-dependence. In the first place, classical German philosophy—
with the possible exception of Schelling—hardly subscribed to the
theme of the death of reason and its resurrection through faith.
It was with this classical German tradition in the West, and not
with the Christian theological tradition per se, that Tanabe, like
Nishida before him and the Kyoto School after him, was exqui-
sitely familiar. Also let us note that, with the exception of Augustine, who was known to Tanabe (cf. his references to "credo ut

intelligam," 6), the other theologians of what Kierkegaard called Religion B appealed explicitly to revelation, Incarnation, and so to scripture, rather than primarily to religious experience for the bases of and the criteria for their renewed reflection. Even Kierkegaard, the one he knew the best, grounded faith on the Absolute Paradox, the revelatory event external to the self, and not internally on the new coming to be of the self. Surprisingly, only two so-called "liberals," Schleiermacher and Tillich, manifest a thoroughly analogous structure of religious reflection, namely one in form philosophical but one essentially grounded, shaped and directed by the rescuing experience of Other-power. With this wider context of differences and similarities in mind, then, let us analyze with more care the structure of Tanabe's "philosophy that is not a philosophy," this reflective self-consciousness of "death and resurrection," or "faith-action-witness."

I

Tanabe's mature reflection begins, so he tells us, with his own involved participation in the historical crisis of Imperial Japan in the war years of 1942 to 1945. In and through that impending social collapse, Tanabe experienced his own personal and vocational collapse, the "death" of his reason and of himself as a philosopher; he was, he says, immobilized and exhausted by doubts and by despair. (One is reminded of Augustine's personal collapse within the larger context of the collapse of classical reason and of Roman civilization in the late fourth century.) But then in recognizing, admitting and, to use Kierkegaard's language, appropriating and surrendering to this "powerlessness and lack of freedom," in humility and repentance, Tanabe experienced a "wondrous power" that both sharpened the consciousness of futility and sin and manifested the presence of a transcendent reality, Other-power, a veritable resurrection. In this union of repentance and renewal, of sin and grace, the stricken self is reawakened, thought begins anew on a new basis, and so philosophy too is reborn. This is metanoetics, or, in his most important term, "mediation," the union of self-power and Other-power, of *jiriki* and *tariki*. Almost unique in Buddhism and rare in Christianity, a deep personal participation in a major social crisis has here resulted in a profoundly new interpretation of interiority and all that is known via interiority: of self, of reason, of community and of ultimate reality (7).

As is clear, there is here a radical breakdown of autonomy, of *jiriki* or self-power. Tanabe insists on the depth and totality of this "death." In sharp distinction to the Kantian critique in which reason remains triumphantly capable, relinquishing only its own excesses of metaphysical and theological speculation, Tanabe's represents an "absolute critique" in which reason comes to a dead stop, a "death" of all of its powers. Nor is this the self-effacement of reason in mystical experience, where gradually the autonomous self, losing its attachments to the finite world and the finite self, voluntarily merges with the Absolute and thus "dies." For Tanabe these represent a self-effected transition, a stripping away by the essential self of its non-essential relations; this is hardly a genuine breakdown or death.

If I read him aright, it is the self or subject which uses, supports and controls reason and which criticizes and directs itself in moral reasoning, it is this very self that is here radically criticized, judged and later rescued. It is, therefore, an inordinate self-power in all its functions, "radical evil" (15), that represents the problem. This "swollen self," what in the Augustinian tradition is called pride or rebellion, is the problem; and it is this radical evil (sin) that must die; the self-centered or autonomous self must end in guilt and doubt, in repentance and total surrender, if anything is to be reborn. Hence—and here is the main point—it is only through some alien power, Other-power, not identical with itself, even with its own real self, that rescue can appear and the self become the true self. It is precisely this experience of Other-power as *other* and yet as renewing—i.e., as grace—that characterizes metanoesis. Hence this is philosophy, and yet "it is not a philosophy."

This is, as we have noted, not at all the end of philosophy. There is a Great Life after the Great Death, provided paradoxically that the repentance and surrender are genuine, that is to say, deliberate acts of self-power. As with Luther, so for Tanabe, a conventional recitation of repentance is of no use, in fact deluding. Thus while the rescuing *tariki* is other, repentance is an act also of *jiriki*; *tariki* joins with *jiriki* to effect rebirth. Genuine repentance is therefore rescued by Other-power; the negation of absolute criticism is countered by a negation of the negation. Or, in Tanabe's own language: *jiriki*, self-power, is reborn through *tariki*, Other-power, and *tariki* becomes embodied, so to speak, through serious *jiriki*, *jiriki-qua-tariki* (107). *Zange*, repentance, is thus an act at once of the self and of Other-power; in Tillich's language, it is theonomous, a union of autonomy and of the divine power, the latter empowering rather than crushing or overwhelming the former. Death, provided it be real death, is followed by resurrection. Again, as in Tillich, alone and separated from its ground, autonomy, self-power on the one hand, and heteronomy, an external divine absoluteness on the other hand, are ultimately either destructive or helpless; only in unity do they become effective, in fact real: creative relative being on the one hand and Absolute Nothingness on the other. *Zange* and its accompaniment, metanoesis, is thus "My act and yet not my act" (li, 7, 170-71), "autonomy determined by the transcendent" (86), "a union of Other-power with self-power" (14, 27), the mediation of the Absolute and the relative. As I have said elsewhere, this is the most elegant and comprehensive articulation of theonomy I have encountered.

It is through this experience of mediation, of *zange* and of metanoesis, that the Absolute makes itself known—as with Tillich the ground of being comes to our awareness through the experience of courage. *Tariki* is experienced through mediation, the union of *jiriki* and *tariki* in *zange* and renewal. It seems that to Tanabe this union—or mediation—takes place at two distinct but analogous levels, although he does not make this point explicit. First, as a universal process, there is the "historicity" of relative things and persons in passage. As in Heidegger—and one might add, in Whitehead—this passage represents a movement from "thrownness," "facticity," being determined, to project, intention, decision and action—or, in Tillich's categories, from destiny to freedom: "History is the transformation of contingency into freedom; contingency is turned into the choice and decision of the subject" (66). This passage of temporality, uniting a determined past to an open future, implies to Tanabe—as it did to Augustine, Thomas, Whitehead and Tillich—an absolute ground, in this case in Absolute Nothingness (71-73). The contingent alone cannot account for either passage or for time since the contingent here dies or is "annihilated" ("passes away" to Whitehead); it must therefore be carried through by a power beyond itself, a union or mediation of Other-power and self-power.

Clearly this universal mediation of Absolute and relative, constitutive alike of the moving world of change and of time, is analogous to, but not identical with, the mediation in special religious awareness of *zange* and renewal, of repentance-faith-action, of death and resurrection so clearly disclosed in Tanabe's personal experience. Both are labeled mediation, and both exhibit the same form, of a creative and cooperative union of *jiriki* and *tariki*. One may hazard that for Tanabe it is through the disclosure of Nothingness in the more personal and religious experience of metanoesis that the universal grounding of all temporal and relative being is itself made known. As in other forms of "twice-born" reflection, the awareness of the universal activity of the Absolute comes through the latter's special manifestation in unique and deeply personal religious experience. While, therefore, the universal and effective role of Nothingness as the source or ground of all relative being is an important aspect of Tanabe's philosophy, this is not, I take it, an example of natural theology, of the uncovering of the Absolute through autonomous reason, through the exercise of *jiriki* alone. Other-power manifests its own mediating presence in temporal passage only as it manifests itself in and to the self humbled by *zange*.

It is even more clear that for Tanabe the Absolute is not known by intuition, mystical or otherwise. Intuition is, he agrees, of *a* being; it is, therefore, of an external entity, and thus the relation to it is an "aesthetic" and not a religious relation. As with Kierkegaard and Tillich, there is and can be no direct experience of the Absolute, lest that which is experienced, in becoming an object or a being, cease to be absolute and relevant religiously. On the contrary, the Absolute is known through participation, to use Tillich's term: in the first instance through the personal and existential participation of the self in *zange* and renewal, in repentance, surrender and new life, in death and resurrection (87); and in the second instance through the self's participation in passage from thrownness to project, from contingency to freedom, responsibility and action (73). Knowledge of the Absolute is thus "the self-consciousness of action-faith" (86), through the "self-consciousness of *zange*" (87-88); and "In the self-consciousness of witness, the self-consciousness of Nothingness is realized" (164).

As a final point on method we should note the intimate and essential union here of religious experience, religious knowledge *and* ethics, even social ethics—again a parallel with the Augustinian tradition where knowledge of God is through faith completed in caritas, or, as Luther put it: faith is the doer, love the deed. If the religious relation is a self-conscious relation of mediation, of the working of Other-power in and through the effective functioning of self-power, and if the latter, self-power, realizes itself in relation to other relative beings, then it follows that the religious relation to Other-power of repentance and faith is completed only when it issues in action and witness "in the world." Mediation is the creative presence of Other-power, of Absolute Nothingness, in and through the realm of relative beings (87): here the Absolute is known, the true status of the relative disclosed, and the relations among the "beings" clarified and purified; resurrection is in this world and for this world, a new being in history among the beings. This message is, so it seems to me, though I can well be wrong here, even newer in Buddhism than it is in Christianity.

II

If there is, as we have noted, a vast array of similarities between Tanabe's Shin or Pure Land philosophy and the Augustinian and Reformation traditions in Christianity, there is also a very great difference between them of which we should be well aware. This has to do, of course, with the nature of the Other-power experienced in death and resurrection. For the entire Christian tradition, and certainly with this Augustinian-Reformation branch, the Other-power known in the experiences of repentance, faith and grace is God, the unconditioned and infinite creator and end of all things now revealed as the forgiving and sanctifying redeemer. In so far, therefore, as God is named ontologically or metaphysically, God is conceived as infinite, unconditioned and omnipotent Actuality or Being—though most of this tradition is essentially uninterested in ontological labels for God. Quite to the contrary, Tanabe insists that this Other-power experienced through *zange* and mediation is Absolute Nothingness and by no means Absolute Being. And further, he argues quite persuasively that the experience of metanoesis, of *jiriki-qua-tariki* (and *tariki-qua-jiriki*) requires Absolute Nothingness and precisely excludes Absolute Being. Since Tanabe's points represent fascinating and important arguments among the representatives of philosophical theology of this sort, let us pursue them now.

Our question is: why does mediation, as Tanabe has defined it, require that Other-power be Absolute Nothingness and not Being? The Absolute appears, we have seen, in metanoesis: in the death and resurrection of the finite, and in the passage of the relative self through time, from fatedness and thrownness into freedom and intentional action. This passage, as we noted, unites self-power and Other-power. It represents an act of the self: in repentance, in rational absolute critique, in faith, in new life, and in action. And yet, as the negation of that self, it is throughout dependent on Other-power. It is this union of *jiriki* and *tariki*, self and Other-power, which, we recall, Tanabe terms mediation, the presence of the Absolute in the relative, the rebirth or renewal of the relative in the Absolute, and its subsequent action in the world. Now the consequence for Tanabe is that mediation so construed requires that Other-power be Nothingness and not Being.

This is a multi-faceted argument, appearing throughout the work in a variety of forms. Let us try to summarize its central thrust. If, says Tanabe, the Other-power is to manifest itself in and through the self-power and so the relative independence of the relative, it must be Nothingness, that is, Other-power that negates itself in "allowing" the other to be (83). Mediation is the active presence of the transcendent in and through the autonomous self-power: the reason, will, decision, and action of the relative. Mediation, therefore, is possible only for Nothingness, because only Nothingness can "step back" or "allow room" for that relative action and relative independence. An Absolute Being present to or within the relative would either swallow the relative into itself; or, if it allowed the other relative independence, it would itself become relative by allowing the other to be beside it; in effect it would become "a being" (101-102, 271-72). Only, therefore, if God be Nothingness (118), can the relative gain freedom through mediation rather than lose it. These are arguments familiar in Nietzsche, and they appear in a number of Buddhist philosophers; they are here, however, much more clearly and "legitimately" articulated since (1) Tanabe has analyzed this theonomy so thoroughly, and (2) he does not, as Zen does, seek to deny the ontological reality of the self; *anatta* here seems to mean *zange*.

Clearly for Tanabe "being" represents a restricted and an undialectical category: it refers to objects, to finite and relative "beings" in the objective system of things, beings which have a determinate identity and relative permanence (cf. 118-19, 257), beings which affirm themselves directly (158); they are, therefore, essentially opposed to or contrasted with other beings. "Being is always relative and can't be absolute" (22). But none of this can be characteristic of *this* Absolute: in Other-power there is neither identity, continuity of a being, nor self-affirmation and opposition. Otherwise, with mediation the relative self-power of the finite would disappear rather than increase. If, argues Tanabe, in metanoesis or mediation there is no identical object, no permanent substance, no distinct or opposing being; on the contrary, there is mediating participation or interpenetration of absolute and relative, a union of other and self power; if all this be so, then the mediating presence must be Nothingness. Only as Nothingness are the transcendence of the one and the autonomy of the other retained. That such participation or mediation of the divine in the finite without compromising the freedom and self-activity of the finite requires in the Absolute non-being as well as being, many in the West now agree; that, however, this requirement precludes the concept of a dialectic or polarity of Being and Non-being in the divine—that is, that Being is an undialectical concept, whereas Nothingness is not—is another question. Tanabe seems to relegate being as quickly to finitude, relativity and opposition, as Western thought had previously relegated Nothingness to mere subservient negation and so to "unreality," if not contradiction. In any case, every aspect of mediation: the self-power of the relative, the transformation of contingency into freedom, the openness of the future, the self-constituting decision of the finite—and the responsibility of the latter for action and its consequences (a point implied but not articulated by Tanabe)—all make the same requirement: the transcendent must be Absolute Nothingness, if it is to unite in this way with the relative, if mediation as theonomy is to be possible.

Tanabe, however, takes this argument one important step further—and so here possibly lies the real force of the concept of Nothingness as well as the authentic Buddhist character of Tanabe's thought. For Tanabe Nothingness *is* only in this mediation. It arises and *is* only in participation in and through the relative, in the mediation of metanoesis and so in the transformation of relative selves and in the interaction mediating that transformation to other selves. Nothingness cannot exist apart or "pre-exist"; then it would become being, Absolute Being, and so quite unreal, that is unknowable and irrelevant (19, 272). Thus the Absolute itself comes to be in mediation just as the consciousness of it comes to be there. (One can feel here the influence of Hegel, as well as of the classical Buddhist notion of *śūnyatā*.) The Absolute is, therefore, as dependent on relative being as the latter is on Other-power. The relation of Absolute and relative is thus quite simultaneous, mutual and reciprocal (23, 94, 118—or "coherent," as Whitehead would say.) It *is* through its mediation in the finite and in no other way (19-20, 183). The Absolute depends on the relative independence of the relative—and hence the possibility of "evil" (24, 159); and "the human gains freedom through the mediation of God while God is realized and made manifest in this mediation" (118).

Thus are Nothingness and finite being, Absolute and relative, correlative or mutually dependent. They realize one another together, in reciprocal relation; and both disappear in negation if they are apart. As Tanabe, who loves contradictions, says, "Since all beings that affirm themselves end in reciprocal negation." (158). Thus "Being is Nothingness, and Nothingness is Being, insofar as being becomes nothingness ('empty being'), and Nothingness being (mediation)—this is a contradiction" (159). One can sum up this view in the phrase: "relative being correlated with Absolute Nothingness" as expressing Tanabe's basic ontology of mutual participation of Other-power and self-power, of transcendence and autonomy, coupled with the deep spiritual requirement of *zange*. This is hardly identical with the Augustinian or the Kierkegaardian traditions of theology, despite their obvious similarities—but it has very much indeed to offer to present participants in these two Christian traditions!

III

Let me conclude with some comments on this fundamental argument for Absolute Nothingness in Tanabe, and also on the issue of language about the Absolute, whatever its "nature." Tanabe's repudiation of an undialectical Absolute Being makes excellent sense. Post-Enlightenment Christian theology, dominated by a new concern for autonomy *(jiriki)*, shows the same insistence which Tanabe manifests: namely, that whatever God or the Absolute may be, the Absolute is the ground and not the antagonist of creaturely autonomy, of authentic self-constitution, effective decision, personal commitment and self-directed action. These ingredients of personal existence are protected, nurtured and celebrated in personalist philosophy, existential theology and process philosophy. Only scientific speculation, itself the major source in the 17th century of the new experience of autonomy, tends to deny these personal categories of autonomy in a splendid and dazzling self-contradiction! For this reason, most modern theology, even that of Barth, is theonomous, speaking of a union or synthesis of divine presence and of autonomous creativity rather than of the providential determination or predestinating election characteristic of the older tradition.

As one signal of the difference between Buddhist philosophy and Christian theology, we may note how these theologians handle the requirements of repentance-faith-grace, requirements that to a Buddhist entail Absolute Nothingness. In modern existential theology, this theonomous experience of grace and freedom discloses not Nothingness but rather the Divine love for the creature and the divine intention for a personal and so mutual relation with the creature. What Tanabe sees as a metaphysical implication towards Nothingness, they see as a disclosure of the wonder of divine AGAPE: of forgiveness, acceptance and empowering grace. Love here replaces Nothingness as the basis of the theonomous, personal relation between the Absolute and the relative.

I agree with Tanabe, and with Tillich, however, that such relations, personal and "religious" though they be, also have ontological implications for our understanding of God. For this reason I have pursued—certainly partly under Buddhist influence—the conception of God as a *polarity* of being and of non-being. Without the latter, the autonomy of the creature and so of historical process itself, is hardly conceivable. And surely the participation of the divine in non-being is made crystal-clear in Christian thinking not only by the implications of the Incarnation but especially, in fact superlatively, in the Atonement and Death of the representative of God as the essential prelude to a triumphal resurrection and victory. At these points "being" in Christian thought is dependent on "non-being" in order to fulfill and complete itself. Thus Buddhist pressure on the Christian tradition to modify the absolute Being in God towards a polarity of being and non-being makes good sense in terms of the integrity of the Christian message itself.

This same potent set of implications, however, runs, so it seems to me, in two directions, not just in one. As the union of *jiriki* and *tariki*, a union in which neither side is compromised, implies to be sure an aspect of non-being, of "stepping-back" in God, so surely the same requirement—namely that *jiriki* not be compromised—requires an aspect of creative Being in God. The relative being—to use Tanabe's term—that exercises *jiriki* exists and is creative; it *is*. Thus it exists over time, establishes and maintains relations with other entities, faces an open future, and, despite its contingency and so vulnerability, acts creatively in and for that future. It is, further, its pride, not its existence per se, that represents its radical evil; for its existence can here be reborn in metanoesis. All this Tanabe freely admits and emphasizes in order that the Nothingness of God be firmly established. But precisely all of this requires "being" as well; in fact it is just this, namely the experience of existing, deciding, acting and relating— of self-constitution through decision and action—that has led to the renewal of the category of being (in Heidegger and Tillich, for example), and that has further led to the necessity of a ground and power of being as the condition for such creative, existing entities in passage.

Even more relevant, creative action in the world, as Tillich has shown, requires the positive presence of the unconditional ground of Being in and through social and cultural activities, an unconditional import or meaning in time that lures out the eros that makes culture possible. It also necessitates the creative and directing role of providence uniting the determined past with the infinite possibilities of the open future so that there is the consistent order and meaning in time that make our social and historical experience possible. All of these are aspects of the divine as Being: as the continuing and necessary source of existence, as the unconditioned order within existence, and as the infinite and novel possibilities necessary for change and particularly for meaningful change. God as ground or source, God as order, and God as novel value are all necessary conditions for *jiriki* to be *jiriki* as

Tanabe describes it, as essential as is the presence of Nothingness. *Jiriki* requires *tariki* for its possibility; but it requires *tariki* as the ground of the real being of *jiriki*, as well as *tariki* as the non-being allowing *jiriki* to be itself. The divine ground, therefore, is both being and non-being, Nothingness and Being, a polarity of the two. This polarity, as the whole of the Kyoto School insists, is implicit already in Nothingness; Nothingness is, they say, not un-dialectical non-being. But they have yet to apply being dialectically or analogically to Nothingness in the way they apply non-being dialectically and analogically to Nothingness. This is, therefore, the step they have to take if they think through Tanabe's arguments, just as Christian theology must take the step of applying non-being dialectically and analogically to God.

As this discussion indicates, much hangs on our use of words at this level of discourse. Clearly Nothingness is a dialectical, an analogical concept; it is not sheer negation at all but a word transposed as a metaphor from the experience of non-attachment, of "death," and of total surrender to the Absolute—qualified, as we have noted, by the continuing needs of *jiriki*. Nothingness thus does not exclude its opposite or antithesis "being" because it is an analogical metaphor and not a literal or univocal concept. To the Buddhists, however, apparently Being cannot be so employed; it applies restrictedly to a being among the beings. Hence applied to the Absolute it connotes and must connote an Absolute Being—and thus inescapably it drowns out *jiriki* in its awesome omnipotence.

Our suggestion, therefore, is that Being is also analogical, and that this is precisely how it has been used in the most perceptive representatives of the Christian tradition. Its reference is thus not to a being, but to the ground and power of the being of all the beings. Thus it establishes and undergirds their autonomy and authenticity, their *jiriki*; it does not and cannot contradict either one. Like Nothingness it is experienced, and it *is*, as the principle of the reality and creativity of autonomy and authenticity. Unlike the pole of Nothingness, that of Being represents the positive basis for the creative self-activity and the positive social and historical relations also essential for *jiriki*. Thus, again like Nothingness, Being is a metaphor applied to the basis of *jiriki* as expressive of the necessary positive side of *jiriki*. Seen from the perspective of Buddhist experience, the Nothingness in the Absolute is emphasized. Seen from the side of Christian experience, the analogical Being in God—as existence, as order, as possibility, and as love—are emphasized. Almost certainly the infinite mystery of the Absolute combines them all.

PART ONE

Shin Buddhism

The Structure of Faith:
Nothingness-*qua*-Love

IT goes without saying that "Absolute Nothingness" is central
to Tanabe's philosophy. This concept indeed forms the common basis of the thought of the philosophers of the so-called
Kyoto School: Nishida, Tanabe, Nishitani, et al. It is true that it
is not necessarily used in completely the same sense by these
thinkers and rather carries different nuances in each of them, but
here I want to investigate the common tenor of this notion.

The concept of Absolute Nothingness does not bear on the
theoretical and speculative problems connected with our knowledge of the world, but on the very practical problems surrounding
the self-awareness and salvation of the subject. It has its axis not
in ontological questions but in the questions of freedom. It is
carried by the conviction that the Good, Freedom, the Absolute
or Unconditioned, at which the fundamental desire and will of
human beings are directed, can be satisfactorily grasped only when
approached from the angle of nothingness — not from that of
being. It does not intend the ontological status of the Absolute
and aim at the negation of its being, but intends the "reality" of
the Absolute for the subject. One could say that it is an expression
of the consciousness of the infinite depth of the practical object
for the subject.

To get a total picture of what Absolute Nothingness means,
we should have to investigate its meaning in the thought of each
of the above-mentioned philosophers but, for lack of space, I must
limit myself here to the concept of Absolute Nothingness in Tanabe. I shall try to throw some light on some of its aspects,
especially the following three: (1) Absolute Nothingness as object
of faith; (2) Nothingness-*qua*-Love as self-negation of the Absolute;
and (3) Immeasurable Life and Pure Land as the root-source of
the working of Nothingness-*qua*-Love.

ABSOLUTE NOTHINGNESS AS OBJECT OF FAITH

While for Nishida the concept of Absolute Nothingness is the object of "action-intuition," for Tanabe it is the object of "action-faith." In other words, for Tanabe nothingness is an object not of intuition but of faith. Hereby a word of explanation may be needed. In *Philosophy as Metanoetics*, Tanabe considers Absolute Nothingness as the "Other-power" which, through the mediation of the act of metanoia, effects the death-resurrection of the subject. Here nothingness is concretized in the figure of Other-power. However, the reason for this does not lie in the idea that since nothingness is the object of faith and the object of faith must have a figure, therefore Absolute Nothingness must appear here as something "being-like," as provided with the figure of Other-power. Tanabe rather sees it the other way around. Something being-like, something with a figure is an object of intuition, not an object of faith. Something becomes an object of faith not because it exists as something being-like, but because it is non-existent or nothingness. What can this mean exactly?

We should begin by noting that, just like the idea of nothingness, so also the idea of faith is not necessarily a clear and distinct concept. As Paul Tillich has it, among all religious concepts there is hardly one "which is more subject to misunderstandings, distortions, and questionable definitions"[1] than the idea of faith. Before it can be used for the salvation of people, this concept must first be saved itself. The reasons for this are not easy to pin down, but one of them is the fact that the reality designated by the word *faith* is so many-sided as to make it hard for its totality to be seen through. Borrowing Tillich's words yet again, we might say that the reality designated by the word *faith* is "the state of being ultimately concerned."[2] And within that reality the promise lies contained that, in the unconditional obedience demanded by our ultimate concern, our quest for ultimacy will come through and be fulfilled. Thus we can find real freedom within the reality of faith. In faith, these two elements or moments, "unconditional obedience" and "the fulfillment of our quest for ultimacy," must

---

[1] Paul Tillich, *Dynamics of Faith* (London: George Allen & Unwin Ltd, 1952), vii.

[2] Tillich, *Dynamics of Faith*, 1.

be profoundly one. When that which demands our unconditional obedience is not really the ultimate, these two moments split apart and, while the quest for the ultimate is not fulfilled, faith becomes warped. Therefore, in order to prevent the quest for the ultimate from lowering its aim to the non-ultimate, a principle of critique or negation must be at work in faith. It is at this point that nothingness connects with the ultimate.

In order to grasp the essential connection between faith and nothingness, an evocation of Kant's idea of "freedom" may be of help. It goes without saying that the concept of freedom lies at the basis of Kant's philosophy. What Kant tries to make clear by this concept of freedom is that we, who as sensual beings belong to the sensual world, in our freedom transcend that world and live in the intelligible world. However, this freedom is not grasped by knowledge *(Wissen)*. We reach the conviction of being free only through the mediation of volitional determination in morality. In Kant's view, that which is grasped by knowledge is, in some sense, given to the senses; in other words, is a "being." Since freedom, which comes to awareness directly within ourselves through the moral law, never falls under the senses, it is called object of faith. Consequently, belief in freedom depends on reason only and not on data obtained other than through reason. Historical belief is also called faith but, since it is based on data given by something besides reason, it cannot be called faith in a pure sense. When looked at more carefully, this "belief" belongs to knowledge rather than to faith.

What follows from this is that freedom, since it is not a "being" that can be grasped by knowledge, must be understood as "nothingness." With regard to this link between freedom and nothingness, Tanabe, for example, writes: "Nothingness is brought to awareness subjectively as the free and selfless self and is symbolized objectively as emptiness."[3] To be sure, Tanabe does not consider his own standpoint identical with Kant's. He rather stresses the difference between the two and describes that difference as follows. While Kant's critique is a critique based on a conviction of the autonomy of reason, "metanoetics" is a critique from a point where all confidence in the autonomy of reason has been negated and destroyed, and is thus an absolute critique. Still,

---

[3] PM, 122.

Tanabe clearly sees an analogy between Kant's standpoint whereby freedom is the object of faith and his own whereby nothingness is the object of faith.

For Kant, since we come to believe in the realm of freedom by the mediation of the moral law, the moral law is considered to be the cognitive ground *(ratio cognoscendi)* of freedom. Likewise for Tanabe, since we come into contact with Absolute Nothingness only through the mediation of the act of metanoia, the act of metanoia is the cognitive ground of Absolute Nothingness. And just as for Kant freedom is the ontological ground of the moral law, so for Tanabe an act of metanoia in the true sense becomes possible only through a working from the side of Absolute Nothingness. However, to say that freedom, the basis of the moral law, belongs to the world of faith means that freedom does not rest on a foundation given by knowledge; in other words, that the ground of freedom is an abyss, a "no-ground" *(Ab-grund)*, "nothingness." This, however, is not a negative nothingness that would throw us into anxiety and doubt. On the contrary, to say that freedom is an unfathomable abyss makes true humility possible and is the condition of the morality of our acts. In Kant's view, if our freedom and God were not objects of faith but objects of knowledge, the primary motives of our human acts would become fear and expectation and in fact their moral character would be lost. In this sense, the fact that freedom is an unfathomable abyss is the *locus* where the will of the subject finally comes to rest.

If freedom is an abyss not based on anything, it is wrong to think that God forms the basis of this freedom. Indeed, it is noteworthy that for Kant God (the Highest Good) himself is inferred from freedom and based on freedom. God is not antecedent to the moral will, but is posited from freedom as the "necessary object of the will determined by moral law."[4] This is not, as is generally thought, debasing God to a mere moral element, but rather presenting God himself as an infinite abyss, and seeing and symbolizing the abyss of freedom as the abyss of God. Consequently, even while freedom, which is Absolute Nothingness, thus obtains a figure as object of faith—the figure of the Highest Good (God, immortality)—that figure is not a "being," that would pre-

---

[4] Immanuel Kant, *Kritik der praktischen Vernunft* (Hamburg, Felix Meiner, 1929), 4.

exist outside of and unrelated to faith and could be clarified by knowledge. It must be thought of as a figure born and developed out of the abyss of nothingness as the object of a faith in the process of deepening. Tanabe saw freedom as Absolute Nothingness and endeavored to grasp the dynamics whereby this Absolute Nothingness develops a figure as object of faith, in the form of "Nothingness-*qua*-Love."

Consequently, a particular figure as object of faith must be understood within Absolute Nothingness. In Shin Buddhism, faith is understood as belief in the Primal Vow Other-power of Amida Buddha, but this Primal Vow Other-power must not be understood as a reality preexistent to faith, as something existing apart from any relationship to faith. If not, faith would become superstition. Thus, in Soga Ryōjin's words, it is something "that faith developed out of itself as its content"[5] in the process of its own deepening; something with Absolute Nothingness as its basis. This applies not only to Pure Land faith but equally to the many figures appearing in the Bodhisattva faith of Mahāyāna. They can all be seen as figures developed from Absolute Nothingness, figures emerging in the process whereby faith reflects deeper and deeper on its own origin, as figures symbolizing, adorning and supporting absolute free will as the inner reality of faith.

As explained above, the particularity of the object of faith is based on the non-being of the object rather than on its being. In the following I would like to give some further thought to the link between faith and nothingness from the viewpoint of the particular nature of the object of faith. The essential characteristic of the object of faith appears to be that there is no distance between desiring it and possessing it, or again between the thought of it and its presence. In the object of faith these two are directly one. This transpires for instance when Eckhart says: "I make God come down to me." In faith, if I truly desire the object, I possess it; if it really occupies my thoughts, it is actually present.

Conversely, the possession and presence of the object of faith is not present apart from the desire for or concern with it. This is the criterium to distinguish between an object of faith and a natural thing that cannot become object of faith; and also the

---

[5] Soga Ryōjin, 曾我量深選集 [Selected Writings of Soga Ryōjin] (Tokyo: Yayoi Shobō, 1970), 5:236.

criterium to distinguish true faith from superstition and magic. Magic consists in trying to find in a natural object the unity of desire and object realized in the object of faith. With natural things, there exists a gap between their desire and their possession that can be filled up only with time and space. Magic originates in disregarding this gap. But when the object of faith is the Good, there is no distance between these two: to intend it is to have it present, and its presence means that it is intended. Thus, while natural objects exist apart from the desire for them, the Good is only present where it is desired. That is why Kant maintains that the Good as object of the will does not exist before being willed and can exist only as "good will." The upshot is that the Good is not an existence in any sense.

In the *image* we can see a familiar case of the unity of desire and possession, concern and presence found in the object of faith. As Sartre says, a condition of the presence of the image is the absence of the object. Sartre finds therein the difference between image and perception. I cannot perceive Pierre if he is not present here and now, but I can evoke an image of Pierre only because he is not here just now. Just as it is illness that makes us aware of health, and children think with love of their mother after she has died, so the image expresses the reality and core of the object in its absence.

This is all the more true in the case where the Good is the object. The Good is real notwithstanding its absence, or even because of its absence. Because of its absence, the desire for the Good and its possession are linked. In this vein, we can say that the object of faith shows, in a higher sense, the characteristics of the image. To call the object of faith an image is not considering it to be illusory. It denotes, on the contrary, that in human life there is a realm that opens up only through images. That is the world of faith.

A deep awareness that the object of faith is characterized by absence, and that it has in a higher sense the nature of an image is precisely what constitutes the purity of faith. It is this awareness that overcomes the ever-present danger: the split between subject and object that distorts faith. It may be good to rephrase the above distinction between true and false objects of faith in Tillich's terms. Tillich writes, for example, that "the ultimate of the act of faith and the ultimate that is meant in the act of faith are one and the same."[6]

In other words, in faith "subject and object are one." And according to Tillich,

> This is symbolically expressed by the mystics when they say that their knowledge of God is the knowledge God has of him-self. . . . Even a successful prayer is, according to Paul (Rom. 8), not possible without God as Spirit praying within us.[7]

If the object of faith is posited outside of faith as an objective reality, the subject-object split thus introduced into faith cannot be overcome. The effort of the subject to become one with the object located outside of itself evokes passion, and supposing even that in this passion the split of subject and object is temporarily overcome, since the object stays located outside the subject, under the outward appearance of unity a fissure is brought about within the personality which may lead to the collapse of the core of the person. Over against this, a keen awareness of the fact that the object of faith is not being but absence or non-being, over-comes the passion inherent in faith and makes the realization of a true unity of the person in faith possible.

In the above, we saw that the fact that freedom has the nature of nothingness and the fact that God is an abyss closed to knowledge are conditions of the possibility of the morality of the human act. In the same way, the fact that the object of faith is absent and has the nature of nothingness is the condition to preserve the purity of faith and to save faith from the idolatry originating in the subject-object split in the object of faith. The reality of the object of faith lies in the fact that it has the nature of nothingness and has as its ground the abyss of Absolute Noth-ingness. When the object of faith has the nature of an image, this image has the openness of nothingness as the background from which it arises and into which it disappears. But what opens up this background is the power of attention at work in faith. At this point we can see the dynamics of faith expressed in "Noth-ingness-*qua*-Love" as the power of imagination become one with the power of attention. As a concentration of attention, faith can

---

[6] Tillich, *Dynamics of Faith*, 11.
[7] Tillich, *Dynamics of Faith*, 11.

also be called prayer, but in the act of faith also, imagination is at work as image-producing faculty. The image that emerges when the power of imagination at work in faith is purified and made transparent by the power of attention is the object of faith. If, in faith, the power of attention can be seen as the working of reflection whereby faith refracts into itself and opens up at its bottom the space of nothingness, then the power of imagination is that which makes the object of faith into an image with that space of nothingness as its background.

In the process of reflectively returning to the bottom of its original inspiration — namely "emptiness," which is the state of absolute freedom reached in Śākyamuni's enlightenment — Mahāyāna Buddhism gave birth to many figures; and within it, in Pure Land Buddhism, especially Shin Buddhism, at the bottom of Śākyamuni's enlightenment the figure of the Primal Vow of Amida Buddha was educed as the adornment of that enlightenment and as what was fulfilled in that enlightenment. By the discovery of the Primal Vow as the adornment and symbolization of Śākyamuni's enlightenment, that enlightenment came to show an infinite depth. It is not sure that the dynamics of Absolute Nothingness, which in Tanabe represents the world of faith, does sufficient justice to that development. But the dynamics of faith as developed in Mahāyāna Buddhism is implicitly contained in Tanabe's synthesis, "Nothingness-*qua*-Love." To this I shall return in my third section.

NOTHINGNESS-*QUA*-LOVE AS SELF-NEGATION OF THE ABSOLUTE

The second aspect of the idea of Absolute Nothingness is its significance as the "self-negation" or "self-emptying" of the Absolute. Tanabe conceives of this self-negation of the Absolute as "Nothingness-*qua*-Love." The entrance of the relative into the Absolute, or the union of the relative with the Absolute, does not obtain unless the Absolute is love. But this love finds its full and manifest realization, not in an Absolute envisioned as an omnipotent God who stands on his rights over against the relative, but in a self-emptying God, a God who contains the principle of self-negation within himself. God's perfection lies in the egolessness and impersonality of his love. By emptying itself, love becomes truth and light. But this self-emptying is not everything of the Absolute. The Absolute must also be a reality that acts on the relative, blows life into the relative and makes it rise from the dead. Tanabe's idea of "Nothingness-*qua*-Love" shows a twofold orientation: that of the Absolute reflecting on itself and perfecting its love by self-emptying and that of the Absolute, having become love, going out of itself to act. In any case, the aspect of self-negation of the Absolute is a very important, even indispensable moment of religious truth. It is from the perspective of the self-negation of the Absolute that I intend to investigate Tanabe's notion of "Nothingness-*qua*-Love."

In Tanabe's view, that the Absolute is nothingness means first of all that the Absolute does not directly act itself but acts by means of the relative. And the fact that the Absolute acts through the working of the relative is called "mediation" or "turn-about" by Tanabe. In order for this mediation or turn-about to obtain, the Absolute must be nothingness. Tanabe expresses this as follows:

> Insofar as it is our absolute turn-about, there is no way of call-
> ing the Absolute but by the name of Absolute Nothingness. . .
> The Absolute is the principle of Absolute Nothingness. But
> Absolute Nothingness is not something that exists directly, but
> something that originates in a turning-about activity that rad-
> ically negates all being. Therefore, as absolute turn-about the
> Absolute must be something that turns-about also itself. It
> must namely turn-about its own nothingness and appear as
> being. This means that precisely by turning-about its very ac-
> tivity of negation and turning-about, it turns itself to the
> other, the relative, and appears there in the form of giving life
> to the relative in a *gensō* 還相 way. In other words, an Absolute
> that is Absolute Nothingness makes the being of relative be-
> ings into its own mediation, thus acting outside itself in a *gensō*
> way, in the form of Nothingness-*qua*-Being.[8]

That the Absolute makes the activity of relative beings relative into its own mediation implies that the Absolute allows the in-dependence and autonomy of the relative which is needed for this mediation. The relative who is allowed this independence carries the sin of egotism in that it tries to affirm itself and set

---

[8] THZ 11:125. Tanabe takes the notion of *gensō* (often translated as "return-ing transference") from Shin Buddhist doctrine and uses it, roughly speaking, to designate the working of Other-power as a breakthrough into this world.

itself up against the Absolute. That the Absolute nevertheless permits the autonomy of the relative denotes the "principle of love whereby the Absolute forgives this while working negation upon itself."[9] According to Tanabe,

> A God who is love is an existence that forever reduces itself to nothing and totally gives itself to the other. In that sense, it is an existence that has nothingness as its principle and does not directly act out of its own will.[10]

As long as the Absolute is absolute, it breaks down the egotistic presumption of the relative being that tries to flout its independence over against the Absolute. Therefore, the Absolute is the "Great Nay" (大否 *daihi*). However, in this Great Nay, the Absolute does not completely negate all working of the relative. This means that it brings the relative, whose self-presumption has been negated and emptied, back to life, raises it from the dead. Then the Absolute makes the activity of this newly resurrected relative being into its own mediation for its ongoing *gensō* working on other relative beings. In this way, the Absolute is also "Great Compassion" (大悲 *daihi*).

Tanabe proposes that the fitting metaphor for this working of the Absolute whereby, assuming the relative, it allows its autonomy and makes it into a mediation of its own working is a net, rather than a bag. A net, while being formless and loose enough to permit the freedom of the things contained in it, at the same time has the power to contain within itself the things that would try to get out. Moreover we, who are thus contained within the Absolute, in turn become each one of the knots of the net and participate in this "loosely containing" working, endeavoring to keep others who would want to escape within the fold.

> Therefore, the knots of a net can exert their role only insofar as they are in a mutual relationship of joint responsibility. For God's net to play its role towards us the sole relationship between God and me is not sufficient. It is absolutely required that we ourselves become knots of the net and thus play a role in God's love embracing and containing all relative beings; in other words that we stand in a relationship of joint responsi-

---

[9] THZ 11:125.
[10] THZ 9:328.

bility. This is the reason why the love of God must be love of neighbor.[11]

What Tanabe tries to make clear by means of that metaphor is the formlessness and emancipatory character of the Absolute that permits the freedom and independence of the relative beings that it embraces within itself. According to Tanabe, this is based on the working of the Absolute whereby it empties itself and negates itself; and that is precisely the love of the Absolute. The idea that the love of the Absolute consists in the self-emptying activity of the Absolute is one facet of religious truth, which is already implied in the idea of creation.

When creation is called "creation out of nothing," one is confronted with a world of nihilum wherein all beings are felt to be no more than dust and clay beset by death and non-being; and then one feels the presence of a great and numinous power that enters that world of nihilum and destroys it, blows its breath into that clay and gives it life, thus bestowing being on all beings. Thereby it is only natural to figure an omnipotent and absolute God on which all beings depend for their very being and survival. Here the feeling of being as a victory over nothingness, of being in spite of nothingness, is strong. The sense of the presence of a power that makes all beings be lies at the basis of the idea of creation.

However, when this created world comes to be felt as covered by the nihilum and evil of man's doing, the reality of that evil and the concomitant sense of nihilum can turn the idea of creation in the opposite direction. The sense of the voidness of this world and of the absence of God from it may make us think of this created world in the light of God's retreat from this world, or of the idea that God has permitted the existence of things that transgress the boundaries of his will. Creation here comes to mean that God has consented to the control of this world by a necessity that lies beyond his will, or has chosen to control this world by that necessity. This could mean that God has abandoned this world, which could amount to a divine crime but, since being love is an indispensable attribute of God, it means that God, by consenting to that, has emptied himself. Thus there is a hidden

---

[11] THZ 11:238.

presence of God's love in the midst of the necessity and void that govern this world. Such an aspect is also part of the idea of creation, and it can be found for example in the works of Simone Weil, who wrote texts like the following:

> Thus the existence of evil here below, far from disproving the reality of God, is the very thing that reveals him in his truth.
>
> On God's part, creation is not an act of self-expansion but of restraint and renunciation. God and all his creatures are less than God alone. God accepted this diminution. He emptied a part of his being from himself in this act of his divinity; that is why Saint John says that the Lamb had been slain from the beginning of the world. God permitted the existence of things distinct from himself and worth infinitely less than himself. By this creative act he denied himself for our sakes in order to give us the possibility of denying ourselves for him. This response, this echo, which it is in our power to refuse, is the only possible justification for the folly of love of the creative act.[12]

The reason I have cited Simone Weil's idea of creation is not to assert that this would be the most fitting understanding of creation, but in order to bring to light an aspect implicitly contained in the idea of creation. All religions are multi-faceted realities. In her words:

> Each religion is an original combination of explicit and implicit truth; what is explicit in one is implicit in another. The implicit adherence to a truth can in some cases be worth as much as the explicit adherence, sometimes even a good deal more. He who knows the secrets of all hearts alone knows the secret of the different forms of faith. He has never revealed this secret, whatever anyone may say.[13]

Therefore, the differences among these religions are not derived from differences in their essence but are based on structural differences, depending on which of the many elements each of them contains are *made the dominant ones* and which stay in the

---

[12] Simone Weil, *Waiting for God*, transl. by Emma Crawford (New York: Harper & Row, 1973), 145.
[13] Weil, *Waiting for God*, 185.

shadow. The aspect of creation which Weil wants to make clear may not be one that is universally recognized in Christianity, but she stresses the point that the hidden elements may be as operative or even much more operative than the ones in the limelight. Often those implicit elements have been made explicit in the writings of Christian mystics. What is brought to the foreground in this case is the aspect of God's kenosis. On this point it can be said that what remained implicit in Christianity has been made explicit in Buddhism. Conversely, there are elements of creation that are explicitly present in Christianity but remained hidden in Buddhism: the aspect of "affirmation of all creatures by God" and that of God's revelation in the creatures. But it can be said that in Buddhism these elements have become more pronounced in Mahāyāna Buddhism and especially in the Pure Land tradition.

Moreover, all authentic religions contain elements of affirmation and elements of negation of reality, and the latter are not less important than the former. According to Paul Tillich, the negative elements contained in religious symbols are the norms of the truth of these symbols of faith. They safeguard the ultimacy of the ultimate which the symbols try to reveal and prevent their falling into idolatry. Therefore Tillich writes: "That symbol is most adequate which expresses not only the ultimate but also its own lack of ultimacy."[14] And recognizing such a symbol in the crucified Christ he comments:

> Christianity expresses itself in such a symbol in contrast to all other religions, namely, in the Cross of the Christ. Jesus could not have been the Christ without sacrificing himself as Jesus to himself as the Christ. Any acceptance of Jesus as the Christ which is not the acceptance of Jesus the crucified is a form of idolatry. The ultimate concern of the Christian is not Jesus, but the Christ Jesus who is manifest as the crucified. The event which has created this symbol has given the criterion by which the truth of Christianity, as well as of any other religion, must be judged. The only infallible truth of faith, the one in which the ultimate itself is unconditionally manifest, is that any truth of faith stands under a Yes-or-No judgment.[15]

---

[14] Tillich, *Dynamics of Faith*, 97.
[15] Tillich, *Dynamics of Faith*, 97-98.

Once we have seen with Tillich that symbols contain the dual elements of affirmation and negation, we can recognize Absolute Nothingness as expressing the aspect of negation and ask the question how therein the Absolute is understood and encountered. For this question we can turn again to Simone Weil. When we see creation as God's kenosis, the only way God can be present in the world is in his absence from the world. In that case, we can meet God only in silence. God's answer to our clamoring to him is then silence; silence is God's language. The reason why we cannot hear silence as God's word is because we have stopped the ears of our heart with noise. In that sense, Weil writes:

> Creatures talk with sounds; God's word is silence. God's secret word of love cannot be but silence. Christ is the silence of God.[16]

What obstructs the access to that space of silence is our human sin.

> Our soul continually makes noise. There is a point in it which is silence but we never hear it. When God's silence enters our soul, pierces it and joins that point of silence, from that moment on we have in God our treasure and soul; and space opens up before us like a fruit that splits in two, for we see the universe from a point located outside of space.[17]

That silence is God's language does not mean, of course, that in silence a particular voice makes itself heard. What is to be found there is only silence, bottomless silence. In that bottomless silence all things present themselves in their naked reality. Take for instance the whiteness and coldness of the snow we touch. This whiteness appears as boundlessly white, this coldness as infinitely cold. Also sadness appears here as bottomlessly sad. This is not alien to what Buddhism understands with *śūnyatā*. Emptiness manifests itself within that sadness, at the point where sadness is infinitely sad.

We meet with this silence of God in sundry places, but Simone

---

[16] Simone Weil, *Pensées sans ordre concernant l'amour de Dieu* (Paris: Gallimard, 1962), 129.

[17] Weil, *Pensées*, 129.

Weil quotes unhappiness and beauty as privileged places wherein we meet with that silence. "Unhappiness" is the fact that, through suffering, all the words that fill the abyss of nihilum that opens up in the bottom of our soul are cut off, and the fact that there comes no answer to the question "why" that wells up from that abyss. Therein the human being comes face to face with absolute silence. That the human being cannot abide in that room of absolute silence thus dug in the bottom of its heart and feels half its soul crushed therein, is due to the sin which natural man harbors within himself. Only they who are able to hear that abyss of nihilum and that silence as the word of God can escape the unfreedom of the crushed soul. "Beauty" is also a form of encounter with God's silence. However, contrary to the case of unhappiness, beauty is a particular instance of meeting God's silence as God's word. Why is it that unhappiness and beauty, which in God are one and the same silence, appear in us as two different categories? Herein the creaturely nature and sin of the human being play their roles.

The ideas that God's word is silence and that beauty is one form of that silence open our eyes to the fact that at its bottom beauty hides "nothingness" and "absence." According to Weil, the condition for extreme beauty is that its object is nearly absent because of its distance and fragility.

> The spectacle of cherry blossoms in spring would not so directly affect our hearts as it does if their fragility would not be so visible. In general, a condition of extreme beauty is to be nearly absent either by distance or by weakness. The stars are immobile but very distant; white flowers are there but nearly destroyed. In the same way, a human being cannot love God with a pure heart unless he or she believes him to be outside of this world, in heaven; or good and well present on earth in the way of human beings, but weak, humiliated, and killed; or again, which is a still greater degree of absence, present as a tiny bit of matter destined to be eaten.[18]

As a pericope wherein God's love and perfection appear as consisting in his self-emptying, the following word of Jesus is often

---

[18] Simone Weil, *Ecrits de Londres et dernières lettres* (Paris: Gallimard, 1957), 180.

quoted: "For he makes his sun rise on the evil and the good, and sends rain on the just and the unjust" (Matt 5:45). Therein God's egolessness and impersonality appear. When we consider our relationship with God, these traits of the divine nature have a positive significance, in that they make a true link with God possible. When we think of God as a personal being, an "almighty person," we can approach God up to a certain point but then reach a limit beyond which we cannot proceed. On the contrary, when we see God's perfection in his egolessness and impersonality, the distance between God and us, which could not be filled up as long as we saw God as a personal being, now becomes crossable. This is because God, while now dwelling in that higher realm of impersonality, enters into our own hearts. In Weil's words:

> To conceive of God as an all-powerful person, or under the name of Christ as a human person, is to exclude oneself from the true love of God.[19]

Earlier we pointed out, following Kant, that freedom and God are objects of faith, not of knowledge; in other words, that freedom and God are infinite abysses whose bottoms cannot be sounded by knowledge; and that this is the condition of the possibility of the moral act. Moreover, we have indicated that the object of faith is not a being that exists previously to and outside of faith itself, but nothingness or something developed from nothingness; and that this is the condition of the possibility of the purity of faith. In the same way, the fact that the Absolute is not directly being but Absolute Nothingness containing self-negation is that which makes possible a truly inner connection between the Absolute and us. Only before a self-emptying God can we, in turn, empty ourselves. If thus Absolute Nothingness reveals the self-negation on the part of the Absolute, metanoia is the self-negation on the part of the relative. When these two self-negations become one and interpenetrate, the working of "Nothingness-*qua*-Love" materializes. Tanabe's "Nothingness-*qua*-Love" expresses one aspect of religious truth. This aspect of religious truth is also present in Christianity, be it in an implicit form. That I have extensively quoted Simone Weil's thought is

---

[19] Simone Weil, *Waiting for God*, p.179.

due to the fact that I have found therein a model that permits a penetrating understanding of Absolute Nothingness as the self-negation of the Absolute.

AMIDA BUDDHA AND THE PURE LAND AS THE DEPTHS OF NOTHINGNESS-*QUA*-LOVE

Tanabe's idea of Nothingness-*qua*-Love contains two aspects or directions. The first is that of self-abandonment or self-emptying. By love reflecting on itself, by the self being emptied by love, love becomes truth and light. This aspect was treated in the above. The second aspect is the orientation whereby nothingness tends to become love and step out of itself to act. Our question now becomes how this second aspect is conceived of by Tanabe.

As indicated already, for Tanabe Absolute Nothingness is the "principle of turn-about." If the emptying of the self in love is the perfection of love, the thorough realization of that "annihilation" is for nothingness to negate itself in turn to become an activity of love and thereby to turn outward. According to Tanabe, since it is not something that directly has its being somewhere, Absolute Nothingness is nothing but going out to act as love, through the relatives entering into it and uniting with it, thus becoming mediations of this working of Nothingness. That means nothingness turning into being. Tanabe sees such working of love, a love that does away with the self, in Christianity's love of neighbor and in Buddhism's Bodhisattva Path. If one can see in this "annihilation" of the self the passive side of love, then one can say that, by its radicalization, this passivity turns into positive activity to appear outside as the working of love. Those are the two sides of one and the same activity. Therein Tanabe sees the turn-about working of Absolute Nothingness as "Nothingness-*qua*-Love."

However, granted that Absolute Nothingness can be seen as the *locus* wherein that turn-about of "Nothingness-*qua*-Love" takes place, nothingness itself cannot be that which brings about this turn-about. For the turn-about to actually occur therein, there must be in Absolute Nothingness a positive principle that impels, realizes, and sustains that turn-about. The turn-about may happen within Absolute Nothingness, but we must look elsewhere for the principle that brings about that turn-about. If, as is often done, Absolute Nothingness is pictured as a vast ocean that embraces all sentient beings, the ocean itself cannot be thought to be itself the power that makes the beings in it float on its surface. It would rather act as the sucking power that draws all beings to its bottom. Therefore, in that vast ocean there must be at work a principle that changes the very nature of that ocean and turns its sucking power into "floating power." Where can we look for that principle in Absolute Nothingness? This is the question which presents itself when we investigate this second aspect of Nothingness-*qua*-Love.

This question is not directly faced in *Philosophy as Metanoetics*. It is true that Tanabe's metanoetics takes its start from the experience of the strong turning-about power of Absolute Nothingness, which Tanabe then qualifies as Other-power. But by reformulating Other-power as Absolute Nothingness, Tanabe loses his grip on the strong turning-about capacity of Other-power. Instead of turning his full attention to Other-power as such and reflectively delving into its depths, Tanabe ends up passing it by. One might be tempted to say that this is the necessary outcome of Tanabe's writing from the standpoint of philosophy rather than that of theology or religion. However, our problem remains: How can we conceive in Absolute Nothingness of a positive principle that causes the turn-about?

As pointed out earlier, Tanabe finds the second aspect of "Nothingness-*qua*-Love," namely that of nothingness becoming love and acting outwardly, in neighborly love and the Bodhisattva Path. However, Tanabe conceives of neighborly love and Bodhisattva Path as the actual form nothingness takes when working in human society, but thereby does not return to that which fundamentally constitutes it. We could say that, in treating the Bodhisattva Path, Tanabe investigates it only in its phenomenal dimension and not in its depths. And not without reason. Since nothingness is not itself directly a being, its working can exist only as the activity of love in the phenomenal level. But, when they are grasped only in their phenomenal level, neighborly love and the Bodhisattva Path cannot appear as powers at work in the depth of the Existenz of the subject. When not grasped in their ground, they may be able to appear as a formal ethical ought, but not as reaching the depth of the religious act. In order for them to originate in the depths of the total person as religious acts, neighborly love and Bodhisattva Path must be backed up by faith in what constitutes their root-source. For the fact of nothingness being at the same time love to become actual reality, faith in Absolute Nothingness must reflect within itself and grasp the principle that effects the turn-about in its ground.

It can be said that within Buddhism, Mahāyāna — and within Mahāyāna Buddhism, especially the Pure Land school — has been engaged in the quest for such a principle. They thereby took Śākyamuni's enlightenment, which can be called the self-awareness of Absolute Nothingness, as their basis and delved towards the Great Wisdom–Great Compassion inwardly attested to in that enlightenment. In other words, they reinterpreted Śākyamuni's enlightenment by returning to what prompted that enlightenment and was realized in it. At this point I would like to leave Tanabe behind for a moment to examine how this principle of the turn-about of Nothingness-*qua*-Love is understood in Mahāyāna Buddhism.

It goes without saying that the core of Mahāyāna Buddhism is the Bodhisattva idea and that love is at the center of that idea. The Bodhisattva idea originated in the process whereby Mahāyāna came to grasp the thread that runs through Śākyamuni's enlightenment as love and to reflect on that enlightenment towards its ground which is love. Among the epoch-making events in Śākyamuni's life, as recounted in the Āgama sūtras, it is the event entitled "the encouragement by Brahman" that is often taken as the symbol of the fundamental spirit of Mahāyāna Buddhism. Therein is related that, after his enlightenment, Śākyamuni fell into deep doubt and distress because he felt that the Dharma he had experienced was so profound and delicate that it would be impossible to communicate it to others. The god Brahman, who feared the world was coming to an end, then appeared and encouraged him to go ahead and preach his Dharma, whereupon Śākyamuni took heart and went to deliver his first sermon in the Deer Park. What appears in this story as a voice of encouragement heard from the outside was in fact the voice of the universe calling for salvation, heard by Śākyamuni within his own heart. When, as a result of sensing that clamor with his whole being, Śākyamuni then decided to start his preaching career, it was love for the entire universe that was the driving force. Thus Mahāyāna came to see the perfection of such love as the outcome of Śākyamuni's enlightenment.

The content of the self-awareness reached in Śākyamuni's

enlightenment is a world of absolute freedom, wide as the sky and without concept or image. The idea of Absolute Nothingness may be said to be an endeavor to grasp the inner depths of that enlightenment. But when this is put before us in an already accomplished form, it finds in us no echo at all. What is expressed in Śākyamuni's enlightenment is also the crystallized and purified form of love, and might be called "truth in charity." By considering Śākyamuni's enlightenment as "shot through" with love or as the clarified form of love, Mahāyāna presented this enlightenment as also available to ordinary people and thus opened it to all sentient beings. In this process the many forms of Bodhisattva thought were born.

Amid the many strains of Mahāyāna Buddhism, it is especially the Pure Land school that looked in Śākyamuni's enlightenment for the root-source of a love that reached thoroughness and clarity. It thus came to the figure of Amida's Primal Vow. Because it is covered by many extraneous things, the love at work in sentient beings looks like it is blind impulse. Basically, however, it is not an opaque and blind impulse. The love at work in sentient beings is, at its ground, penetrated by Amida's Primal Vow. Amida's Primal Vow is eternal life, immeasurable life and light, at work at the bottom of the life of sentient beings. But since our life and love is covered by the dust of our passions, the root-source of our life does not become transparent to us. That which becomes clear and transparent, rises to self-awareness and becomes fulfilled, is Śākyamuni's enlightenment. Thus, for the Pure Land school, Śākyamuni's enlightenment goes back to, and is based on, the Primal Vow of Amida Buddha. This enlightenment is thus reinterpreted from Amida out, as the fulfillment of Amida's Primal Vow. Therefore, Śākyamuni is the enlightened one but not simply one among many enlightened ones. He is at the same time also the "savior." Thus Mahāyāna Buddhism, in the process of reflecting within itself the Great Wisdom–Great Compassion attested to in Śākyamuni's enlightenment, came in one of its strains, namely the Pure Land school, to the Primal Vow of Amida Buddha.

Hence Mahāyāna Buddhism is not something that originated after the time of Śākyamuni; in a sense, it predates Śākyamuni. Historically speaking, Mahāyāna is of course later than Śākyamuni. Since human thought as a rule develops from the simple to the complicated, so Mahāyāna must be seen as a doctrine which transformed the original tenets of the Buddha by introducing into it a lot of speculation and products of imagination and by interpreting it freely. But according to a representative theologian of Shin Buddhism, Soga Ryōjin, Mahāyāna is to be located before rather than after Śākyamuni, and originated not by a free interpretation of Śākyamuni's doctrine but previous to Śākyamuni's enlightenment as the ground out of which that enlightenment arose. By pursuing the inner necessity of that enlightenment, Mahāyāna remounts to the time before Śākyamuni. From a historical standpoint, Mahāyāna is to be situated after Śākyamuni, but from the standpoint of faith which is that of the self-awareness of Śākyamuni, Mahāyāna comes first. Soga explains this as follows:

> Mahāyāna is not a Buddhism that developed and originated after Śākyamuni. Buddhism is not a doctrine that originated later by theorizing and ontologizing, or again idealizing and mystifying the original tenets. Buddhism exists only as the vast and limitless background in space and time of Śākyamuni's unique self-realization; as that which makes that self-realization truly into self-realization. I think that what is called the Buddha land or the Pure Land denotes precisely that background.[20]

What then is that Mahāyāna as the precedent or ground of Śākyamuni's enlightenment? In other words, what would be this "vast and limitless background" of that enlightenment? That is the Primal Vow of Amida Buddha and the Pure Land as its home-land. As mentioned before, in all sentient beings there is at work a desire to reach enlightenment. That is the demand to awake and reach a self-awareness of absolute freedom. Śākyamuni felt that desire in himself and became a Buddha by fulfilling that desire in his enlightenment. But that desire is not simply at work in that one individual, Śākyamuni only. It transcends him to work all through the consciousness of all humanity, all sentient beings, and constitute their inner life.

It is not only mountains and rivers, sun and moon, stars and planets that maintain their majestic being; the stream of life of sentient beings that has upheld itself in time through countless reincarnations is not inferior in vastness and limitlessness to the

---

[20] Soga Ryōjin, *Selected Writings*, 5:407.

course of sun and moon, stars and dragons. And also the desire for awakening that pervades that limitless life is itself limitless. It can be called the fundamental impulse or instinct at work throughout all sentient beings. This must have its roots somewhere beyond the sense consciousness and sensual life, but cannot be fathomed since it too is limitless. It is therefore grasped symbolically as "the Primal Vow of Amida Buddha" or "the Primal Vow of Dharmākara Bodhisattva." Because of the limitlessness of the life of sentient beings, it is said that Dharmākara Bodhisattva, in the pursuit of the fulfillment of his desire for enlightenment, spent five kalpas in deep thought and then became Amida Buddha.

Thus Mahāyāna, especially in its Pure Land strain, sees as the vast and limitless background of Śākyamuni's enlightenment the Primal Vow of Amida Buddha (in the Primal Vow of Dharmākara Bodhisattva). As such, his enlightenment is "adorned" by that background. Shinran's words, "The reason for Śākyamuni's coming into this world was solely to reveal the ocean of Amida's Primal Vow," express this basic insight of Mahāyāna Buddhism. In that sense, Pure Land Buddhism sees it as the main task of Mahāyāna to make clear "the real intention of Śākyamuni's coming into the world" as the fulfillment of the Primal Vow of Amida Buddha.

As said in the above, the content of Śākyamuni's enlightenment is a world of non-concept and non-thought beyond all objects and the ego infecting these objects. It is emptiness. It can also be called the self-awareness of Absolute Nothingness and stands, beyond all oppositions, right at the beginning of all things. However, Mahāyāna, specifically Pure Land Buddhism, locates this beginning of all things, the Primal Vow of Amida Buddha and the Pure Land, in the background of that enlightenment as its homeground. Hereby Śākyamuni's enlightenment becomes two-leveled: Śākyamuni himself becomes the reincarnation in this world of Amida Buddha and his enlightenment becomes the proof of the realization of the Primal Vow. This has a twofold consequence. One, by being backed up and adorned by Amida Buddha, this enlightenment ceases to be the philosophical self-awareness of one practical philosopher, to assume the character of salvation for others. It thus takes on a deeply religious character. And second, by becoming something attested to and realized in Śākyamuni's enlightenment, Amida's Primal Vow ceases to be an abstract idea of another world and obtains a real foundation. And both deepen one another by echoing and refracting one another from the other world to this world and back. And right in between the partners of that "holy *commercium*" stands the figure of the Primal Vow of Dharmākara Bodhisattva to mediate that mutual correspondence and evocation. Śākyamuni feels in himself Amida Buddha as his background through feeling in himself the Primal Vow of all sentient beings as Dharmākara Bodhisattva. And since Amida Buddha's Primal Vow flows into the Primal Vow of Dharmākara Bodhisattva, Śākyamuni can sense Amida Buddha in Dharmākara's Primal Vow. And moreover, since Śākyamuni's life is linked to the life of Dharmākara, his own former personality, it is through Dharmākara that Amida's Primal Vow reaches Śākyamuni. And in a process of clarification, Dharmākara's Primal Vow finds in the two poles of Śākyamuni and Amida Buddha its realized form. Thus Dharmākara Bodhisattva becomes the *locus* of the mutual correspondence and exchange between these two poles. In this way, Mahāyāna Buddhism, especially the Pure Land school, conceives of Śākyamuni, Dharmākara Bodhisattva, and Amida Buddha in the form of a triune structure.

In our search for the principle that underlies the turn-about of Nothingness-*qua*-Love in Absolute Nothingness, we have left behind Tanabe's Bodhisattva Path, turned then to Mahāyāna Buddhism and have finally found the root-source of that principle in the Primal Vow of Amida Buddha in Pure Land Buddhism. Since the principle of the turn-about that brings the human being from nothingness to being is something of an extremely religious nature, it can be grasped at a sufficient depth not in philosophy but only in theology or myth. The reason why in Tanabe the positive character of the principle of the turn-about is not sufficiently clarified is also due to the fact that Tanabe sticks to the standpoint of philosophy, refuses to bring myth into philosophy and tries to keep all myth away from philosophy. That same attitude appears for example also in Tanabe's interpretation of Christianity, where he bases himself solely on the theology of Jesus with the exclusion of the theology of St. Paul. However, myth is the only language that can bring to consciousness and articulate the depth (or the beyond) of human Existenz—a region inhabited by our human existential demands and not accessible to philosophical language—and the other shore that lies beyond the human horizon. Therefore, if philosophy wants to penetrate to the depths of the human Existenz, it must receive from myth its wealth and life. However, because of the duplicity of the language it uses, myth covers up and hides its wealth and life within its literal meaning. Therefore, philosophy must, while participating in the life that is contained in an *an sich* form in the myth, decipher the myth and emancipate it from its literal meaning, in order to bring that life to the light of day.

It goes without saying that the Primal Vow of Amida Buddha, as developed in the Pure Land school, is a myth. However, this myth is rooted in the achings that well up from the depths of religious Existenz and has its *raison d'être* in the depth of faith. Therefore it must also be understood that we should not, at a distance from faith, treat that Primal Vow as existing somewhere outside of faith and chatter away about its objective reality.

How then can we, from a philosophical standpoint, theorize about Amida's Primal Vow and Pure Land? It was said above that the content of Śākyamuni's enlightenment is no-thought, no-form; it is emptiness free from the limitations of form. The content of faith can be said to be a pure and absolutely free will, embracing enough to fill the vast and limitless universe. When this unhindered and pure will touches sentient beings and is taken up in their feelings, it takes on the form of love. Amida's Primal Vow could be said to be the outcome of such a pure religious will, or of faith having come into contact with feeling, and in the light of this having taken on form. Similarly, the Pure Land would be the result of such a formless religious will, which could also be called Absolute Nothingness, being cast in the image of a world wherein we can live by being taken up by feeling. This is an image come about by the absolutely free will reflecting within itself. It is within the human being, within feeling that can also be called the human corporality, that the absolutely free will refracts within itself and gives birth to the image. And when thus taking on image and form in our feeling, this pure religious will has the power to move and sustain us humans. The Pure Land then can be said to be the image that Absolute Nothingness shows when it meets people. In other words, the Pure Land is a symbol of Absolute Nothingness, and we can come into contact with Absolute Nothingness through the image of the Pure Land.

How then is the Pure Land treated in Tanabe? The question of the Pure Land is certainly not sufficiently developed in Tanabe, but on the other hand we can say that the seeds for such a treatment are there, namely in his "logic of species." Let us, finally, delve into that possibility in Tanabe.

As said before, in Tanabe, Absolute Nothingness is a matter of faith and not an object of intuition. This is because we cannot come into contact with Absolute Nothingness directly but only through the mediation of the act of metanoia. And Tanabe expresses this by saying that we can meet Absolute Nothingness only as a differential part and never as an integral whole. However, as long as Absolute Nothingness is something that can be met as a differential point in the act of metanoia, we have therein a relationship of individual and universal, but not a mutual relationship of individuals. In other words, the relationship of individual and universal is not mediated by a relationship of individual to individual. Consequently, even while Tanabe understands the form of love whereby the individual comes into contact with Absolute Nothingness, and this in turn works in the individual as Nothingness-*qua*-Love, as the Bodhisattva Path, this Bodhisattva Path remains, as it were, on the level of the moral ought of the individual and the aspect of a true communication among individuals is only dimly present. The Absolute Nothingness that acts as a differential part in metanoia does not have an image or form that has the power to give rise to a real communion among individuals, and to that extent is still abstract. That is how Absolute Nothingness still appears in *Philosophy as Metanoetics*. In a word, Absolute Nothingness there can only be met, indeed, by mediation, but the mediating instance is only the act of metanoia unsupported by any symbol.

On the other hand, Tanabe interprets the fact that Absolute Nothingness cannot be met unmediated in the framework of the relationships of genus, species, and individual, and gives special attention to the importance of the particular or species as the mediator between the universal or genus and the individual. This concept of species is so rich that it can embrace all kinds of contents, not only state and people, but also culture and traditions of all sorts. And, since they are inseparable from tradition, religious symbols can also find a place therein. The species is the real foundation whereon concrete relationships among individuals are built, the cornerstone of community. However, Tanabe came to his appreciation of the importance of the problem of the species because he was looking for the basis of concrete communities like state and people, so that spiritual, cultural, and religious communities, which may lie outside the realm of actual societies, did not necessarily get sufficient attention. As a result, state and people as species mediating individual and universal were one-sidedly absolutized and the mediation between universal and individual not sufficiently clarified.

However, in his later works, Tanabe succeeds in bringing these two kinds of mediators together and thus to overcome the abstractness of both. Into the relationship of universal and individual, which in the act of metanoia was still a single point purely within the realm of the individual, is now introduced the idea of the community wherein mutual relationship and communication among individuals is contained. And at the same time, in this logic of species, into the real mediating communities of state and people, is introduced the moment of metanoia which negates and transcends them. Thereby "expanse" is added to the point-to-point relationship of individual and universal in the former category of mediators, and "depth" to the relationship of individual and universal in the latter. There the species as the mediator between individual and universal becomes the pure and self-aware community or home-land, which gives rise to true communication and existential community among individuals. Therein we can find the seeds of a Pure Land conception in Tanabe.

Tanabe did not develop such a conception of the Pure Land in his *Philosophy as Metanoetics*. It is only later that Tanabe came to the insight that participation in Absolute Nothingness cannot reach clarity and thoroughness if solely mediated by the act of metanoia of the individual; that existential mutual communication and community must be contained within that act. And Tanabe then widens this existential community into a world of communication that embraces not only the actual world of the living but also the dead. And by going beyond the world of the living to reach also the world of the dead, this world of communication appears as a world of greater purity and higher reality. Therein the existential communities in the world of the living become two-layered, and an existential community linked in its background to the world of the dead opens up. Therein the "Pure Land" opens up as a world wherein existential and pure mutual community obtains. A thoroughgoing conception of existential community goes beyond the actual world wherein we live and opens up in the depths of this world or on its other shore a home-land, a land which gives rise to and sustains true existential community. Tanabe develops this idea with the help of the Christian idea of the "communion of saints."

It has often been pointed out, however, that this last evolution in Tanabe's thought was, in fact, occasioned by the death of his faithful wife. Nishitani formulates this as follows.

> The dialogue (in the world of memory) between Tanabe and his deceased wife expanded the world of mutual communication beyond the world of the living to include also the realm of the dead. And this widened communication was experienced as having much more reality than that among the mere living. After the death of his wife, while living alone with her ashes, Tanabe experienced how, from his recollections, his wife gradually emerged vividly, impressing upon him a strong sense of her reality. In his dialogue with his deceased wife, he felt a world open up wherein the realm of life and the realm of death interpenetrate.[21]

The wall separating the realm of the living and the realm of the dead gradually became transparent, and while the dead appeared with an extraordinary vividness in the heart of the living, the actual presence of the living extended into the dwelling place of the dead. To borrow Nishitani's words again, Tanabe experienced there a world as described by Shōtoku Taishi with the words, "The world is illusion, only the Buddhas are real"—the feeling that only the realm wherein the Buddhas intercommunicate is the true and real world. Just as through the moral law it becomes clear that this world is connected with the intelligible world of freedom and with the yonder world, so it is through the dialogue between the living and the dead that the link between this world and the yonder world is clarified. As just mentioned, Tanabe explains that dialogue and communication with the help of the notion of the "communion of saints." Absolute Nothingness then becomes the *locus* of this communication and existential communion, which clarifies the link that connects this world and the world of the beyond.

---

[21] Nishitani Keiji, NKC 9:283.

As pointed out by Nishitani, however, by becoming such a *locus* of existential communion, Absolute Nothingness loses its character as a differential point to become something with an integral expansion. In other words, Tanabe's Absolute Nothingness is no longer merely the world of the sole relationship of the self and God, but becomes the *locus* wherein that relationship comes to embrace the various other existential relationships and wherein among them all a reciprocal, empathic correspondence obtains.[22] As such, it takes on the nature of the realm wherein the myriad Buddhas recognize and praise one another; in other words, it has the character of the Pure Land as symbolized in the 17th Vow by the "Praise of all the Buddhas."

As "Nothingness-*qua*-Love," Absolute Nothingness has the potential to develop and concretize itself into the Pure Land through the mediation of the existential community.

[Translated by Jan Van Bragt]

---

[22] Nishitani Keiji, NKC 9:283.

Shin Buddhism and Metanoetics

Taitetsu UNNO

D OWN through the centuries Shin Buddhist scholars have developed sophisticated arguments for the validity of the *nembutsu* 念仏 (invocation of the name of Amida Buddha) *within* the circle of Japanese Buddhism, vis-à-vis other Buddhist schools, but in an age of religious pluralism and diversity, it is incumbent upon them to break out of their self-enclosure and demonstrate their claims in relation to the other schools of Asian Buddhism and within the broader context of world religions. One of the rich resources to which they may turn for direction is the Kyoto School of Philosophy, which has ventured, consciously or unconsciously, to rethink and reformulate traditional Buddhist thought in the language of Western philosophy and theology. For Shin Buddhism to pursue such a course means to confront its past, clarifying its origins in Mahāyāna Buddhism, and to face the future, the spiritual crisis of modernity and secularism which it has yet to do.

In this paper I shall limit my discussion to a central figure in the Kyoto School, Tanabe Hajime, and his seminal work, *Philosophy as Metanoetics*, which, as he asserts repeatedly, was inspired by the thought of Shinran. By analyzing Tanabe's philosophical appropriation of this thirteenth-century thinker we may elucidate aspects of Shinran's insights and make them relevant for contemporary people because of the approach taken:

> Shinran's valuable thought goes largely unexplored and undeveloped, when it should be investigated thoroughly in a spirit free of the bonds of sectarianism. It needs to be reinterpreted in the light of our current spiritual situation and brought to bear on the religious needs of today (PM, 225).

In order to explicate the significance of the *nembutsu* which is claimed to be the simplest yet the most superior practice leading to supreme enlightenment I shall focus on two significant topics in Tanabe's work. First is the relationship between the absolute and relative which in Buddhist language may include form and emptiness, *saṃsāra* and *nirvāṇa*, this world and Pure Land, all manifesting *śūnyatā* which is also the heart of *nembutsu*. Second is the bodhisattva ideal which vows the salvation of all beings, formulated as *gensō-ekō* 還相廻向, "returning to this world," by Shinran and utilized by Tanabe to give content to his logic of species as the basis of a world community based on non-ego made possible by a transcendent Other whose essence is compassion:

> It is here that the Great Compassion of the absolute, which revives the relative self by its transcendent power, realizes its quality of absolute mediation: it makes independent relative beings a skillful means (*upāya*) to serve the workings of its own Great Nay, and yet allows them their relative existence as an "other" to serve as mediators of absolute Other-power (256).

Tanabe's heroic efforts to reconstruct philosophy by "Metanoetics, as the transrational resurrection of reason" (28) naturally leads him to develop his thought along lines that separate him from Shinran, whose original insights arose from the depth of religious life, touched by Immeasurable Life and Immeasurable Light. That should not, however, detract from his creative endeavors, from which we can learn much.[1]

I

Hōnen established the singularity of *nembutsu*, superior to all other practices, when he proclaimed:

> The *nembutsu* of the Primal Vow stands by itself and no auxil-

---

[1] For the study of Tanabe's place in modern Japanese intellectual history, see Ienaga Saburō, 田辺元の思想史的研究 [*An Intellectual History of Tanabe Hajime*] (Tokyo: Hōsei Daigaku Press, 1988, 2nd edition). Ienaga traces Tanabe's deepening involvement in the study of Shinran, 178-213, the major impact that Soga Ryōjin had on his interpretation of Shinran, and his subsequent journey into Christianity and Marxism. The only substantial Western study on Tanabe and Shinran is Johannes Laube's "Die Interpretation des *Kyōgyōshinshō* Shinrans durch Hajime Tanabe," *Zeitschrift für Missionswissenschaft und Religionswissenschaft* 65/4 (1981): 277-93.

iary practices are necessary. Those who pursue auxiliary practices will be born on the fringe of the Land of Bliss. Auxiliary practices refer to cultivating wisdom, upholding precepts, aspiring for enlightenment, and practicing compassion as aids to emancipation.[2]

This was confirmed by Shinran and his tradition, as formulated by Rennyo in his famous statement concerning the object of worship:

> In other schools, rather than the Name (*nembutsu*), a painted image (of the Buddha) is preferred, and rather than a painted image, a wooden statue is preferred. But in our school, rather than a wooden statue, a painted image is preferred, and rather than a painted image, the Name is preferred.[3]

What, then, is the significance of this symbol, *nembutsu*, the Name embodying supreme enlightenment, from the standpoint of Mahāyāna Buddhist thought?

First of all, the *nembutsu*, Namu-amida-butsu, has no objective referent, neither a being called Amida Buddha nor any kind of metaphysical absolute. Second, it forms the totality of Shin awakening, confirmed in the saying of *nembutsu*. Third, in thus living the *nembutsu*, the simultaneous realization of the absolute and relative takes place. When couched in traditional Pure Land language this means that the Primal Vow of Amida Buddha, accomplished in the timeless past, and the Pure Land, established in the timeless future, both come to complete realization for the first time in the *nembutsu*, here and now.[4] And finally, the *nembutsu* so experienced liberates a person condemned to the infinite finitude of samsaric existence, making possible the freedom to become truly human within the very midst of karmic limitations.

In sum, the absolute realizes itself through the relative, becoming a concrete manifestation in history, and the relative becomes itself truly with humility and gratitude by virtue of the

---

[2] 昭和新修法然上人全集 [*Collected Works of Hōnen: Shōwa Shinshū Edition*] (Tokyo: Jōdoshū Shūmuchō, 1955), 462.

[3] 蓮如上人御一代記聞書 [*A Collection of the Sayings of Rennyo*] , 69. 真宗聖教全書 [*Shinshū shōgyō zensho*] (hereafter SSZ), Volume III, (Kyoto, 1964), 549.

[4] For this formulation, see Nishitani Keiji, "The Problem of Time in Shinran," *The Eastern Buddhist*, 11/1 (1978): 13-26.

absolute. Thus, the *nembutsu* consummates the non-dual realization of the absolute and relative, of *nirvāṇa* and *saṃsāra*, of the compassionate working of Amida's Primal Vow and the foolish, evil self drowning in the ocean of birth-and-death.

In spite of this realization, however, history has shown that in both orthodox Shin doctrine and individual religious experience a constant wavering between the two poles of the absolute and the relative occurs. When the absolute in the form of Amida Buddha is reified without full awareness of one's karmic evil, as orthodoxy sometimes tends to do, a proclivity towards moral laxity and spiritual inertia on the part of the relative is inevitable. Tanabe describes this precisely when he writes that "by placing too much emphasis here on Other-power, we end up in the usual position of claiming that whatever action sentient beings perform is done *qua* the Great Action of Tathāgata" (274). It is also prone to a static faith, grasped within a subject-object dichotomy that keeps self-delusion intact:

> The temptation surfaces again to harden genuine faith into an abstract notion that quickly contents itself with the status quo and forgets the need for ongoing transformation and conversion (206).

On the other hand, when the weight is placed on the relative, all kinds of deviations, rooted in the massive self-centeredness called karmic evil, appear. Included in this are different kinds of heresies, such as the antinomian tendency of so-called "licensed evil" and the mistaken pride in the Primal Vow, referred to as *honganbokori* 本願ぼこり by Tanabe (14).

The Shin tradition developed two central doctrines in order to sustain the creative tension between the absolute and the relative, such that a one-sided emphasis could be avoided: *kihō ittai* 機法一体 and *butsubon ittai* 仏凡一体. Both of these concepts, however, need to be unraveled and articulated in terms of Mahāyāna Buddhist thought so that they can be given new life. *Hō* and *butsu* in the respective concepts both refer to the absolute under different names, Dharma and Buddha; *ki* and *bon* both point to the relative, practitioner and foolish person, respectively. If we translate *ittai* literally as "oneness," the terms may be understood as the oneness of practitioner and Dharma, or the oneness of Buddha and foolish person. But this oneness is not a oneness that dissolves the distinction between the absolute and relative; rather, the distinction becomes even more pronounced as their interdependence is realized. In Buddhist terminology, it is a relationship characterized as "non-dual" within which an on-going, creative tension is maintained.

Tanabe is perceptive in pointing out that this "oneness" in Shin Buddhism does not point to any kind of self-identity with the absolute, whether considered as nothingness or being, as found in Zen and some forms of mysticism. Tanabe is highly critical of such an identity as leading to stasis and asserts the necessity of a dynamic interplay between the absolute and the relative, such that the "relationship of opposition and mediation between the relative and the absolute in which the two are neither identical nor different, neither one nor two, comes about through transformative action" (175).

In Shin Buddhism *kihō ittai* is generally understood as the primary *relationship* between practitioner and Dharmic reality as a fundamental fact, whether conscious or unconscious; and *butsubon ittai* denotes the content of religious experience in which a radical *transformation* of a foolish, evil being into its opposite takes place. Let us now turn to Tanabe's explication of the absolute and the relative which may help us gain a better appreciation of the Shin teaching of *nembutsu*, Namu-amida-butsu, within which is contained the totality of Buddhist salvific truth. Anything realized outside of this is a subjective fabrication, an arbitrary conception, a sentimental religiosity.

II

For Tanabe "the absolute is essentially nothingness" (257) whose function is "the negation and transformation—that is, conversion—of everything relative" (li). Absolute nothingness is thus the Dharmic reality that underlies *kihō ittai*, a manifestation of *śūnyatā* that can never be objectified or grasped conceptually but can be totally and completely realized. The absolute does not exist, for example, in the non-mediated form as found in the ontic versus ontological distinction made by Heidegger (82). Tanabe formulates it as follows:

Nothingness cannot, however, exist directly, for anything that exists directly belongs to being. Nothingness must manifest it-self in the mediation of negative transformation. . . . Nothing-ness does not allow itself to be treated ontologically (82).

This nothingness is also called Other-power, referring to its dy-namic, transformative activity. "When we speak of Other-power, the Other is absolute precisely because it is nothingness, that is, nothingness in the sense of absolute transformation" (18). Since nothingness effects transformation, bringing to realization the one-ness of practitioner and Amida Buddha, it is ultimately experi-enced as compassion. Thus, "Nothingness-*qua*-Great Compassion" is the working of Amida's Primal Vow bringing to life the oneness of practitioner and Amida Buddha. Tanabe makes this point, stressing the realization that "Nothingness is practiced and wit-nessed to in gratitude for Great Compassion and *reaches self-con-sciousness in the core of the self*" (141, emphasis added). The absolute as Great Compassion means radical-negation-*qua*-radical-affirma-tion of the relative:

> The self bears witness within itself to an absolute conversion; that self that has been abandoned is now rescued; what has died once again lives. Because the self bears witness to this res-urrection, the absolute can be spoken of as Great Compassion, which is surely more than a new construct based on the ab-stract notion of self-negating love (141).

This understanding makes it clear that the absolute cannot exist by itself alone. In the oneness of practitioner and Dharmic reality, the latter becomes real through the former, just as the former realizes itself through the latter.

The term for the relative, *ki* 機, has been understood tradi-tionally as connoting 1) all beings, including nature, 2) beings who strive to lead an ethical life, and 3) beings who are religiously awakened. Metaphorically, the three have been likened respectively to 1) the tension before the arrow is released from the bow, 2) the potentially explosive moment of release, and 3) the explosive moment itself. The third connotation is also contained in *butsubon ittai*, wherein the foolish being realizes itself completely in the oneness with the Buddha.

In all three cases the significance of the relative in its rela-tionship to the absolute is underscored: "Nothingness entails the mediation of being and cannot imply the negation or annihilation of mediation" (143). Tanabe articulates the role of the relative positively when he writes:

> The existence of the relative is a *sine qua non* for the absolute as nothingness. And precisely because the absolute *is* nothingness, the relative can exist as being. Conversely, because the existence of the relative is "being as *upāya*" (*hōben*) in the sense that it alone serves a mediating function with regard to nothingness and because it is absolutely relative in the sense that it is a being related to other beings in relative reciprocity, it is able to serve as the medium for the absolute mediation of nothingness and thus enables nothingness to realize itself (23).

Now, "the absolute makes room for the independence of relative being" (272) by affirming the nature of the relative as karmic evil. Not only is this crucial for the absolute, but "In it we see the very core of Pure Land faith with its distinctive profession of participation in *nirvāṇa* without extinguishing our evil passions" (227). While the followers of monastic Buddhism made a concerted effort to destroy evil passions in order to attain supreme enlightenment, the Pure Land path did not see what is essentially human as an obstacle to ultimate realization. In fact, its distinctive quality was that *nirvāṇa* could be attained without sundering delusion. Here we see the identity of *saṃsāra* and *nirvāṇa* in its ultimate form.

In sum, absolute nothingness is the basis on which the absolute and relative each becomes real, existentially and religiously, for the first time. Both affirm their respective identities in this realization: "Mediation is not a relationship in which one party is subordinated to the other, but one in which both enjoy and maintain an independence made possible by the other" (272).

The Shin view concerning the absolute and relative, the simultaneous realization of *kihō ittai*, has various shades of complementary meanings that have developed over the years. Zonkaku (1290-1373) establishes the fundamental relationship between the two as follows: "having entrusted oneself to the Buddha's Primal Vow, practitioner and Dharmic reality are in oneness, and subject and object are in non-duality."

He continues:

> The Buddha's supreme enlightenment (*shōgaku* 正覚) is accomplished by the birth (*ōjō* 往生) of a practitioner and the birth of a practitioner is accomplished by the Buddha's supreme enlightenment. Therefore, since practitioner and Dharmic reality are in oneness and the subject and object are non-dual, the life-span of the Buddha and the life-span of a practitioner are identical, and there is no difference in their transcending impermanence and realizing permanent reality.[5]

Here we see the simultaneous realization of Dharmākara becoming Amida Buddha and the ultimate awakening of a practitioner, referred to as the attainment of birth (*ōjō*), occurring here and now. Zonkaku establishes this unity of the absolute and relative on the basis of Shinran's twofold aspects of faith, inherited from Shan-tao: the simultaneous insight into the evil nature of self and the boundless compassion of Amida. The same point is reiterated in the *Anjinketsujōshō* 安心決定鈔 , reputed to be a text of the Seizan Branch of Jōdo-shū but cherished by successive Shin masters. Its central point is that "When the vow and practice of practitioners in the ten quarters were fulfilled and birth was attained, the supreme enlightenment that is Namu-amida-butsu, the oneness of practitioner and Dharmic reality, was accomplished."[6]

Rennyo (1415-1499) really brought this oneness of the absolute and relative closer to daily life, when he popularized the *nembutsu* as the religious practice *par excellence* which could be upheld anytime, anywhere, and by anyone. He taught that *namu* is the person (relative) who is lost and seeks a real home which is to be found in *amida butsu*, Immeasurable Life and Immeasurable Light (absolute). When the two attain union, it is confirmed in the saying of the Name, "Namu-amida-butsu," which erupts spontaneously.

The *Anjinketsujōshō* expresses the permeation of Amida's vow and practice by graphically describing that every particle obtained by pulverizing both body and mind contains the oneness of practitioner and Dharmic reality.[7]

---

[5] SSZ III, 366.
[6] SSZ III, 615
[7] SSZ III, 622.

The noetic dimension of this oneness is stressed by Kakunyo (1270-1351) when he writes,

> Having been nurtured by the Light that illuminates reality, a sentient being experiences true entrusting and spiritual joy. This is the oneness of practitioner and Dharmic reality. Although that which illuminates and that which is illuminated appear to be two different things, they are actually non-dual.[8]

Here the suggestion is that at the core of oneness is found an illumination or awakening which enables a person to see things, including oneself, as they truly are. True wisdom, granted to a person through Amida's compassionate working, is what makes possible the recognition of karmic evil within.[9]

When we turn to *butsubon ittai*, the focus is on the religious transformation at the heart of this realization. This transformation is not self-generated but occurs by virtue of Other-power. Kakunyo explains the basis for this as follows:

> Since *shinjin* 信心 is read as "true and real mind" (*makoto no ko-koro*), it does not refer to the deluded mind of a foolish being. It is nothing but the mind of Buddha. When this Buddha mind (that is true and real) is placed on the mind of a foolish being, it is called *shinjin*.[10]

According to tradition, when the true and real mind of the Buddha is placed on the foolish mind of delusion, it is called *shinjin* from the side of the Buddha, but it is called foolish, evil nature from the side of human beings. While the foolish mind remains just as it is, in the oneness with the Buddha mind, "the evil mind of the practitioner is made identical to the good mind of the Buddha." This paradoxical experience is beyond rational comprehension but occurs at the core of *shinjin*. In the words of Shinran, "To be transformed means that evil karma, without being nullified or eradicated, is made into good, just as all waters, upon entering the great ocean, immediately become ocean water."[11] The

---

[8] 願願鈔 *[Treatise on the Vows]*, SSZ III, 46.

[9] Yoshifumi Ueda and Dennis Hirota, *Shinran: An Introduction to His Thought* (Kyoto: Hongwanji International Center, 1989), 214-15.

[10] 最要鈔 *[Treatise on the Essence]*, SSZ III, 50.

[11] *Shinran*, 237.

transformation of evil into good is one of the most important among the ten benefits received in the awakening of *shinjin*.

The awareness of karmic evil is also at the heart of *zange* 懺悔, which is crucial for Tanabe. He describes *zange* as a "disciplined way towards one's death" (4) and "a despair in which we renounce all hope for and claim to justification" (5) as the working of absolute nothingness. He writes:

> Although *zange* is an act of the self, it does not belong to the self but is an act of self-surrender and must be an act of absolute nothingness. Thus, *zange*, as distinguished from the despair of arrogance, includes the despair of submission in which no self-assertion of the ego performing *zange* remains (7).

Yet, as Tanabe is fully aware, it is still prone to ego-assertion, just as the *nembutsu* (the 18th vow) can easily become misapprehended as an act of self-assertion, whether self-willed (the 19th vow) or unconscious (the 20th vow). He is therefore correct in concluding that "The only way to avoid such a pitfall is through continual *zange*, wherein the activity of Other-power works its transforming mediation" (207).

Continual *zange* was for Tanabe the key term which differentiated his philosophy from that of Nishida. In direct contrast to Nishida, who developed absolute nothingness into the logic of topos wherein "action-intuition" takes place, Tanabe sees absolute nothingness activated through action-faith-witness. That is, "absolute nothingness does not allow itself to be treated ontologically. It is simply brought to faith-witness through action. . . . Self-witness is prior to self-consciousness of nothingness" (272).

Although Tanabe ascribes the source of his awakening of *zange* to Shinran, he seems ambivalent about the role that it plays in Shinran himself. On the one hand, speaking of Shinran's *magnum opus*, he writes that "even though *zange* is not a formal part of the *Kyōgyōshinshō*, it constitutes the whole basis and background, only occasionally breaking through the surface" (20). On the other, he states that "Shinran's teaching is completely reliant on Other-power. In this doctrine *zange* does not figure as a special mediating element in salvation but serves only as a background" (17).

Furthermore, in spite of Tanabe's relentless negation of self-power and absolute faith in Other-power, traces of self-will remain in his act of *zange*. He writes, for example, that

> it is necessary that the *an sich* action of metanoesis be prior to faith in order for self-power to be emptied out, brought to self-negation, and made into a mediator of Other-power. . . . In itself, faith in the Original Vow may be prior, but for us it is metanoesis that is prior (252).

For Shinran the sense of remorse and shame is not a precondition for *shinjin*, for man is not capable of such self-emptying; it is only through the experience of *shinjin*, wherein occurs the mediation of the absolute, that transformation occurs. Self-power can only be negated by Other-power.

A similar problem exists when, for example, Tanabe asserts that "the conversion from the twentieth vow to the eighteenth vow is also mediated by the performance of *zange*" (209) and "the *sangantennyū* 三願転入 means that the future-oriented desire for rebirth is transformed by metanoesis for the past into the sincere mind of 'action of no action'" (221). This assumes that the performance of *zange* leads one to become free of sin and evil, enabling a person to acquire the sincere mind capable of the "action of no action." For Shinran the depth of his karmic evil was fathomless, beyond human comprehension and requiring the working of Other-power. This depth was alluded to when Yuien spoke of his teacher Shinran as the one who made him "deeply realize that we do *not know* the depth of karmic evil and that we do *not know* the height of Tathāgata's benevolence, all of which cause us to live in utter confusion."[12]

Although Tanabe repeatedly stresses that metanoetics is for ordinary, ignorant, and sinful people like himself, thoroughly conscious of finite and relative limits, his *zange* in the final analysis appears to be yet another path for sages and saints, performed in self-will, even though Other-power is operative. It lacks the dimension of religious depth in which is found the foolish, evil self unable to undertake true metanoesis that becomes the primary object of great compassion. Perhaps this was inevitable because of Tanabe's dedication to his philosophical enterprise: the death and resurrection of reason.

---

[12] Taitetsu Unno, 歎異抄 *Tannisho: A Shin Buddhist Classic* (Honolulu: Buddhist Study Center Press, 1984), 36.

III

The bodhisattva path in Mahāyāna Buddhism, according to Tanabe, is "given a grounding in doctrine" (280) by Shinran, specifically in the concept of *gensō-ekō*, a powerful movement of returning to this world born out of irrepressible compassion. Tanabe utilizes this concept to fortify his logic of species—"social existence as an important orientation for the Other-power philosophy of metanoetics" (282). Here again Tanabe's interpretation deviates from that of Shinran, yet his ideas are suggestive for Shin Buddhists to develop an "ethic which is not an ethic" parallel to his "philosophy which is not a philosophy."

According to Shinran, the dynamic working of the Primal Vow results in two forms of empowerment among people. First is *ōsō-ekō* 往相廻向, going to the Pure Land, which is made possible by the teaching (*kyō* 教) that expounds the practice or activity (*gyō* 行) of Amida Buddha, causing a person to entrust (*shin* 信) the self to Amida, and thereby attain unsurpassed enlightenment (*shō* 証). And the second is *gensō-ekō*, returning to this world from the Pure Land for the sake of all beings through the working of Amida Buddha.

While the former is spelled out carefully in Shinran's *Kyōgyō-shinshō*, the latter receives only a brief discussion, probably because it was seen as belonging to the realm of enlightenment, beyond any discursive understanding. Social consciousness as we know it today was no more present in the Orient of the thirteenth century, when Shinran lived, than it was in medieval Europe, but the crises of global survival compel every religious tradition now to address the complex issues facing humankind.

Traditional Shin scholarship, developed during the Tokugawa period (1600-1868), clearly states that birth in the Pure Land occurs after death, and thus only after attaining Buddhahood in the Pure Land does one return to *saṃsāra* to save all beings. This does not accord completely with Shinran's thought, since he considered "birth in the Pure Land" to be twofold: simultaneous with the awakening of *shinjin* and the attainment of Buddhahood with death.[13] Some contemporary interpretations, clearly dissatisfied with this traditional, futuristic view, suggest that *gensō* activities

---

[13] *Shinran*, 240.

are carried out in this life by people of Shin faith who work for the welfare of fellow beings and spread the teachings to others. But this also counters Shinran's understanding, for it lacks the radical negation of self-assertion which creeps into even the noblest of human deeds.

While Tanabe would be aligned to the latter group, he speaks of *ōsō-qua-gensō* 往相即還相 (211, 216) at the core of which is relentless *zange*, differentiating him from an easy identification of *gensō* with the activities of the faithful. According to Tanabe,

> Only the "natural" (*jinen-hōni* 自然法爾) activity of relative being serving as a mediatory element for the absolute can become an *upāya* for absolute transformation, that is, for the work of salvation which belongs to the absolute alone. Only such an "action of no-action," an action performed *without an acting self*, can participate in the absolute's work of saving others (214, emphasis added).

Here we see that Tanabe's *ōsō-qua-gensō* is based upon action "without an acting self" which is the essence of compassionate bodhisattva activity. Nevertheless, he also speaks of *gensō* as the possibility of the relative performing salvific acts:

> Relative sentient beings can serve others as *upāya* for salvation by acting as a temporary axis of absolute transformation. In this function, each relative being enjoys the power to make its own *gensō* a skillful means for the salvation of others, and thus an independent existence vis-à-vis others (219).

This "power to make its own *gensō*" is the basis for his scheme that "the work of salvation is mediated by the *gensō* of the more advanced, who provides guidance and instruction to the less advanced. . ." (276). The model for such an action, he states, is the discipline of Dharmākara Bodhisattva, the symbol of absolute *gensō* (275). But he also seems to suggest that anyone who has undertaken *zange*, who has entered the "rightly established state" (*shōjōju* 正定聚), can engage in *gensō* activity to lead others as the representative of the absolute (285).

While such an interpretation might have been essential for Tanabe, who sought to reinforce his logic of species in contradistinction to Nishida's logic of topos, it differs from the view of Shinran, for whom both the going to the Pure Land and the returning to this world are made possible only by the overwhelming compassion of Other-power, not by any willful calculation. This is connoted by the term *ekō*, which is crucial for both *ōsō* and *gensō*. This term is almost impossible to translate into English (210) but is usually rendered as "merit-transference" or "directing of virtue." Its fundamental meaning is that the accumulated power and virtue of Amida Buddha is given over to a person, such that one not only acquires the cause and effect of supreme enlightenment in the Pure Land but instantaneously returns to this world to work for the salvation of all beings. All this is part of the dynamic working of *dharmatā* which excludes any form of willful calculation.

As long as karma-bound, foolish and evil beings are concerned, the only movement possible is *ōsō-ekō*, going forward to the Pure Land. Thus, for Shinran the only *gensō-ekō* bodhisattvas were those who, returning from the Pure Land, guided, aided, and sustained him on his own journey to the Pure Land. The paradigm of *gensō* is Śākyamuni Buddha:

> Those who attain the Pure Land of peace and bliss
> Return to the evil world of Five Defilements
> And like Śākyamuni Buddha
> Benefit sentient beings without end.[14]

But for Shinran the *gensō* bodhisattvas were also other historical personages, such as the Seven Patriarchs of Pure Land Buddhism of whom he writes:

> Appearing from the ocean of great mind
> Was truly the teacher Shan-tao
> For the sake of sentient beings in the Latter Ages
> Requesting that all Buddhas bear witness.[15]

> In many births of countless aeons
> I never knew the way of liberation;
> Without my teacher Hōnen
> This life, too, would have passed in vain.[16]

---

[14] *Jōdo wasan* 浄土和讃 *[Hymns on the Pure Land]* 20, SSZ II, 488.
[15] *Kōsō-wasan* 高僧和讃 *[Hymns on the Patriarchs]* 62, SSZ II, 508.
[16] *Kōsō-wasan* 101, SSZ II, 513.

Although Shinran late in his life identified the person of *shinjin* with Maitreya Bodhisattva and saw such a one as the equal of Tathāgata, he saw himself as nothing but a being of karmic evil on the way to the Pure Land, unable to fulfill the miraculous salvific powers of a *gensō* bodhisattva. Shinran, quoting T'an-luan, defines the work of such a bodhisattva:

> With great compassion, one observes all sentient beings in pain and affliction, and assuming various transformed bodies to guide them, enters the garden of birth-and-death and the forest of blind passions. Sporting freely there with translucent powers, one attains the stage of teaching and guiding.[17]

Only Buddhas and bodhisattvas who assume the "transformed bodies" to engage in compassionate activities, completely free of willfulness and blind passion, can be called beings of *gensō*.

This, of course, does not mean that the person of *shinjin* lacks compassion; in fact, he or she manifests true compassion precisely because of the mediation of the absolute. This is suggested in the famous passages in *Tannishō* IV:

> There is a difference in compassion between the Path of Sages and the Path of Pure Land. The compassion in the Path of Sages is expressed through pity, sympathy, and care for all beings, but truly rare is it that one can help another as completely as one desires.
>
> The compassion in the Path of Pure Land is to quickly attain Buddhahood, saying the *nembutsu*, and with the true heart of compassion and love save all beings as we desire.
>
> In this life no matter how much pity and sympathy we may feel for others, it is impossible to help another as we truly wish; thus our compassion is inconsistent and limited. Only the saying of *nembutsu* manifests the complete and never ending compassion which is true, real, and sincere.[18]

To realize that "our compassion is inconsistent and limited" is to admit the failure of self-power to accomplish an authentic, thoroughgoing love and compassion. This realistic appraisal of human

---

[17] 教行信証 *Kyōgyōshinshō* SSZ II, 106-107. English translation, *The True Teaching, Practice, and Realization of the Pure Land Way* (Kyoto: Hongwanji International Center, 1987), III, 390-91.

[18] *Tannisho*, 9.

limitation is shown to us by Amida's wisdom and compassion which leads to humility and an openness to true compassion. As soon as we become receptive to the working of the Primal Vow, having departed from self-power, we are in the midst of that dynamic, on-going process, beginning here and now, which is "to quickly attain Buddhahood, saying the *nembutsu,* and with the true heart of compassion and love, save all beings as we desire." Such a person, mediating great compassion, manifests true solidarity with all of life; thus, Shinran, who disclaimed having a single disciple, could proclaim that we are all involved one with another, for "all beings have been fathers and mothers, brothers and sisters, in the timeless process of birth-and-death."[19]

All this occurs in our movement towards the Pure Land by virtue of *ōsō-ekō.* While Tanabe would ascribe all this to the beings of *gensō,* they are qualities already found in the beings of *ōsō,* as enumerated by Shinran in the ten benefits received by the person of *shinjin* in this life.

The ten benefits which result from the mediation of the absolute in relative beings are as follows.[20] The person of *shinjin* 1) constantly receives the protection of unseen powers, 2) manifests the highest virtues, 3) transforms evil into good, 4) receives the protection of all the Buddhas, 5) is praised by all the Buddhas, 6) is embraced by the Light of wisdom, 7) is filled with joyful happiness, 8) possesses a grateful heart that desires to repay the world, 9) always does the work of great compassion, and 10) enters the group of the truly settled, destined for supreme enlightenment in the Pure Land.

Here we see clearly that the person on the way to the Pure Land, without his or her knowledge, has become a mediator of true compassion. In such a person karmic evil is transformed into the highest good, joyful happiness abounds, humility and gratitude are spontaneous, and the work of great compassion is constantly manifested. All this, of course, is due to the working of Other-power, which is nothing but absolute nothingness appearing in the person of *shinjin* and manifesting itself in the interdependence and interconnectedness of all life.

The true metanoia of a foolish, evil person is endless, and

---

[19] *Tannisho,* 10 and 11.
[20] *Kyōgyōshinshō,* SSZ II, 72. Also, *Shinran,* 297-98.

therefore the compassion of Amida that grasps and illuminates such a person is also endless. As such, we live out our karmic life on this earth cherishing each moment, grateful to the working of true compassion, and experiencing solidarity with all beings who are also sustained by that same compassion. Although it awaits to be more fully articulated and related to contemporary concerns, the vision for global survival is clear. In the words of Tanabe:

> To seek existence for oneself alone by destroying all others is to forfeit one's own existence as well. Only by giving life to those who exist as others, by seeking coexistence despite the tension of opposition, and by collaborating for the sake of mutual enhancement can the self find life in its fullness. . . . The absolute is absolute mediation, mediating relative beings to one another and thereby mediating itself as well. And this process means continual transformation for relative beings; grounded in a nothingness that ensures mutual self-transcendence, each relative being finds itself in every other (290-91).

This vision is implicit in Nishida's logic of topos and explicit in Nishitani's circuminsessional interpenetration. All three thinkers in their respective ways formulate the bodhisattva ideal of Mahāyāna Buddhism for the contemporary world.

Tanabe's Metanoetics and Shinran's Thought

UEDA Yoshifumi

ANABE'S reliance on Shinran's thought in his *Philosophy as Metanoetics* is unequivocal, as when he states that I "can only express my gratitude to Shinran for being my precursor and teacher in the philosophy of metanoetics. In fact, I firmly believe that Shinran has returned to the world—performed *gensō*—to teach me this truth" (PM, 29). This basic stance remains throughout the work; thus he states towards the end:

> In the dialogue with Western philosophy, this metanoetic philosophy of *tariki* leans in a special way on the guidance and instruction provided by Shinran's faith in Other-power.... In this sense, Shinran is truly the master and the teacher of my philosophy (260).

Tanabe, without any question, draws heavily upon Shinran, citing such crucial terms peculiar to his writings as *jiriki* 自力 (self-power) and *tariki* 他力 (Other-power), *ōsō* 往相 and *gensō* 還相 , *ekō* 廻向 (merit-transference), *tenkan* 転換 (conversion), and *gyō-shin-shō* 行信証 (action-faith-witness). Moreover, he gives a detailed analysis of the theory of the Three Vows (*sangantennyū* 三願転入) in Chapter Six and the theory of Three Minds (*sanshin* 三心) in Chapter Seven. In brief, *Philosophy as Metanoetics* at first appears to be a modern version of Shinran's major work, *Kyōgyōshinshō*.

It seems to me, however, based upon my own understanding of Shinran, that Tanabe fails to faithfully incorporate so much as a single concept in its entirety from Shinran, and that his interpretations of the Three Vows and Three Minds differ radically from those of Shinran. Perhaps this is unavoidable because his views are based on his version of *zange* (懺悔), which is non-existent in Shinran and radically different from the latter's *zangi* (慚愧). We will first clarify this difference and demonstrate how it affects our understanding of Shinran's thought.

The original Sanskrit for *zange* is *kṣama* or *kṣamaṇa*; it consists of *zan* (transliteration of the Sanskrit) and *ge* (translation into the Chinese). It means to regret and to make changes or to seek forgiveness. *Zangi*, in contrast, is composed of *zan*, from the Sanskrit *hrī*, and *gi*, from the Sanskrit *apatrāpya*. It means to feel a sense of shame so as effectively to stop evil actions.

The former, *zange*, is used in Buddhism generally to connote the elimination of evil, but Shinran does not use it and prefers the latter, *zangi*. The basic reason for this is that *zange* has the connotation of "repentance" (which according to *Webster's New World Dictionary* means "to feel so contrite over one's sins as to change, or decide to change one's way; be penitent"), while Shinran's usage of *zangi* is completely lacking in the idea of doing away with evil and cultivating good, as evident, for example, in *Tannishō* Sections XIV and XVI.

Thus, *zangi* contains simply the sense of being humbled or being ashamed—the forceful Japanese phrase is *muzan-mugi* (無慚無愧), "without shame, without remorse"—and contains no idea of repenting or turning over a new leaf. The implication is that a truly human person who feels ashamed about his or her conduct would naturally, without coercion, cease from pursuing it or repeating it. Both *zan* and *gi* do have the connotation of stopping evil, a sense also found in Shinran, but it does not come from a willful effort; rather, evil is naturally avoided as the consequence of feeling ashamed of oneself.

The fundamental standpoint of Buddhism—"Not to do evil but practice good and purify the mind; this is the teaching of all the Buddhas"—is to be realized by the practitioner through dedicated effort. In the case of the Other-power teaching of Shinran, however, the same goal is accomplished without consciousness of any ethical imperative but as the result of a sense of humility and the natural working of Amida's Primal Vow. According to D. T. Suzuki, such a person "is entirely relieved of all effortful activities which grow out of a contriving consciousness. He is living an effortless life. The effortless life is the perfection of passivism."[1] And in the words of Shinran, "though people of the diamond-like mind neither know nor seek it, the vast treasure of virtues com-

---

[1] *On Indian Mahayana Buddhism* (New York: Harper and Row, 1975), 113.

pletely fills them; hence, it is likened to an ocean of great treasure."[2]

In contrast, in Tanabe's way of *zange* or metanoesis what is central is the repentance for wrongs committed, realizing the powerlessness of self, and the experience of Other-power which comes into play to cause the birth of a new self. Such is the "conversion-resurrection experience" (PM, li) central to his philosophy. For Shinran, who has abandoned the self completely, there is no resurrection as implied in metanoesis. When self-power is completely abandoned, it is left behind forever and one enters the ocean of the Primal Vow which is Other-power. There is no room at all for self-power; all is the working of Other-power. Shinran describes such a life poetically: "When one has boarded the ship of the Vow of great compassion and sailed on the vast ocean of light, the winds of perfect virtue blow softly and the waves of evil are transformed."[3]

In Tanabe's metanoesis it would seem that even though the self admits to powerlessness when saved by Other-power, the strength to begin a new life is restored. For Shinran no power remains intact within him that can lead to a new life; he has completely departed from self-power and now lives within Other-power, in the ocean of Amida's Vow which alone sustains and guides him. We cannot but conclude that Shinran is more thoroughgoing than Tanabe in the negation of self-power. That this abandonment of self-power is absolute means that Other-power is also absolute. We shall have more to say about this later. In any event, for Shinran the working of Other-power is fully realized because self-power admits to its powerlessness. But in metanoesis the self that is newly born advances on a new path aided by Other-power, giving us a "unity of *jiriki* and *tariki*."[4]

Other-power is realized only where there is no working of self-power. In the words of Shinran, "Other-power means to be free of any form of calculation."[5] As long as there is even an iota of self-power working, Other-power cannot be found. Shinran is

[2] Yoshifumi Ueda and Dennis Hirota, *Shinran: An Introduction to His Thought* (Kyoto: Hongwanji International Center, 1989), 271.

[3] *Shinran*, 284-85.

[4] Langdon Gilkey, "Tanabe and the Philosophy of Religion," *see above*, 74.

[5] *Letters of Shinran* (Kyoto: Hongwanji International Center, 1978), 39.

precise on this point: "Since the person of self-power, being conscious of doing good, lacks the thought of entrusting himself completely to Other-power, he is not the focus of the Primal Vow of Amida."[6]

As long as one thinks that one can, or should, do good by self-power, there is no entering the ocean of the Primal Vow of Other-power. When Shinran refers to the person of profound karmic evil or of abundant blind passion, he is referring to a person who is incapable of performing even the slightest good by self-power, or uttering even a single *nembutsu* that is true and real. For that very reason such a person becomes the primary *object* of Amida's Primal Vow.

From the standpoint of the movement from Other-Power to self-power, the person who has "boarded the ship of the Vow of great compassion and sailed on the vast ocean of light" no longer has any need to swim with his own powers. Although the Other-power in the way of metanoia is said to be transcendent and absolute, its effectiveness is limited, because even though one is saved by such a power, one must exert self-power in order to swim. In short, that the negation of the relative is not thoroughgoing means also that the absolute is not completely and absolutely absolute. Can an absolute that requires the working of the relative be called truly an absolute in the full sense of that word? The absolute in Shinran embraces the relative completely and functions in the world by itself, permitting no room for the activity of the relative. There is no way to obscure the radical difference in the understanding of the absolute between Shinran and Tanabe.

According to Tanabe, "The conversion from the twentieth vow to the eighteenth vow is also mediated by the performance of *zange*" (209). But in Shinran that conversion means the complete abandonment of self-power (20th vow) and entering Other-power (18th vow); here there is no performance of *zange* whose structure is said to be one of self-power and Other-power, *tariki-qua-jiriki* 他力即自力 (7). That is, the relationship of self-power and Other-power in *zange* is *both/and*, whereas in Shinran it is *either/or*. Furthermore, the *zangi* in Shinran occurs after the conversion into Other-power; that is, it is born from his reflection as he lives

---

[6] Taitetsu Unno, *Tannisho: A Shin Buddhist Classic* (Honolulu: Buddhist Study Center Press, 1984), 8.

within Other-power. Thus, conversion is prior to *zangi*. This is the opposite of *zange*, which—according to Tanabe—effects the conversion, making it prior to conversion.

Tanabe thus speaks of conversion as being the essence of metanoia, turning pain into joy and repentance into gratitude. In Shinran, however, rather than such a conversion taking place, *zangi* remains just as it is while at the same time gratitude is deeply felt. The profound remorse of *zangi* felt by Shinran remains, but an ever greater sense of gratitude to compassion is experienced. Let us analyze this simultaneous occurrence of remorse and gratitude.

People generally live with some kind of morality as the basis for their daily life, and they believe that they are basically moral and good, and, therefore, they are not evil. Thus, they feel no sense of shame, which would not be the case if they only knew themselves truly. When one has no awareness of the Buddha's compassion, there is no knowledge of the profound karmic evil carried within the self. Hence, there is no humility. Within Shinran's *zangi* is a penetrating insight into his true nature, because he sees himself with the eyes of wisdom. He can see himself as he truly is, because, having entered the ocean of Amida's vow, his blind passion has been transformed into great compassion, and it has become of "one taste" with true wisdom (which is none other than *shinjin* 信心). Since his mind has been transformed into the mind of great compassion, he is called "equal to Tathāgata," and it is this mind that reflects upon the profound nature of karmic evil within, leading to *zangi*. That person who is said to be equal to Tathāgata is the very person aware of profound karmic evil. Here karmic obstacles and virtues, evil and great compassion, are one. To attain such a realization is to be grasped, never to be abandoned (the working of Amida), which also means the awakening of *shinjin*.

As long as we live out our karmic lives, we must confront the evil within. But Shinran states that "Even though we do evil, we should even more think of the power of the Vow. Then the thought of tenderness and forbearance will become manifest by virtue of 'made to become so by itself.'"[7] Even though one is aware of karmic evil tendencies within the self, one does not

---

[7] *Tannisho*, 31.

willfully try to overcome them; rather, as one entrusts the self still more to the Primal Vow, the mind of compassion, flexible and tolerant, will become manifested naturally as the working of the Vow. Since the person of true and real *shinjin* lives within the Primal Vow of Amida, even though blind passion may arise, before it is manifested externally, the Vow works to transform the blind passion or karmic evil into the content of enlightenment. This is the meaning of the statement that "though people of the diamond-like mind neither know nor seek it, the vast treasure of virtues completely fills them; hence, it is likened to an ocean of great treasure," and "In one-thought moment (of *shinjin*) one inevitably receives unexcelled virtues without seeking it and receives immense benefits without knowing it."[8] Such is the reason that Shinran proclaims that "no other form of good is necessary, for there is no good that surpasses the *nembutsu*."[9]

In regard to the ideas of *ōsō* and *gensō* there is also a fundamental difference between Shinran and Tanabe. According to metanoia, both activities are to be carried out in this life. The *gensō* taught by Shinran, however, becomes a reality only after one attains unexcelled Buddhahood, when "in the one moment of death, one transcends and realizes the supreme *nirvāṇa*." In the *Notes on 'Essentials of Faith Alone,'* Shinran writes:

> When a person attains this enlightenment, with great love and great compassion immediately reaching their fullness in him, he returns to the ocean of birth-and-death to save all sentient beings; this is known as attaining the virtue of Bodhisattva Samantabhadra.[10]

The ultimate realization of great love and compassion is attained in the "rank of perfectly benefiting others" in which nothing is lacking in serving others. Such a thing is impossible for human beings in this life, even if a person of *shinjin* is said to be the equal of Tathāgata. Shinran's *ōsō* and *gensō* both extend beyond this life, transcending birth-and-death, and touch the dimension of the timeless or eternal. The way of metanoesis is "a

---

[8] *Shinran*, 353, ll. 1-2.

[9] *Tannisho*, 5.

[10] *Notes on 'Essentials of Faith Alone,'* ed. by Yoshifumi Ueda (Kyoto: Shin Buddhism Translation Series, 1979), 33-34.

philosophy which is not a philosophy," but it is not "a religion which is not a philosophy." This distinction is directly related to the differences in the understanding of ōsō and gensō, which in turn are rooted in the different understandings of Other-power.

This also touches upon the notion of shō (witness) in action-faith-witness (gyō-shin-shō). In Shinran shō denotes supreme enlightenment which is to be realized as the one thought-moment of death (hence, "witness" is a misleading translation, although it fits Tanabe's purposes). As long as we are living in this world, even if we attain the stage of non-retrogression, also referred to as being equal to Tathāgata, it is not shō in Shinran's sense. But in Tanabe's metanoesis action-faith-witness is to be repeated in this life. Just as there is a difference in gensō, whether it reaches the timeless or not, so also the same difference exists in the understanding of shō. Here again we see the basic distinction between a philosophical witness and a religious awakening.

As in the case of shō, so also a similar gap exists in the interpretation of gyō and shin. In Shinran the essence of gyō (practice) originates with Amida Buddha; hence, it is called Great Practice. He states that "Great Practice is to say the Name of the Tathāgata of unhindered light."[11] This practice is the saying of "Namu-amida-butsu" or "Kimyō-jinjippō mugekō-nyorai." Activities undertaken by people, no matter how noble or selfless, cannot be the cause leading to supreme enlightenment; thus, they cannot be called true and real practice. In this sense the way of metanoia, undertaken as a joint effort by self-power and Other-power according to Tanabe, is fundamentally different from the practice central to Shinran's thought.

"Saying the nembutsu" is not simply a matter of vocalization, for it is the "nembutsu selected by the Primal Vow" (senchaku-hongan 選擇本願) as the most superior of practices. The fact that the nembutsu originates from the Primal Vow is clarified in the Chapter on True Entrusting (shin) in the Kyōgyōshinshō. Although the official title of this work, Kyōgyōshō monrui 教行証文類 (Collection of Passages on the Teaching, Practice, and Realization), omits mention of shin, this chapter is central to Shinran's purpose in writing this work.

---

[11] Kyōgyōshinshō, SSZ II, 5. The True Teaching, Practice, and Realization of the Pure Land Way, Volume I, ed. by Yoshifumi Ueda (Kyoto: Hongwanji International Center, 1983), 71.

He felt that it should not be equated to the three chapters of Teaching, Practice, and Realization, because True Entrusting is an elaboration on the chapter on Practice. For this reason he adds a separate preface to the chapter on True Entrusting, regardless of the fact that a general preface already exists at the very beginning of the work.

The disciples of Shinran all understood the role of the chapter on *shin*; thus, they constantly refer to this work as *Kyōgyōshō* and not *Kyōgyōshinshō*. When we understand the reason why *shin* is not part of the official title, we will see the intimate connection between Practice (*gyō*) and True Entrusting (*shin*) and know that the practice of saying the Name arises from the Primal Vow. To suppose that the popular title, *Kyōgyōshinshō*, more adequately describes the work is to betray a shallow understanding of how the Primal Vow works in our life.

Not only is Shinran's understanding of practice different from Tanabe's, but the same holds true for True Entrusting (*shin*). For Shinran *shin* denotes first of all "the true and real mind" of the Buddha; this is central in his constant reference to *shinjin*. The principal characteristic of Shinran's religious thought is that "the true and real mind" is limited to the mind of the Buddha, affirming its non-existence in human beings. Shan-tao and Hōnen still felt that people are capable of attaining a mind that is true and real, and they embraced the Three Minds expounded in the *Meditation Sūtra*, in contrast to Shinran, who, realizing their complete absence in human beings, opted for the Three Minds taught in the *Larger Sukhāvatī-vyūha Sūtra*. When a person, devoid of that which is true and real, realizes the true and real mind of the Buddha, it is called gaining *shinjin* (*shinjin gyakutoku* 信心獲得). From the side of the Buddha, it means the transference of the true and real mind of the Buddha, the mind of the Primal Vow, to all beings. When *shinjin* is thus granted to a person, the Name, Namu-amida-butsu, is also given. Hence, the assertion that the practice of saying the Name arises from the Primal Vow of Amida. In the case of Tanabe, however, True Entrusting seems to be a matter arising from the human subject:

> I entrust my entire being to Other-power (*tariki*), and by practicing *zange* and maintaining faith in this Power I confirm the

truth of my own conversion-and-resurrection experience
(PM, li).

For Shinran both practice (*gyō*) and entrusting (*shin*) are the manifestation of Amida's Primal Vow and are given to all beings. In
one of his letters to a disciple he wrote, "You should know further
that there can be no *nembutsu* separate from *shinjin*. Both should
be understood to be Amida's Vow."[12] Because both practice and
entrusting come from the Buddha, they provide the efficient cause
for beings to attain supreme enlightenment. Thus, both the cause
leading to enlightenment and the effect of Buddhahood, *ōsō* and
gensō, are transferred from the Buddha to sentient beings. That
the teaching is given to people is common to both self-power and
Other-power paths, but in the latter practice and attainment are
also given to them. Thus, the opening lines of *Kyōgyōshō monrui*
reads:

> Reverently contemplating the true essence of the Pure Land
> way, I see the Amida's directing of virtue to sentient beings has
> two aspects: the aspect of our going forth to the Pure Land and
> the aspect of our return to this world. In the aspect of going
> forth, there is the true teaching, practice, *shinjin*, and realiza-
> tion.[13]

The whole tradition of Pure Land Buddhism is contained in
the singular activity of *ekō*, rendered variously as merit transference, giving over, or directing of virtue, whereby all the compassionate workings of the Buddha are performed on behalf of
humankind. In sum, in the teaching of Shin Buddhism one completely abandons self-power and attains supreme enlightenment
by virtue of the working of Other-power.

In regard to Shinran's notion of transformation (*tenzu* 転ず)
I have elaborated upon it elsewhere,[14] but the crucial point is that
it takes place in the meeting of the mind of Buddha and the
mind of man, unlike the conversion in metanoia. Transformation
occurs within a basic structure whereby the true and real mind

---

[12] *Letters of Shinran*, ed. Yoshifumi Ueda (Kyoto: Hongwanji International
Center, 1978), 40.

[13] *The True Teaching, Practice, and Realization of the Pure Land Way*, Volume I,
63.

[14] *Shinran*, 152ff.

of the Buddha encounters the impure and defiled mind of sentient beings. This encounter is *ekō*, the directing of virtues, granting great practice and *shinjin*, to beings (from the side of the Buddha), and it is none other than gaining *shinjin* (from the side of beings). Transformation forms the core of Shinran's thought and has elements in common with the thought of Nāgārjuna, Asaṅga, and Vasubandhu in India, and with Chih-i of T'ien-t'ai and Fa-tsang of Hua-yen in China, demonstrating that Shinran's thought is in the mainstream of Mahāyāna Buddhism.

For Shinran, transformation occurs when sentient beings enter the ocean of Amida's Vow, or when a person enters the world of the 18th Vow from the 20th Vow. In other words, it takes place when the defiled mind of sentient beings enters the pure mind of the Buddha. Tanabe talks extensively about the absolute and the relative, but he is unclear about how the former relates to the latter. If the absolute enters the relative, as he seems to assert, how can one know that it is the absolute? If the absolute thus becomes the relative, then the absolute which is one with the relative cannot be a true absolute. If, on the other hand, the absolute enters the relative but retains its absolute nature, how can that be possible? The structure of the relationship between the absolute and the relative needs to be explicated. In Shinran the process of transformation clarifies how the defiled mind of relative beings enter the absolute, pure mind of the Tathāgata.

Tanabe also speaks of the absolute as nothingness, but since the relative is being, how does nothingness enter being and retain itself? Nothingness and being are mutually negating. The absolute transcends the relative and at the same time the two are in opposition as nothingness and being. Then the question becomes: what is the relationship between the absolute transcending the relative and the absolute standing opposed to the relative? These questions remain vague in Tanabe's way of metanoesis. In contrast, in Shinran the relationship between the relative and the absolute, between the defiled mind of beings and the ocean of Amida's Vow, is very clear. One cannot help wondering whether the absolute in Tanabe can be called truly an absolute.

Let us now turn to the theory of the Three Vows, referred to as *sangantennyū* (evolution through the stages of the Three Vows). This phrase is uncritically used today, but Shinran himself did not coin this expression. When he referred to the movement from the 19th Vow to the 20th Vow, he called it "turning and entering" (*e-nyū* 回入); and only when speaking of the transition from the 20th Vow to the 18th Vow did he use "transforming and entering" (*ten-nyū* 転入). The movement from the 19th to 20th Vow still remains within the realm of self-power, and the structure for transformation does not exist.

When one who has been relying on self-power to cultivate various practices (19th Vow) decides to abandon them for the single practice of *nembutsu* (20th Vow), there is a quantitative but not a qualitative change. But in the case of transformation (*tenzu*) one departs forever from self-power and enters Other-power, having been embraced by the Primal Vow of Amida. Hence, the relative which is a samsaric, temporal existence comes into contact for the first time with that which transcends time, namely, Immeasurable Life. Thus, Shinran states, "*One thought-moment* is time at its ultimate limit, where the realization of *shinjin* takes place"[15] and "One thought-moment expresses the ultimate brevity of the instant of realization of *shinjin* and manifests the vast, inconceivable mind of joyfulness."[16] Here samsaric time reaches its ultimate, bringing about a radical transformation, such that the person no longer falls back into *saṃsāra*. This is the stage of non-retrogression. The transformation is not quantitative but qualitative, and there occurs a leap, a discontinuous continuity.

Shinran was the first person in Pure Land history to affirm the attainment of the non-retrogressive state in the realization of *shinjin* here and now in this life. There are various points of difference between Shinran and the earlier Pure Land masters, but the most significant is the emphasis on this-worldly attainment of the stage of non-retrogression. Central to the Pure Land tradition until this time was the belief that non-retrogression was to be attained after birth in the Pure Land; even his teacher Hōnen saw that it was to be realized in the Pure Land. Shinran, however, clarified that by gaining *shinjin* people could realize here and now the timeless or eternal which is none other than the attainment of the stage of non-retrogression. Pure Land Buddhism took a radical turn from a futuristic faith to an awakening to reality here and now.

---

[15] *Shinran*, 196.
[16] *Shinran*, 297.

Such is the transformation that occurs in the movement from the 20th Vow to the 18th Vow, and there is no comparison to be made with the transition that takes place from the 19th Vow to the 20th Vow. The latter transition was the problematic for Hōnen, who through a series of negations selectively rejected all the Buddhist practices to finally selectively adopt the sole practice of *nembutsu* for the people of his age. This meant, in effect, the total negation of the whole history of Buddhism from Śākyamuni to Hōnen, an unthinkable and abominable act in the eyes of the established Buddhist Church. Thus, Hōnen and his disciples were persecuted by both the church hierarchy and the political powers; they suffered banishment, exile, and in some cases even capital punishment.

In the history of Buddhism many monk-scholars and priests rejected paths other than their own as inferior, but all paths were invariably included in the final scheme of salvation. This practice, known as the classification of doctrine (*kyōhan* 教判), never negated the entire Buddhist tradition as did Hōnen. It was upon such a foundation that Shinran formulated his Buddhism of absolute Other-power. In so doing he resurrected the various paths rejected by Hōnen and labelled them as *upāya*, liberative means to attaining reality, that could eventually lead people to the Other-power path. This is reflected in the movement from the 19th to the 20th to the 18th Vows. This not only depicted the evolution of Pure Land Buddhism but also marked the stages of Shinran's own religious pilgrimage. That is, he too moved from the various stages of *upāya* as found in the 19th Vow into the true teaching of Pure Land, and eventually he moved beyond the 20th Vow, the exclusive *nembutsu* practice preached by Hōnen, into the world of the 18th Vow, the Other-power Buddhism expounded by Shinran.

Shinran writes that this "*shinjin* becomes the diamond-like mind because of Amida's grasp. This is the threefold *shinjin* of the Primal Vow of birth through the *nembutsu* and not the three minds of the *Meditation Sūtra*."[17] Here he clearly rejects Shan-tao's and Hōnen's teaching based on the *Meditation Sūtra*. One must pass through the stages of the 19th and 20th Vows and enter the 18th Vow in order to realize that which is true and real, for the true and real mind of the Buddha becomes completely manifest

---

[17] *Notes on the 'Essentials of Faith Alone,'* 45.

only in the 18th Vow. This transformation into the true and real means returning to the timeless or eternal, called Immeasurable Life. For this reason the realization of *shinjin* is called "time reaching its ultimate limits." This returning to the true Buddha, the Tathāgata of Inconceivable Light, and the true Land, the Land of Immeasurable Light, is also called "immediate attainment of birth in the Pure Land." Once a person attains the true and real, there is no regression into the *upāya* stages, so it is called the stage of non-retrogression.

Tanabe sees the transition from the 19th to 20th to 18th Vows as a kind of logical progression and not as a historical or religious transformation. He writes:

> Thus the twentieth vow mediates the nineteenth and the eighteenth vows through *zange*, thereby not only elevating the *nembutsu* of the twentieth vow to that of the eighteenth but also mediating a circular movement in which the *nembutsu* of the twentieth vow is degraded to that of the nineteenth and then raised to the level of the eighteenth (207).

The transformation into the 18th Vow in Shinran is the movement from *upāya* to truth, and this movement is irreversible (from truth to *upāya*), the stage of non-retrogression attesting to this fact. The logical structure of the Three Vows developed by Tanabe is nowhere to be found in Shinran.

A huge difference also exists between Shinran and Tanabe regarding the theory of the Three Minds. The three refer to Shan-tao's interpretation of this concept in the *Meditation Sūtra*, in which he states that anyone wishing to be born in the Pure Land must cultivate the three attitudes of sincere mind, deep mind, and mind aspiring for birth. Anyone aspiring for Buddhahood must have a sincere mind, a mind free of falsehood and untruth; a deep mind which includes a belief in the karmic evil of the self and faith in Amida's salvific Vow; and an aspiration to be born in the Pure Land by transferring the merits of good karma past and present. Shan-tao and Hōnen not only encouraged their followers to cultivate these Three Minds, but they probably were convinced about their own ability to accomplish them. We know this by what they themselves taught and what their disciples recorded.

Shinran, however, while being a devoted student of Hōnen,

came to eventually realize his inability to develop the Three Minds of the *Meditation Sūtra* for a truly meaningful spiritual life. Thus, he turned to the Three Minds or threefold *shinjin* found in the 18th Vow of the *Larger Sukhāvatī-vyūha Sūtra*; namely, sincere mind, sincere faith, and desire to be born of the Primal Vow. According to Shinran, the latter teaches that foolish beings completely lack the sincere mind and only the Buddha's Three Minds are true and real. At the beginning of his *Notes on the Inscriptions on Sacred Scrolls*, he gives a detailed exegesis on the 18th Vow in which he reveals the lack of sincere mind in beings and urges all to entrust themselves to the true mind of the Buddha. Shinran unifies the threefold *shinjin* into "one-mindedness" (*isshin* 一心), claiming that true and real *shinjin* is none other than this one-mindedness.

What Shinran realized through the 18th Vow was that he completely lacked the sincere mind necessary for birth in the Pure Land. That his karmic evil was so profound, that he lacked the sincere mind taught in the *Meditation Sūtra*, was a reality shown to him by the 18th Vow. Thus, he rejected the Three Minds of the *Meditation Sūtra* as provisional, for it presupposes that a person can cultivate them, whereas the complete lack of the Three Minds was the true reality for Shinran.

Tanabe writes:

> This makes it amply clear that the whole of the Three Minds is based on the transformation and mediation of metanoesis and thereby enjoys the unity expressed in the saying, "Three Minds-*qua*-One Mind." Shinran sheds light on the inner dialectic of the relationship between the Three Minds (or Three Faiths) and the transforming mediation of immanence-*qua*-transcendence that stems from this relation when he redirects Zendō's demand for a moral ideal into the transforming action of *zange* (245).

As we saw earlier, when Shinran abandoned the Three Minds of Shan-tao and relied upon the threefold *shinjin* (which is none other than "one mindedness" of *shinjin*) of the *Larger Sukhāvatī-vyūha Sūtra*, he intended nothing less than an absolute departure from self-power and return to Other-power. Thus, Shinran's understanding has no connection with Tanabe's metanoia, which is said to be the joint effort of self-power and Other-power. I believe that the dialectical structure of Three Minds and the transforming mediation of immanence-*qua*-transcendence have no relevance to Shinran.

Tanabe's realization of evil at the core of the self that has realized the inability to meet the ethical demands of the Three Minds of Shan-tao and the subsequent negation experienced in the bankruptcy and abandonment of the self parallels Shinran's experience. But there is a vast gulf between the two regarding what happens after that radical negation. In the case of Tanabe the self that has been negated undergoes metanoia and with the help of Other-power is resurrected to walk on a new path in life. For Shinran, on the other hand, his life is sustained by Other-power alone, leaving no room for the operation of self-power. He writes that "Other-power means above all that there must not be the slightest calculation on our part."[18] The slightest calculation, even as tiny as a particle of dust, does not exist where Other-power is working. As previously mentioned, in Shinran self-power and Other-power exist in an either/or relationship, and existence of one rules out the other. The negation of self-power is absolute, which as a realization in a person is the admission of powerlessness in the face of insurmountable difficulties in life.

After entering the ocean of Other-power, one simply lives entrusting the self to Other-power, as if riding on a huge vessel, then by virtue of the natural working of *jinen* all the evil obstructions are transformed into the substance of highest virtue. In the words of Shinran, as stated earlier, "Though people of the diamond-like mind neither know nor seek it, the vast treasure of virtues completely fills them; hence, it is likened to an ocean of great treasure."[19] There is a universe of difference between this and the way of metanoia where the self with the aid of Other-power undertakes endless *zange*.

This completes my analysis of Tanabe's metanoia. Lest the reader be left with the impression that my only concern was to subject

---

[18] *Letters of Shinran*, 42. This English translation should be more accurately rendered as follows: "Just because there must not be the slightest calculation, even as tiny as a particular of dust on our part, the term 'Other-power' is used."

Philosophy as Metanoetics to criticism, I ought perhaps to add that I find no meaning in merely criticizing the thought of a highly respected philosopher of the past. I undertook a review of the work with the idea that among those who have learned about Shinran through the lens of metanoia, there may be those who would like to see Shinran as he is. And that is what I have tried my best to present, fully aware that my understanding may differ from the reality. In this regard, I am grateful for the opportunity to carry out a comparative analysis of Shinran and metanoetics, for it has led me to reflect on several matters of which I had not been fully aware.

[Translated by Taitetsu Unno]

Conversion in Shinran and Tanabe: Undergone or Undertaken?

Jean HIGGINS

TANABE Hajime, the celebrated philosopher of the Kyoto School, late in life underwent a conversion experience that had profound consequences for his personal and professional life. This experience, which he expresses as a *metanoesis*, revealed to him two things in particular: 1) the limits of philosophical knowing; and 2) the unlimitedness of the Absolute. Autonomous reasoning had taken him to the outer boundaries of relative, philosophical knowing. Philosophical reasoning, converted to faith, took him across the border to a mediated experience of the Absolute. The Absolute Tanabe discovered in this experience was not Being with a capital *B*, nor anything that could be defined substantially. It was "Nothingness," "Absolute Nothingness"; an Absolute infinitely open as relation, brought to reality in relation, and bringing to reality (fullness) all that is relative.

Tanabe's conversion experience, its consequences for him as philosopher and believer, and its implications for East-West dialogue are found expressed in his *Philosophy as Metanoetics*, a work that continues the remarkable and successful efforts of the Kyoto School to engage the West in mutually fruitful dialogue. Like others in the Kyoto School, he brings to this task a fidelity to traditional Mahāyāna thought, a substantial knowledge of modern Western (European) philosophy, an acquaintance with Christianity (at least in the form in which it is presented by this philosophy), and a concern for the inescapable confrontation of traditional religion with secularized modernity.

While Tanabe remains faithful to the goals of the Kyoto School in his *Philosophy as Metanoetics*, he strikes a note of discontinuity in his interpretation of "Absolute Nothingness," a designation created by and central to that School's philosophy of religion. Setting aside the Kyoto School's previously Zen-influenced understanding of this concept, Tanabe turns for his interpretation to the Pure Land sect of Buddhism. "Absolute Nothingness" is linked now with "Other-Power," the Pure Land savior-figure compassionately involved with the existential sufferings of sentient beings. This new interpretation is of great consequence for East-West exchange. In contrast to dialogue based on the "self-power" Zen mode, Shin brings into focus the universal elements of "other-power" religions which it shares with Christianity. Irrespective of the cultural modalities of these basic religious realities, this shift in interpretation of "Absolute Nothingness" creates a more accessible point of entry for Westerners into the world of Buddhist thought.

Philosophy as Metanoetics invites dialogue among theologians, philosophers, and social ethicists East and West. Its interplay of philosophical reasoning, religious subjectivity and ethical action centers on a conversion experience which radically alters the relation of existential relative being to Absolute being. It does so primarily by revealing the rootedness of this relationship in nothingness (both on the side of relative being and of Absolute being), and by positing relative being as the point of contact with, and the communicator of, the Absolute to the relative. In its setting up of relative beings as mediators of a compassionate, self-giving Absolute in societal context, Tanabe's book suggests a timely "bodhisattva-ethic" for the secular world.

I

Of particular concern to Shin scholars is Tanabe's unrelenting claim that Shinran, the founder of this tradition, is "the master and teacher" (PM, 260-61) of his philosophy. Tanabe rests this claim on his study of the Shin Buddhist sacred text, the *Kyōgyō-shinshō*, Shinran's masterful summation and interpretation of the teachings of the patriarchs of the Pure Land tradition. That study left him deeply convinced of one thing: that he and Shinran shared a common existential crisis and a common philosophy of religion rooted in *metanoia*.

"Shinran's faith and thought," he writes, "are metanoetical to the core . . . . Metanoetics alone provides the key to understanding the *Kyōgyōshinshō*" (PM, 225-26). Tanabe is in no way deterred by the fact that the Japanese word for metanoia (*zange*) is but scarcely found in Shinran's major work. He himself adverts to this when he writes, "Yet even though *zange* is not a formal part of the *Kyōgyōshinshō*, it constitutes the whole basis and background, only occasionally breaking through the surface" (PM, 20).

Various of the contributions included in this collection give some idea of Shin Buddhist reaction to the presentation of Shinran and Shin teaching in Tanabe's *Philosophy as Metanoetics*. The tacit assumption on which they all rest, it is worth observing, is that Shin Buddhism is a salvation religion. Shinran held not only that human beings were weak, sinful, inclined to evil, but that they were depraved. As depraved they could make no contribution toward attaining birth in the Pure Land.

This pessimistic view of human nature was not shared by Shinran's Pure Land predecessors. Prior to Shinran, sentient beings were understood to cooperate with Other-Power (Amida Buddha), accumulating merits for good works by virtue of self-power. Attaining to birth in the Pure Land was clearly a joint affair. Self-power and Other-Power worked in tandem. Shinran himself had functioned under this cooperative system. But not very well. Despite heroic spiritual labor, anxiety and insecurity attended all his efforts. He found himself up against the wall of human limits, starkly confronted with his own moral and religious depravity and powerlessness.

Shinran's existential crisis found resolution in the contemplation of a particular text in a particular context. The context was the age of *mappō* (a term indicating a Latter Day Age, in which Shinran believed he lived). It was an age of degeneracy in which no one, neither lay nor monk, could live up to the demands of the 18th Vow, which required realization by the believer of sincere mind, joyful faith and desire for birth in the Pure Land. The text was the *Larger Sūtra of Immeasurable Life*. There, in the portion dealing with the 18th Vow, Shinran came to the insight that the impossible that appeared to be *demanded* of degenerate foolish being was in fact not demanded but *given*. Salvation lay beyond the power of the human. It lay alone with Other-Power, the Giver of all saving gifts.

This shift in soteriological understanding necessitated a shift in traditional Pure Land teaching on merits. With not a little exegetical maneuvering of the texts on merit-transference, Shinran places its directing entirely with Amida, a step that followed logically from the rejection of *jiriki* (self-power) and the centering of salvation solely on *tariki* (Other-Power). The process of realizing *shinjin* (coming-to-faith) also took on new character. No longer did one arrive there by the plodding path of human effort. *Shinjin* was now seen to be realized in a "one-thought-moment." It was more an instantaneous event than a process, in the sense that it was solely the work of Other-Power and not the laborious, cumulative achievement of foolish being.

In *shinjin*, one had to let go of grasping and let oneself be grasped, never to be abandoned. In a mutuality of negation the self was emptied out and became the receptacle for Amida's self-emptying (of heart and mind). With the gift of Amida's sincere, real mind and heart, the "impossible" demands of the 18th Vow were realized. Illumined by this new mind, Shinran was able to see clearly the true nature of reality: the abyss of karmic evil and the abyss of Amida's compassion irrevocably conjoined. Relative and Absolute become one while remaining two in an illogical yet real identification.

As a response to this encounter of abyss with abyss there arises the *nembutsu* (an abbreviated invocation of the Name of Amida: Namu-amida-butsu). The *nembutsu* is an uttering — etymologically an "outering" — of a transformed inward state of mind and heart. It says all there is to say about the illumination that is *shinjin*. It expresses *total entrusting, boundless gratitude,* and *assured peace of mind* (indicating the conviction of having been born — here and now and irrevocably — in the Pure Land).

Such was Shinran's conversion experience. Possessed by the heart and mind of Amida, he experienced liberation from self-circling calculation and anxiety about his spiritual state. Anxiety was simply out of place in the person of *shinjin*. In fact, anxiety could surely be read as mistrust of the compassionate saving act, mistrust of the power of the Primal Vow. What did one's state of vice or virtue matter when one was grasped, never to be abandoned? Whether one was good or evil in the past or in the present or in the future mattered not one bit. All of time ran together in *shinjin*, that out-of-time encounter of wisdom-compassion with sincere acknowledgment of radical karmic evil and human powerlessness. All was held and healed in the grasp of Transforming Power.

II

Against this background of grateful, trusting, carefree abandonment to Other Power, one can understand Professor Ueda's reaction to Tanabe's claim that *zange* (understood as repentance and the desire to rectify) lies at the core of Shinran's major work. Professor Ueda is curt and to the point: *zange*, as understood by Tanabe, is simply not there. While the closely-related *zangi* (expressing shame and remorse) *is* to be found in Shinran, it in no sense implies repentance. A clear distinction has to be made between the two.

The distinction Professor Ueda calls for is crucial, for it gets to the heart of the soteriological insights that led to the founding of the True (*shin*) Pure Land tradition: human nature is radically evil and will never be anything other than evil; despite all the good will in the world, sentient beings cannot do good; despite the acutest intellection possible, they are not able to grasp that they cannot do the good they will. Only under the illumination of Amida Buddha can foolish being come to knowledge and acknowledgement of these basic truths of human existence. Faith in the compassionate power of Other-Power is the sole means to birth in the Pure Land. Depravity and inability are not obstacles. One is saved not only *despite* them but *because* of them.

It is clear from this Shin view of sentient being and Other-Power that *zange* as repenting/rectifying falls out of pattern. It suggests self-power still subtly at work. From the Shin perspective, the attempt to rid the self of its wrong is simply wrong-headed, for it is as much an activity of the self as the self-activity it is trying to correct. There is no action that sentient being can perform that can turn around the deep-rooted evil of human nature. Primal Vow Other-Power alone can work this transformation, and to such extent that "karmic evil, without being nullified or eradicated, is made into the highest good."

Shinran's *zangi* on the other hand coexists quite comfortably with awareness of his radically evil nature and his inability to do anything about it. He has no concern for rectifying. To be so concerned would return him to the self-power state of uncertainty from which his conversion insight released him. In *shinjin* he has been "made to become so" (*jinen*), made to become "one taste" with the mind and heart of the Vow-Maker. Sharing that heart and mind turns him from contemplation of his spiritual state to gratitude and joy. It provides him the possibility of becoming fully human and serving as a conduit of Amida's compassion to others.

For Shinran, *shinjin* is a radical transformation that is *undergone* not *undertaken*. His reforming insight was rooted in the belief that *jiriki* and *tariki* were mutually exclusive. This is not at all the case with Tanabe. Tanabe's *zange* is not Shinran's *zangi*. Had it been, we would not be gathered here for a symposium on Shin Buddhism; for Shinran would have remained peacefully within his inherited tradition with self-power playing its apportioned role in attaining to birth in the Pure Land.

In his unequivocal denial of Tanabe's claim that *zange* is a "core" element in Shinran's work, Professor Ueda has struck a blow at the keystone (metanoia) of *Philosophy as Metanoetics*. But he does not stop there. He goes on to say that "Tanabe fails to faithfully incorporate even a single concept in its entirety from Shinran" (134). But does Professor Ueda really mean to leave Tanabe nothing? Is the difference between Tanabe's understanding of *zange* and Shinran's understanding of conversion so fundamental that other aspects of Tanabe's thought cannot be true to Shin Buddhism? Suppose Tanabe has made an historical error, or an error of interpretation—is it not possible he has made a valid or valuable discovery of his own? After all, many people claim that Shinran misinterpreted or misunderstood (whether volitionally or not) the sūtras on which *he* commented and by which he was inspired. Yet in his very "misunderstanding," he made a valuable contribution which brought Shin Buddhism into being. Could not Tanabe be historically wrong, yet religiously right? Has Tanabe, as a contemporary interpreter of Shinran, nothing worthwhile to say to Shin Buddhists or to Westerners interested in dialogue on Jōdoshinshū?

III

That Tanabe's *Philosophy as Metanoetics* provides a new opening for the dialogue of Shin Buddhism and Christianity, is clearly something of a mixed blessing to traditional Shin Buddhists. Professor Unno's paper settles for the more positive part of the "blessing." He applauds Tanabe's reinterpretation of Shinran's thought, if not for its fidelity, at least for its attempt to share the richness of Shinran's insights with a contemporary world in spiritual crisis.However, Professor Unno (with Professor Laube) is quite right in pointing out that Tanabe, as philosopher, did not necessarily undertake to elucidate the thought-world of Shinran. His *Philosophy as Metanoetics* attempts to develop a philosophy for the contemporary period with assist from one (Shinran) with whom he feels kinship in existential crisis and in the proposed solution to that crisis. Even when his philosophical approach sets him on a track other than the purely religious, Professor Unno does not necessarily see this as detracting from Tanabe's creative contribution. If nothing else, the publication and translation of *Philosophy as Metanoetics* has obliged Shin Buddhists to leave their self-enclosure and confront the need for reinterpretation of Shin Buddhism for the contemporary world.

What is of particular interest to Professor Unno is the manner in which Tanabe's understanding of the relationship between relative and Absolute addresses the contemporary spirit. This relationship is presented as a unique (for the Shin tradition) balancing of dependence and independence. Each becomes itself only in and through relationship, each provides the opportunity for the other to become "nothingness" (in the mutual act of self-emptying), and each, in the final analysis, realizes the other. It is a relationship of "twoness" in "oneness" (despite the radical karmic evil of the relative) in which the identity and independence of each is preserved. In the interests of showing continuity with the Shin tradition, Professor Unno sets Tanabe's contemporary interpretation of this Absolute/relative relationship in historical and doctrinal perspective. He locates it first and foremost in "living the *nembutsu*." He then notes that the creative tension of this relationship is sustained and protected against extremes in the Shin tradition by means of *kihō ittai* and *butsubon ittai*, two central concepts which he interprets along the lines of traditional Shin interpreters such as Zonkaku, Rennyo, and Kakunyo.

Professor Unno considers Tanabe's *Philosophy as Metanoetics* a meaningful contribution to the development of a much-needed contemporary Shin Buddhist ethic. Of particular significance is the socio-religious role ascribed the relative as mediator of the Absolute-qua-Great Compassion to all beings. Again with an eye to contemporary spiritual/ethical needs, Professor Unno lauds Tanabe's updating of the Mahāyāna bodhisattva-ideal formulated as

gensō-ekō. While noting that Tanabe deviates from Shinran's interpretation, he nevertheless finds Tanabe's contribution "suggestive
for Shin Buddhists to develop an 'ethic which is not an ethic'
parallel to his 'philosophy which is not a philosophy.'"

Professor Unno joins Professor Ueda in his discomfiture with
Tanabe's interpretation of *zange*. Even though Tanabe shares Shinran's insight into the depth of karmic evil and consequent human
incapacity for meritorious action, he nevertheless betrays this insight in the positive role he ascribes to self-power in the act of
zange. Professor Unno also questions Tanabe's description of a
progressive movement towards *shinjin*. Tanabe sees the act of *zange*
prior to the moment of *shinjin*, and the self as major actor in that
act (PM, 252, 209). This appears to differ little from the traditional
understanding of self-powered, gradual progression from one stage
of spiritual attainment to another, which Shinran's conversion left
behind.

In this context, I have three critical questions to raise. First,
Professor Unno criticizes Tanabe for doing an interpretation of
Shinran that depends totally on a concept: *zange*, which is all but
absent from the text of the *Kyōgyōshinshō*. My question is whether
kihō ittai and *butsubon ittai*, on which Professor Unno's own analysis
and defense of the *nembutsu* depends, are important in the *Kyōgyōshinshō*. All the references he gives to those notions in his paper
are drawn from later writers in the Shin tradition.

Secondly, I feel the need for a further elaboration of Shin
Buddhist hermeneutic principles. While many authors from the
tradition are cited, it is not clear what weight their authority holds
for a contemporary interpretation. Among Professor Unno's cita-
tions is one that he describes as "reputed to be a text of the
Seizan Branch of Jōdoshū but cherished by successive Shin masters" (124). What are the limits to drawing on material from
outside the tradition to establish doctrinal points within the tradition?

Finally, I think that most Western readers would have serious
trouble with Professor Unno's answer to his own question, "What
is the significance of the symbol, *nembutsu*?" He replies: "First of
all, the *nembutsu*, Namu Amida Butsu, has no objective referent"
(119). Since for most Western philosophers, the claim that a statement has no objective referent means either that the statement
has no significance or that the statement is false, further elucida-

tion seems in order. I am aware of Professor Unno's warning that "This paradoxical experience is beyond rational comprehension (125), but—to paraphrase a frequent line in Tanabe—if it is beyond rational comprehension for a sage and saint like Professor Unno, how much more for us foolish and sinful ones?

IV

Professor Hase carries forward in his paper the Kyoto School's preoccupation with "Absolute Nothingness," a designation for the Absolute which results from the melding of modern Western philosophy and theology with traditional Mahāyāna Buddhism. Hase follows Tanabe in turning to Shin rather than to Zen for the Buddhist interpretation of this concept. With this turn, appeal can be made to universal elements in the salvation religions of Shin and Christianity, thus enhancing dialogue with the Christian West.

Professor Hase explicitly states that he shares Tanabe's conviction that the Primal Vow, Amida Buddha, Dharmākara, and so forth are all myths. He accepts the standard analysis in terms of philosophy of religion, familiar to many Westerners from the work of Paul Tillich and others, according to which the psychological reality of faith cannot help but throw up images, which in turn become the central figures of the various religions.

These images express what is at the heart of faith—here, Absolute Nothingness, the psychological reality of being face to face with infinite depth. Professor Hase avoids the word *being*, which he understands with Kant as a term properly confined to objects in the world of sense-perception. The transcendent realm, to which Absolute Nothingness belongs, is reached only by faith. One also senses here the echo of Tillich's sedulous efforts to avoid referring to God as a "being." In any case, for the pure philosopher, the objective observer of reality from outside, the matter stops there.

But it is different with Tanabe, who insists that any pure philosophical "outsider's view" is an existential impossibility. Persons engaged in East-West dialogue possess no neutral vantage-point from which to serenely contemplate the range of the world's religions. Rather they come to dialogue only because they are already within one or another of the traditions. Dialogue consists in a person within one tradition becoming so aware of the values available in another that the question seriously arises, How can I make those values my own? Perhaps even, Why am I not myself in that tradition rather than in my own?

In the more specific context of Shin Buddhist reactions to Tanabe's metanoetics, I have to ask myself whether taking Tanabe as Professor Hase has taken him (accurately, I think)—namely, the relativization of Amida and his vow, of Other Power—is an existential option in the religious sphere. Can a convinced, faithful, devout, prayerful, religious Shin Buddhist be convinced that Amida and his Vow do not pre-exist his own faith in them? Can a devout Shin Buddhist give up all reliance on self-power to put all his or her hopes on the promise of Amida Buddha and at the same time know philosophically that Amida is only an image cast up by his own faith? Can a Shin Buddhist be sure of salvation through the Primal Vow of Amida and at the same time be convinced that to think of Amida as an objective reality is superstition? Can one build one's life on the recitation of the *nembutsu*, preach it to others as the key to salvation, and at the same time think and teach that Amida is parallel to hundreds of other Mahāyāna images in hundreds of other Mahāyāna traditions; parallel, indeed, to the images at the center of non-Buddhist traditions as well?

In short, can faith still be faith after having been submitted to this sort of philosophical analysis? After the images of one's faith have undergone a *Religionsphilosophisch* relativizing such as we find in Tanabe (as well as in Hase, Tillich, James, et al.), after all vestiges of superstition and magic have been removed from them, can those images continue to function to transform a human life?

If one leaves matters where Professor Hase seems to leave them, I doubt that they can. To contribute significantly to the dialogue of religions, he would have to add one further step. He would have to tell us why a religious person, having reflected philosophically on how similar are the psychological structures of the various religions, then can go on to ask himself or herself plausibly and intelligently: Why then do I take my Shin Buddhist tradition with absolute seriousness? Why do I pray as a Shin Buddhist? Why do I trust in the promises of Amida? Why do I hope for the Pure Land? Why not abandon all these outdated traditions and simply strive to live in the philosophical awareness of Absolute Nothingness?

Professor Hase does touch on this topic in quoting Tillich's reference to the Christian cross as an absolute expression of divine self-emptying love. But he immediately mentions that he himself finds Absolute Nothingness a more compelling image. He also touches the question I suggest when he speaks of the Christian God standing on his rights, as opposed to the loving compassion of the bodhisattva. Such discussions, brief as they are, imply that there are criteria by which the religions can be judged, something philosophical or psychological, more basic than the symbols of this religion or that. This area needs more exploring and development if one is to contribute to the dialogue among the religions.

Karl Rahner's early masterpiece, *Hörer des Wortes*, attempted the further step I am calling for here, offering criteria of concrete ways of salvation which a philosophical analysis of human being would lead one to look for. As Rahner was a committed Christian, there is nothing surprising in the fact that his criteria would be met in a reformed Catholic Christianity. I see no reason why they could not be met in a purified Shin Buddhism. Rahner's book ends, however, without making any specific applications, simply leaving the reader waiting, alert, ready to take seriously a religious tradition whose imaged account of reality can meet the human needs that have been articulated and tie up all the loose ends which philosophy alone must leave unraveled. (Tillich's "method of correlation," I would add, comes down to the same thing.)

Professor Hase's reading of Tanabe does not close the door on these questions. He portrays human reality in its helplessness, the miseries from which it suffers, the perfection to which it aspires. He expresses these in terms of a philosophy of Absolute Nothingness, and then affirms that the images of the Shin Buddhist tradition, if they too are understood in terms of a philosophy of Absolute Nothingness, meet the needs and aspirations of that human nature. Of course this implies the need of a reform in Shin self-understanding, in order to lay a greater emphasis on the fundamental role of Absolute Nothingness. In the dialogue among the religions there will be those who say that this is a call for reforming Shin in the direction of Zen. Whether that in itself is religiously acceptable to Shin Buddhists, is not for me to judge.

PART TWO

Christianity

The Metanoetics of
Inter-Religious Encounter

James FREDERICKS

I

IN an address given at the Nanzan Institute in Nagoya and subsequently published in the collection *God and Absolute Nothingness*, Nishitani Keiji raises the modern problem of universality and uniqueness for inter-religious encounter.[1] Introducing his remarks, Nishitani highlights the problem of fruitful dialogue between Buddhism and Christianity as especially perplexing, due to the fact that both religious traditions constitute separate "worlds" capable of responding to the entire human being as a universal and exhaustively meaningful "world religion." Historically, although both Buddhism and Christianity emerged from narrow ethnically and geographically determined cultural contexts within Palestine and Northern India, in their maturity these traditions have not only provided the spiritual foundations for ecumenic civilizations but also religious visions of a universal humanity that is the progeny of these civilizations. Reminiscent somewhat of Jaspers and Voegelin,[2] Nishitani notes that in the world religions, we witness the emergence of the *humanum* as such *(ningen toshite ningen* 人間として人間*)* out of local ethnicities. Perplexingly, these world religions hold out differing images of what it is to be human. It is this historical fact that is in urgent need of interpretation today.[3]

The rise of the world religions corresponds to the geograph-

---

[1] Nishitani Keiji, 仏教における 「向上」 の立場 ["The Standpoint of 'Ascent' in Buddhism"] in ZMK, 150-80.

[2] For Karl Jaspers, see *Vom Ursprung und Ziel der Geschichte* (München: Piper Verlag, 1949). For Eric Voegelin, see *Order and History*, vols. 1-4 (Baton Rouge: Louisiana State University Press, 1954-1974).

[3] Nishitani, "The Standpoint of 'Ascent'," 151-52.

ical diffusion of interpretations of the human situation which are no longer restricted ethnically: universal paradigms for ethical action, artistic creativity, political expediency and religious realization, which potentially, at least, are capable of encompassing and sustaining every human being. Today, the spread of these universalisms has progressed to the point of a crisis, not sufficiently recognized, but a crisis all the same. Nishitani conceives of it as a problem of "universality" and "uniqueness." In a way which is without precedent in their separate histories, Buddhists and Christians can no longer regard the universality of their respective religious traditions as unique and unparalleled. This is a new fact for us today, a fact which increasingly should alter the course of our future self-understanding. As universalities, world religions are capable of including all human groups within their compass and charging them with the possibility of unlimited religious realization. But in our current period, despite their many features in common, religious universalities have begun to confront one another with deeply conflicting symbols. Without losing any of their universality, the encounter between world religions calls into question their own claims to unparalleled and unsurpassed uniqueness. Religions which once experienced themselves as unchallenged universality now experience themselves as relative. What was once the unparalleled has now become rivaled. In past eras, in order to maintain their uniqueness, religious traditions have worked out various strategies for denying other religions. At times, the need for denial becomes violent. After commenting on the "collisions" between Christianity, Judaism, Islam, Buddhism and Hinduism over the centuries as well as in current events, Nishitani once again affirmed his belief in the increasingly urgent need to interpret the meaning of religious universality anew. Since there is not as yet one world with a unified history and humanity, conflicts of this religious and cultural nature will continue. Nishitani's gloomy prediction makes inter-religious understanding imperative even as it underscores the difficulty of the problem.[4]

With Nishitani's concerns regarding religious universality and uniqueness as a backdrop, various strategies for inter-religious dialogue present themselves. I will discuss three options,[5] without

---

[4] Nishitani, "The Standpoint of 'Ascent'," 153-54.

[5] These "options" should not simply be identified with Christian theological

pretending that they are exhaustive, in the interest of developing Nishitani's concern for universality and uniqueness as well as looking to Tanabe's metanoetic philosophy as a source of insight into the problem.

Clearly, one option available to those engaged in inter-religious dialogue is what might be called "exclusivism." Herein, religious truth is simply identified with the uncompromisable uniqueness of symbols. The symbols of other traditions may be humane and praiseworthy, and they may represent sizable human achievements, but they are ultimately inadequate when set alongside the unique and unsurpassable symbols of one's own tradition. As might be expected in the light of Nishitani's insight into religious universality and uniqueness, this strategy comes easily to world religions precisely because of the universal character of their truths. Universality is equated with unparalleled uniqueness readily and without difficulty. To say the least, this approach has a stultifying effect on inter-religious dialogue. At worst, it leads to what Joseph Kitagawa has dubbed a "simultaneous monologue" between dialogue partners.[6] At best, it trades the danger and creativity of authentic dialogue for the safety of merely clarifying points of academic agreement and difference. Curiously, as much as Nishitani's attention to religious universality helps us to understand why this option comes so easily to committed believers in a world religion, at the same time, it underscores the fact that the results of this strategy for dialogue are wholly unsatisfactory. Buddhism and Christianity, for instance, despite certain similarities, make profoundly conflicting, yet universal truth-claims. To merely highlight these points of contradiction, and leave it at that, seems to suggest that we are dealing with tribal religions, and not world-religious universalities. Ultimately the problem of universality and uniqueness cannot be placed in abeyance.

A second strategy for dialogue, "syncretism," brings with it its own difficulties. The syncretistic strategy tends to protect the

---

options for interpreting non-Christian religions. They represent instead intellectual strategies adopted by Christians and non-Christians alike who are engaged in inter-religious dialogue. In this respect, I hope to reflect the spectrum of Christian "theologies of religions" while at the same time doing some justice to non-Christian interpretive patterns as well.

[6] Joseph Kitagawa, *The History of Religions* (Atlanta: Scholars Press, 1987), xix.

universality of religious truth by sacrificing the uniqueness of the various religious traditions. Often the result is a highly intellectualized pseudo-religious philosophy, which ironically, by being wrenched from a specific cultural context, is no longer truly universal either. In understanding religious universality, we must be attentive not only to the vapors, but to the precipitate as well, for it is distilled from both. Casting aside the strong points and rough edges of a religious tradition in the interest of identifying a putative "lowest common denominator" which unites it with other religious traditions, is to abstract a religion from the cultural specificity which is the basis for concrete religious life. Hegel is the great example of the illusory universality which results from this strategy. Kierkegaard reminds us that demythologizing religious symbols into the abstract language of metaphysics is both a gain and a loss. When compared to the specific existential fullness of a concrete religious tradition, the ersatz universality of metaphysics does not suffice as a basis for an encounter in depth among religions.

A third strategy is "inclusivism." Often this approach is promoted as a middle ground which avoids the problems attending exclusivism and syncretism. Certainly this strategy has found a following among Christian theologians. Karl Rahner and Paul Tillich, to take two salient examples, argue for a wide understanding of general revelation in which all world religions can be affirmed as salvific, even while Christianity retains the pride of place as the final and definitive revelation.[7] Other religions are to be respected, even honored, for it is the truth of the Christian God revealed there. The inclusivist strategy also has its champions among non-Christians as well. There are Hindus, for instance, who interpret Christianity as a variety of mystical "panentheism" which locates Christianity within the pale of Hindu truth.[8] Once

---

[7] For Rahner, see *inter alia*, "Christianity and the Non-Christian Religions," *Theological Investigations* Vol. 5 (Baltimore: Helicon, 1966), 115-34. For Tillich, see *Systematic Theology* (Chicago: University of Chicago Press, 1951-1963), Vol. 1, 137-44, 218-30; Vol. 2, 78-88; Vol. 3, 98-106.

[8] For instance, the so called "Neo-Hinduism" of Tagore and Radhakrishnan apparently is willing to sacrifice itself as a particular religious tradition (presuming that other religions do the same) in order to be transformed into a new universality, without limitation of culture, cult, dogma, etc. Despite the claim to a pan-religious perspective, the "new religion" being suggested seems rather

again Nishitani's views on universality and uniqueness are illuminating. The inclusivist strategy seeks to preserve the uniqueness of one religion without sacrificing the universality of the others. In order to do so, however, it pays the unacceptable price of reducing the significant differences between the world religions to simply "more of the same." By domesticating the "otherness" of the world religions, the menace and threat of religious plurality are likewise rendered harmless.

Nishitani's views on universality and uniqueness raise one more important issue for dialogue between religions. Today, world religions are not the only movements which offer their own vision of universal humanity and unequaled truth. The Western enlightenment, for instance, claims for itself an interpretation of the human situation which is not only universal and unique but also non-religious. It offers modern human beings not only a mythology ("progress") and soteriology ("technology") but an ethics ("pragmatism") as well. It too presents itself as a universal truth (the cosmic universality of scientific law) whose uniqueness is heralded by its own prophets. The political totalitarianisms of our century must also be included in non-religious (or perhaps more accurately, "quasi-religious") options for a universal humanity. These non-religious or quasi-religious options constitute an important new factor in the current encounter between religions. Not surprisingly, that this novel situation presents the world religions with a new mutuality has not been lost on various commentators.[9]

This "new mutuality" might easily be mistaken for the emergence of a new religious universality. Even though this would be premature, a better understanding of the "mutuality" of religions vis-à-vis anti-religious or quasi-religious universalities will no doubt have the beneficial effect of leading our dialogues to a recognition of the need for a renewal of religious commitment and, I think

---

Hindu all the same. For Radhakrishnan, see *The Hindu View of Life* (Allen and Unwin, 1952-1953). For Tagore, see *The Religion of Man* (New York: Macmillan, 1953).

[9] In this respect, to deny a specifically religious meaning to National Socialism in Germany, the Stalinist brand of Marxist-Leninism in the Soviet Union and State Shinto in Japan is to misinterpret these political phenomena systematically.

somewhat surprisingly, may lead to a profound distrust of any "easy pluralism" as a solution to the problem of universality and uniqueness among the world religions.[10]

The current situation of religious pluralism confronts us with a Janus-faced dilemma. In order to overcome the violence linked to the profound differences separating religions, we are menaced by the loss of our own religion's uniqueness. Ecumenical tolerance is purchased at the terrible cost of religious relativism. More frighteningly, our century offers abundant examples of an unwelcome relativism leading to the eruption of the demonic. Intolerance is often preceded by an easy pluralism. The fanaticism of Iran's "Islamic Republic," the "Christian America" envisioned by the extreme religious right in the United States, and "Protestant Ulster" are all signs of an intolerable pluralism and the religious and cultural relativity which results from it. It is a peculiar truth that fanaticism and fundamentalism cannot be successfully resisted with more relativism. Only by the assertion of ultimate values can extremism be confronted. For adherents of the world religions, this means that the total world of meaning that the fanatic would impose by violence can be countered only by means of a religiously grounded commitment. What is more, the commitment required arises from within the believer's own religious "world" of values, symbols, loyalties and traditions. Without such commitment to a specific tradition, religiously grounded resistance to fanaticism is diluted by the relativism which gives rise to the fanaticism in the first place.

Recognition of this fact leads to a paradoxical conclusion: in order to respond responsibly and creatively to the current situation of religious pluralism, both a certain type of relativism and a certain type of uncompromised commitment are required. Religious traditions must be understood in terms of a paradoxical juxtaposition of relativity and absoluteness. As the violence of religious plurality leads us in the direction of ecumenical cooperation

---

[10] For instance, the problem of anti-religious ideologies is the paramount concern of Paul Tillich on the question of Christianity and the encounter with world religions. This has also been a recurring theme in the writing of Masao Abe. For Tillich, see *Christianity and the Encounter with World Religions* (New York: Columbia University Press, 1963). For Abe, see *Zen and Western Thought* (Honolulu: University of Hawaii Press, 1985), 231-75.

and tolerance, so also it requires us to re-assert forcefully the religious symbols specific to our tradition. In order to be religious, concretely, existentially and historically, especially given the atrocities of non-religious and religious fanaticism today, we need a standpoint of ultimate concern, an absolute standpoint from which to believe and act. At the same time, this absolute standpoint must be relativized if it is not to become yet another odious fanaticism. We need to envision with one another, as concretely as possible, new interpretations of our differing religious traditions as "paradoxical universalities" and as "relative absolutes."[11]

II

It is not inaccurate to say that Tanabe was concerned throughout his life with the problem of universality and uniqueness. For instance, along with his older colleague Nishida Kitarō, Tanabe felt deeply the dilemma faced by Meiji Japan in attempting to import Western technology while seeking to maintain its indigenous religious-cultural synthesis. The problem of an untenable religious and philosophical pluralism forms one of the earliest and most forceful motivations of the Kyoto School. Even more directly to the point, Tanabe's "logic of species" reflects his concern with absolute truth and its concrete embodiment in cultural specificities.[12] In the measure that his metanoetic philosophy grows out of his earlier concern with "species," the logic of "absolute mediation" as well can be related to the issue of cultural and religious pluralism.

I am going to offer an interpretation of Tanabe's metanoetic philosophy as a helpful way to clarify the metaphysical underpinnings of the "relative absolute" introduced above. The hope that lies behind this strategy is that metanoetics might better illuminate our understanding of the "paradoxical universality" of the world religions today.

---

[11] In addressing himself to this same issue, Langdon Gilkey uses the phrase "relative absoluteness." See his "Plurality and its Theological Implications" in *The Myth of Christian Uniqueness*, John Hick and Paul Knitter, eds. (Maryknoll, New York: Orbis Books, 1987), 37-50, esp. 44-46, 47.

[12] Tanabe suggests as much in the final chapter of *Philosophy as Metanoetics*, 269.

At the center of Tanabe's metanoetic philosophy is his notion of "absolute mediation." I believe that Tanabe's insistence that there is no unmediated absolute addresses Nishitani's concerns about modern religious pluralism. Not only does Tanabe recognize the metaphysical possibility of a "relative absolute," he also understands it as a religious event that is historical, concrete, ethically mediated and existentially transforming. The former point helps us in developing a creative interpretation of the pluralistic situation of world religions today. The latter point might have something to teach us about the praxis of inter-religious dialogue. Since the absolute has no unmediated existence or reality in any sense, it cannot be known immediately apart from the relative. Therefore taking Tanabe seriously will require a fundamental reevaluation of the absolute truth-claims of religious traditions. This reevaluation will include the status of religious language, the phenomenology of symbols and the hermeneutics of texts. I also believe that it will require a new understanding of the universality and uniqueness of the world religions. These factors suggest Tanabe's *zange-dō* as a possible model for creatively guiding the encounter between religions.

Two points are especially important to the question at hand. First, according to Tanabe's metanoetic philosophy, the absolute has no unmediated existence apart from the relative. Absolute truth is present only indirectly in the medium of our symbols and texts. It cannot be simply fixed in the word, the concept or the text. It cannot be named directly by language as an object is named, nor is it amenable to the direct exercise of critical reason as in "self-power" philosophies. Second, Tanabe insists that the absolute arises only in the existential transformation of subjectivity by the grace-event of Other-power *(tariki* 他力 *)*. Therefore, he is unwilling to dissociate the reality of the absolute in any way from the awakening of self-consciousness. This means that what he calls "authentic religious action" is an event that is always concrete, historical and existential. The absolute cannot be known immediately, because it has no separate reality apart from the transformation of subjectivity itself. Both of these issues must be explored in relation to the problem of religious pluralism.

Tanabe's first claim, that the absolute has no unmediated existence apart from the relative, implies that the absolute establishes relative being as its mediation. For Tanabe, this means that the absolute cannot be understood as "being" (which leads to an emanationist metaphysics incapable of sustaining true mediation). Instead, it must be understood as absolute nothingness. Were the absolute present immediately, it would be being and not absolute nothingness since it would in fact be some "thing" that could be named directly by language and understood in the direct exercise of self-identical reason. Therefore, the logic of absolute mediation subscribes in its own way to Nishida's maxim that "the true absolute is not opposable to the relative."[13] Relative being is constituted as such not by being negated by an "absolute" which stands over-against it as absolute being, but by standing over-against another relative in the mutual mediation of the absolute. Tanabe insists that this mediatory action of relatives is the only reality of the absolute.[14]

Venturing a bit beyond the text of *Philosophy as Metanoetics*, we might ask if this means that mediation can be thought of in two different ways. In the first case, the relative, through its practice of metanoia, acts as the mediation of the absolute. In the second case, two relatives, encountering each other in mutual contradiction, come to mediate the absolute to one another by practicing metanoia.[15] In this second scenario, the "other" ceases being mere contradiction and negation and through the transformation of Other-power becomes the actual historical occasion of the experience of salvation by the absolute. Might not something similar occur in the current encounter between conflicting religious traditions? Religious universalisms, through the praxis of metanoia, would become for one another the paradoxical experience of absolute truth without ceasing to be contradictions. Experienced metanoetically, world religions would in fact be the

---

[13] Nishida Kitarō makes this assertion in several texts. See, for instance his final essay, translated by David Dilworth in *Last Writings: Nothingness and the Religious Worldview* (Honolulu: University of Hawaii Press, 1987).

[14] PM, 18ff.

[15] Tanabe himself seems to be moving in this direction in his discussion of using metanoetics to achieve a religious interpretation of society. In contrast to the "heroic individualism" of European existentialism and Samurai Zen, Tanabe suggests that social existence can find fulfillment in "love," which he understands as a concrete transforming mediation of the absolute between relative being and relative being. The specific context is a discussion of the master-disciple relationship. See PM, 265, 276.

"paradoxical universalities" and "relative absolutes" that were discussed above.

This leads us to Tanabe's second claim, viz., that metanoetic cognition arises only in the existential transformation of subjectivity by the grace-event of Other-power *(tariki)*. In his treatment of the "absolute critique" of reason, Tanabe draws attention to the fact that pure reason inherently strains for absolute knowledge. Given the ease with which religious traditions infer the absolute and unparalleled uniqueness of religious truth from the universality of that truth, we might say that something analogous is the case with world religions as well. Finite reason, striving for absolute knowledge, is forced to its limit (the Kantian antinomies) in its encounter with the real. By submitting to its own self-negation *(zange)*, reason undergoes a transformation in which it is not restored to its original status, but rather resurrected as "empty being" which acts as the mediation of the absolute. Once again analogously, religious traditions, in their own encounter with the "real" (in this case, the "real" is the other religious universalities), experience their own relativity at first negatively (as the contradiction of their claim to uniqueness) and then affirmatively (as the grace of the absolute mediated by the other religions). In other words, religious traditions are not exempt from the "radical evil"[16] in which the relative mistakes itself as the absolute. The easy equation of universality with uniqueness makes it necessary for the world religions to learn again and again that authentic religious existence is a matter of conversion *(zange)* and subsequent transformation through Other-power.

Tanabe's metanoetic philosophy gives us a way of approaching Nishitani's problem of universality and uniqueness critically. The true absolute is always experienced as a "relative absolute" for two reasons. It is experienced as a "relative absolute" first because it is always mediated in specific, contingent cultural symbols, while never being simply identical with them. Second, it is always experienced as a "relative absolute" because the plurality of unparalleled and unique "absolutes," by taking the "path of metanoia" *(zange-dō)*, can break out of their simple contradiction and negation in an increase of self-consciousness which leads to their absolute affirmation. This affirmation is a concrete event in history, a dis-

---

[16] PM, 4.

closure of new meaning and value, a religious event, the experience of a transforming power *(tariki)* not identifiable with finite being. In Tanabe's metanoetic view of social existence, this event would be characterized by a rejection of violence, intolerance and fanaticism. It might lead to that in which Nishitani places his hopes, viz., the creative appropriation of religious pluralism and the mutual transformation of world-religious universalities in the restoration of their religious vitality.[17]

With this possible restoration in mind, let us turn our attention to the way Tanabe's metanoetics might re-configure our practice of inter-religious dialogue.

III

Tanabe's philosophy of absolute mediation illuminates some of the problems of inter-religious dialogue outlined above. First, absolute mediation acts as a critique of the exclusivist strategy for dealing with religious pluralism. Tanabe's notion of authentic religious action stands against all naive religious beliefs in an unmediated absolute. Since the absolute is never experienced directly without the mediation of relative being, fundamentalisms of any sort are ruled out as possible candidates for an authentic religious subjectivity. Truth cannot be determined literally in a text or doctrine. Fundamentalisms must reject conflicting truth claims since they pose a serious threat to the unparalleled uniqueness of their symbols. This amounts to artificially restricting the religious quest for absolute truth: the religious interpreter becomes a mere apologist with his or her imagination under orders.

But in keeping with Tanabe's interest in carrying the Kantian critique of reason to its logical and existential conclusion in the "absolute critique," like pure reason, a text or symbol cannot supply its own foundation guaranteeing its absolute truth. Instead, the truth of a symbol is measured by its ability to "die" to its literal meaning in disclosing through mediation what (literally speaking) it is not, i.e., the absolute. In the praxis of metanoia, the religious quest is set free for its ultimate crisis of self-contradiction, self-surrender, and resurrection as mediation of the absolute. As Tanabe believes that the path of metanoia *(zange-dō)* is

---

[17] Nishitani, "The Standpoint of 'Ascent'," 160.

not an arbitrary route for philosophical inquiry, so also we might ask if it is not merely one alternative for inter-religious dialogue to take in confronting fundamentalism and fanaticism, but rather the path leading to a contemporary renewal of authentic religious subjectivity itself.

Second, metanoetics holds the syncretistic tendency up for criticism as well. Repeatedly, Tanabe insists that, after passing through its absolute crisis and transformation, the contradiction of reason remains. Reason is not transformed into a universal point of view capable of synthesizing contradictions by negating them, but into the mediation of absolute nothingness which is no longer restricted by contradictions but preserves them as "empty being."[18] Contradiction remains, but the intellect is brought back as the mediator of absolute truth which is the basis of religious communication between individuals.[19] It is the contradiction itself which acts as a mediation of the absolute. Thus, Tanabe foresees neither an intellectual synthesis of religious differences (along the lines of the Hegelian *Aufhebung*), nor a religious "lowest common denominator" achieved through philosophical abstraction. Both reflect the standpoint of self-power philosophy. Otherness and contradiction must remain in order for the true absolute to be realized in the metanoia of mutually contradictory relatives. It is Tanabe's paradoxical notion of the true absolute, what I have been calling a "relative absolute," that precludes syncretism as a viable option for inter-religious dialogue.

The major problem attending the syncretistic tendency applies to the inclusivist strategy as well. This tendency in inter-religious dialogue seeks to affirm the uniqueness of one tradition while refusing to negate the universality of the others. If, as Tanabe argues, the absolute has no existence apart from its mediation in the relative, then the contradictory otherness of the relative must be preserved in order for there to be true mediation arising in the experience of transformation. The contradictory, the unfamiliar, the unintegrated, the sheer otherness of that which confronts cannot be annulled if there is to be authentic religious action. The inclusivist differs from the syncretistic tendency in its attempt to leave the present interpretation of one's own tradition's symbols

---

[18] PM, 55.
[19] PM, 40.

intact, by claiming that the symbols of the other religions in fact express the same truth. For instance, if in fact Buddhism reveals the truth of the Christian God, what is called for, then, is a creative reinterpretation of Buddhism and not a rethinking of Christian theism. Dialogue, carried out metanoetically, will be suspicious of any attempt to reduce the genuine differences between world religions to merely more of the same. To do so would be to bring the conversation to a premature end by refusing to place the symbols of one's own tradition at risk.

More positively, understanding inter-religious dialogue as a *zange-dō* makes available to us a way to respond to religious fanaticisms and non-religious ideologies. Perhaps ecumenical tolerance need not be purchased at the cost of an intolerable religious relativism. But this much seems certain: religious and political fanaticism cannot be successfully resisted simply by administering more doses of relativism and pluralism. Instead, it must be met with commitment to ultimate values. It is not without significance to our inquiry that Tanabe consistently locates the concrete, historical mediation of the religious in the ethical.[20]

The current situation of religious pluralism drives us toward ecumenical community at the same time that it requires of us a renewed commitment to the specific values and symbols of our respective religious traditions. Tanabe's metanoetic path shows how this paradoxical juxtaposition of commitment and tolerance might be realizable. If the encounter with the otherness and contradiction of religious traditions not our own can be experienced as the event of our self-awakening to the paradoxical reality of the true absolute within our own tradition, then perhaps ecumenical community with serious commitment to religious symbols specific to a particular tradition can become a concrete possibility for dialogue partners. This, of course, will require a revision of the absolute claims of our particular religious traditions. Religious self-understanding will have to be reconfigured along the lines of Tanabe's paradoxical experience of the "true absolute" mediated in the "relative absolute."

To look to Tanabe's metanoetics as a model for creative encounter between religious universalities today is to recognize dialogue as a form of praxis that arises out of the experience of

---

[20] PM, 152-156.

existential transformation by Other-power. This would suggest that dialogue is not really possible for the fanatic or for the uncommitted.[21] Thought of as praxis, dialogue has two moments. The first moment is that of self-surrender *(zange)* in which the symbol (understood naively as an unmediated absolute) is strategically exposed to its contradiction by other claims to unmediated truth. The second moment is that of affirmation in which the symbol is resurrected as the mediation of the true absolute. To think of dialogue as praxis is not to make this "resurrection" automatic. In Tanabe's view, the "Great Compassion" of Other-power is always experienced as grace. All the same, I believe that it can be thought of as praxis in that the transformation of the relative by Other-power does not arise apart from its mediation by the self-surrender of the relative.[22]

The resurrection of the symbol requires that our appreciation of religious claims undergo its own metanoia. By clinging to the doctrine of *pratītyasamutpāda* as a mere metaphysical position *(dṛṣṭi)*, this religious symbol no longer mediates to the Buddhist the truth of existential release. By believing literally in the kingdom of God coming at the end of time or in a *creatio ex nihilo* at the beginning of time, these religious symbols no longer mediate to the Christian the protological and eschatological meaning of salvation. Tanabe believes that religious doctrines, symbols, texts, etc. become "empty being" in genuine religious action in order to work as a "skillful means" *(upāya)* to salvation.[23] Somewhat similarly, for Tillich the symbol participates in revelation by relativizing itself, because in sacrificing itself *(zange)* it points beyond itself. The unauthentic

---

[21] While I would exclude the fanatic and the uncommitted as participants in the model of inter-religious dialogue I am developing, it is also true that not all commitment is commitment to a specific religious tradition or religions as such necessarily. Christian theologians and their non-Christian counterparts have no monopoly on the interpretation of religious symbols. The danger and risk of authentic inter-religious dialogue are often enhanced by the contributions of non-religious but existentially committed participants. What is more, the contribution of existentially uncommitted historians, textual critics, phenomenologists, etc. are likewise not to be underestimated.

[22] Tanabe expresses the meaning of metanoetics as praxis in his reliance on the Pure Land Buddhist doctrine, *tariki-soku-jiriki* 他力即自力 . In this respect, metanoetics is both a religious path to be practiced *(jiriki)* and a grace *(tariki)*.

[23] PM, 22, 41-2.

symbol refuses to die and becomes demonic.[24] Paul Ricoeur's investigations into metaphor theory also bear certain affinities with Tanabe. He explains the rhetorical functioning of tensive metaphors in terms of the self-destruction of the literal meaning in order for there to be a disclosure of a "surplus meaning."[25] To what degree, we might ask, does Ricoeur's sense of a "second naivete" correspond to Tanabe's views of the transcendence of the noetic by the metanoetic in which relative being is resurrected from its self-negation in order to function as *upāya*? To what extent does the meaning of the cross lead Christian believers to the silence of the Buddha?

Finally, Tanabe takes pains to speak of the transformative action of Other-power as a "manifestation" and as an event in history. This too is helpful in coming to terms with the meaning of the contemporary encounter between religions. Might the manifestation of which Tanabe writes herald a step in the direction of a common history, a common humanity, a common religion? On this question, caution seems most appropriate. As noted above, Tanabe's notion of mediation, if correctly employed, will alert us to the dangers of a premature syncretism of religious outlooks. Participants in inter-religious dialogue are well advised to be as attentive to the meanings which separate religious traditions as they are to those meanings which they share. Tanabe has helped me appreciate that it is the unrelenting "otherness" of Buddhism which instructs and indeed transforms my Christianity. Without this appreciation of "otherness," the vitality of the Buddhist heritage becomes merely "more of the same" vis-à-vis my Christian belief. Still, it is a peculiar sign of our times that, because of the creative encounter between religions in dialogue, some Buddhists and Christians feel a solidarity with their dialogue partners that they do not share with their co-religionists. Instead of premature talk of a new religion, Tanabe's metanoetic standpoint seems to suggest that we look to where creative individuals are "breaking through" to a new awareness of the mutual service that religions render to one another. Increasingly, because of the "paradoxical universality" of Christianity, Christians must realize the importance

---

[24] Paul Tillich, *Systematic Theology*, Vol. I, 238-39.
[25] Paul Ricoeur, *Interpretation Theory: Discourse and the Surplus of Meaning* (Fort Worth: Texas Christian University Press, 1976), 45-69.

of Buddhism for discerning the future of their tradition in the century to come. Likewise, some committed Buddhists have come to look gratefully on Christianity as the "skillful means" *(upāya)* for realizing their own salvation in the religiously pluralistic situation in which they find themselves today. Herein lies the existential and religious basis for authentic dialogue and encounter in depth.

In his reflections on the problem of universality and uniqueness, Nishitani outlined his own hopes for the restoration of the power of religion.[26] Importantly, Nishitani does not suggest that this restoration is to be found in a new religion. He looks instead for the world's great religious universalities to become "living things" *(ikita mono* 生きたもの *)* once again. The revival of the power of the religious in our day, Nishitani believes, will take place through a reform from within. At the same time, however, Nishitani thinks that this revival is tied to the willingness of religious traditions to engage in creative dialogue with other religious traditions. In working out his metanoetic philosophy, Tanabe Hajime cautioned that religion degenerates when mediation is not full,[27] but he also held out the hope that, through the praxis of metanoia, we might participate in the "renewal of reality itself."[28] Ultimately what is manifest in metanoetic cognition is the "direction toward which actuality moves." For Buddhism and Christianity, might this not mean that the future of both great religious traditions lies in their mutual transformation?

---

[26] Nishitani, "The Standpoint of 'Ascent'," 160.
[27] PM, 152.
[28] PM, 41.

Metanoetics and Christian Spirituality

Donald W. MITCHELL

I N this paper I would like to approach Tanabe's idea of metanoetics from the viewpoint of spiritual theology. I will begin
by looking at the ultimate cause of metanoesis as Tanabe
understands it. Next, I will consider Tanabe's analysis of the dynamics of the life of metanoetics. And finally, I will examine what
Tanabe sees as the results of this transformation, particularly as
they bear on social concerns in the light of his logic of species.
At each step of the way, I will attempt to point out similarities
with and differences from Christian spirituality.

THE CAUSE OF METANOESIS

At the outset of his *Philosophy as Metanoetics*, Tanabe defines metanoesis *(zange)* as "the activity of conversion and transformation
performed by Other-power *(tariki)*" (lx). Clearly, it is an idea
informed to a large extent by Pure Land Buddhism: "My experience of conversion—that is, of transformation and resurrection—
in metanoesis corresponds to the experience that led Shinran
(1173-1262) to establish the doctrine of the Pure Land Shin sect
(Jōdo Shinshū)" (lii). In fact, the advance of Tanabe's own philosophy toward metanoetics was, on his own account, the result of
Other-power acting in and through his personal *zange* as he
faced the horrors of war in Japan in the early forties. In a letter
to Takeuchi Yoshinori written on July 7, 1944, Tanabe said:
"The national mood is extremely somber, and yet I feel a strange
sense of light streaming over me that fills me with indescribable
gratitude."[1]

It was certainly this type of experience of spiritual transfor-

---

[1] "Translator's Introduction," PM, xxxvii.

mation, so characteristic of authentic spirituality, that led him to
write:

> Once I have submitted myself to this requirement and devoted
> myself to the practice of *zange*, I am met by a wondrous Power
> that relieves the torment of my shameful deeds and fills me
> with a deep sense of gratitude. *Zange* is a balm for the pain of
> repentance, and at the same time the source of an absolute
> light that paradoxically makes the darkness shine without ex-
> pelling it. The experience of accepting this transforming
> power of *zange* as a grace from Other-power is . . . the very core
> of metanoetics (2).

> In the life of the spirit . . . "resurrection" must mean regen-
> eration to a new life. I no longer live of myself, but live because
> life has been granted to me from the transcendent realm of
> the absolute which is neither life nor death. Since this absolute
> is the negation and transformation — that is, conversion — of
> everything relative, it may be defined as absolute nothingness.
> I experience this absolute nothingness through which I am re-
> born to new life as nothingness-*qua*-love (li).[2]

For Tanabe, this "life of the spirit" is not achieved by the
effort of the will, or what Buddhism calls "self-power" *(jiriki)*, but
through the mediation of the transformative Other-power *(tariki)*.
He says that this Other-power "that acts within me exercises its
power in a way so overwhelming that it obliges me to perform
zange" (3). It is the dynamics of this life of metanoetics that constitute the subject matter of *Philosophy as Metanoetics*. This dynamic
life is a process of living, or better, being enabled to live, the
"practice of death-and-resurrection." I say being enabled to live
this way because such a life is the result of Other-power. So before
looking at the life of metanoetics that Tanabe calls "death-and-
resurrection," we should first see what exactly this Other-power
is for Tanabe and what its relation is to Absolute Nothingness in
Buddhism and to God in Christianity.

While Pure Land Buddhism conceives of Other-power as the

---

[2] Note that the divine qualities referred to here and in the previous quotation are "absolute light" and "new life." Amida Buddha worshiped in Shin Buddhism as the personification of Other-power is the Buddha of infinite light and
life.

power of the Buddha, particularly the power of the vow of Amida Buddha, to transform one's existence through grace, Tanabe takes a middle path between this Pure Land position and that of Zen Buddhism (172). While he recognizes that religious faith can conceptualize Other-power in a theistic manner, his approach is from the philosophical point of view that understands this phenomenon in a very different way. For Tanabe, "the absolute subject of Other-power is absolute nothingness" (8). The transformation of the self through death and resurrection is an absolute transformation because it is the dynamic functioning of Absolute Nothingness. This functioning of Absolute Nothingness is Other-power as the absolute transformation of the forms of life. Therefore, all things including ourselves exist through the mediation of Absolute Nothingness, that is, through the absolute transformation of Other-power. This mediation sets up a relationship of mutual transformation between self and world that just is the dynamic of Absolute Nothingness understood as Other-power. In this way, Tanabe sees each being as a mediation of Other-power, or as "a mediative moment of absolute nothingness" (68).

It is important to note that for Tanabe, Absolute Nothingness cannot function apart from this dynamic of being. It is similar to what Nishitani Keiji calls a "near-side" reality; Other-power is not something beyond and outside the transforming process of being. So while this process transforms the person in terms of death-and-resurrection, it breaks into the person as grace, but grace emerging from within the depths of the self. Other-power is not a something that confronts the self, but it is an "action seen as the transformation of the self" (235). It is the "force" of Absolute Nothingness that converts the self and restores it to a new life through death-and-resurrection. While it may be experienced as transcendent, it is at the same time immanent.

It is clear then that Absolute Nothingness for Tanabe is not a reality that can exist apart from beings: "Nothingness cannot function apart from the cooperation of being" (121). There is a Zen-like reciprocal penetration between Absolute Nothingness and beings. This penetration in one's self-consciousness is experienced as the grace of Other-power. For example, Tanabe says that "I am graced with a personal experience of emancipation from the eternal darkness of mind, as if a serene light had poured forth from eternity into my mind" (124). Yet for Tanabe, this pouring forth of light that brings new life is not from a personal God, but is the dynamic of Absolute Nothingness as absolute transformation or Other-power. The God of theism seems to Tanabe to be a transcendent absolute that is experienced directly without any mediation (19). This in Tanabe's mind would make God a relative Other-power, that is, existing apart from the process of transforming action and affecting it directly through its transcendent will. For Tanabe, to place the absolute in opposition to the relative is to make it another relative. On the other hand, Absolute Nothingness as Other-power is the absolute mediatory activity of transformation itself.

If we compare Tanabe's notion of Other-power to the Christian notion of God, it is clear that while the notion of God includes this dimension of immanence within the process of transformation, it also includes a transcendent dimension as well. The Other-power of Absolute Nothingness that generates the transformation of existence is similar to the power of the Holy Spirit of God that Christians understand to be the source of transformation through death into new life. However, for Christians this Other-power experienced in the transformation of one's existence is like the *gensō*, or "returning to the world," of Christ. It is the returning to the world of this new life poured forth from the heart of the Trinity. And this trinitarian reality can never be simply identified with creation. So God is perhaps similar to Absolute Nothingness in that creation can be understood as the "kenosis," or self-emptying, of God. But this kenosis is not a complete or absolute emptying out of God *as* creation.[3] This would empty out Christian hope. In Christian spirituality, one is opened up to something more than the transformation process itself. For the Christian, the end of the transformation process is not to be reborn into it, but to live its fruits of joy, gratitude, freedom, compassion, love and unity forever in paradise in the heart of the Trinity. To empty out this reality completely as creation would be to lose the ultimate goal of Christian spirituality.

Tanabe's reluctance to posit the Other-power as a theistic God makes it clear that he intends to maintain a notion of absolute mediation that is compatible with the broader Mahāyāna notion

---

[3] Here I have in mind Masao Abe's widely circulated essay, "Kenotic God and Dynamic *Śūnyatā*" (unpublished).

of Emptiness. Other-power is thus transforming mediation, and can only function as that mediation of Absolute Nothingness. This in turn means that each person is an "axis of transformation" (22). That is, each person is a mediator of Absolute Nothingness and thus serves as an axis of transformation for others. And here we find the heart of the matter. Tanabe says that this brings us to the meaning of life:

> The world exists for no other reason than that of *upāya* ("skill-ful means"): it is the world of mediation through which such a reciprocal transformation enables relative beings to move toward nothingness and to return to the world to serve as a means of enlightenment and salvation for others. Metanoesis is the mediatory activity of transcending being in terms of "being as *upāya*" (22).

It is through our reciprocal mediation of absolute transformation that we are ourselves transformed through death-and-resurrection and are enabled by that process of Other-power to be an expedient means of that death and new life for others. To be "mediative moments" of Absolute Nothingness one must be transformed by Other-power into what one truly is through dying and rising to new life.

THE LIFE OF METANOETICS

This brings us to the second part of our analysis of metanoetics, namely, the dynamics of metanoesis, or the dynamic of "death-and-resurrection" that is produced by Other-power. The first thing to note about this dynamic of metanoesis is that it is not something that a person *does* so much as something that *is done to* a person. One can try to achieve this goal through the exercise of will or "self-power" but if pursued to the end, action no longer belongs to the self. Rather a higher action is manifest, what Shinran calls the "Great Action" *(taigyō)*. For Tanabe, this is the Other-power action of Absolute Nothingness that transforms the person into an "empty being" (81). This graced kenosis of the self makes the self empty and thus enables it to function as a true mediator of Absolute Nothingness. The action of the self is empty and yet expresses a new life, the life of compassionate transformation. Again this is not based on will or self-power, but on a "faith" *(shin)* "in which the self abandons itself and submits obediently to absolute nothingness, the faith of a self-conscious action based on total self-abandonment" (81). In this way the metanoetic practice of self-abandonment cooperates with Other-power which can then transform the self into a true mediator of Absolute Nothingness.

In this way the mediation of Absolute Nothingness "realizes" itself in relative beings in a manner that is transformative for others. This is the "returning to the world" *(gensō)* so important in Shin Buddhism. Actually given the grace of Other-power, one's return to the world is a "being returned" to the world: "As a true bodhisattva cooperating with the Great Compassion of nothingness, the self performs the action of gratitude toward the Great Compassion of nothingness" (143). In fact, Tanabe says that the very movement into nothingness is the action of absolute *gensō*. He quotes Pascal's comment that "Instead of saying: 'If God were not merciful, we should have to make every effort towards virtue,' we should on the contrary say that it is because God is merciful that we must make every effort" (194). Tanabe explains this in Buddhist terms. In Shin Buddhism, *ōsō* means "going toward" the Pure Land, and *gensō* means "returning to" this world from the Pure Land in order to help others. Metanoetics is the philosophy of *gensō*. That is, metanoesis is itself a kind of absolute *gensō* of Other-power in that it is a power that acts within one in such a way as to overwhelm the self obliging it to perform conversion: "the absolute as a 'returning to' this world is the motivating force behind our performance of *zange*" (10).

It is interesting to note that Tanabe contrasts this notion of *gensō* with Christian mysticism which he calls the "path of *ōsō*." He states that mysticism is a self-power path that seeks, through methods of contemplation, to achieve sainthood. However, I am reminded here of the work of Jean-Pierre de Caussade (1675-1751) entitled *Abandonment to Divine Providence*.[4] Caussade taught that true spirituality involves entrusting oneself to God with total self-abandonment. Caussade, like Tanabe and like Shinran, also taught that one's own efforts to generate transformation will fail: "God's

---

[4] See Jean-Pierre de Caussade, *Abandonment to Divine Providence* (New York: Doubleday, 1975).

[5] *Abandonment to Divine Providence*, 29.

action is boundless in its scope and power, but it can only fill our souls if we empty them of all false confidence in our own ability."[5] And like Shinran and Tanabe, Caussade says that even the ability to practice this kenotic self-abandonment is itself a grace. In this sense, it is what he calls "an art without art." To quote Caussade at some length:

> There is a time when God desires to animate the whole of the soul and bring it to perfection secretly and by unknown ways. . . . After several experiences of the folly into which it is led by its efforts to guide itself, the soul recognizes how helpless it is and . . . it abandons itself to God so that it can have only him and receive all things through him. It is then that God becomes the source of its life. . . .[6]
>
> Now it is surely obvious that the only way to receive the impress of this idea is to put oneself quietly in the hands of God, and that none of our own efforts and mental strivings can be of any use at all. This work in our souls cannot be accomplished by cleverness, intelligence, or any subtlety of mind, but only by completely abandoning ourselves to the divine action. . . .[7]

These words certainly echo the teachings of Shinran who also rejected any self-power "calculative thinking" in spirituality. We see, then, that the mystical path in Christianity is not necessarily the path of *ōsō* as Tanabe thought. Growth in the mystical life comes from the *gensō* of the "love of God that has been poured out in our hearts through the Holy Spirit who has been given to us." (Rom. 5.5) The kenosis of Christ produces the *paradosis*, or pouring forth, of the Holy Spirit who as Other-power re-creates us in the image of God: "All of us . . . are being transformed from glory to glory into his very image by the Lord who is the Spirit." (2 Cor. 3.18) This sanctification does not result from human effort, but from the *gensō* of Christ, the returning to the world of new life through the kenosis of the Cross. The discipline of the religious life in Christian mystical practice may look like the path of *ōsō* from the outside, but in essence it is simply the cooperation of the person with the Other-power of God.

---

[6] *Abandonment to Divine Providence*, 110.

[7] *Abandonment to Divine Providence*, 56.

A second aspect of the transformation process according to Tanabe is that its dynamic of "death-and-resurrection" changes the moral human condition. Tanabe's description of how this is so has obvious parallels to Christian thought. For example, he argues that this metanoesis is necessary because of the given condition of humanity which is constituted by a "radical evil" that is the consequence of our freedom (4). Here he means that our identity is established by acts of free self-assertion. One has the freedom to determine one's identity and this can lead one to forget one's relativity and presume to be absolute. The natural emergence of the individual self entails a displacement of one's primordial center and in its place there develops a position of self-centeredness. Tanabe terms this innate human tendency toward arrogance "original sin." And, he points out that this tendency is grounded on a misuse of freedom. The freedom we enjoy "is rooted solely in the grace of the absolute" (4). On the other hand, the grace of the absolute can also negate this freedom and the identity one creates through it in order that one may find "true freedom" in the resurrection of new life. This is the dynamic Tanabe calls "death-and-resurrection." It is in entrusting oneself to this process that one acquires true freedom and true identity.

Metanoesis is the self-negation of one's rebellious being in self-surrender to grace. And through that negation one's being is affirmed and rediscovered. The negation of death is transformed into the affirmation of new life. Again this negation-affirmation is not something one does, but is done to one by Other-power. Therefore the activity of Absolute Nothingness is called by Tanabe "Great Nay-*qua*-Great Compassion" (8). Thus the kenosis of the self is not an activity of the self only, but it is an emptying of the self that is the self-determination of the Great Nay. And since that Great Nay is the Great Compassion, the kenosis is not left in negation, but empties out through a negation of the negation into new life. Real kenosis is accomplished by the power of the Great Nay of absolute transformation.

However, Tanabe also feels that this does not free the person from the inclination to evil. The disposition to isolate oneself from the absolute and others in the absolute is grounded in the principle of our freedom to differentiate ourselves. Given this situation, one must constantly practice metanoesis in the continuous entrustment of self to this ongoing process of kenotic negation and Grand

Affirmation. In this regard, Tanabe quotes Buddhist and Christian sources: "to be restored to life again once and for all immediately after dying the Great Death" and "to come to life by dying with Christ on the cross" (158). This coming to new life is in the kenotic mode of an "empty being" that becomes the true axis of transformation for others. It is a life of *upāya* that mediates the kenosis of negation and affirmative compassion of Other-power for the good of all living beings.

This brings us to the third aspect of metanoesis that I wish to consider, namely, that metanoetics leads to mediation, or that through metanoetics one's life can be transformed so that one can mediate the absolute to others. Now this is important to Tanabe because Other-power is in need of our "cooperation" to bear fruit: "The absolute, which consists solely in absolute mediation, cannot function without their mediative cooperation: it requires the self-negation of their self-power. The former is realized only correlatively with the latter" (155). However, even this cooperation of the self is brought about by the Other-power.

In this way, a dialectic of mediative cooperation is grounded and Tanabe can speak of "*jiriki*-qua-*tariki* and *tariki*-qua-*jiriki*." The self is needed for the realization of mediation, and must exercise its freedom to cooperate with that mediation; and the self needs Other-power in order to cooperate in the first place and thus to achieve its own transformation in the dialectic. Metanoetics is not grounded on self-power as such, then, but on the negation by Other-power that enables a kenosis that leads to resurrection of "empty-being" that mediates Absolute Nothingness. Tanabe writes:

> The way of *zange* . . . does enable the self to be transformed into a new being within the absolute . . . so that one is allowed to exist by the grace of Other-power and to cooperate as the mediator of the absolute. Metanoesis is action performed by the self, but at the same time it is the practice of abandoning the self. Hence, it originates in the Great Compassion of Other-power. Nevertheless, it is actually the self that submits itself voluntarily to Other-power and performs this action. Paradoxically, metanoesis both is and is not the action of the self (170-71).

Here we see that Other-power is a power of compassionate enablement. It is not an autocratic monarch that rules by direct unmediated power. (This unfortunately is how Tanabe sometimes describes the theistic idea of a personal God.) The absolute, he notes:

> is not an ideal or goal that ultimately sublates the relative; it is, rather, a principle that supports us continually wherever we stand and makes it possible for us to engage in authentic action. It is . . . the very force that moves us here and now. Wherever the relative exists, the absolute is there as its correlative" (95).

This absolute force that moves as the life-force of relative existence enables us to participate in the dynamic of our own transformation that in turn enables us to be mediators of the absolute. Our freedom is in need of an enablement that moves one from metanoesis to mediation. This metanoetic transformation is that "in which the self is enabled to perform the genuine activity of nothingness, even though it is the force of absolute nothingness that does the enabling by turning the self into a mediator of nothingness" (119).

In Christian spirituality, the transformation by the Holy Spirit also enables one to express the life of God to others. However, all beings mediate the absolute to some degree, that is, they are the vehicles of God's providence. To quote Caussade about divine providence again:

> It is offered to us all the time and wherever we are. All creatures, friends or foes, pour it out in abundance, and it flows through every fiber of our body and soul until it reaches the very core of our being. . . . God's activity runs through the universe. It wells up and around and penetrates every created being.[8]

Thus, all creatures mediate the absolute to each person through God's providence: "The actions of created beings are veils which hide the profound mysteries of the workings of God."[9] And for this mediation, Caussade says that we should be "grateful to all creatures, cherish them and thank them silently for their good

---

[8] *Abandonment to Divine Providence*, 25-26.

[9] *Abandonment to Divine Providence*, 36.

[10] *Abandonment to Divine Providence*, 37.

will in helping us, by God's design, toward perfection."[10] For Caussade, each present moment mediates this Great Action of God transforming one's life. He calls this the "sacrament of the present moment." But for it to do its work fully and in a "genuine" sense, as Tanabe puts it, one must abandon oneself to its transformative power. It is in need of our "acceptance," "surrender" and "cooperation," in short our "gentle and wholehearted submission to providence."

The "touch," as John of the Cross calls it, of this action is the Holy Spirit within the heart of the person. It may be mediated by another, but it is, as Tanabe noted, an immanent phenomenon that transforms the person from one's deepest Center and enables the person to be more purely a mediator of God for others. This is what Tanabe calls the movement from metanoesis to mediation. John of the Cross speaks of this effect of the Holy Spirit in the Center of the person as one that "transforms and clarifies it in its whole being, power and strength and according to its capacity, until it appears to be God."[11] Here John emphasizes the mystical experience of both "transformation" and "manifestation."[12] The Holy Spirit dwells in the Center of one's being: "Do you know that your body is a temple of the Holy Spirit within you?" (1 Cor. 6.19) And when it transforms a person, that person is clarified so as to reflect or manifest this reality of God to others. In this movement from transformation to manifestation, we see a Christian parallel to Tanabe's notion of moving from metanoetics to mediation.

In this way, the Christian is enabled to image God, to be a purer image of God. Paul points out that the transformation by the Spirit re-makes us in the image of Christ: "All of us . . . are being transformed from glory to glory into his very image by the Lord who is the Spirit." (2 Cor. 3.18) And this, for Paul, results in a manifestation of God in the transformed person:

> For God, who said, "Let light shine out of darkness," has shone
> in our hearts, that we in turn might make known the glory of
> God shining on the face of Christ (2 Cor. 4.6).

John of the Cross uses the metaphor of a crystal to explain this

---

[11] *The Living Flame of Love*, 1.13.
[12] *The Living Flame of Love*, 1.13.

transformation and manifestation. He says that when a "pure light" shines on a clean crystal, the light concentrates within it and the crystal becomes brilliant so that it seems to be all light: "And then the crystal is indistinguishable from the light, since it is illuminated according to its full capacity, which is to appear to be light."[13]

Paul and John of the Cross, like Caussade, also make the point that this is not achieved by us, but by the transforming power of God. It is this "Other-power" that enables us to participate in the new life of the Risen One that in turn makes us new persons. Paul calls this "sharing the image of the Son." In this way we are "redeemed," that is, "rescued" from our old ego-self such that we "recover" our true or original self as a new self in the image of Christ. (Rom. 8.29) We are enabled by the transformation of the Holy Spirit to manifest this Christ image in our own unique ways. Using the metaphor of light, as does Tanabe, Paul says that in this way one "inherits the light" so that the Holy Spirit takes "us out of the power of darkness and creates a place for us in the reign of the Son that he loves." (Col. 1.13)

Now we come to the fourth point of comparison between Tanabe and Christianity on the dynamic of transformation. It has to do with what Tanabe calls the "trinity of action, faith, and witness *(gyō-shin-shō)*" (6). "Action-faith-witness," so important in the Pure Land tradition, is interpreted in a dialectical fashion by Tanabe. The action that precipitates faith which in turn issues in witness is in fact the action of Other-power. This action is the transformation of the Great Nay-*qua*-Great Compassion that is realized in the religious consciousness of faith-witness. In one's faithful entrustment to this metanoesis, one is transformed and this transformation *itself* gives witness to the action that brought it about. For example, two modes of this witness to the action of Other-power are joy and gratitude. Joy is not something that comes after the transformation but is part of the process itself. That is, joy is not a feeling that results from a change brought about by the process of metanoesis, but it emerges from the Other-power in the process of transformation. This is because while the negation of the process empties the self, the affirmation of one's empty-being is one of joy. And this joy witnesses to Other-power

---

[13] *The Living Flame of Love*, 1.13.

and in turn leads to gratitude which moves one to cooperate with the Other-power in being an expedient means *(upāya)* in helping others to share in this joy. This becomes the life of compassionate witness that is founded on faith and ultimately on the action of Other-power. The compassion here is a mediation of the Great Compassion. Gratitude for the radiant joy originating in the Great Compassion "issues in an enthusiasm to act on behalf of others *(gensō-hōon)*" (45).

There is a spiritual depth to the notion of joy in Tanabe's philosophy because of the negation through which it arises:

> The self-surrender . . . produces the grace of a resurrected self that brings with it the joy of a regenerated life. Needless to say, the suffering of *zange* is accompanied by the bitterness of repentance. . . . This profound pain, however, is at the same time the medium of joy and the source of bliss. Joy abounds in the midst of pain . . . because *zange* turns us toward the bliss of *nirvāṇa*, however sinful and perverted we may be. The joy and gratitude that stem from our being included in the compassion of the absolute and thus redeemed from our original sin arise neither apart from the pain of *zange* nor after it. The joy and pain of *zange* interpenetrate each other (6-7).

In the midst of the pain suffered through the Great Nay of the kenosis of self, there is joy and gratitude through the affirmation of the Great Love of the Other-power. Death-and-resurrection, understood by Tanabe, is a total process in each moment of the life of metanoesis. Metanoetics for Tanabe means to submit "obediently" to the process of transformation that brings the pain of kenosis and at the same time the joy and gratitude of new life.

We find something similar to this phenomenon in Christian spirituality. That is, in Christian spiritual life, one also experiences the joy of the resurrection life in the midst of everyday sufferings. And as Tanabe points out, this joy is not just a feeling caused by the transforming process, rather it is a quality of the transforming resurrection life itself. The action-grace of God enables one to live this new life of joy, the joy of the absolute, in relative existence. Like the Pure Land Buddhist who receives the mind of

---

[14] See my discussion with Kobori Nanrei Sōhaku, "Dialogue with Kobori Nanrei Sōhaku," *Japanese Religions*, 14/2 (July, 1986): 19-32.

Amida, the Christian receives the "mind of Christ" (1 Cor. 2.16) with the qualities of that Christ-reality which include the kind of joy about which Tanabe is talking.[14] These qualities, such as joy, are the Great Action of God mediated by the person. Therefore, these qualities of new life witness to a faith that is itself the action of God.

A fifth aspect of the dynamic of metanoetics is related to this way of action-faith-witness. It entails the development of freedom: "only when the way of action-faith-witness opens up before us does freedom becomes manifest to us" (123). This freedom (*jinen*) is not the unmediated freedom of human will, but the freedom of Absolute Nothingness mediated in the selfless person. Just as the joy and compassion mentioned above are not simply human feelings but rather the concrete expressions of the joy and compassion of the absolute, so too *jinen* is the "naturalness" of the free functioning of Absolute Nothingness. The relative being in its kenosis lives the freedom of the absolute through the transformation of Other-power. This type of freedom is the selfless action of new life which in Buddhist terms means "action of no-action" or "action without an acting self" (204). That is, the action of the self is no longer merely the doing of the self, but it is the Great Action mediated by the self. Here again the Buddhists appreciate the statement of Paul implying that it is no longer he who acts but Christ within him who acts.

Hence for Tanabe, the affirmation of freedom or naturalness is mediated by the negation of kenosis. Therefore he says that it demands the "blood and sweat" of kenotic religious discipline. It is not something "beneath ethics," but "beyond ethics" in a Kierkegaardian sense. That is, one must exert oneself to the utmost and then with an awareness of one's powerlessness submit oneself to the *jinen-hōni* of Other-power. In the resulting metanoetic negation, one is enabled by Other-power to live the true freedom of new life: "to submit oneself to the absolute and serve as its mediator means to be free in the true sense of the term" (80). The kenosis of self is completed by grace so that the freedom of new life is made possible. But it is important to note that Tanabe quickly adds that this transformation does not empty out our humanness into angelic perfection: "By following the way of *zange*, we ordinary fools can participate in that freedom just as we are, with all our ordinariness and folly. Once we have set foot on the path of *zange*, access to freedom through the Great Compassion is ours" (128-29).

One might be inclined at this point to object to this notion of freedom. That is, it seems that one is giving up freedom in submitting one's will to an Other-power. However, Tanabe points out that the Other-power in Buddhism is grounded in Absolute Nothingness so that the agent that moves one by Other-power is just the absolute transformation of one's life. There is no "being" as an agent outside the self. Other-power as absolute transformation is a "naturalness" *(jinen-hōni)* that is beyond the opposition of self and other. In fact, it is in this regard that Tanabe criticizes Christianity. He feels that in Christianity, God is a personal other so that submission to his will makes freedom impossible. The Christian God is outside the transformation process and so cannot be the absolute grounding of the spontaneous freedom of *jinen*. I might add that Tanabe includes Pure Land Buddhism in this critique insofar as it too posits a personal relationship between Amida Buddha and sentient beings (172, 213).

At one point, however, Tanabe does say that "if we identify the will of God with the love of God, and divine grace with the working of divine love, then grace, far from destroying human freedom only draws it out as it fosters and sustains the activity of human will" (82-83). This seems to be verified in the lives of Christian saints. For example, Teresa of Avila says that in the highest state of spiritual life, Christ becomes the very life of the soul.[15] Here there is a great freedom that is natural, simple and characterized by "self-forgetfulness." Unusual mystical phenomena such as raptures and visions cease and one seems focused on living compassion and charity for others. This care for others is not pursued in a busy and willful manner, but is a free and spontaneous functioning of the mind of Christ being mediated by the person for the benefit of others.

In this mystical life, one feels free and fully actualized as a person because one's will is conformed to the will of God in all things. So, while this Christian life resembles the absolute medi-

---

[15] See also my essay, "Shinran's Religious Thought and Christian Mysticism," *The Pacific World: Journal of the Institute of Buddhist Studies*, 4 (Fall, 1988): 15-22. This essay is a reworking of a paper published in Japanese: "Christian Mysticism and Shinran's Religious Philosophy," *The Shinshūgaku: Journal of Studies in Shin Buddhism*, 74 (June, 1986): 27-45.

ation of Absolute Nothingness, to be understood properly it must be placed in context. And this context involves the existence of a personal God. For Christian spirituality, it is important that the transcendent or "far side" of God's reality be maintained as the source of true freedom. True freedom for the Christian is a living of the resurrection life of the Risen One. So the Christian believes that the process of transformation into freedom involves a participation in the life of the Trinity. The process of the sanctification of humankind is not self-contained, but is the result of the pouring out of that new life from God. This does not deny human freedom but opens it up to its fulfillment in God. The transformation does not lead only to rebirth within its process, but to an eternal life of endless joy, gratitude and freedom within paradise. The negation of kenosis and the affirmation of new life lived by mediating that transformation to others is not, in Christian spirituality, an end in itself. It is a taste of the resurrection life of paradise and thus demands an Other-power with a transcendent dimension that pours this life forth into human existence and also enables one to participate fully and forever in it in paradise, in the heart of the Trinity.

We have been looking at the dynamics of the life of metanoetics according to Tanabe and making some comparative comments along the way. But as we examine such things as joy, gratitude, compassion and freedom, we are also looking at the results of metanoetics. This is because metanoetics means transformation by Other-power, and these qualities are just the action of Other-power taking shape in the individual. At the beginning of this paper, I said I wanted to explore (1) the cause, (2) the dynamics and (3) the results of metanoetics in Tanabe's thought in relation to Christian spirituality. So we have already begun to talk about the third part of this exploration. Accordingly, for the rest of this paper, I want to look at a particular result of metanoetics that has great social relevance today.

METANOETICS AND SOCIAL TRANSFORMATION

So far we have been looking at metanoetics as an individual phenomenon, that is, as involving the personal transformation of the individual. But it has a social dimension as well. Tanabe refers to true freedom as "ecstatic" in that it involves a kenosis of self, a "breaking through" of the self into a deeper experience of selfhood. This *ekstasis* is the breaking of the limits of self in free action. That is, in active freedom, the self is ecstatic in that it is no longer merely itself but the realization of Other-power. It no longer acts according to its own plan but acts in a way that manifests a "higher spontaneity" (81). This "action of no-action" is an expression of the Great Action mediating grace for all living beings. It is certainly this ecstatic condition of freedom that is witnessed to by joy and gratitude. And being restored by metanoesis to "empty-being" *(kū-u)*, one is enabled to exist as "being as *upāya*." Tanabe compares this state to the person who works for the "Kingdom of God" by submitting to "divine providence" (50, 206). It is similar to the negation of the negation of self by Other-power that affirms the self as mediator of the absolute which according to Tanabe is the middle path of "true emptiness, wonderful being" (183).

For Tanabe, people who live this way, as builders of the Kingdom of God, can work together as "co-workers of God or the Buddha." They can cooperate with God or Buddha even in the midst of pain, suffering and evil as mediators of spiritual peace, joy and gratitude, and the freedom of new life in a social context. Working together to build the Kingdom of God through social action is therefore another aspect to the new life of action-faith-witness. This collective activity of faith gives witness to the unity of love "wrought by the Great Compassion." For Tanabe, one of the most important results of metanoetics is that within the unity of the Great Compassion, transformation moves the kenotic self to reconciliation with other selves issuing in "social solidarity" (140). Persons are drawn into this unity by their reciprocal kenotic love, or what Tanabe calls their "reciprocal negation." The important thing for Tanabe is that this unity is not contemplated but lived, made real in social action.

This communal dimension of new life is understood by Tanabe in Pure Land terms. He points out that the salvific work of Amida Buddha is actualized in the context of the community of many Buddhas. In fact, he says that Amida Buddha is "nothing other than this 'communion' constituted by the absolute mediation between one Buddha and another" (215). The unity of compassion pervades the relationship between the Buddhas. And the communion between relative beings can be the context of the actualization in this world of this unity between the Buddhas. Therefore, unity in the human community can be the realization of Amida Buddha. The reciprocal negation of the members of a community in love and unity precipitates the "reciprocal mediation" of the love and unity that exists among the Buddhas. Tanabe says that this "spiritual community of Buddhas and believers" provides the context for mutual transformation. Again this is because the community makes present the transforming presence of Amida Buddha. He, as the *Tathāgata*, "is present in the community of Buddhas engaged in praising one another and reciting the name of Amida Buddha, and in the derivative mutuality of sentient beings teaching and guiding one another for the sake of salvation" (220).[16] Thus Tanabe recognizes the importance of communal or social transformation as well as personal transformation in spirituality. The latter involves the presence of Other-power within one's individual life, and the former involves the presence of Other-power in the midst of the life of the community.

Tanabe philosophically develops this communal dimension of metanoetics through his logic of species in a manner that clearly shows the influence of Hegel. Tanabe's logic of species also rejects Nishida's logic of place. For example, he says that each individual does not exist as just a particular form of the universal, as a particular form of Absolute Nothingness. Between the genus and the individual is the mediation of the species, namely, in our case, a human community. Contrary to Nishida's thinking, Tanabe believes that we do not exist as unmediated forms of, and in the "place" *(topos)* of, Absolute Nothingness. Rather, we exist in a community (species) that mediates the universal to us. This makes society, and its ability to mediate the absolute and its unity, of crucial importance to Tanabe. And because of this, he feels that the pressing problem of modernity is the conflict between various societies or communities of humanity. These conflicts keep the unity of the absolute from being mediated by its various social forms to humankind as a whole.

In this regard, Tanabe mentions the example of liberal democracy in capitalist countries and real socialism in communist countries. He says that, given the ideals of the French revolution

---

[16] This notion of the Buddhas praising Amida is based on the 17th vow of Dharmākara Bodhisattva as explained in Pure Land Buddhism.

(freedom, equality, and fraternity), freedom in capitalist countries has led to great inequality, and the equality in communism has led to a loss of freedom. Tanabe feels that the unifying factor that can conserve both of these ideals is fraternity. This concrete unity should be the goal of modern society. So the modern philosopher must take up the challenge to establish an ontology of a unified social existence that can overcome the present divisions in our world.

In his philosophy of metanoetics, Tanabe takes up this challenge in the following way. He posits a religious view of society which holds that "only the joy of a trans-individual unity of mutual reconciliation and instruction at work within the human community of individuals mediating individuals" can give meaning to human existence (264). This is only achieved through love which is the concrete relationship of transforming mediation where kenosis leads to affirmation. And this love can only reach its fulfillment in social existence where it creates unity or "the joy of social harmony." Given this unity, the members of the society will live freely and equally with others for the good of the whole community. That is, they will be enabled by the Other-power to live united in freedom and equality. And in the ideal sense, this unity that affirms freedom and equality will extend between communities, overcoming the divisions of humankind.

Tanabe points out that for Augustine the meaning of history lies in the establishment of the City of God where love is the pivotal mediator of unity. In this way, God's love is mediated by love of neighbor and God's unity is realized on earth. In Buddhism, Tanabe says, the "mutual correspondence among Buddhas" has a social implication for humanity. It can be lived out in the social solidarity of Dharma fellowship. And if this dimension of religion is not maintained, praxis vanishes into contemplation and religion becomes an opiate of the people: "A religion of the people must offer peace of soul and inspire trust in action" (284). While Tanabe makes it clear that it is only through the action of self-offering for the sake of others that one can be delivered from self-centeredness and return to the absolute, he also notes that one's growth in this Bodhisattva way is in the context of the social interrelatedness of self and other in mutual mediation of Absolute Nothingness. In commenting on the Biblical passage, "He who finds his life will lose it, and he who loses his life for my sake will find it," (Lk. 17.21) Tanabe says:

> Everything in this world exists correlatively to everything else. To seek existence for oneself alone by destroying all others is to forfeit one's own existence as well. Only by giving life to those who exist as others, by seeking coexistence despite the tension of opposition, and by collaborating for the sake of mutual enhancement can the self find life in its fullness (290-91).

Insofar as unity is realized by a community or state, that species represents, according to Tanabe, a particular determination of the Kingdom of God on earth. It mediates the absolute and expresses it in its culture. A transformed culture is a particular social form but also express the universal and so can communicate with other cultures the common bond of love and unity that reaches out to all humanity. From all this Tanabe concludes that:

> The absoluteness of nothingness that brings us into this society of brotherhood is love; it is Great Compassion. Nothingness is love; and the Great Nay of absolute transformation is the Great Compassion. The action-witness of this fact is itself the building of the Kingdom of God and the fulfillment of faith in rebirth into the Pure Land. It is here that we find the meaning of history: that the Kingdom of God is made actual in the course of history through the action-witness of nothingness (292).

So it is through the kenosis of the Great Nay that one is enabled by the grace of Other-power to pass into the Great Affirmation of the new life of joy, ecstatic freedom, gratitude, peace, love and unity. This Great Action realizes itself in the faith-witness of new life whereby one mediates Absolute Nothingness to others. And this mediation in the context of community is a communitarian life of love and unity that can be realized through the mutual kenosis of its members. This community has present within it the presence of the *Tathāgata*, the Buddha-reality as the power of light, truth, compassion and love that illumines and guides its members into a deeper participation in its new life. This community can then become the mediator of this new life to all humanity in a way that overcomes divisions and conflicts in the modern world and builds the Kingdom of God on earth.

To conclude, one can certainly see Christian elements in Tanabe's notion of social transformation by Other-power. For example, I think there is something similar in Christian spirituality to the notion of the unity of the Buddhas being realized as a unification of the human community. Jesus' last prayer for his own community was, "That they all may be one, as you Father are in me, and I in you, that they also may be one in us . . . that they may be one, even as we are one. . . ." (Jn. 17.21, 22) Here Jesus is praying that society reflect the unity of God which in trinitarian terms is the unity of the Persons of the Trinity. Given this trinitarian view, if humanity was created in the image of a triune God, then all humanity was created as a single whole to image together the love and unity of the Trinity. And it was for this unity of social solidarity realized in community life that Jesus was praying.

Christians would also agree with Tanabe that this unity is not produced by human willfulness, but by the presence of Other-power in the midst of the community. Just as the person is transformed by the Other-power within him or her, so is the social organism transformed by the Other-power among its members. In communal Christian spirituality the love and unity of the Trinity can become the life of the community through the power of the presence of God in the midst of that community: "For where two or three are gathered together in my name, there am I in the midst of them" (Mt. 18.20).[17]

This presence is what makes the community to be the Church, the mystical body of Christ animated by the Holy Spirit with the new life of the Risen One. And in this way, the Church can be a *sign* of the Kingdom of God for which it works. The love and unity of that Kingdom is signified by the love and unity of the community. But the community is made a sign by the presence of God in its midst. The Church carries a transforming and uniting presence of God so that it is a *sacrament* for its members and for the unity of humankind. And in this way, the Church is also a *servant* to the world for the building of the Kingdom of God. As sign, sacrament and servant, the Church is a social form of the Christ-reality of death-and-resurrection offering itself, in full co-

---

[17] As an example of a communal spirituality that seeks this ideal, see: Chiara Lubich, *May They All Be One* (New York: New City Press, 1984).

operation with persons of other faiths, for the liberation and enablement of all humanity, especially the poor and the oppressed, so that all humankind can become full sharers in a more just and united pluralistic world community.

Finally, I must say that Tanabe has enabled me to understand and appreciate more fully the soteriological presence of Other-power in the Buddhist tradition. He has shown the importance of this power not only for the personal transformation of the individual, but also for the communal transformation of society. And he has demonstrated how in Buddhist spirituality, metanoetics is not only converting, but is also healing, refreshing, enlightening, enriching, empowering and encouraging. It provides what I believe may very well be a fruitful basis not only for interreligious dialogue, but also for interreligious collaboration toward the kind of social-historical transformation that Tanabe correctly perceived to be so necessary in today's world.

Metanoetics and Christian Theology

YAMASHITA Tadanori

NO doubt the publication of *Philosophy as Metanoetics* in 1946 marked a watershed in the life of Tanabe Hajime as a man, a teacher, and a philosopher. Previously he had worked in logic, the philosophy of science, and Kantian and Hegelian critical idealism. Out of these studies he created his "logic of species," which attempted to chart a realm between affirmation and negation, the universal and the individual. Before this time, too, he had used his concept of species to express his idea of the ideal state—in particular, the militaristic and expansionistic Japanese state that existed during the Second World War. In 1944, when the war was coming close to an end, Tanabe gave a series of lectures in one of the war-torn lecture halls of Kyoto University. In the course of these lectures, he made clear his complete desperation with his previous philosophic system and his willingness to begin a new philosophy which he called "a philosophy that is not a philosophy" or "philosophy as metanoetics." Up until then, Tanabe had been a philosopher and logician, but from that point on he became a philosopher of religion. Where he had once, wittingly or unwittingly, been an advocate of a militaristic Japanese state, he now put his efforts into the construction of a new state like Augustine's "City of God" or Shinran's "Pure Land here on earth."

The significance of Tanabe's *Philosophy as Metanoetics* lies "in the midst of contradictions." This was how the Christian theologian Kitamori Yoshizō introduced Tanabe's philosophy in a popular article that appeared in the *Asahi Journal* some twenty-five years ago.[1] Tanabe tried to strike a balance between contradictories like the rational and the irrational, affirmation and negation.

---

[1] 日本の思想家 —3 ["Thinkers of Japan"] 朝日ジャーナル *[Asahi Journal]* (1963): 271-85.

Both before and after the pivotal point of 1944, Tanabe had ranged through a wide variety of religious teachings in search of religious truth. At the time of the publication of *Philosophy as Metanoetics*, he was deeply immersed in the teachings of Shinran. Soon after World War II he published a book entitled *The Dialectics of Christianity*,[2] in which he seemed to be asserting the superiority of Christianity to all other religious ways. This trend continued in his *Introduction to Philosophy*.[3] Toward the end of his career, he seems to have returned to his inclination to favor Zen Buddhism, as we see in an essay entitled "An Existentialism of Life or a Dialectics of Death?"[4] in which he argued for the bodhisattva ideal. It is often pointed out that Tanabe had no close affiliation with or commitment to any one particular religious tradition. His abstinence was deliberate in that it allowed him to speak from the higher perspective of the philosophy of religion. Professor Laube's comment on this point, that Tanabe is an unchurched religious vagabond, is amusing as a caricature but does not exhaust the complexity of Tanabe as a man of "philosophical faith," in the words of Karl Jaspers.[5]

In order to get a grasp of just what this philosophical faith of his was, it may help to read Tanabe's *Philosophy as Metanoetics* from a different point of view. In this essay I shall not attempt to analyze Tanabe's new philosophy of religion as expressed in that book, nor to trace the course of his pilgrimage as a philosopher or religious thinker. I would rather like to engage in my own religious philosophy as it is stimulated, educated, and guided by Tanabe's metanoetics. From his works, it is clear that Tanabe was influenced by Shinran's Pure Land Buddhism and Biblical Christianity in the formulation of his own philosophy and in the erection of his impressive philosophy of religion. Allowing Tanabe to do the same for me, I hope at least to erect a small hut for myself.

---

[2] キリスト教の弁証 , THZ 10.

[3] 哲学入門 , TZH 11.

[4] 生の実存主義か死の弁証法か , TZH 13:525-76. On this point, see the excellent survey done by Himi Kiyoshi, "A Study of the Later Tanabe," parts 1 to 9, 奈良県立短期大学研究季報 *Research Proceedings of Nara Prefectural Junior College*, 1985-1989. I am indebted to this series of articles for a grasp of the general flow of Tanabe thought.

[5] James W. Heisig, "Foreword" to *Philosophy as Metanoetics*, xxiii.

My method is basically that of Biblical theology. The terms and concepts that Tanabe used in his metanoetics often coincide with those used in the Bible, even when no direct reference was intended. To trace them back to their origins in Christian scriptures and tradition can be a stimulus for theological discussion.

To some extent, the conclusion to some of the questions I shall take up are already present in the fifteen volumes of Tanabe's *Collected Works*, which have been edited and commented on by distinguished scholars in the field. But our purpose here is not to engage in historical research on the thought of Tanabe. Tanabe would not himself have wanted that. He would rather have us "search for truth and it alone" in the area of philosophy of religion.[6]

TANABE AND CHRISTIANITY

In the introduction to *The Dialectics of Christianity*, Tanabe recalls how in his high school days he often used to read the Bible by himself but found himself unable to accept the Christian teaching of salvation based on the mythical event of the resurrection. This was in 1901 when he was 16 years old.

It is worth noting here that in his earliest writings, he quotes Saint Paul, showing his familiarity with the Bible. The following passage is taken from a 1917 essay, "Once Again on Freedom in Morality":

> Do we really have true freedom in morality as Kant thought? Or do our inclinations not rather put us in the position of Paul who says, "For I do not do what I want, but I do the very thing I hate."[7]

The passage from Romans 7:15 is repeated in a 1922 essay on "The Idea of Culture."[8]

Tanabe's familiarity with Christianity is obvious throughout

---

[6] The allusion is to the epitaph inscribed on Tanabe's memorial stone in Kita-Karuizawa; see Heisig, "Foreword," vii.

[7] THZ 1:133-34, as cited in 家永三郎 Ienaga Saburō, 田辺元の思想史的研究 *[A Study of the History of Tanabe's Thought]* (Tokyo, 1974), 256, n. 9. All Biblical quotations are from the Revised Standard Version.

[8] THZ 1:444-45.

the development of *Philosophy as Metanoetics*. His principal source of inspiration there is Shinran's *Kyōgyōshinshō*; but, as we will see later, his interpretation of Shinran contains a great deal of Christian doctrine. In Tanabe's mind, Christianity and Shinran's Pure Land Buddhism are like the two wheels of a cart, each needing the other in order to move. We see a good example of this balance in an essay of his on "Christianity, Marxism, and Japanese Buddhism,"[9] which was composed immediately after *Philosophy as Metanoetics*. In that piece he sees Christianity's emphasis on social action as almost equal to that of Marxism, and yet maintains high esteem for the spirituality of the Christian religion as equivalent to that of Japanese Buddhism. That he saw Christianity as primarily a practical, ethical religion received greater emphasis in his *Introduction to Philosophy* than any other writings, especially in the section on ethics.[10]

Throughout his life, Tanabe consistently relied on Christianity as an important resource along with Japanese Buddhism and Western philosophy for his philosophical and religious thinking. However, the kind of Biblical theology he was familiar with has since by and large become obsolete. Tanabe was particularly interested in Albert Schweitzer and his eschatological interpretation of the New Testament. Schweitzer's research had a profound impact on Biblical research in the twentieth century, but a great deal of new work has been done since. Tanabe had some acquaintance with Bultmann's demythologizing approach to the New Testament, but this did not seem to affect greatly his own reading of the New Testament. What is more, Tanabe's interest in the Old Testament is far more casual and off-handed than we might expect of a scholar. As influential as the Christian scriptures were to Tanabe's thought, the Bible is not a static document but one that depends on ever new interpretations as it is transmitted from one generation to the next.

THE CONCEPT OF METANOIA

The most fundamental concept of *Philosophy as Metanoetics* is the idea of *metanoia*, which Tanabe makes the beginning and end of

---

[9] TZH 10:271-324.
[10] See TZH 11:153.

his philosophy. Indeed, his whole philosophical system is a process of *metanoia. Metanoia* is not only repentance for past sins but also a preparation for a new era by overcoming oneself. Tanabe uses the German word *Durchbruch* (breakthrough) to describe this.

Let us begin with a closer look at the Biblical concept of *metanoia*. The Japanese word that Tanabe uses is 懺悔 *zange*, which he takes as equivalent to the Greek word μετάνοια. The term appears in the New Testament 22 times in substantive form; in the verbal form μετανοέω, 32 times; and in the alternative verbal form μεταμέλομαι, 6 times. It occurs very frequently in the Old Testament, where the simple word *šub* is most commonly used for the meaning of repentance (the Septuagint translation being ἐπιστρέφων). The Old Testament has another word for repentance, *naḥum*, to which we will return later.

In the New Testament, the word *metanoia* means "to feel remorse for deeds committed in the past," or "to change one's mind to a new direction" in the sense of conversion. The Gospel of Mark reports that Jesus preached this message at the beginning of his ministry:

> The time is fulfilled, and the kingdom of God is at hand; repent, and believe in the Gospel (Mark 1:15).

From this passage, we can assume that the arrival of God's kingdom and belief in the Gospel take place simultaneously with repentance, and that this is the basis of Jesus' ministry.

Joachim Jeremias observes that the parable of the prodigal son in Luke 15 expresses the meaning of repentance in the clearest language.[11] The prodigal son repented his sins, returned to his paternal home, and begged his father's forgiveness. Jeremias notes that the scripture describes the sons's turning point with the words εἰς ἑαυτὸν δὲ ἐλθὼν (Luke 15:17). Behind the phrasing may lay the Aramaic expression *hădar bēh*, which does not mean, "he returned to a rational state of mind," but simply "he repented."

Another example of repentance in the New Testament appears in the contrast between the penitent tax collector and the self-righteous Pharisee. The former, too ashamed to raise his eyes

---

[11] J. Jeremias, *The Parables of Jesus* (London: SCM Press, 1958), 103-106; see also his *New Testament Theology* (New York: Charles Scribner's Sons, 1971), 152.

to heaven, only beat his breast saying, "God, be merciful to me a sinner!" Of this man Jesus repeats the proverbial saying, "Everyone who exalts himself will be humbled, but he who humbles himself will be exalted" (Luke 18:9-14).

These two scenes of repentance in the New Testament speak eloquently to the question Tanabe is addressing. Throughout his book he notes again and again that repentance means "going beyond oneself" or "abandoning oneself." According to the original Aramaic, the expression "he comes to himself" in Luke's Gospel would not mean, "he turns to his rational self," as the Greek translation may mean, but rather, "he went beyond himself," or simply, "he repented." As one who had struggled long and hard with Kant's *Critique of Pure Reason*, Tanabe saw *metanoia* as a self-negation that takes one beyond oneself—and beyond Kantian pure reason. What Tanabe is trying to say with expressions such as "self-negation-*qua*-self-affirmation" is well expressed in Jesus' parables and in the saying, "Everyone who exalts himself will be humbled, but he who humbles himself will be exalted."

Another important factor in the case of New Testament *metanoia* is that it is not a half-hearted but a total negation, as Tanabe puts it. Only after such total negation can one return to a new affirmation, to recognition of Other-power as one's new master. Jeremias quotes the parable in Matthew 12:43-45 (the parallel of which is found in Luke 11:24-26) that tells of an unclean spirit going out of a man. The unclean spirit, finding no place to rest, decides to re-enter its old house which is now "empty, swept, and put in order." The parable goes on to say that the evil spirit brings with him seven other spirits who enter in and take possession of the empty house.

The parable shows two important characteristics of *metanoia*. First, as we mentioned earlier, repentance must not be half-hearted but it requires total negation. And second, it requires a new master or a new direction. On this point, Jeremias concurs with H. S. Nyberg:

> Verse 24 is to be understood as a conditional sentence and should be translated: "If the demon returns and finds the house empty, then he will return with sevenfold reinforcements." Seven here is the number of totality. Jesus is not, therefore, speaking of an inevitable consequence, as though

every exorcised person were helplessly bound to suffer re-
lapse; rather he is speaking of the consequence of a half-
hearted repentance. . . . A new master must take up residence
in it, the shining light must take possession of it.[12]

These words recall the familiar saying of Jesus:

You are the light of the world. . . . Let your light so shine before
men, that they may see your good works and give glory to your
Father who is in heaven (Matt. 5:16).

Having come this far, one can hardly fail to recall the images
of Infinite Light (無礙光 *mugekō*) and Mysterious Light (不可思議光
fukashigikō) which appear frequently in the tradition of Pure Land
Buddhism on which Tanabe was drawing so heavily. These meta-
phoric allusions to light in the New Testament and Tanabe are
not fortuitous, but demonstrate clearly how both describe the state
of an individual after radical *metanoia* in exactly the same manner.

THE MOTIVES OF METANOIA

The most conspicuous characteristic of Tanabe's metanoetics is
that it is based on what Pure Land Buddhism calls Other-power
(他力, *tariki*). Tanabe relied heavily on Shinran's interpretation
of this idea, and in particular on his major work, the *Kyōgyōshinshō*.
He explains the dependence of his metanoetics on Other-power
by way of two theories: that of the three vows (三願転入) and
that of the three minds-*qua*-one mind (三心一心). Let us consider
these two ideas in their biblical context as we reinterpret them.

THE THEORY OF THE THREE VOWS

The theory of the three vows stems from Shinran's reinterpretation
of 48 vows of Bodhisattva Dharmākara.[13] Shinran believed that
the 18th Vow represents the final state of total dependence on
Other-power, having passed through the ethical stage of the 19th
Vow and having accumulated the merits of invoking the name of

---

[12] *New Testament Theology*, 154. H. S. Nyberg, "Zum grammatischen Ver-
ständnis von Mat. 12:44f," *Arbeiten und Mitteilungen aus dem neuetestamentischen
Seminar zu Uppsala* (Lund, 1936), vol. 4, 22-35.

[13] See chapter 7 of *Philosophy as Metanoetics*.

Amida Buddha *(nembutsu)*. The process is very much like Kierke-gaard's idea of "the religious transcendence of the ethical."[14]

Jesus' concept of *metanoia* in the New Testament goes through the same process as the theory of the three vows. Here again the coincidence is hardly fortuitous. According to the synoptic Gospels and even more so in the Fourth Gospel, John the Baptist appears on the new scene as forerunner of Jesus, and Jesus as the antithesis of John. According to John's Gospel, the Baptist "came from God to bear witness to the light, while he himself was not the light" (John 1:6-8). According to Matthew, John the Baptist preached repentance but urged the people to "bear fruit that befits repentance." Furthermore, John the Baptist resorted to threats, proclaiming:

> Even now the ax is laid to the root of the trees; every tree therefore that does not bear good fruit is cut down and thrown into the fire (Matt. 3:10).

Matthew describes the beginning of Jesus' preaching of repentance in compeletely different fashion. He opens with a quotation from the prophet Isaiah:

> The people who sat in darkness
> have seen a great light,
> and for those who sat in the region
> and shadow of death,
> light has dawned (Matt 4:16, Isaiah 9:1-2).

The dawning of the light has nothing to do with those sitting in the darkness. While they were waiting, the light automatically dawned on them. This is totally God's doing and not man's.

One must not forget that the passage comes from the prophet Isaiah who has totally lost his confidence in the ability of humans to help themselves. A few verses previously, the prophet had said:

> Be broken, you peoples, and be dismayed;
> Give ear, all you far countries;
> Gird yourselves and be dismayed (Isaiah 8:9-10).

---

[14] Takeuchi Yoshinori had earlier compared Kierkegaard's idea to that of Shinran in his 教行信証の哲学 *[Philosophy of the Kyōgyōshinshō]*, Gendai Bukkyō meicho zenshū 6 (Tokyo: Ryūbunkan, 1965), 71.

One may describe Isaiah as nihilistic, critical, or desperate. How-ever appropriate these descriptions may be, his message was sin-gleminded and clear: "O Immanuel, God is with us." The prophet Isaiah is the prophet of Other-power, the *tariki* prophet.

Quite unlike John the Baptist, Jesus never expected repen-tance to bear fruit. Repentance comes to people from Jesus, not directly from people themselves. The anecdote of the conversion of the chief publican Zacchaeus points to this. Jesus of his own will goes to the home of Zaccheus as a guest. The story ends with the famous saying, "For the Son of Man came to seek and to save the lost" (Luke 19:1-10).

A more dramatic "religious transcendence of the ethical" is seen in the Old Testament prophets. This is true not only in Isaiah, whom we have just considered in connection with Mat-thew's Gospel, and in Jeremiah, for whom Tanabe had a great sympathy, but also in other prophets such as Amos and Hosea.

Here we may return to the meaning of the Hebrew word, *naḥom*, the equivalent of *metanoia*. Hebrew lexicons usually refer to two different meanings of the word *naḥom*. The first is a turn-about, which would include the sense of repentance, and the second is compassion.

It was Jörg Jeremias who pointed out the remarkable fact that in the Old Testament these are not two separate meanings but one and the same.[15] There God himself changes his mind and repents, and this itself is God's compassion. Just before the great flood, God saw how great the wickedness of human beings was and so grieved that he repented of having created them (Gene. 6:5-8). Or again, God repented for having made Saul the first king of Israel before David (I Samuel 15:35).

The prophet Amos repeatedly tells Israel to return (*šub*, in Hebrew, the same word as *metanoia*) to the Lord. As Tanabe notes, Israel's classical prophets, among whom Amos belongs, de-manded of Israel a national repentance—proving a prime example of his idea of "species." Amos says that God changed his mind and repented about his impending judgment. Just as God is pre-paring a storm of locusts to rain upon the earth, Amos intercedes:

---

[15] Jörg Jeremias, *Die Reue Gottes*, Biblische Studien 65 (Neukirchener Verlag des Erziehungsvereins, 1975).

> O Lord God, forgive, I beseech thee! How can Jacob
> stand?
> He is so small!
> The Lord repented concerning this;
> "It shall not be so," said the Lord (Amos 7:2-3).

Once again, God was calling for a judgment by fire and Amos implored him:

> O Lord God, cease, I beseech thee!
> How can Jacob stand?
> He is so small!
> The Lord repented concerning this;
> "It shall not be," said the Lord God (Amos 7:4-6).

In both passages, the word "repented" can be replaced by "felt compassion." The God who punished his own people on ethical grounds turns into a God of compassion without any warning or explanation in the book of Amos.

The same transition is more dramatically presented in chapter 11 of the Book of Hosea. The prophet Hosea, as was the custom in Israel from of old, recites the history of Israel beginning with Exodus and then he laments over Israel's rebellion and apostasy. At the moment, out of nowhere, a sudden change takes place.

> How can I give you up, O Ephraim!
> How can I hand you over, O Israel!
> How can I make you like Admah!
> How can I treat you like Zeboiim!
> My heart recoils within me.
> My compassion (naḥum, metanoia) grows warm
> and tender.
> I will not execute my fierce anger,
> I will not again destroy Ephraim (Hosea 11:8-9).

The only reason which Hosea gives for God's changing his mind is this:

> For I am God and not man,
> the Holy One in your midst,
> and I will not come to destroy (Hosea 11:9).

Because God changes his mind, he is compassionate. This is characteristic of God.

The prophetic notion that God changes quickly from a God of judgment to a God of compassion is not exactly the same as Shinran's doctrine of the three vows. Shinran emphasizes the transition from the ethical to Other-power, while Amos and Hosea the suddenness of the transition. Nevertheless, both are affirming a doctrine of the Other-power. Humans cannot save themselves unless God changes his mind. God must undergo *metanoia*.

THE THEORY OF THREE MINDS-*QUA*-ONE MIND

Tanabe takes a further hint from Shinran's doctrine to support his idea of Other-power. He begins by quoting from the *Meditation Sūtra*:

> If there are sentient beings, who wish to be born thither into the Pure Land, they can satisfy their wishes by establishing Three Minds. What are these three? The first is the Sincere Mind; the second, the Deep Mind; and the third, the Mind of Aspiring for Birth by Merit-transference. With these three Minds they can surely be born in the Pure Land.[16]

That is:

1. Sincere Mind
2. Deep Mind
3. Mind of Aspiring for Birth

$$1 + 2 + 3 = \text{Faith in Other-power}$$
$$= \text{One Mind}$$

Here Tanabe is following Soga Ryōjin's interpretation of temporal structure, according to which the three minds represent the past, present, and future. That is, the three minds are three times, subsequently becoming one time and one mind, and this one mind is faith in Other-power, faith in the transformation of the Original Vow.[17]

The doctrine of the three minds-*qua*-one mind reminds us of the central core of Judaism, *shema'*. As we read in Deuteronomy 6:4-7:

> Hear, O Israel: the Lord our God is one Lord; and you shall

---

[16] PM, 229-34.
[17] *See* PM, 233.

love the Lord your God with all your heart, and with all your soul, and with all your might. And these words which I command you this day shall be upon your heart; and you shall teach them diligently to your children, and shall talk of them when you sit in your house, and when you walk by the way, and when you lie down, and when you rise.

That is:

1. All your heart
2. All your mind
3. All your might

1 + 2 + 3 = Love of One God

All three—heart, mind, and might—are equated with love of the one God. That is to say, with all three faculties, we are to love the one God. This is cut of a single cloth with Shinran's theory of the three minds-*qua*-one mind. What is more, it is this same Deuteronomic theology that emphasizes God's power to love and choose Israel. It is God's doing and not Israel's. It is Otherpower, *tariki*. Immediately after setting up the doctrine and practice of *shema'*, the Deuteronomic author discusses the issue of Israel's election:

For you are a people holy to the Lord your God; the Lord your God has chosen you to be a people for his own possession, out of all the peoples that are on the face of the earth . . . But it is because the Lord loves you, and is keeping the oath which he swore to your fathers, that the Lord has brought you out with a mighty hand . . . (Deut 7:6-8).

Here again it is Lord God who takes the initiative, not Israel. And here again, too, we see an obvious parallel between the Deuteronomic concept of time and that of Pure Land Buddhism as noted by Soga and Tanabe. In the Deuteronomic structure of time we find clearly the past (the Exodus and the receiving of the Commandments), the present (the time of Mosaic sermon at Mt. Pisgah, and/or the time of Deuteronomic reformation in 621 BCE), and the future (the time when you, your sons and daughters, and your children's children live and keep the Commandments). The Deuteronomic unity of the three times is expressed as one time, "this day" *(hayyom hazzeh)*, a typically Judeo-Christian notion.

The same concept of time is dramatized in eucharistic sayings in the Christian tradition and in the Passover *haggadah* in Jewish tradition. Indeed, it is so Judeo-Christian that one might even argue that any interpretation of Buddhist doctrines that uses it is more Judeo-Christian than Buddhist. The interpretation of the three minds by Soga and Tanabe seem to fall under the umbrella of this judgment. But whether such a notion of time be Christian or Buddhist, the deep understanding of salvation in terms of time and eternity bears witness to a profound philosophy of religion.

THE REALIZATION OF METANOIA

As *metanoia* is the beginning, it is also the end. It is the cause of philosophy as well as its finality and the process that intervenes. Yet from the point of view of our discussion here, *metanoia* is realized as final goal on the level of practice, ethics, and the care for the world. Tanabe's strong preference for Christianity because of its deep social and ethical concerns has already been noted. This becomes much clearer as his life-work progresses after *Philosophy as Metanoetics* but is clear already in that work. Tanabe devotes the final chapter of the book, "Metanoetics as a Religious View of Society," to this question.

Tanabe's idea of ethics pivots about his reflections on Shinran's teaching on "return," consisting of the return to the world from the Pure Land *(ekō)* and the return from the Pure Land to this world *(gensō)*. Already from the Preface, references to *ōsō* and *gensō* abound, making it patent that the doctrine is to be one of the pillars of his metanoetics. Just as Shinran began the *Kyōgyō-shinshō* with references to *ōsō* and *gensō*, so did Tanabe begin his *Philosophy as Metanoetics*.

Is there any comparable doctrine in Christianity so fundamental and yet so conclusive as to formulate ethics as its beginning and end? The Johannine concept of incarnation as ascent and descent is no doubt both similar and entirely compatible, and like the notion of *parousia* points to the same religious reality.

Let us examine the Johannine formulation of the idea of incarnation more closely. The prologue of John's Gospel sounds almost like one of the three Pure Land sūtras:

The true light that enlightens every man was coming into the world. He was in the world and the world was made through him, yet the world knew him not. He came to his own home, but his own people received him not.... And the Word became flesh and dwelled among us, full of grace and truth; we have beheld his glory, glory as of the only Son from the Father (John 1:9-14).

Or again later:

God sent the Son into the world, not to condemn the world, but that the world might be saved through him. He who believes in him is not condemned; he who does not believe in him is condemned already, because he does not believe in the name of the only Son of God. And this is the judgment, that the light has come into the world, and the man loved darkness rather than light, because their deeds were evil (John 3:17-19).

In both passages we find a clear statement of the idea of incarnation in the New Testament, in which the linear concept of time has been radically modified. Creation is mentioned, but not so much in the sense of the physical formation of the materialistic world in the beginning but in the sense of the primacy of the Word before the world. As Bultmann has noted,[18] eschatology is interpreted not as the judgment at the end of world history but as the consequence of disbelief in the Word. The Word, which is one with God, turns towards this world to share in the destiny of the world. This concept of incarnation in the Fourth Gospel is almost identical with Shinran's concept of *gensō*. The ethics based on the Johannine incarnation idea is the New Commandment to love one another. The giving of the New Commandment in the 13th chapter marks the high point of the Fourth Gospel.

The commandment to love one another is also presented in the context of the Son of Man being glorified (John 13:31). The Fourth Gospel equates "glorification" with "being lifted up" on the cross, or being in a position between ascent and descent—in Shinran's terms, between *ōsō* and *gensō*. After the presentation of the New Commandment, John proceeds to the promise of sending

---

[18] Rudolf Bultmann, *Theology of the New Testament*, vol. 2 (New York: Charles Scribner's Sons, 1955), chs. 2, 3.

the Counselor, the Holy Spirit, the spirit of truth (14:17) who will administer love and peace (14:21,27).

Finally the realization of *metanoia* is a resurrection experience. Tanabe frequently refers to resurrection throughout his *Philosophy as Metanoetics*.[19] *Metanoia* takes place, he says, "by abandoning oneself through resignation and by the submissive awareness of having been restored to life while dying to oneself."[20] Tanabe's concept of *metanoia* is most clearly manifested in his "negation-*qua*-affirmation," which appears in the Christian gospel as the crucifixion-resurrection event.

---

[19] See references in the index, PM, 312.
[20] PM, 49.

Metanoetics and the Encounter among Religions: A Brief Reflection

Quentin QUESNELL

IN his treatment of interreligious dialogue, Fredericks suggests that a philosophy of metanoetics could provide the key to how Christian theology might face up to the reality of other world religions. He lists three typical models of Christian response to world religions (syncretism, inclusivism, exclusivism), indicates the defects of each, and then concretely reflects on how each of them might be improved by adopting the point of view of philosophy as metanoetics.

A central issue is the elimination of exclusivism. For this, Fredericks demands a certain difficult combination of qualities in the dialogue partners: a readiness to let contradictions remain, a commitment to the symbols of one's own tradition, but a commitment which is without fanaticism. This commitment will be compatible with "a revision of the absolute claims of our particular religious traditions," a readiness to modify or surrender details of religious symbols which connote exclusivism. He mentions "the Kingdom of God" and "creation out of nothing," but his words would apply as well to any literal understandings of Amida Buddha, the Pure Land, or the efficacy of the Nembutsu.

Fredericks knows the suggestion is not new. It preceded the current dialogue with Buddhists and the subtleties of Tanabe and the Kyoto School. It is the approach of Liberal Theology, even demythologization. And while that is one Christian position, it will hardly solve the problem of dialogue if it merely brings liberal, demythologizing Christians together with Buddhists who are liberal and who demythologize.

This becomes clear when Fredericks writes of a future common religion that may arise among those Buddhists and those Christians who already feel solidarity with their dialogue-partners. If some Christians and some Buddhists are drawn to this future union, while the majority of each religious body remain untouched, the result will not be dialogue between two religions but the creation of a third religion, not recognized as authentic by either of the original two.

Some of the ambiguity may lie in Fredericks's conviction that "fundamentalisms of any sort are ruled out as possible candidates for an authentic religious subjectivity." Ruled out? If fundamentalism means taking the symbols literally, surely many heroes of sanctity in all traditions have demonstrated its compatibility with authentic religious subjectivity. Being trapped in error or in ignorance does not rule out authenticity. Fundamentalism is overcome through education. The needed conversion is not religious but intellectual.

There is something of the same problem with Fredericks's warnings against fanaticism. Is not every martyr a fanatic, holding a single doctrine more precious than life itself? Would it really promote interfaith understanding and dialogue to forget about those religious heroes of the past? Or would some of the best in each tradition be lost in the process?

Mitchell, also writing as a Christian theologian, incorporates metanoetics into his Christian theology of spirituality, explaining in metanoetical categories the progress of the person toward God. He uses Tanabe in order to help Christian readers understand their own lives by acquiring another perspective on their spiritual growth experiences.

In the second half of his article he manages to describe in Tanabe's terms the whole Christian reality of death, resurrection, and salvation, including the reality of the Church. But, though he is describing Christianity, he sees that others can equally well use Tanabe's language to describe their own religious institutions. This is possible because Mitchell grants Tanabe's point that the Christian theologian, the Buddhist, the psychologist and the philosopher all deal with the same phenomenological reality of spiritual growth.

Again some questions arise. Is this not a reaching for a least common denominator, after the manner of the syncretism against which Fredericks warned us? Or how does it differ from

Fredericks's "inclusivism," if it says the Buddhists are doing essentially the same things as the Christians? If they are, why *not* call them "anonymous Christians"?

In other words, when it seems most clear to us that some other tradition is really engaged at a deep level in exactly what our own is, should we congratulate ourselves that now at last we have understood the other? Or should we precisely then most suspect that we may be missing the other's point? The question is methodological. It cannot be solved by inspecting data or examining concrete instances.

But there is another risk. One of Tanabe's main points is that what he is doing is philosophy and no more. He does not admit any reality beyond and behind the transformation experience — neither Mitchell's Christ or Spirit, nor Shin's Amida Buddha. Tanabe explicitly renounces as mythologies all theological interpretations of religious conversion. For him such myths serve no useful purpose. If that is literally true, then the religious traditions themselves serve no useful purpose. To overcome this problem, Mitchell at every point adds explicitly or implicitly: "But I mean more than that; I even experience more than that; or at least as a Christian I must interpret experience as more than that." And of course believing Buddhists or Muslims or Jews say and must say the same.

But the real problem is that Mitchell and Fredericks may both be deceived, for Tanabe's route may inexorably lead to holding to the psychological phenomena, explaining these purely philosophically, while abandoning every particular revelation. No religious tradition will be comfortable going that route, since it is the road to complete secularization.

Yamashita is saying that anything good in Tanabe's account already existed and can be found in the Christian bible. He gives such instances as Other-power, conversion, or repentance. This is very useful for explaining to Buddhists how near to them is much of Christian biblical thought. It is also useful for showing Christians how some Buddhist ideas, apparently so strange and remote, simply discuss in new terms certain realities they have been familiar with all their lives. But again, how is this eagerness to remove the strangeness of the other methodologically different from what Fredericks called "inclusivism"?

The fact that Yamashita can point out biblical parallels to what Tanabe describes merely underlines the fact that Tanabe does a good job of describing the phenomena in a way which various religious traditions can recognize as competent. It adds no information which might help confirm either the biblical tradition or the Tanabe analysis.

To touch the most basic issue, the Christian biblical tradition may say with Tanabe that one must go beyond philosophy. So do all religious traditions. That is their nature. What the religious traditions, including the biblical, do not ordinarily say is that one is to go beyond philosophy *and remain philosophical*, limiting one's judgment to what one has observed.

The religions say there must also be faith. Tanabe uses the word, but not as they do. The religions call for faith (whether as intellectual assent or as simple trust) in something definite, something real that is not merely part of ourselves, not merely called up from our own inner depths. Their faith is not merely a name to cover our experience, but a real reference to Another. They do not simply feel *as if* they were helped by another; they affirm that they really are helped, and it is important to them that this is true.

William James long ago described this in psychological terms, suggesting that a person is saved by an inner-power which never goes into action, unless the person thinks of it as an outer-power. But the religions do not say, one's own inner-power must be conceived as if it were an outer-power. They say, what comes and saves *is* the power of another. That is very different from Tanabe's ultimate analysis. When the religions dialogue with one another, they ask, "Are we saved by Other-power X or by Other-power Y?" Or "Is Other-power Y another name for Other-power X?" They are not usually willing to say, "We are basically just putting different names on one purely human phenomenon."

It is hard to find the right categories to describe the goals of interfaith dialogue. We may be less than sure of what we hope for. But we do know what we are experiencing in the midst of the dialogue, and perhaps we can describe that accurately.

It seems to me that any sincere commitment to the symbols of one's own religion implies at least as much exclusivism as is contained in the judgment "These things are true." Commitment also implies "inclusivism" to the following extent: that if one accepts one coherent set of symbols as a true and right account of the whole with which religion deals, then one will of course try to explain all other successfully functioning religions as somehow fitting under those symbols.

Does this leave any room for authentic and respectful pluralism? It does when one adds to it the further realization that what is true of one's own commitment is true of others' commitments as well. Their theologies too are all-encompassing explanations of reality, so they are practicing inclusivism in my regard. They define me in their theology in terms of their symbols, as I define them in terms of mine. We simply try to propose honestly to one another the world-picture that results. What new values, inspirations and motivations our account or theirs may give rise to in the souls of the participants is beyond our ability to predict.

This pluralism abandons neither faith nor the symbols of faith. It merely adds to them the realization that every human statement and understanding (even of a divine revelation) is imperfect and incomplete in ways which at any given moment we cannot know.

PART THREE

Philosophy

The Logic of Species
and the Pursuit of True Reality

KAWAMURA Eiko

SCIENCE AND RELIGION

IT is often said that ours is an age of irreligion, an age that puts science and technology above all else. The current tendency to one-sided scientific development poses a threat to true humanity, reducing people as it does to little more than cogs in a great technological machine.

To be sure, modern technology has enriched human life in any number of ways. Medical science, for example, has increased the human lifespan by many years, and electric appliances have eliminated hours of labor from the round of daily household chores. But if we ignore the many and difficult problems associated with the advance of science, we risk not only forfeiting its benefits but even working ruination on humanity and the natural environment.

In this paper I would like to consider some of the implications of these problems from the perspective of Tanabe's "logic of species as the dialectic of absolute mediation," particularly as it is transformed to the religious dimension through the philosophy of metanoetics.

MODERN SCIENCE AND TECHNOLOGY

Modern science and technology has brought countless problems in its wake: radioactive contamination caused by the testing of nuclear weapons and mishaps at nuclear power plants; pollution of the air through automobile exhaust and factory emissions; poisoning from the leakage of industrial waste; social and moral confusion brought about by the development of artificial intelligence, robotics, and other technological innovations; and so forth. Meantime, modern medical science has raised its own host of complex ethical issues with the introduction of techniques for gene splicing, organ transplants, and so on. If these questions are not addressed seriously, we may well land in a confusion that could spell the eventual destruction of the human race.

COSMIC ANXIETY AND TRUE FREEDOM

Consciously or unconsciously, all of us who inhabit the contemporary world carry within us a great anxiety for the future of mankind. It is an anxiety that falls outside the various definitions provided by Paul Tillich in his *The Courage to Be* or the existential anxiety that Kierkegaard takes up in *The Concept of Dread*. It is not even encompassed by the metaphysical anxiety that Heidegger discusses in *What is Metaphysics?* — the *Grundstimmung* that makes its presence felt during periods of ennui, thoroughly negating our sense of wholeness in the world.

This "cosmic anxiety" lurking within us seems to have little direct connection with the relationship between human beings and the transcendent. It is a result of our refusing to face issues on the horizontal dimension that are unrelated to the transcendent. In short, it seems to be no more than the form of anxiety peculiar to the extraordinary scientific and technological development of our age. At the same time, it has the potential of playing a role equal to anxiety of the vertical dimension, if — by way of Tanabe's logic of absolute mediation — it can be shown to lead to true freedom and true reality (though the same anxiety could also, of course, lead to the destruction of these very things).

Cosmic anxiety may well be for us, in this age of extreme scientific and technological development, the vehicle of negative mediation to true freedom and reality, like the consciousness of sin in Christianity, the self-awareness of absolute nothingness in Nishida's philosophy, or the sense of deep guilt in Pure Land Buddhism. As we shall see presently, cosmic anxiety does not arise directly from the dimension of self-pursuit or inner self-reflection, but from the horizontal dimension. As a horizontal anxiety, it is neither the same as vertical anxiety nor entirely separate from it. In other words, we in the modern world have to come to grips seriously with both the vertical and horizontal dimensions of the problems resulting from modern science and technology. Refusal to do so is to put both ourselves and the world at risk. And if there is any doubt about the gravity of the risk we are currently running, one needs only look at the current state of experiments in genetic manipulation which has made possible human-animal hybrids, the *in vitro* fertilization of persons with high IQ's, the changes in weather due to the greenhouse effect, etc.

There are two ways to face our cosmic anxiety: one vertical approach and one horizontal. The former leads us to the field where self and the transcendent are related as a "self-identity of absolute contradictories." In this approach the confrontation with the problems of modern science is more religious than ethical (here *vertical* indicates the dimension dealing with the relationship between self and the transcendent, and *religious* indicates the mode of dealing with horizontal dimension problems that involves the relationship between the transcendent and the self which has experienced the great death). The horizontal approach, in contrast, is one that makes use of the activities of everyday life as ways of mediation. Things like scientific and academic research, ethical and artistic pursuits, and ordinary work are made mediating elements. In this approach the relationship between self and the transcendent is set aside as it were until reason has undergone a metanoesis. In that sense the horizontal approach leaves out the relationship between self and the transcendent. Hence the confrontation with the problems of modern science takes on a more ethical aspect (*ethical* here indicates the way of confrontation of the person who is defined not by absolute but by historical actuality).

The vertical approach and the horizontal approach share the common goal of overcoming cosmic anxiety through the attainment of that absolute openness where all things are as they are (自然法爾). The vertical approach is represented by Nishida's philosophy, whose starting points are "pure experience,"[1] which develops into "intellectual intuition," and "place," which takes form as "dialectical universality" and ultimately attains to the logic of absolutely contradictory self-identity between self and the transcen-

---

[1] For Nishida, "pure experience" refers to the strict integration of consciousness and primordial experience at a dimension preceding the separation of subject and object and the disjunction of intellect, feeling, and will. Here humanity, nature, and the transcendent are in a state comparable to a sphere of infinite circumference or a circle every point of which is the center. This state of being, a state of absolute openness, is called by Nishida the "place of absolute nothingness," because everything is non-substantial and everything can become the true self through the absolute negation of self.

dent, between the relative and the absolute (理事). Tanabe's philosophy represents the horizontal approach, where each intellectual pursuit, each art, each occupation that people engage in has the potential of becoming the mediation to true reality.

Every occupation or pursuit is associated with one of three dimensions: humanity, nature (the world), and the transcendent. When a sincere attempt is made to pursue true reality in the dimension associated with one's chosen place, one becomes increasingly aware that that place is associated with the other two dimensions as well. This enables the conversion of human reason through the thoroughgoing pursuit of the path chosen by each individual. Tanabe, for example, became aware in an absolutely negative and subjective manner of the self-negative movement of scientific thought through his study of mathematics and the natural sciences, and developed this awareness into his philosophy of "knowledge-*sive*- act." Tanabe, in other words, advanced through "the logic of species as the logic of absolute mediation" to the philosophy of metanoetics.[2]

THE LOGIC OF PLACE AND THE LOGIC OF SPECIES

The vertical approach aims at the oneness of humanity, nature, and the transcendent, and then looks at all anew from the perspective of their realized unity, i.e. the place of absolute nothingness.

Nishida's philosophy has its beginnings in the latter part of this approach, the section dealing with unification. Tanabe's philosophy has a superficial resemblance to the first element, but differs in that his logic of species views mediation as consisting not of the pursuit of self, but of thoroughgoing involvement with one's chosen place or occupation. Human beings, in other words, concern themselves with a certain place of study or work, and, through profound inquiry into that place, ultimately integrate the three dimensions of humanity, nature, and the transcendent, so that true reality can make its appearance. When one becomes aware of this fact, as Takeuchi Yoshinori notes,[3] philosophy as metanoetics is manifested and the bounds of speculation and theory are transcended. Tanabe's philosophy thus recognizes natural

---

[2] THZ 7:255.
[3] See ZMK, 196ff.

science, scientific logic, ethics, art, and various occupations as potential ways of mediation, and attains to a metanoetics through
the "logic of species as the dialectic of absolute mediation."[4] In
this case the word *mediation* indicates self-negation,[5] so that "absolute mediation" means absolute self-negation. Moreover, the eternity in which absolute mediation is realized is absolute nothingness
functioning as a "conversion principle" whereby self-negation is
transformed into self-affirmation.[6]

For Tanabe, the scientist who carries out absolute negation
comes in the end to a subjective awareness of the element of
self-negation inherent in science. This develops into the philosophy
of "knowledge-*sive*-act,"[7] which in turn is transformed into a sense
of individual sin and collective (or national) guilt. Metanoetics
opens to the religious dimension when the unification of human
beings, nature, and the transcendent is realized and true reality
appears.

The problems posed by modern science with which we began
provide an entirely new set of negative motivations for the attainment of oneness. Nishida's approach, which has its starting point
in unification through the pursuit of self, is always available as
an immutable, universal way. Each age, however, has its own
particular problems that cry out for attention and offer a way to
the attainment of true reality. None of us can avoid dealing with
the world. Even those who achieve to the universal unification
taught by Nishida must eventually confront the problems of the
age they live in. Similarly, those who take Tanabe's way are im-
pelled by the absolute dialectic inherent in the logic of species to
seek unity among humanity, nature, and the transcendent, however unrelated they may at first appear to be.

In this way the vertical and horizontal approaches are both
concerned with the integration of humanity, nature, and the transcendent. In other words, both approaches necessarily have a point
of mutual contact in the integration of these three dimensions.
Moreover, we always find outselves at a crossroads of the vertical
and horizontal approaches. All human beings, as Kierkegaard says,
are composed of the finite and the infinite, of the necessary and

---

[4] THZ 6:343.
[5] THZ 6:304, 480.
[6] THZ 7:117.

the possible, of the mutable and the eternal, of the relative and the absolute; and it is therefore impossible to limit oneself to either the vertical or the horizontal dimension.

The vertical approach, where the problems raised by science and technology are dealt with from the perspective of a new integration rising from the "thinking of no-thinking,"[8] is the way of religion. The horizontal approach, where the problems raised by science and technology serve as a form of negative mediation leading to the integration of humanity, nature, and the transcendent, is the way of the philosophy of metanoetics as manifested through the academic and occupational pursuits of life.

For true reality to be attained, both approaches must strive to come together through confronting the problems peculiar to one's age—each in its own way. In the horizontal approach one tries to achieve integration through negative mediation, as in one's occupation or place of study. In the vertical approach one tries to attain immediate integration through the mediation of absolute nothingness. It is vitally important in this approach to experience self-awareness of the self (that is, the self sees the self in itself) as simultaneously a self-awareness of the world (that is, the world, through self-negation, becomes the individual), and vice versa.

Tanabe lived the majority of his life the years preceding World War II, a time when the principal negative mediation was the issue of nationalism. Tanabe felt that Japan, in its fierce competition to secure a place for itself in the modern world, had to adopt an ethic of "being-*qua*-duty" based on a premise of "duty-*qua*-being." This was accordingly the central issue in his thought.[9] While he did see science and ethics as dialectical ways of negative mediation that lead to true reality, he viewed them as a parallel means for understanding the logic of being of the state. This was how he made use of quantum theory, for example.

Applying Tanabe's thought to the situation in our own age, however, impels us rather to the ethical issues arising from science and technology. When we undertake a thoroughgoing search for a new ethics capable of resolving not only existential, ontological, and metaphysical anxiety but cosmological anxiety as well, we are

---

[7] THZ 5:213.

[8] Cf. the 坐禅箴 ("Admonitions for Zazen") chapter of Dōgen's *Shōbōgenzō*.

[9] THZ 7:98.

led to an "absolute conversion" through "the logic of species as the dialectic of absolute mediation," and transcend the dimension of speculation through our metanoetics. As mentioned above, the term "mediation" refers to self-negation, and absolute mediation is, as dialectic, the principle of self-awareness.

A word should be added about the distinct meanings the notion of "self-awareness" had for Tanabe and Nishida. For Nishida, self-awareness means that the self-awareness of self and the self-awareness of the world form a self-identity of absolute contradictories, achieved in the absolute death of each individual in the place of absolute nothingness. The "place of absolute nothingness" is a mode of being that he was fond of likening to a sphere whose center is everywhere, where "form is emptiness and emptiness is form" (色即是空, 空即是色). In Tanabe's philosophy, absolute mediation is the pivot of self-awareness. That is, when one is engaged in a particular occupation or academic pursuit and penetrates to the bottom of what one is doing to draw close to true reality, the self-negative internal movement of one's realm of activity acts as a mediator that unfolds, through absolute negation, into subjectivity. Through metanoetics, this becomes a philosophy of "knowledge-*sive*-act," and finally attains to the religious dimension.

THE RELATIONSHIP BETWEEN DIMENSIONS

WHEN THE VERTICAL DIMENSION CROSSES THE HORIZONTAL

When the vertical dimension crosses the horizontal, the resultant relationship is of the greatest importance. Nishida's philosophy stresses the vertical orientation, following the path outlined in the "Ten Oxherding Pictures"[10] of the Zen priest Kakuan. There one seeks true reality through absolute death, without reliance on the mediation of matter or being. But even such a one cannot remain indifferent to problems arising at the horizontal dimension

---

[10] Cf. D. T. Suzuki, *Manual of Zen Buddhism* (New York: Grove Press, 1960). The ten pictures are titled as follows: 1. Searching for the Ox; 2. Seeing the Traces; 3. Seeing the Ox; 4. Catching the Ox; 5. Herding the Ox; 6. Coming Home on the Ox's Back; 7. Ox Forgotten, Leaving the Man Alone; 8. The Ox and the Man Both Gone Out of Sight; 9. Returning to the Origin, Back to the Source; 10. Entering the City with Bliss-Bestowing Hands.

(i.e., science and technology) insofar as living in the world implies living at a crossroads of two.

Those on the vertical path who attempt to ignore the problems of the horizontal dimension come to a halt—as the Zen saying has it—at the top of a hundred-foot pole, refusing to leap free and find new life. Their position corresponds to the seventh stage in the "Ten Oxherding Pictures," which represents a state of ecstasy where the individual has not yet thoroughly died to the world. It is possible at this stage to retain one's attachments to wealth and political power, to display hypocrisy, self-righteousness, and hedonism.

Those who take the vertical path strive to maintain a state of unobstructed absolute openness. This fact can provide inspiration and guidance for those experiencing difficulty on the horizontal path.

WHEN THE HORIZONTAL DIMENSION CROSSES THE VERTICAL

The crossing of the vertical dimension by the horizontal is the situation addressed by Tanabe's logic of species, where the academic and occupational pursuits of daily life become ways of mediation leading to a metanoetic philosophy. This is described in the parable of "The Poor Son of the Rich Man" in the *Lotus Sūtra*.[11] It begins not with the self-negation of the world or the death of self, but with the acceptance of the world's existence and of occupational or academic pursuits which serve as a way of mediation opening the way (consciously or unconsciously) to true reality. In the horizontal approach the relationship between self and the transcendent is not taken into consideration, and there is usually no conscious undertaking of religious discipline.

In Nishida's philosophy, pure experience is the starting point. Pure experience becomes self-aware with the insight that "pure experience is the only reality," and finally develops into philosophy with the awakening of the desire to explain everything on the basis of this insight. In other words, for Nishida the primordial religious fact of pure experience opens, widens, and deepens to the philosophical dimension through individual self-awareness, which is at the same time the world's awareness of itself. Nishida

---

[11] See 大乗仏典 *[Mahāyāna Canon]*, ed. by Nagao Gadjin and Kajiyama Yū-ichi (Tokyo: Chūōkōron-sha, 1984), 4/1, 123ff.

was thus able to explain, on the basis of his logic of absolute nothingness, such concepts as the nonexistence of absolute time and absolute space as posited in Einstein's theory of relativity, or the non-absoluteness of the law of causality as theorized in Bohr and Heisenberg's quantum mechanics.

Tanabe's view is that the antinomy and methodical contradiction inherent in scientific systems give rise to a negative movement within science itself.[12] A subjective awareness of this fact grows in scientists, and develops into philosophy through the dialectics of absolute mediation. This outlook can not be seen in Heidegger's philosophy,[13] but it can be clearly discerned in the thought of C. F. von Weizsäcker,[14] his uncle V. von Weizsäcker,[15] and Whitehead,[16] all of them natural scientists and / or mathematicians in addition to being philosophers. With such support, Tanabe's view of the relationship between science and philosophy has come to seem more obvious than when it was first proposed.

The supreme desire of the human mind is to understand what in principle lies beyond its grasp (Kierkegaard).[17] In this sense, science cannot but develop into philosophy, just as love must grow from selfishness to non-egoism. We find this same

---

[12] THZ 5:213.

[13] Heidegger attempted to resolve the problem of technology by returning it to its roots in philosophy, then reconstructing it more in the direction of art (in Greek, "technology" and "art" have the same etymological root).

[14] See C. F. von Weizsäcker, *Der Garten des Menschlichen* (Munich: Hanser, 1978).

[15] See V. von Weizsäcker, *Gestaltkreis* (Stuttgart: George Thieme, 1950).

[16] See A. N. Whitehead, *Process and Reality* (London: Collier-Macmillan, 1978).

[17] The pre-Socratics considered nature to be preeminent, with the transcendent and the human dimensions subordinate to nature and integrated by it. From the time of Socrates until the end of the classic age the human dimension was considered supreme, integrating the other two dimensions within it. In the Middle Ages this position was attributed to God, the transcendent.

The humanism that arose in early Renaissance Italy recognized only the human dimension, ignoring the other two. With the development of natural science in the seventeenth century the natural dimension was emphasized to the exclusion of the others, and following the reformation God came to have a narrow, independent existence. Whenever any of these three dimensions takes on independence, it inevitably falls into nihilism. This was expressed by Jean Paul Friedrich Richter (1763-1825) in the form of a dream in a novel, and by

movement in Kant's thought. The dialectic of the "critique of pure reason" shows the need to recognize, through a logic of shadows, the superiority of practical reason over pure reason. From there human understanding must progress to the "critique of practical reason," as Tanabe himself also says.

In Nishida's philosophy, everything—including science and technology—is defined by absolute nothingness. Science and technology are seen to be far removed from pure experience and yet to consist of the abstraction (or noetic objectification) of pure experience. Tanabe, in contrast, sees science as leading to philosophy through an internal self-negating element. The concerned researcher becomes subjectively aware, through absolute negation, of this movement by means of the antinomy[18] and self-contradiction[19] inherent in science, and as this awareness increases it causes a turn to philosophy.

A sense of the oneness of humanity, nature, and the transcendent has, of course, been present in philosophy up until the time of the Italian Renaissance at the beginning of the modern age. But once civilization has shut itself up in a single dimension, the approach to true reality requires breaking through to absolute openness (where one dimension exists in unity with the other two) by making use of the self-negating element inherent in all three dimensions.

Nishida's philosophy addresses the issue of why human beings cannot confine themselves to the dimension of the transcendent in the quest for true reality. Self-awareness in Nishida's philosophy

---

Nietzsche in his philosophical prophecy.

The everyday world in which we live consists of the integration of humanity, nature, and the transcendent. Even if we are concerned with only one area the other two inevitably become relevant when we attempt to attain true reality, as reality cannot be experienced in any of these three dimensions alone.

[18] The antinomy in Kant's *Critique of Pure Reason* provides a good example of this.

[19] Consider, for example, modern physics's awareness of the interrelatedness of observer and observed, as in the quantum which changes position the instant it is illuminated for the sake of observation. Moreover, as Murakami Yōichirō 村上陽一郎 points out in his 非日常性の意味と構造 *[The Meaning and Structure of the Non-Everyday]* (Tokyo: Kaimei, 1984), "Science itself has been supported by enormous prejudices, biases, and value judgments" (38). Also relevant is the subjectivity recognized in animals and plants. See von Weizsäcker, *Gestaltkreis*.

is not only one's own awareness but also the world's awareness. That is, in self-awareness self and world are absolute contradictories formed into a single self-identity. In the same way, existence in "absolute openness" must needs confront the problems of the horizontal dimension.

The question why it is that one cannot confine oneself to the world of nature while trying to attain true reality is taken up by V. von Weizsäcker (who recognizes subjectivity in animals and plants), by Whitehead (who regards not only animals and plants but also inorganic substances as actual entities), and Tanabe.

Nor can a seeker of the truth remain within the human dimension. Art, as we see in the case of a Goethe or a Bashō, attests to this fact. The artistic masterpiece achieves absolute openness as an integration of the three dimensions, independently of whether the artist happens to be conscious of it or not. Of course, the possibility always exists that the follower of the horizontal path might, in the process of breaking through from the horizontal to the vertical dimension, form attachments to wealth and power. This is liable to happen particularly when one does not engage in true metanoetics through the death and resurrection of human reason. By the same token, one who follows the vertical path runs the risk of forgetting the suffering of others (不化衆生) in the drive to enlightenment (上求菩提). Both of these paths are fundamentally one and the same, the inside and outside of the same event. But the horizontal way, as the way of absolute mediation, offers a means of correcting arrogance, falsehood, and hypocrisy.

TRUE REALITY

As noted earlier, we human beings dwell at the crossroads of the vertical and horizontal dimensions. How, from this position, are we to countenance the problems that the extraordinary development of modern science and technology throw up at us? The search for true reality and the confrontation with the problems of the modern world seem to be mutually exclusive — if not outright contradictory — undertakings.

In fact, true reality is absolute openness, manifesting itself as the integration of humanity, nature, and the transcendent in confrontation with the problems of the world at the crossroads of the vertical and horizontal dimensions. As explained, there are two paths to the openness leading to true reality. One is the way of integration from the vertical dimension towards the horizontal; the other, the approach from the horizontal dimension through the dialectic of absolute mediation towards philosophy as metanoetics. Obviously, each path runs its own dangers. The follower of the vertical path must guard against fleeing the confrontation and reintegration demanded by the problems of the horizontal dimension. The follower of the horizontal approach must avoid a metanoetics based on an incomplete death and resurrection.

With these warnings in mind, we must address the problems of the modern world in all their global implications so that we can come to a contemporary understanding of absolute openness appropriate to the twenty-first century. Different ages understand true reality in different ways and express what they have understood in different terms. In Nishida's philosophy true reality is the experience in which the absolutely contradictory self-identity of the one and the many becomes manifest through active intuition. In Tanabe's philosophy, true reality is viewed as the realm manifested through philosophy as metanoetics, which in turn develops from the "logic of species as the dialectic of absolute mediation" based on active self-awareness.

In conclusion, then, it seems clear that true reality is attainable not only through a logic of place based on absolute nothingness, but also through a logic of species, also based on absolute nothingness. Surely these two ways differ for us who live at the crossings of the ways, but only as differing ways of manifesting the same true reality. The logic of place attempts to reveal reality through the relationship between self and the transcendent; the logic of species attempts to express it from the point of view of mediation. Both approaches are not only inseparable but mutually indispensable, as both manifest the same reality from different dimensions. In the age of science and technology the importance of the logic of species cannot be overemphasized. It is for each era, however, to discover the form taken by the integration of the two approaches when they cross in the absolute openness of the place of absolute nothingness.

Metanoetics and the Crisis of Reason: Tanabe, Nishida, and Contemporary Philosophy

John C. Maraldo

TANABE Hajime died in 1962, yet he remains a living philosopher, alive not only in the hearts and words of many
contributors to this volume, but also in the discourse of
many contemporary philosophers who have never heard of him.
For he shares a major concern with them: the crisis of reason,
our greatest critical faculty. But he lives in them in a surreptitious
way, as a sometimes deeply repressed demand to bring their philosophical problems in touch with their personal lives. My concern
here is to bring Tanabe into an engagement with contemporary
philosophy. And since the predominant form of philosophical engagement on Anglo-American soil is challenge and response, it is
appropriate that Tanabe's philosophy be presented as a challenge,
in order to see what counter-challenges might be forthcoming. I
focus first on the crisis of reason in contemporary philosophy and
Tanabe's version of it, which he calls "absolute critique." I consider
next some analogues to Tanabe's resolution of the problem he
faced, and then some possible counter-challenges from the viewpoint of contemporary philosophy. Finally I challenge Tanabe's
implicit critique of his former mentor and older colleague, Nishida
Kitarō, in order to relocate his philosophy in the political context
of his time.

TANABE'S ABSOLUTE CRITIQUE AND THE CRISIS OF REASON

Tanabe's absolute critique was precipitated by a personal crisis
that found a personal but not private solution. The crisis was
the inability of reason to resolve the conflict between care for
his compatriots and criticism of an oppressive government during

World War II. Any act of overt criticism could, Tanabe believed, exacerbate the oppression and make one an accomplice instead of a reformer. Tanabe's solution was not to throw up his hands in despair but to open his heart and surrender to the compassion of Other-power. The solution was intensely personal, but because he saw every genuine philosophical problem as affecting the individual person, his solution was also a universal model. It took concrete form not only in the space of Tanabe's mind, but also in a public work, a book written in the wartime crossfire of traditions, Japanese and Western. There are two things to note about its philosophical significance: it implies that resolutions of philosophical problems require personal transformation; and it suggests that such transformation, in the form of self-surrender, is ethically potent. One's impotence in the face of severe personal and ethical crisis is transformed into the power to change people and society. Even though most philosophers still invoke the Socratic dicta that the unexamined life is not worth living, and that one must know oneself, it is extremely uncommon today for a philosopher to speak of self-transformation, if not of social transformation.

But what prevents this personal philosophy of self-surrender to "Other-power" from becoming merely an esoteric exercise or an appeal to convert to a particular brand of religion? The point of this question is blunted as soon as the reader of Tanabe's work recognizes two of its features: it gestures the surrender or letting-go of reason only after coming to grips with the crisis of reason, and it gestures in the direction of experiences not confined to traditional philosophy, much less the Japanese Pure Land tradition. Tanabe chose the term *metanoetics* as a critique of philosophy, a "going beyond" noesis or philosophy based upon reason and practiced as the discipline of reason. His absolute critique is a critique of reason that results in the transformation of reason.

There are several ways to understand the crisis of reason. One way is to notice cultural rifts in the concept of reason. It is reputedly reason that we humans have in common; it is reason that allows us to understand that others have views different from our own and that therefore our own views are perspectival and limited by what I, or the culture I belong to, understands to be reasonable and what not. We posit reason in common, and it reveals our differences, even differences about the extent of reason. Whatever its extent, Tanabe means to take it as far as it will go.

Another way is to view reason historically within the tradition that has most emphasized it. This was Husserl's way. In modern times the model for reason became the natural sciences and their methods of investigation. But the natural sciences cannot answer the "big questions" of the meaning of life and death, or of the origin and nature of good and evil. As the categories of the natural sciences spread throughout the world, so did a sense of meaninglessness, of nihilism. The modern ideal of reason had lost its Socratic moorings in personal examination and had become an impersonal investigation that was impotent in the face of the irrationalities and cruelties of human history. In lectures delivered in 1939, Tanabe, too, had emphasized that history involves problems that cannot be treated impersonally like questions of engineering.[1] Husserl ended by affirming the necessity of faith in reason and its infinite task of humanization.[2] Tanabe, on the other hand, proposed that we take reason to its limits and then be ready to give it up, indeed to give ourselves up.

Martin Heidegger also understood the crisis of reason historically within Western tradition. The history of *logos*, of reason, has culminated in a *Technik* or technological drive that seeks to expose all things to control and mastery. No space is left for leaving things hidden, mysterious, outside human control. This same drive has exposed humankind to unfathomable environmental atrocities. Technological reason cannot provide the solution to the immense problem that it itself has become. To use the words of Tanabe, it is the ultimate collective *jiriki* 自力, the total presumption of self-power. Heidegger, in his middle years, proposed the gestures of openness, letting-go, and simply waiting as antidotes; later he seemed to grow more impatient, and said (in his famous *Spiegel* interview) that Zen was not the answer, but that we must wait for a god. Tanabe's god was not even Amida, but absolute nothingness. And we do not passively wait for it; it breaks upon us just when we have exerted reason to its limits.

---

[1] See his 歴史的現実 ["Historical Reality"], THZ 8:117-69.

[2] These themes are most explicit in Husserl's work, *The Crisis of European Sciences and Transcendental Phenomenology* (Evanston: Northwestern University Press, 1970), especially 391.

The crisis of reason also raises the possibility of the end of philosophy. Heidegger thought of the end of philosophy as the culmination of metaphysics, of the search for truth solely in the *logos* (the reasoned statement) of what is; but this culmination is a frustration, not a fulfillment, of that search, because reasoned statements about what is inevitably leave out the reason we look for reasons.[3] That has simply been our historical destiny, and it is so pervasive that the very critique of metaphysics or traditional philosophy must rely upon reasoned assertions. (We ask, for example, "*Why* was the search necessarily incomplete"? And we answer, "Because . . . .") Jacques Derrida, who has both extended and broken off Heidegger's "destruction of metaphysics," used the term "disruption" for the event of recognizing that the critique must employ the terms and methods under attack. Not only is the history of philosophy disrupted when the critique of the tradition begins; the critique itself is disrupted because it is bound to repeat traditional moves.[4] Even Derrida's brilliant analysis of this circle is a logical exercise ("the critique is disrupted *because* . . . "). But then, why shouldn't it be? Are we to abandon reason just when we begin to recognize its boundaries? Tanabe's metanoetics is a disruption of reason that explicitly demands not its removal but its transformation by a power removed from it, never under its sway. It demands a disruption of the self, the center of the power to reason, that does not leave the self as it was, that is not its repetition. Is this not a totally unreasonable demand?

Heidegger's and Derrida's recognition of the historicity of reason has a parallel in the effort of critical theorists like Jürgen Habermas and Karl Otto Apel, who criticize the notions that reason is transhistorical and that knowledge is disinterested, affirming rather a model of reason as communication. Reasoned discourse is the way to address practical social problems, and the practice of reasoned discourse requires that we acknowledge the plurality

---

[3] This is my extrapolation from points Heidegger makes in "The End of Philosophy and the Task of Thinking," in *On Time and Being* (New York: Harper and Row, 1972), 56; and in *Der Satz vom Grund* (Pfullingen: Neske, 1957), 63-75.

[4] This is my paraphrase of Derrida's point in "Structure, Sign and Play," *Writing and Difference* (Chicago: University of Chicago Press, 1978), 280. Derrida does not explicitly address the issue of reason in that text, but he does mention Heidegger's destruction of metaphysics and analyze structuralism, a type of discourse or *logos*.

of our interests and norms as well as the universality of some interest and some ability that brings us together to talk. The model is already inherent in our very invocation "we," a community or communities in dialogue. It is critical of reasons, but does not do away with reason; one cannot argue against reason without employing it in the very act of arguing. Similarly, neo-pragmatists like Richard Rorty define ideal rationality as the rule or practice of sane, reasonable conversation which does not necessarily follow pre-established criteria or even know what its goal is. Rorty directs his critique against the old (i.e., modern) paradigm of rationality that identifies it with the selfless pursuit of objective facts and responsibility toward nonhuman truth. He suggests as a replacement the humanist reign of tolerant persuasion and open discussion, and claims that he "would like to drop the idea that human beings are responsible to a nonhuman power [such as nature]."[5]

Such critiques of reason tie truth claims to people making and receiving them; they connect rational discourse to human subjects and stress the necessity of commitment. For none of the critics is reason a transpersonal power detached from particular subjects. Some would stress more than others the interdependence of truth and subjectivity. And most would emphasize community and communication, rather than individual subjectivity, as the locus of rationality. But all recognize the contribution of individual persons to rational discourse and therefore the political dimension of rationality—the dimension of persons speaking together. Neither the exercise nor the critique of reason is neutral for these philosophers. The positive role here assigned to personal commitment seems similar to Tanabe's metanoetic act; both call for self-transformation. But Tanabe's "action-faith-witness" does not arise from the will of the subject; it is not an act whereby I take a stand and commit myself. It is rather like a leap into something unknown that I give myself over to. Tanabe describes it in terms of obedience, surrender, submission, admission of powerlessness and impotence. A far cry from the practice of rational discourse! Does metanoetics make any sense?

The critiques of reason and traditional philosophy referred to above take the form of textual analysis and theoretical discus-

---

[5] Richard Rorty, "Science as Solidarity," in John Nelson et al., ed., *The Rhetoric of the Human Sciences* (Madison: University of Wisconsin Press, 1987), 45.

sion, but current interests do not end there. The formation of influential fields of applied philosophy with their focus on practical social issues, and the turn to "Eastern philosophies" for a wisdom based more directly on experience, are likewise critiques of reason, even when that word never appears. The move to connect philosophy with temporal concerns—the care of the environment, of the body, of each other—speaks against the legacy of impersonal, detached, eternal reason even when it is silent about that legacy. These tacit critiques loudly proclaim that the only future for philosophy is to let philosophical issues be personal issues, because the most important personal issues are philosophical ones. Tanabe's philosophy as *zange* 懺悔, as confession and not merely impersonal contemplation of past faults, would seem to be the next logical step. Metanoetics, however, enters as an absolute disruption of this current move as well. It comes from another shore, as it were, and its turn to the "real world" is a return (*gensō* 還相) to it from an act of transcendence that leaves the person behind. Philosophy as metanoetics is so radical that it requires *my* conversion, which is the death of me and the resurrection of a new self.

Yet another sweep of contemporary philosophical concerns reveals initial parallels with Tanabe's philosophy that are soon disrupted by the challenge of metanoetics. The death of the subject as a centered self-identity is foretold in Heidegger's analysis of the history of subjectivity, Derrida's account of the de-centered self, and Michel Foucault's attempt to represent voices other than those of the rational subject. Once again, however, metanoetics demands more than the premature notification of this demise, more even than the awareness that the writer too, as the analyst, lies on his deathbed. *Zange* is more than philosophy's "gigantic confession" that it cannot take in what is opposed to reason, more even than Derrida's personal confession of his own fragile self-consciousness in undertaking a critique of the limits of reason (a personal confession, incidentally, which soon slips from that of "I" to "he," that is, into the confession of some general subject).[6] Metanoetics demands not the death of the subject but *my* death and restoration. And restoration!

There are, then, two points that multiply the differences be-

---

[6] Jacques Derrida, "Cogito and the History of Madness," in *Writing and Difference*, 62, 31.

tween Tanabe's absolute critique and the critique of reason of these others. First, metanoetics is a disruption of reason, of the self-willing subject or ego, of self-identity, but it does not leave the self dead or impaired. It effects a resurrection and restoration not of the self as it was, but a self with a difference. Its negation or Great Nay is followed by an absolute affirmation of Great Compassion, compassion as the greatest value. This value, however, is grounded in nothingness, in the continual negation or emptying of being and of self-asserted values. Compassion in effect is not grounded in anything absolute (that is, in any thing, any being). It seems therefore a value acceptable to our nihilistic age. We understand it as an emotive capacity to feel with, suffer with, even if one feels powerless to change things. Tanabe seems to ask for more, for a recognition that we can do nothing more on our own, that the compassion is not ours to give but is being directed toward us who "suffer with." Compassion is the denial of my power, a surrender of my power and my interests, not to the other party but to something entirely other to both or all of us, to us and to them, a surrender to the Other of having interests and employing power. In comparison, Foucault's reminder that knowledge is inseparably linked to power, and Habermas's recognition that knowledge is always bound to human interests, remain within the confines of both noesis and "self-power." Meta-noesis calls for the practice of faith in and witness to Other-power. (The play on the word *power* is deliberate here; it works equally well in English and Japanese.)

Secondly, the death, denial, surrender, must actually be mine. Each of us must be able to say, as did Shinran, "Amida's vow is made for me alone." A confession that replaces me with some subject in general will not do. But in saying this, are we not slipping into an uncritical appeal to some traditional, even (to us) esoteric religion? Tanabe's absolute critique seems to have precedents only in religion and thus leaves itself open to suspicion even for the critics of reason today. It demands *my* conversion for the solution to problems both practical and conceptual. What madness is this? (To be sure, metanoetics is not religion as usually accepted; it is in fact an a/theism which is neither a theism nor an atheism in the usual sense of those terms. It is certainly a hard opiate to swallow for believers in a personal God, since the "Other" of Tanabe's "Other-power" is not a being one can confide in, pray to, expect anything from. But Tanabe's avowal of God as absolute nothingness, empty of any determination, can also be challenging to those who would define God as love and find God in other people. Unbelievers, on the other hand, who expect the only Other simply to be other humans, will balk at Tanabe's talk of an Absolute mediated by relative beings.)

Before we give way to the madness (non-rationality) of absolute nothingness, let us revisit the question of a reasonable critique of reason. Tanabe, like Kant, sees enlightened reason as self-critical, reflecting on and aware of its own bounds, criticizing itself as a safeguard against exceeding those bounds.[7] The familiar "antinomies" express those limits; they are contradictory but equally tenable positions whose truth cannot be decided by reason. For Tanabe the recognition of the bounds of reason is simply not enough. The self-critique of reason keeps us in line but forbids us from speaking with assurance about crucial matters, such as the reality of freedom, or of God—matters that are still today philosophically undecided. By leaving important matters perpetually open for debate, if not up for grabs, the exercise of self-critical reason forfeits an immense area of jurisdiction and mitigates its role as universal arbiter. Not only that, but this exercise of perpetually reflecting on reason's own limits engages in a kind of infinite regress: a critique of critique of critique . . . Today's critical theorists like Habermas and Apel take this perpetual self-criticism of reason as a positive task, but the necessary incompleteness of this task is at odds with reason's assigned role as universal arbiter of disputes. Even if all problems fall within rational discourse, some parties may refuse to reason. Consider situations such as the civil war in Lebanon, the conflict between the Palestinians and Israel, or the ideology of Islamic terrorists. Reason seems to have been brought to its knees, powerless to arbitrate such disputes, at least in the form of reasoned conversations and negotiations between disputing parties.

From Tanabe's perspective, however, there is another way out. When we come up against the limits of reason in solving problems both conceptual and practical, we can "pull the plugs" and let reason die, that is, no longer insist upon its rule. Absolute critique puts an end to reason's self-criticism. It acknowledges

---

[7] PM, especially p. 63.

reason's limits, not prematurely, but only after exercising reason to its full extent, letting it live as fully as it can. How full that is cannot be decided beforehand, but if we recognize that reason is not infinite wisdom, then we do not necessarily curtail its life by cutting it off at some (probably arbitrary) point. The exercise of self-critique could go on forever, so there is no impulse within this exercise to stop. The impulse must come from without, from somewhere else, from an*other* power.

Could the disruption come from emotion, or from the volitional aspect of humans, or from the body? All these are commonly set in opposition to the rule of reason. Leaving the possibility of the interruptive (disruptive) role of emotions or the body aside for the time being, we can say that volition will not do the job. The death of reason cannot be willed. The exercises of willing and of reason have in common the impulse to guide and control. The disruption of reason must come from an Other-power that is not the force of will. It is attendant upon an "I give up," a resignation of self-assertion and a reliance upon . . . something unnameable to which we give the name "nothingness." (Tanabe's "action-faith-witness" is not faith in a personified absolute Amida, but in Amida as *muryōju* 無量寿, infinite life, that is, the negation of life as we know it.) It is not a resignation to someone or something definable (though perhaps something in each case definite), but a surrender of the self-willed activity and of the willing subject, the ego.

ANALOGUES TO SELF-SURRENDER

Some interesting parallels to this self-surrender can be drawn in terms of the body. These analogues are significant because they indicate that Tanabe's resolution is neither passive nor sectarian. It will be important, however, to consider how far the parallels reach.

People adept at a martial art such as *aikidō* describe an ideal state, acquired at the peak of their training, in which they execute actions will-lessly. Put more precisely, they seem to yield to a situation so completely that "they" do not act at all, even while under attack, but rather give themselves over to the energy of the opponent and the environment in order to redirect it. Now there may be significant phenomenological differences between

metanoetic surrender to Other-power and this peak state of yield-
ing to and redirecting other forces in a martial art, but do the
two not have in common an equally significant surrender of self-
willed activity?

Accomplished athletes report entering a state that has come
to be called "the zone," a state of relaxed concentration in which
"things go right" because there is no resistance to the conditions
under which one must perform. Once again, in this state it is not
so much that one performs as that one acquiesces to the limits
of one's ability and turns those limits to one's advantage. A master
archer, for example, describes a particularly successful day when,
as she says, "I didn't feel like I was shooting my shots, but like
they were shooting themselves." Her coach encourages his students
to acknowledge that their sight is always in motion and to acqui-
esce to that movement. "If you *let* your sight move, you'll shoot
within the arc of its movements. But if you *try* to hold it . . . "
catastrophe! Likewise, "releasing the arrow must not be an act of
decision or will. The great enemy for an archer, as perhaps for
any athlete, is conscious intervention." It is a great mistake to try
to make your arrows hit the target "rather than *letting* them go
in."[8] Such insights are of course familiar to us from Eugen Her-
rigel's classic *Zen in the Art of Archery*, and are now being applied
widely to the psychology of sport. Once again, for all the differences between competitive sports and religious metanoesis, I think
we can find in both a surrender of self to something beyond the
power of the self.

Martial artists and athletes trained in techniques of letting go
frequently practice meditation, an approach Tanabe seems to align
with self-power. There is no question that he is critical of Zen
for its self-power approach, although he qualifies his criticism by
remarking that it may be right for some (namely, sages and saints)
and that Zen practice also involves *kōan* practice, which is a form
of metanoetics insofar as it takes one to the limits of reason. *Zange*,
however, is a "total *kōan*", one not restricted to saints and sages.[9]

---

[8] Reported by Lawrence Shainberg, "Finding 'The Zone' " in *The New York
Times Magazine*, April 9, 1989. In pointing out structural similarities between the
athlete's and Tanabe's gestures of self-surrender, I would caution against any
equation of the former with Buddhist liberation.

[9] PM, 128.

For my part, I have the feeling that Tanabe misses the metanoetic quality of *zazen* practice. That practice may be self-initiated, but it certainly calls for self-abandonment and transformation. Letting go of thoughts, feelings, good and bad experiences, and of the subject of such experiences, is the core of *zazen*. The practice of letting go of *any* self assertions is embodied in every detail of the meditative posture. Tanabe is fond of Dōgen's notion of *genjō-kōan* 現成公案, realizing reality as a *kōan*, a sign of a deep concern for the actual world, similar to that of metanoetics. But is not Dōgen's *shinjin datsuraku* 心身脱落, dropping off body and mind, also a metanoetic act of self-abandonment, certainly not accomplished through self-power? Tanabe quotes Zen sayings that speak of a return to the world, similar to his *gensō*, and he recognizes that Zen involves self transformation. His appraisal that the sages and saints who have accomplished the Way in Zen leave most of us behind may be correct, but I think he overlooks the metanoesis of the *zazen* practice that some like Dōgen identify with the Way accomplished.

The major difference between Tanabe's metanoetics and all these *other* experiences is, to my mind, not that between self-power and Other-power, between having an aim and giving it up, or between worldly and truly religious activities. It is rather the difference the body makes in the practice of Zen, the martial arts, and athletics. The role of the body in metanoetics is unspecified. Although we would not expect it to be identified with Other-power, the body, viewed in the mainstream Western tradition as "everything opposed to reason"[10] would certainly seem to play a significant role in the absolute critique of reason. As an opponent to the tradition, Nietzsche's fictive Zarathustra plays the role of the body, the "great[er] reason"; but Tanabe's critique of Nietzsche does not touch upon this parallel to his absolute critique. For Tanabe, presumably, it is not bodily experience that initiates metanoesis, not even the emotive quality of the "change of heart" that translates *metanoia*. It is the exercise of reason until reason is exhausted, helpless in the face of contradictions like that between

---

[10] Descartes, *Passions of the Soul*, No. 47 (Indianapolis: Hackett, 1989).

[11] Tanabe writes, in the Preface to *Philosophy as Metanoetics*:

In such a critical situation, where there was no time for delay, would it not be disloyal to my country to keep silent and fail to express whatever ideas I had

speaking rightfully against a war and thereby encouraging more division and conflict.[11] The power to overcome such an impasse breaks in upon one not from the strength of the body but from a completely other source. The resultant action (*gyō* 行) is not a discipline or practice of bodily exertion (*shugyō* 修行), but an attitude that issues into faith and witness, which are postures of mind or consciousness. The self-surrender of martial arts or athletics or even Zen would seem to fall short of the Other-power of metanoetics precisely insofar as they are disciplines that try to reach a completely other source.

Nevertheless, this comparison of practices secular and religious is pertinent to Tanabe's project in two ways. First, Tanabe does not limit transformation to models provided by established religions. His entire emphasis on Other-power as nothingness, rather than as a personified force or entity called Amida Buddha, is indication of his non-traditional approach. There is no attempt to confine action-faith-witness to the practice of religion per se, although there is an interest in defining the heart of religion. And it is not the denial or transcendence of this world, but on the contrary *gensō*, a return to the world and historical actuality, that characterizes authentic religion. True religion embraces the ordinary, everyday world in which we live, and its practice is possible for ordinary human beings, not just saints and sages. For us ordinary human beings, the examples of "secular" activities such as martial arts or meditation are important, if imperfect, analogies to metanoesis because they provide access to the understanding of Tanabe's Buddhist religious language.

Secondly, the analogies highlight a point that Tanabe makes about the contradiction of metanoetics. Metanoesis demands something that I cannot demand of myself. As a surrender to Other-power, it is beyond me, "out of my hands." It is not within my power to demand that Other-power hold sway. Is it within my power to give up my power? This question is misleading. It is not that I should or can give up my power, but that in exerting myself to my fullest capacity I come to my limits. It is not within

---

on reform? On the other hand, there seemed something traitorous about expressing in time of war ideas that . . . might end up causing divisions and conflicts among our people that would only further expose them to their enemies (xlix-l).

my power to compel Other-power, but does Other-power enter without my total exertion? The way of Other-power, unlike that of exclusive self-power, is open not just to sages and saints, but to "us ordinary, ignorant humans." Yet exerting oneself to the utmost is a requirement of "being just as one is," being "natural." Naturalness (jinen-hōni 自然法爾) is realized only by "those who, having exerted themselves to the utmost, experience despair over the powerlessness of their own being and submit themselves to it obediently."[12] Self-exertion is definitely part of self-surrender. Similarly, the disciplines of meditation, martial arts, and athletics obviously require self-exertion, a degree of mastery and of will. They are not resignations before one has tried. If they fall short of metanoesis, it is because they have not been totally exhausted by trial.

TURNING THE TABLES: SOME CHALLENGES TO TANABE

As demanding as it is, metanoetics is meant for the "ordinary, ignorant person," not "the sage" addressed by the theoretical critics. The erudite Tanabe considered himself one of the ordinary and ignorant, like the "fool" (gutoku 愚禿) Shinran thought himself to be. In his own words, a conversion (transformation and resurrection) similar to Shinran's led him to the philosophy of metanoetics.[13] A startling central thesis of that philosophy is that it is impossible to philosophize apart from one's personal and historical situation. This raises the question of the scope and relevance of Tanabe's philosophy: does it remain confined to Tanabe's personal metanoia and to the circumstances of his time and place? What happens to the universal scope and validity of philosophy? What happens to the transpersonal, transsocial, transhistorical claims of truth that are sought by philosophers? In the light of the crisis of reason that we have examined, this question of course must be asked of critics besides Tanabe; but his is a unique resolution that deserves response.

Obviously, Tanabe is not just talking to himself. He addresses Kant, Schelling, Hegel, Nietzsche, Heidegger, and he addresses us in an invitation to think about their issues and his. He means to

---

[12] PM, 155.
[13] PM, lii.

tell the truth, and he knows that this truth for all is always mediated by times, circumstances, and fallible persons. His book begins with a personal confession, but it does not belong to a confessional genre; it speaks for all. Do not his pages upon pages of rational analysis exceed the limits he has repeatedly drawn, the limits of the power of reason to convert? In what form, besides a strong utterance of faith and surrender, can a philosophy of metanoesis speak?

Tanabe's discourse is exceedingly abstract, particularly to "ignorant and ordinary" folk. I have of course been reading *Metanoetics* here as a book addressed to contemporary philosophers, but even they would find its language remote from concrete analysis of experience or social problems. Tanabe's analysis of religion, for example, does not delve into a study of particular historical religious institutions; nor do the views on society analyze any particular societies, even by way of example. Locutions such as "reason forced to recognize itself"[14] repeat the language of abstract reason. Is Tanabe's discourse applicable only to the degree in which it is abstract, not limited to temporal concerns, like Kant's and Hegel's works? What language would make the "concreteness of absolute mediation" concrete and expedient to contemporary philosophers, if not to "the ordinary and ignorant"? Or is the conversion demanded by metanoetics really an adversion, a turning away from the specific concerns of our times? The language of metanoetics suggests that what philosophers need is not to return to the world (*gensō* 還相) but first to turn to the absolute (*ōsō* 往相).

I have wanted Tanabe's work to speak to philosophers today and to their present concerns, worldly or not. Ultimately, however, the removal of *Philosophy as Metanoetics* from its concrete historical situation in wartime Japan raises the specter of massive deception and betrayal. Tanabe's acquiescent response to his situation may have been appropriate. If, however, we say in general that the direction of concrete socio-historical transformation is determined by "Other-power," do we not leave ourselves open to being duped by ideologies imposed on us from without that have horrendous consequences? Have we not learned some lessons from history? Do not the dangers of "passivity," "obedience," and a submission to one's "impotence" call for a different response today? People

---

[14] PM, 43.

often surrender themselves to something that turns out to be evil and truly self-destructive, destroying the possibility of their emerging from the situation as new beings. Often it turns out that I am only obeying others who would exploit, oppress, destroy. How do I know that I am not giving in to the irrational forces of ultranationalism, imperialism, racism and sexism? In such cases I would of course be surrendering to something relative that masks as the absolute. Yet in a generalized metanoetics, the absolute never appears by itself, unmediated, but always in some relative form or another. Ordinary reason cannot guide us through such crises with impunity, but neither can Tanabe's reason transformed, for it is transformed only after one's total submission. Is metanoesis possible only as repentance for the past? This question is sharpened by an examination of Tanabe's critique of an adversary he never names in his book, his older colleague and former mentor, Nishida Kitarō.

EXCURSUS: TANABE'S CRITIQUE OF NISHIDA

I am continually puzzled by the tacit but acute critique of Nishida in *Philosophy as Metanoetics*. There are numerous places in Nishida's texts that, on the face of it, indicate Tanabe's misunderstanding or distortion of him. Yet it seems implausible that the brilliant critic Tanabe did not understand Nishida better than I do. This discrepancy makes me want to look for other than evident reasons for Tanabe's disagreements with Nishida.

Let us first consider the principal complaints of Tanabe with regard to Nishida. James Fredericks has summarized them admirably in his recent article "Cosmology and Metanoia," and Christopher Ives has replied on Nishida's behalf to some of them, while conceding others.[15] Critic Tanabe, commentator Fredericks, and respondent Ives, however, all refer rather indiscriminately to ideas in different periods of Nishida's thought and largely overlook its evolution. I think it is important to take up the main issues again, because they are central not only to the thought of both philos-

---

[15] James Fredericks, "Cosmology and Metanoia: Buddhist Path to Process Thought for the West," and Christopher Ives, "Non-dualism and Soteriology in Whitehead, Nishida and Tanabe: A Response to James Fredericks," EB 22/1 (Spring, 1989): 111-27, 128-38.

ophers but to the relevance of either to contemporary Western philosophy.

Tanabe frequently accuses Nishida of "intuitionism," that is, of placing absolute nothingness as the object of aesthetic intuition, instead of encountering it in the event of the subject's transformation by way of "Other-power." Tanabe states that if nothingness is something that can be intuited, it is being rather than absolute nothingness. Again, if it is spoken of in terms of "place" (*basho* 場所), it suggests an immediate noetic object and not a meta-noetic and absolutely mediated transformation. If Nishida's nothingness is "pure experience," that is to say, if it is purely experienced in an immediate presence of unified (or not yet opposed) subject and object, then the mediatory character of absolute nothingness drops out of the picture, and instead being is absolutized. If it is placed in an "absolutely contradictory self-identity," it clearly privileges self-identity and totality, which are qualities of being, over difference, disruption and transformation, which are the entries of absolute nothingness. The practical consequences of Nishida's mistakes, whether he intended them or not, are an assertion of self-power and absolute subject, and a neglect of the role of the concrete history and reciprocal, ethical action of relative beings.

Let me try to untangle these issues and take up the relevant notions roughly in the order in which they appear in Nishida's philosophy. Pure experience comes first, and we do well to recall that Nishida abandoned this notion quite early in his career, and that while he employed it, the notion of absolute nothingness was not in use. He abandoned it not only because, as he believed, it lent itself too easily to a psychologistic view of a subject having an experience, but also, I think, because of internal logical difficulties with the language of pure experience. He calls it "immediate experience" (*chokusetsu keiken* 直接経験) as well, but implies that this does not mean that it is unmediated in the sense of being either contentless or unconditioned. It is possible to view (a) pure experience as constructed out of the past, so it is not temporally or historically unmediated. What makes an experience "pure" is foremost its unitary character: no split between subject perceiving and object perceived, or differentiation between feeling, intention and will. Even thought can exhibit this unitary character, as Nishida makes clear in the second chapter of *An Inquiry into the Good*.

Similarly, Nishida would not consider pure experience to be an immediate experience of nothingness, even if he were to use that term in this context. The very first examples he cites, hearing (a) sound or seeing (a) color, before the disruption into perceiving subject and perceived object, imply that *something* is experienced. On one account this would seem to mean that it is being and not nothingness that is "purely" experienced. Both Tanabe and Nishida, however, would view this as a "relative nothingness," opposed to being, and not absolute nothingness which exists only in relation to being. On another account we could read this example as an experience of nothingness manifested in, i.e., *mediated through,* such "things" as color or sound. We could even see, in Nishida's example of color *(iro* 色, also pronounced *shiki)* a Buddhist tint of *shiki soku ze kū, kū soku ze shiki* 色即是空 空即是色, form is emptiness and emptiness is form; in other words, there is no (experience of) color (or sound, or any sensible form) without nothingness, and vice versa. This view of course reads into early Nishida the terms and interests of his later periods, but I think that it is consonant with the early philosophy of pure experience. In his Preface to *From the Acting to the Seeing,* the work of 1927 often cited as a major turning point in his philosophy, Nishida speaks of "seeing the form of the formless, hearing the sound of the soundless."[16] This too clearly implies that it is not an unmediated formlessness (nothingness) that is seen or heard.

Nishida, then, never writes of the pure or immediate experience of nothingness. Thus a major question for both Tanabe's and Nishida's philosophies is in what sense nothingness can be "experienced." It is certainly not experienced as an object, and yet the "experience of nothingness" would not mean that nothing is experienced, that there is simply an absence of experience. To speak of nothingness experienced *in or through,* i.e., *mediated by,* something else comes closer to Tanabe's meaning and may approximate early Nishida's intention as well, but begs the question of whether it is nothingness that is experienced. For the later Nishida, I think, it would be more apt to speak of nothingness as an (objectively unexperienced) condition for the possibility of experience. But this turn of phrase could not be taken in the Kantian sense of a structure of a pre-existent and self-identical

---

[16] NKZ 4:6.

transcendental ego. It might be even more appropriate to say that it is nothingness that experiences. In fact Nishida remarks that experience precedes and gives rise to the individual, not that the individual has experiences,[17] and he later uses turns of phrase such as the self-awareness of nothingness (*mu no jikaku* 無の自覚), that is, nothingness's self-awareness (or experience). But to try to speak of experience without a subject doing the experiencing runs up against the limits of language. It was for this reason also, I believe, that Nishida soon abandoned the language of pure experience.

Intuition is another term Nishida used in this context and continued to use. (Perceptual) intuition and intellectual intuition are synonymous with pure or immediate experience in many passages of the early works. In *Intuition and Reflection in Self-Consciousness*, the primary form of intellectual intuition becomes self-consciousness, the activity of self seeing itself within itself, thus constituting its own self-identity and derivatively that of other things in the world. To the extent that these notions suggest self-power, at least of the self as an activity, I suppose they fall prey to Tanabe's criticism. Yet even in this work Nishida says that the self comes from nothingness and returns to "creative nothingness," a (non-relative) nothingness that is being (*mu ni shite u* 無にして有), so that we are not dealing with a substantial self or being.[18] Later of course Nishida developed the notion of actional intuition (*kōiteki chokkan* 行為的直観) as a way to stress that intuition, as a foundation for the creation of self and world, is not passive receptivity; but neither again could one say that it arises from the self-power of a substantial self. In Yuasa Yasuo's interpretation, acting intuition springs from the base or unconscious layer of body-mind, where the "self becomes an instrument or empty vessel receiving [an] intuition, [simply acting] as no ego."[19] (The athlete's ability to "enter the zone" that I alluded to earlier,

---

[17] NKZ 1:4.

[18] See NKZ 2:272; trans. by Valdo Viglielmo, Takeuchi Yoshinori, and Joseph O'Leary as *Intuition and Reflection in Self-Consciousness* (Albany: State University of New York Press, 1987), 134.

[19] Yuasa Yasuo, *The Body: Toward an Eastern Mind-Body Theory*, trans. by Nagatomo Shigenori and Thomas P. Kasulis (Albany: State University of New York Press, 1987), 199.

would exemplify Nishida's active, creative intuition.) Nor is nothingness considered a direct object of the self's intuition, be it intellectual, actional, or aesthetic—as Tanabe purports. At best Tanabe's criticism could touch the idealism suggested by the spontaneous creation of self and world, an idealism inconsistent with the imperative of self-transformation. But cannot one also see already in the notion of returning to nothingness a parallel to Tanabe's "death and resurrection"? And cannot one continue to find, in Nishida's later view of the self as a continuity of discontinuities, parallels with Tanabe's "disruption of the self" that does not leave the new self the same as the old?

Tanabe further attacks Nishida's metaphor of "place" (*basho*) and his dialectic of an absolutely contradictory self-identity. Both supposedly presume an "aesthetic intuition into the undifferentiated immediacy of being"[20] and not a mediation of absolute nothingness. Nishida first developed the notion of *basho* as a metaphor for ever more inclusive universals enfolding subjective and objective poles of experience, e.g., the worlds of art, or biology (life), or physics (matter / energy). The ultimate enfolding place is absolute nothingness. (Here *basho* might better be rendered "open space" and is perhaps analogous to Heidegger's *Lichtung*, the clearing wherein beings are free to appear.) I do not see how this metaphor implies "aesthetic intuition into the undifferentiated immediacy of being." In fact, it seems to displace any (transcendental) subject who might so intuit things and thereby constitute the unity of the world. Even the intermediary *basho* of consciousness, as the place of judgments about (grammatical) subjects and objects, is displaced by "absolute nothingness," the context or "place" beyond linguistic determination, wherein subject and object, knower and known, acting self and objectified self are negated. Nishida's mature notion of the *basho* of absolute nothingness is an explanation of how individuals can be absolutely different from one another, not specifiable by any number of predications, but self-determining by being continually self-negating. Precisely because the individual is grounded in nothingness, that is, ultimately ungrounded, it is not a fixed self-identical entity; and precisely because absolute nothingness determines itself by negating itself, it is absolute only in relation to relative individuals, only in mediation. The self-de-

---

[20] This is Fredericks's formulation, 122.

termination of individuals out of nothingness takes place as the mutual determination of a plurality of individuals, as a mediation of differences. Perhaps "place" is too static a metaphor, but Nishida's dialectic of self-determination clearly includes the dynamic mediation of differences that *remain* as differences, held together in an absolutely contradictory self-identity.

Often Tanabe's critique of Nishida seems directed more at Nishida's use of terms than at underlying ideas. For example, Tanabe implies that self-identity is a category proper to being, not to nothingness, which means that Nishida's "self-identity of absolute contradictories" is misspoken and that we should rather speak of a "unity of absolute contradictories based on nothingness." Yet for both Tanabe and Nishida, the contradictories held together remain contradictory. Both proclaim that the absolute must not oppose but rather include the relative. After 1935 Nishida also emphasized that the absolute touches the relative only through other humans, other relative beings. Nishida deemphasized this intersubjectivity in his last essay, "The Logic of Place and the Religious Worldview," but it is also questionable whether Tanabe was familiar with the content of that essay and thus whether he was criticizing Nishida's final position. A glance at the problem of death in that work suggests that Tanabe's reasons came from elsewhere.

Tanabe feels perhaps that Nishida does not sufficiently emphasize the necessity for a self-transformation that cannot arise from one's own power. But the awareness of one's own death (in Nishida's last essay) is parallel to Tanabe's surrender to Other-power, for death means the end of ego and self-will. I might will my death and attempt suicide (out of despair), but what I intend is an end to my plight, not a continuation of my wants. I throw myself into the unknown, which is better than this suffering I know. Or if I commit a suicide of protest or apology or the like, I do it as a last will, the last thing I can will, the end of my willing. Tanabe explicitly discounts suicide from the sense in which one becomes "the efficient cause of one's own death."[21] Death always reaches me as that over which I have no power, as Other-power. Death furthermore has a positive significance in Nishida; akin to the Great Death of the self in Zen that Tanabe refers to

---

[21] PM, 162.

approvingly, it signifies not the end of one's life but the beginning of self-creation. How different is this from Tanabe's death-and-resurrection?

Tanabe, then, does not differ from Nishida as much as he thinks. Much of his criticism applies better to Nishida's *terms* than to the context of his ideas. He does not take into account the development in Nishida's philosophy. On the one hand, we must acknowledge the influence that Tanabe had on Nishida's development, particularly the growing recognition in Nishida since 1931 of the role of concrete historical and social reality. On the other, it is possible that Marxists like Tosaka Jun, whose influence on Nishida was even stronger at that time, also steered the direction of Tanabe's own philosophy toward the role of history.

Why then does Tanabe so strongly disagree with Nishida in *Philosophy as Metanoetics*? Does Tanabe in his heart judge his revered colleague deficient in *zange*, in repentance for being an accomplice, intended or not, to wartime government propaganda? Is the exhortation to personal transformation not strong, not explicit enough in Nishida's later works? And this urgent exhortation on the part of Tanabe—is it his own calling or a calling from the other side / other shore / Other-power? If it is an exhortation wholly on his part, it seems to me that it could elicit from Nishida only a repentance for the past, but not an openness for present fallibility.

EPILOGUE

This synopsis of challenges posed between metanoetics and contemporary philosophy has omitted many important themes in Tanabe's book, among others, absolute mediation, freedom, and Pure Land faith. Moreover, as a synopsis or broad look at some themes, it remains a kind of witness that is not accompanied by transformative action or committed faith. For all I know, my essay is not true to its source, which is its Other. Though I will not pretend that my confession of uncertainty is a metanoetic act, I hope that it elicits open-minded inquiry.

Tanabe and the Dialectics of Mediation: A Critique

Whalen LAI

AS with Nishitani Keiji's *Religion and Nothingness*, the translation of Tanabe Hajime's *Philosophy as Metanoetics* has provided us with the major work of one of the leading thinkers of the Kyoto school in the tradition of Nishida Kitarō, and at the same time introduced a new thinker to Western philosophers. If Nishida's idea of Absolute Nothingness may be called a Zen-inspired dialectics of paradox/identity (after the model of what he calls "absolute contradiction in *an sich* total identity" 絶対矛盾自己同一), Tanabe's interpretation of Absolute Nothingness as Other-power offers a Pure Land-inspired dialectics of mediation.

In this essay, I would like to begin with a Heideggerian summary of Nishitani's central thesis as a lead-in to Nishida's idea of Absolute Nothingness. From there, I will try to set that notion in the wider context of Buddhist thought. Next, I will attempt to see both Nishida's and Tanabe's dialectics as variations of Tendai *hongaku* 本覚 thought. Finally, turning back once more to Heidegger, I will note how Tanabe's reading of his thought differed from Nishitani's, and propose yet another reading of my own in response to both Kyoto philosophers.

THE PROMISE OF ABSOLUTE NOTHINGNESS

We might consider Nishitani's *Religion and Nothingness* as an answer to the problem of the human that Heidegger, his one-time teacher, raises in *Being and Time*. Nishitani begins with the question "What is Religion?" and answers it much as Heidegger answers his basic question, "What is Metaphysics?" For both, the answer is not something that can be stated objectively, but rather lies somewhere in the peculiar structure of that query itself. Heidegger builds his fundamental ontology on the phenomenon that only humans can ask about (show concern for) their own being. In similar fashion, Nishitani considers the key to religion to lie in the very act of wondering what religion is about. The religion of awakening (*kaku no shūkyō* 覚の宗教 , i.e. Buddhism) regards ignorance (*avidyā*) a function of knowledge (*vidyā*).[1] Ultimately, religion, like Being, is not an object outside of human beings; it is as much a part of us as our flesh and bones. We are the "there" of Being to Heidegger. For Nishitani, too—and here he follows Zen—the depth of our doubt 大疑 is proportional to the depth of our awakening 大悟 .[2]

At the same time, Nishitani sees nihility as the threat that religion faces in our time. Nihility is partly due to our modern capacity, through science, to objectify the world, which in the process also objectifies and dehumanizes us ourselves. It used to be, in medieval Christendom, that human beings and the world (nature) both had a place in God's creation. Life had a purpose; the world was guided by Providence. But with the Renaissance and the redefinition of the human and natural worlds as opposites—as subject and object, after Descartes—the human became alienated from God and from the world by virtue of its free will (Kant). Nature was ruled by blind necessity, and God withdrew to a deist inactivity. At first, this human sovereignty was still sanctioned by God, for it was God who gave Adam dominion over all of creation, and God who told Edison "let there be light." But in time, even these deist assumptions proved unnecessary; the machine could work well enough without a *deus ex machina*. The result was the severing of the vertical axis that tied creation to the creator. Left to their own on the horizontal axis, human beings made themselves masters of the world. With that, the old salvation history was called into doubt and replaced with the nineteenth century ideal of unending progress. After two world wars, this ideal had turned into a nightmare and in its place, nihilism reared its ugly head. It is in this context that Sartre paints his portrait of the lonely individual with no ground to stand on except what one freely wills oneself within an otherwise meaningless universe.

---

[1] In Indian (as in Aristotelian) logic, the privation of knowledge (or good) assumes the reality of knowledge (or the good).

[2] Thus, too, in terms of the Buddha-nature, the no-self is the True Self.

Like Nietzsche, Nishitani ultimately lays the blame on the Christian God who, by creating the world *ex nihilo,* deprived it of all intrinsic value. The world of medieval Christendom offers no refuge for modernity. Indeed, it is itself the problem, since its idea of *creatio ex nihilo* leads to modern nihilism. And like Nietzsche, the hopeful pessimist, Nishitani welcomes contemporary nihility as a possible harbinger of a transvaluation of everything by Absolute Nothingness. Absolute Nothingness would overcome the "relative nihility" of a world *ex nihilo* just as it had once overcome the world-denigration of the Hīnayāna Buddhist. And just as Mahāyāna once resanctified *saṃsāra* by seeing how it is as *nirvāṇa,* so Absolute Nothingness may bridge the ontological divide between the divine and the human. All things, all opposites, can find an immediate unity in the *topos* of Absolute Nothingness.

WHAT IS "ABSOLUTE NOTHINGNESS"?

The term *Absolute Nothingness (zettai mu* 絶対無 *)* is a creation of Nishida Kitarō. It is not, nor was it ever intended to be, entirely Buddhist in scope. Still, a look at the history behind this idea may help to clarify its meaning.

Of the eighteen forms of *śūnyatā* (emptiness) in Mahāyāna, two have captured the Chinese imagination more than the others: *śūnyatā-śūnyatā* (the emptiness of emptiness, a double negation that reaffirms the real); and *atyanta-śūnyatā* 空竟空 or "ultimate emptiness."[3] The latter is a total Emptiness all around, and in that sense, is a precursor to our absolute nothingness.

In the Sanron school, the highest emptiness is *zettai kū*: the Emptiness that terminates all relativities. *Zettai* was then written 絶待 (without dependence) and not yet as 絶対 (without opposites). The former usage is derived however from the more classic expression *hsiang-tai* 相待 (mutual dependence) which nowadays is expressed as *hsiang-tui* 相対 (what is relative; literally, facing each another). Kuo Hsiang (d. 312), in his commentary on the *Chuang-tzu,* speaks of the Tao as *mu-tai* 無待, meaning that it is "non-de-

---

[3] The eighteen forms of emptiness all refer to the same emptiness, but each points to its different implications in different contexts. "Ultimate emptiness" is the emptiness in all dimensions. See the entry under 十八空 in the 仏教代辞典 *[Buddhist Dictionary]* of Mochizuki Shinkō 望月信亨, 3:2356b-57c.

pendent" on anything. Everything less than this "unmoved mover" is naturally dependent (u-tai 有待) on it. This is where the meaning of zettai kū comes from. Everything that is has a logical opposite, an antithesis upon which the thesis depends. Only zettai kū knows no polar extremes; it puts an end to all opposition.

Crucial as this idea was to the Sanron school, the Sanron school did not continue to exist beyond the Sui dynasty. Although it is now thought that Sanron influences the Ox-head branch of early Zen 牛頭宗, no one has suggested any direct connection between this early tradition and the modern discussion of Absolute Nothingness by Nishida, whose philosophical inspirations included a strong dose of German Idealism.

Moreover, Nishida used the term zettai mu, not zettai kū. Kū 空 was what Kumārajīva settled on to render śūnya and śūnyatā.[4] Kumārajīva's avoidance of the term mu 無 was prompted by his recognition that the śūnyatā negates nonbeing as much as being. Both are equally empty 有無皆空.

In reverting to the term mu, Nishida might appear to be reviving the Taoist concept of nonbeing. And indeed in one sense, this nonbeing has always been deemed by the Taoist as the Absolute. The Tao-te-ching regards it as the mother of all beings.[5] But when Lao-tzu says that being comes from nonbeing 有生於 無,[6] the image of nonbeing he had in mind was not so much that of a literal void as of a nebulum of infinite potentia, a womb pregnant with the forms of all things. Historically, it was Wang Pi (d. 248), the neo-Taoist, who first took nonbeing as denoting a virtual void.[7]

But all this is too far removed in time from the modern Kyoto school. We do better to look at the use of the word mu

---

[4] Chinese words do not have that Sanskrit recension to distinguish the verb "to empty" and the noun "emptiness." This might have affected past and present usage of the term mu.

[5] See chapter 1. This interpretation depends on the reading that punctuates the line 無名万物之母 not as 無名 万物之母 but as 無 名万物之母.

[6] See chapter 40. This line, however, is absent from one of the Ma-wang-tui text of the Lao-tzu.

[7] Wang Pi might have been influenced by Mahāyāna. And ironically, śūnyatā as a mathematical concept does denote "zero" though Śūnyavāda as a school teaches more than just nihilism. See Wing-tsit Chan, A Source Book in Chinese Philosophy (Princeton University Press, 1963), 321-24.

within the circles of Japanese Zen to which Nishida's philosophy has known ties.[8]

In Japanese Zen the *mu* kōan in the *Mumonkan* 無門関 has been widely influential. Although the collection stems from Sung China, it has never been as central in China as in Japan. Its use of the notion of *mu* is not in reference to a nebulous nonbeing, but often as a sharp, cutting verb *mu* as in the famous first kōan in the collection, "Jōshū's *Mu*":

> A monk asked Jōshū, "Has a dog the Buddha Nature?" Jōshū answered, "*Mu*."[9]

Here the word *mu*, whose root meaning is "there is not," is a resolute "No!". It evokes the Śūnyavāda call to negate, to "void" all theses.

And because the kōan *Mu* is meant also as an icon for meditation, it is more than a sign. It is a symbol that participates in the Nothingness that it seeks to disclose. The kōan *Mu* is an extended metaphor. Taken literally, it is an untruth; ignore it altogether, and you miss the beauty of the kōan. In between is that dissonance that demands the mind to work through the impertinence of the language. One finds that which lies beyond words through the power of the particular kōan before one.[10] The experience is described as a "thick fog of doubt" that oppresses the mind but which, once dispelled, brings on the Great Enlightenment.

DIFFERENT SHADES OF *SAMSĀRA-SIVE-NIRVĀNA*

Absolute Nothingness is, of course, more than an icon. It derives from a larger philosophy, and indeed represents the central mystery in Mahāyāna. It is the paradox often expressed as "form is emptiness—emptiness is form," a formula that calls to mind the

---

[8] This remains true despite the rightful claim of the Kyoto philosophers themselves that their philosophy, as philosophy, is not restricted to Zen.

[9] Cited from K. Sekida's translation in *Two Zen Classics* (Tokyo: Weatherhill, 1977), 27.

[10] The model here is that whereas a symbol points beyond (Tillich), a metaphor doubles back upon itself. It is the collision of two incompatible images (for example, "original face" and "before you are born") that opens up a vista within that conjunction.

similar formula, "*saṃsāra* is *nirvāṇa*, *nirvāṇa* is *saṃsāra*." To see how Nishida and Tanabe could have derived two different dialectics from this latter expression, we need to examine different levels of understanding the formula.

> 1. The simplest reading takes *saṃsāra* as the unreal and *nirvā-ṇa* as the desirable. *Saṃsāra* can then be *nirvāṇa* because in fact the former has been annihilated.

This, however, gives us the relative nihility of the Hīnayāna position. A true dialectics requires two poles; to erase one of them is to take away the necessary tension. Accordingly, it is better to say:

> 2. There is *saṃsāra*, there is *nirvāṇa*. This sets up a coincidence of opposites between the two.

The problem with this solution is that it leaves itself open to the charge of accepting a prior dualism of *saṃsāra* and *nirvāṇa* before discovering their non-duality. To avoid that pitfall, we might say:

> 3. There is only one reality *(unus)*, a *saṃsāra-sive-nirvāṇa* unity which the deluded mind mistakes for two realities subsequently conjoined into one *(unio)*.

Position 1 says that "There is no reality" and that absence of the real is *nirvāṇa*; Position 2 says that "There is an apparent reality, but that it is really empty." Position 3 accepts only one reality, but a reality that appears at one moment as real and another moment as unreal. This latter position may in turn be faulted for a lapse into monism. This suggests that we do better to combine Positions 2 and 3, which gives us:

> 4. *Saṃsāra*, without being any less "this side," is somehow immediately identical with *nirvāṇa*. *Nirvāṇa* forfeits nothing of its belonging to the "far side" and yet is also *saṃsāra*.

This view is known as "attaining *bodhi* (wisdom) without cutting off the *kleśa* (defilements)." It can be further refined so that not only the limit of *saṃsāra* is equal to the limit of *nirvāṇa* — which is the *prajñāpāramitā* teaching — but any item in *saṃsāra* can also be fully *nirvāṇa*. In Tendai, this is the view that "Every form and every aroma are no less the Middle Path." The Hua-yen or Kegon school takes an even more extravagant position in claiming that "every item is every other item in the universe."

At every level, the general purpose of the dialectics of emptiness is to free the mind from clinging to absolutes. This yields a wisdom, a freedom from cognition and also from all concepts like "God" or "Buddha," "*saṃsāra*" or "*nirvāṇa*." The Buddhist premise behind this position — and this is a premise that is far from self-evident — is that many of life's problems are due to a misperception of reality. Wisdom comes through living without illusions, through seeing reality as it is.

Of the various proponents of emptiness, the Sanron school keeps closest to a pure negation of other positions without staking out a position of its own *(prāsaṅgika)*. In China and Japan, this is considered an extreme position. All other proponents of emptiness tend toward some kind of positive thesis, such as that of a Buddha-nature.[11] For his part, Nishida constructed his dialectics on Position 4, but in envisioning an independent philosophy, he moved beyond the "pure negation" of Sanron and hence should be numbered among the more positive majority. But how does Tanabe derive a philosophy of Other-power from the formula of "*saṃsāra-sive-nirvāṇa*"?

THE ROOTS OF ABSOLUTE NOTHINGNESS AS OTHER-POWER

In replacing Nishida's dialectics of "paradox/identity" with his own dialectics of mediation, Tanabe is modifying a wisdom formula to fit the requirements of a faith in Other-power. At first, this change seems unfounded. How can the non-dual allow itself to be posited as a pole in a new duality of the Thou and the I in which the Other empowers the ego? But the move is not without precedent.

Mahāyāna, with Mādhyamika as its central philosophy, has long adapted the emptiness dialectics to express the element of faith. In the Far East, Nāgārjuna is even counted as a venerable patriarch of the Pure Land school and author of the distinction between the "hard" and "easy" paths. T'an-luan (Jpn., Donran) had declared the Unborn *(anutpattika-dharma-kṣānti,* a synonym for

---

[11] Whether this Buddha-nature is real or a synonym for emptiness is, of course, open to debate and a variety of dialectical formulations.

emptiness) as none other than the Born (in the Pure Land). Faith finds justification in wisdom.

Tanabe's understanding of the Pure Land faith is not, however, "orthodox" on Jōdo or Shin standards. The roots of his dialectics are more accurately traced to Tendai.[12]

Tendai practices a dialectics of reciprocity, in which everything there is forms a single interlocking whole "in the round." The round is the key symbol to this school. Everything in the circle is in balance with everything and related to it in perfect reciprocity. Nothing—not the Real, not the Empty, and not even the Middle—is granted ascendancy over anything else. The perfect balance applies alike to mind and matter, to the one and the many. In the case of self-power and Other-power, the two are to crisscross, wisdom forming the vertical ascent and faith (in Amitābha) the horizontal exit.

The ascent is gradual and methodic; the exit cuts across and moves quickly. Rather than decide between the two, Tendai regarded both necessary, even making a point of practicing Zen meditation (the upward ascent) and Pure Land devotion (the horizontal exit).[13] This model was the norm in Heian Japan, before Zen and Pure Land broke off as independent sects in the Kamakura era.[14]

If we draw a spectrum of Emptiness dialectics—with nonduality at one extreme (Zen), Other-power at the other (Pure Land) and a balance of the two in perfect reciprocity in the center (Tendai), we are better able to gauge where Tanabe's dialectics falls (see following page). At the two extremes we find self-power and Other-power, Zen and Pure Land. On the Zen pole, any sudden or abrupt interruption of the normal consciousness or flow of events leading to awakening is deemed the self-awakening of an *a priori* enlightenment *(hongaku* 本覚 *)*. On the Pure Land side, the same transformation will always be attributed to Amida's Vow.

---

[12] Chinese T'ien-t'ai, based on the *Lotus Sūtra* and Mādhyamika philosophy, has always had a niche for Pure Land piety.

[13] Tendai, however, does not consider the upward path "sudden," as Zen might; and it would not call the exit across "true," as the Pure Land school would. The "quick exit" is only an expedient means.

[14] The either/or position of sectarianism is regarded by Tendai as "biased." In fact, Chinese Ch'an and Pure Land did not take the either/or position in the strict sense of the term.

Nishida is to be placed at the self-power pole. For him, Absolute Nothingness is tied to trust in immediate self-awareness.[15] It is an all-encompassing *topos* — or in Nishitani's term, a standpoint — of Nothingness[16] where *śūnyatā-śūnyatā* as "double negation"

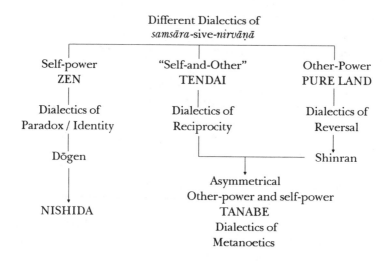

negates only to reaffirm. There may be what Nishida calls acting intuition, but one does not speak here of "negation and transformation." It is enough to affirm the *is* of reality "as it is."

Since other essays in this volume deal more directly with the other pole, represented by the position of Shinran, we need only note here that Shinran's dialectics may be characterized as a dialectics of reversal in which all credit in the transformation of the self is assigned to the Buddha.[17] Thus Jōdo Shinshū does not even

---

[15] See James Heisig's discussion on this above, 27-28.

[16] Nishitani seems closer to the view of Nāgārjuna, whose theory of the "two truths" does not refer to two realities but to variant views of a single reality.

[17] The notion of reversal is borrowed in part from Paul Tillich, whose *Theology of Culture* speaks of religion of faith as a religion of paradox. "To be saved because of one's sins" *(akunin shōki* 悪人正機 *)* is a statement of faith as well as a statement of paradox. Given Zen's insistence on the importance of paradox, however, we need to tie reversal to a "logic of (self-) negation" wherein the paradox is premised on an existential difference between the (sinful, impotent) self and the (good, powerful) Other. In this way, we avoid confusing this reversal with the reversibility of *saṃsāra* and *nirvāṇa* in the wisdom end of the spectrum, a reversal premised upon epistemic nonduality. I will return to this below.

see *shinjin* 信心 (faith) as a function of the human mind but as entirely the working of Amida's grace. That it also turns the naturalness due self-being (*jinen* 自然) on its head into a naturalness due self(-power)-lessness and accepts the *bodhicitta* and Buddha-nature only as a gift of faith[18] gives an indication of how this intentional dialectics of reversal works. Be that as it may, we need to look more closely at the central position, the Tendai dialectics of reciprocity,[19] before we are able to locate Tanabe on the spectrum.

The Tendai dialectics "in the round" insists on balancing the contribution of self-power and Other-power to work for one's liberation. A Sung sub-commentary on a commentary on the *Meditation Sūtra* attributed to Chih-i expresses that perfect correlation of mind and Buddha, self and Other.[20]

| *Chi-hsin nien-fo* | 即心念仏 | Recall the Buddha *sive* mind. |
| *Yüeh-hsin kuan-fo* | 約心念仏 | Meditate on the Buddha *via* mind. |

The words 即 (*sive*) and 約 (*via*) are so exact, their nuance so fine, that they are not interchangeable despite the extreme ease in transposing the words. It also makes for difficult translation into English. The point, simply put, is this: Practice *nembutsu* but to avoid falling into total reliance on Other-power, do so *sive* mind, i.e. in recognition that the Pure Land is only a correlate of your pure mind. This way you do not reduce mind to Amida's grace (the Pure Land bias) or reduce the Pure Land to mind (the Zen bias). Similarly, one should meditate on the Buddha through visualization *via* the mind, that is, by engaging the mind. *Via* denotes a correlation, not an identity like *sive*. Because *nembutsu* meant

---

[18] This is much the same as how the Spirit in the Christian faith represented what has been "freely given" as opposed to what has been "won through human effort."

[19] This is our term. Tendai calls the dialectic "round" 円 , a symbol of perfection. We use "reciprocity" to draw out its implication in mediating self-power and Other-power and similar pairs of polar opposites. Tendai actually uses a tripolar scheme, so that reciprocity would seem too two-dimensional for it. For the same reason, Tendai does not use the formula of bipolar reversibility. It prefers a tripartite rhetoric of 即空 即仮 即中.

[20] The guiding principle here is taken from the *Vimalakīrti Sūtra*'s idea that "as the mind is pure, the Buddha land is pure" 随其心浄則仏土浄 —and its reversal. See Mochizuki, *Dictionary of Buddhism*, 4:3137b-38b.

originally "keeping in mind the Buddha," it should be done *sive* mind. Because visualization assumes an object seen, the mode is the distanced engagement of *via*. This is how Tendai keeps the correlation between Buddha and Mind perfectly balanced.

Unlike Shinran, Tanabe insisted on an element of self-power. And unlike Dōgen, he put great stock in Other-power. Despite occasional comments to the contrary, to the effect that "self-power is Other-power," his overall dialectic of mediation is not perfectly balanced. Other-power is clearly given precedence over self-power. Amida is not *totaliter aliter* from the human,[21] but neither is Amida ever said to be totally the same as the human. For Tanabe, the sin-ridden human individual needs Amida to become whole far more than Amida needs men and women.[22] The mutual mediation is thus asymmetrical, favoring a greater role for Amida.

All of this would seem to place Tanabe somewhat off center, to the right of Tendai and to the left of Shinran.[23] His stress on Absolute Nothingness as Other-power does not mean that Tanabe gave up the rhetoric of *saṃsāra-sive-nirvāṇa*. The two formulae are not incompatible, for him, as they would have been for Nishida, because Tanabe has reshaped Absolute Nothingness for his dialectics of mediation.[24] For example, the samsaric individual (the human being) deemed "empty" is also left as-is (sin-ridden) even as it is drawn into the orbit of the all-encompassing Other-power. At the same time, the Other-power which is not completely Other needs to be mediated by human beings in order to function. We may phrase their relationship as follows: *Other-power as Absolute*

---

[21] Such utter transcendentalism, which is commonly attributed to the Christian God, is deemed to run counter to both the dialectics of Absolute Nothingness, which negates such an absolute Being, and to the idea of mediation, which always requires a common ground.

[22] For a Tendai-like Pure Land faith in which Amida is as dependent on human beings as they are on Amida, one may consider the case of the Jishū or Seizan-ha sects of Jōdoshū.

[23] Many of the terms favored by Tanabe — "empty reality," "relative being," "*upāya*," and so forth — come directly from Tendai usage.

[24] The reverse can also be attempted. D. T. Suzuki was able to draw out the similarity between Zen naturalness and Shinran's idea of *jinen hōni* by reading the reversal of faith as a Zen paradox. The left end of the spectrum in the diagram tends to stress the subject and to psychologize religious beliefs, words being only poor substitutes for experience; the right end trusts in the objective Dharma and guards its words, doctrines, faith from excessive psychologism.

Nothingness standing in relation to the ordinary sinner as relative being both negates and affirms its subjectivity—negates in the sense of exposing it as "empty being", affirms in the form of leaving its humanity intact. Making full use of the upāya leverage of his confession to the limits of the freedom of self-power, Other-power transforms the action-faith of the penitent and brings it into conformity with the natural flow (jinen hōni) of Nothingness-qua-Love, which as the Great Nay-qua-Great Compassion recalls such a one to moral action in the world (gensō).

HONGAKU NONDISCRIMINATION, *SHIKAKU* DISCRIMINATION

In accepting as necessary the distinction between self and Amida, Tanabe injected a tension into that nonduality of *saṃsāra* and *nirvāṇa* that lies at the heart of Absolute Nothingness. He in effect qualifies *hongaku* with *shikaku*. Since these two terms have special meaning in the Buddhism of the far East in general and Tendai in particular, we should pause to consider them briefly.

Hongaku (本覚 Chin., *pen-chüeh*) is a Chinese term meaning "a priori enlightenment." It is an idea that was not intrinsic to the *prajñāpāramitā* wisdom tradition with its *saṃsāra-sive-nirvāṇa* formula. Rather *hongaku* derives from the doctrine of a universal Buddha-nature found in the *Nirvāṇa Sūtra.*[25]

Although they were at one point separate, the two strands of *mahātman* and Emptiness fused. Zen knew both; it speaks as often of Emptiness as of Buddha-nature. The Kyoto philosophers still echo the paradox of their synthesis in their insistence on "the no-self that is the true self."

As a term, however, *hongaku* appears for the first time in the *Awakening of Faith* where it is said that the mind of sentient beings is as such already suchness or *tathatā*. It is both real and empty. Because of this mind, there is a priori enlightenment. Not realizing this, a person might seek after wisdom, believing in the possibility of *shikaku* (始覚 Chin., *shih-chüeh*) or incipient enlightenment. Ultimately, though, wisdom is not acquired. It is in us, such that what is perceived as *shikaku* is actually grounded upon and promoted by *hongaku*.

---

[25] The sūtra postdates Nāgārjuna but the idea of a seed (cause) to enlightenment—which is what *buddhagotra* means—has been faulted for being full of antinomies by Nāgārjuna's *Madhyamaka-kārikā.*

The Chinese T'ien-t'ai patriarch Chih-i, who was committed to Mādhyamika and critical of Yogācāra idealism, was reluctant to incorporate this *hongaku* idea. After all, the *Awakening of Faith* is an idealist text teaching a doctrine of "mind only" that Chih-i, who perfected the dialectics of reciprocity, saw as "biased" toward mind at the expense of matter (*rūpa*, form). But the influence of the *Awakening of Faith* was such that its *hongaku* thought infiltrated T'ien-t'ai by the time of the Sung. In Japan, a commentary on the work (大乗止観法門) was even attributed to Chih-i's teacher, Hui-ssu, and accepted as such, so that the idea became an inseparable part of Tendai *hongaku* thought.

Basically, *hongaku* promises the assurance of wisdom for all. It says that there never was a time when we were not enlightened. If one should suppose that one needs to look for enlightenment, then one has already distinguished oneself from the Buddha by falling into the discriminating model of *shikaku* thought. An example of this difference can be seen in the *Platform Sūtra*. Hui-neng, for whom "the Buddha-nature is always pure," understood the *hongaku* idea. His opponent Shen-hsiu, who still worried about "wiping the dust off the mirror," was still languishing in *shikaku* thought — and judged the worse for it. During the Heian period, Japanese Tendai developed the *hongaku* ideology still further.

True to its name, the early years of the Heian period were a time of peace and tranquility. In line with this, Tendai exuded a sense of confidence that all sentient beings had never been alienated from their innate Buddhahood. Though Tendai prized the *Lotus Sūtra* and practiced its own Lotus *samādhi* (meditation), the school was so committed to an all-inclusive faith that it would not refuse legitimacy to any path in the pursuit of the truth. It exhibited a special affinity to Pure Land piety, partly because of Chih-i's alleged commentary on the *Meditation Sūtra* referred to above. The Heian nobility are remembered for "reading the *Lotus* in the morning and chanting Amida in the eve." The latter, performed *sive* and *via* the mind, was no departure from the overall *hongaku* optimism of the time.

The late Heian, however, was a time of calamities, making the earlier peace and tranquility rarities. From the year 1052 onwards,[26] eschatological anxiety over *mappō* (the age of the de-

---

[26] This figure is arrived at by dating the death of the Buddha in 948 BCE and

generate Dharma) had people worried. The omnipresence of wisdom could no longer be assumed. Pure Land confraternities at Mount Hiei began to favor the greater ease of Amida pietism over the more demanding path of the Lotus *samādhi*. Still, no one came forward directly to challenge the *hongaku* ideology—until Hōnen, that is.

Going beyond the Tendai patriarch Genshin,[27] Hōnen set out to dismiss the assumptions of *hongaku* thought. By disowning all availability of the *bodhicitta* in this last age, he ruled out the sage's path of attaining *nirvāṇa* by way of wisdom. No one had ever taken such a radical position before or after. *Bodhicitta*, the aspiration for enlightenment, had simply been accepted as a prerequisite for all Mahāyāna bodhisattvas.[28] Once Hōnen came out in favor of *shikaku*, all major Kamakura thinkers were forced to come to terms with both traditions and to forge their own dialectical combinations of *hongaku* and *shikaku*. Tamura Yoshirō, has worked out a schema classifying the principal figures in Kamakura Buddhism in these terms, and has suggested that to the extent that the Kyoto philosophers are heirs to this unique development in Buddhist thought in Japan, they could also be so classified: Nishida belonging to the *hongaku* idea, Tanabe to the *shikaku*.[29]

A statement made by Tanabe in his *Philosophy as Metanoetics*

---

having the age of the True Dharma 正法 begin in the 1,000th year thereafter, and then the age of the Counterfeit Dharma 像法 in the 1,000th year after that.

[27] Genshin, better remembered in Jōdo circles for popularizing the love for Pure Land and the fear of hell in his *Ōjō-yōshū*, belonged to the Eshin school 恵心流 of esotericized Tendai. Writings bearing his name still aligned Pure Land with mind and considered the chant of the name A-mi-da to be a *mantra* capturing the three truths of the Empty, the Real, and the Middle—that is to say, that the *nembutsu* was itself a psychic realization of the dialectics of the round.

[28] In a Japan heavily influenced by Shingon, it was all but equivalent to enlightenment itself. This is because, according to the *Vairocana Sūtra*, the arousal of this mind of enlightenment virtually guarantees the attainment of enlightenment itself.

[29] Tamura Yoshirō 田村芳朗, 鎌倉新仏教思想の研究 *[Studies in the Thought of the New Buddhism of the Kamakura Era]* (Kyoto: Heiraku-ji, 1965). A more general discussion can be found in a work he co-authored with Umehara Takeshi 梅原 猛, 絶対の真理—天台 *[Absolute Truth: Tendai]* (Tokyo: Kadokawa Shoten, 1970). See also Y. Tamura, "Critique of Original Awakening Thought in Shōshin and Dōgen," *Japanese Journal of Religious Studies*, 11/2-3 (1984): 243-66.

captures his difference from Nishida in this regard. There Tanabe remarks that he would accept "discrimination of nondiscrimination" but not its reverse (56). Here "nondiscrimination" refers to Nothingness as the nondual Absolute absolving all distinctions. "Discrimination within that nondiscrimination" allows for existential distinctions like that between sin and grace, that is, distinctions that may be mediated but not denied. To erase the distinction by reversing the formula—i.e., by the nondiscrimination of discrimination—is possible in *hongaku* thought. There, claims can be made like "I am the Buddha," or "I am Māra," or "Buddha and Māra are one and the same." Tanabe vehemently rejects this strategy, arguing that it quickly leads to antinomianism by making light of one's sinfulness and rendering the grace of Amida irrelevant.

Yet it is just such a distinction that Nishida's "self-identity of absolute contradictories" implies. For Tanabe, however, such a unity-in-identity belongs to the realm of the "aesthetical," which falls short of what Kierkegaard called the "ethical," whose burden can in turn be resolved only through the "religious." The aesthetical is the luxury of the *an sich*, the realm proper to the sage who finds liberation without "returning to this world" for the sake of others.

TWO RESPONSES TO HEIDEGGER—AND A THIRD

We began our discussion with Nishitani's response to Heidegger. Let us now contrast his *hongaku*-inspired response with Tanabe's *shikaku*-defined critique.

Nishitani's work was not restricted to a critique of "ontotheology," but in the crucial final two chapters of *Religion and Nothingness*, offered an alternative to the salvation history of the Christian West.[30] Noting how the unidirectional history of the Christian story—a history with a beginning and an end—is predicated upon a self or soul, he paints a very different sense of history and time when that self is emptied into the "no-self" (*anātman*). Suddenly what is disclosed to the empty being is a temporal infinity with no beginning and no end, and yet an infinity in which past, present, and future can at any moment mys-

---

[30] It is worth noting that the later Heidegger, no longer obsessed with death, spoke instead of the self-disclosure of Being in history, in thought, in words.

teriously interpenetrate each other. It is a worldview that most Buddhologists would see as reminiscent of the Kegon idea of the phenomenal world *(dharmadhātu).*

Where Nishitani used *Being and Time* as a foil to his metaphysics of the "standpoint of *śūnyatā,*" Tanabe took up the moral issue of freedom as his focal point. The freedom that was the pride of the Enlightenment has been given a radical reformulation by Heidegger. Kant had postulated that the rational individual would honor all other, like-minded, free-willing individuals as ends in themselves, and hence aspire naturally for the common good. Such a basically essentialist view of the human equates reason with morality (moral reason). In Heidegger, however, the ontological distinction between the human being with free will and the beast ruled by necessity is reduced to the *possibility* the human has for being concerned about such a distinction that the beast does not. It is of course only a "possibility," since one can also behave like a beast *(Das Mann).* Denying any fixed essence to the human being[31] and insisting rather on the mere possibility of being, Heidegger also takes away all (moral) "content" from that human concern. Sartre's Caligula, for example, opts for evil. One can only hope that in realizing its finitude in the face of its own death, human Dasein will be concerned enough to choose the good.

Heidegger also challenged another modern bias: that things have essences and that humanity has a history. In his early writings, the dimension of history is so severely delimited by the mortality of Dasein that it becomes no more than biography. Still, time was seen as an avenue of self-transcendence. Whereas animals are trapped by their past, human beings have the option of being a mere creature of circumstance or of laying claim to authentic existence and will, that is, "pro-ject ahead" the project of humanity itself. By running ahead to face death, Dasein awakes to its fallen lot—that it has been thrown into the world with no known purpose and fallen among things that made it regard itself as a thing among other things, forgetful of its ontological distinction. Realizing the contingencies of one's past, one is able to be concerned

---

[31] One is reminded here of Ernst Bloch's remark in *Das Prinzip Hoffnung* that the human being is an "unfinished being," much as the French Revolution remains an unfinished revolution.

with the present. The freedom of the human will here is not tied to any moral law but only to the existential project (future) of overcoming its thrown-ness (past). In the end, of course, given the inevitability of death and the limits to human choice, it is no more than a finite freedom for a finite transcendence.

After reviewing the whole history of the idea of freedom from Kant to Fichte, Tanabe concedes to the realism of Heidegger's analysis, but finds his finite solution suffocating. For him, a greater freedom conjoined to a transcendental good is possible. From that vantage point, Heidegger's freedom appears as ōsō, too concerned with its own death and showing too little compassion for others. Death, the curtailing of possibilities, is only a relative *Nichts*. The freedom of the "project" that it promotes is only a self-powered, finite freedom, whereas an encounter with ultimate denial, Absolute Nothingness as Other-power, promises the true freedom. The self dies only to be resurrected in love. Self-concern is transformed into compassion for others. The overcoming is at once an immediate returning.

In turning to a religious solution to the dilemma of human finitude, Tanabe has in one sense turned back from Heidegger to Kierkegaard, albeit without endorsing the "leap of faith" and the total elimination of works of self-power. For him, this was as much a mistake as pure mysticism. The dialectics of reversal or paradox/identity escapes into irrationalism. Reason is retained better in the dialectics of mutual mediation. The self wills to ground itself in a greater Other—Amida—and the resultant unity of wills can then almost magically lift the finite self into accord with the Great Nay that is cosmic love. The right side of the diagram at the top of the following page is meant to depict Tanabe's nondual but asymmetrical dialectics; the left, to show in rough form Nishida's dialectics of paradox/identity.

The asymmetry is due to Tanabe's belief that slavery to the past (evil or karma) prohibits the human individual from carrying out the project of freedom alone. One needs the assistance of Other-power. Freedom is no longer a human project so much as it is Amida's project. Without realizing it, Tanabe altered Heidegger's analysis of time as an existential flow from the future to the past coming to term in the present. Tanabe rather stresses the power of contingency and its accompanying temporal flow from the past through the present to the future, and then counters

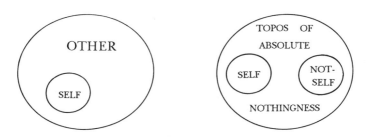

that profane time with the "presence" of the "project" of the "past" Vow of Amida, seeing that vertical interruption of time as the one and only assurance the human being has of a "future" and of ultimate transcendence.

This structure is visible in his reading of the theory of the Three Minds.[32] Originally, the Three Minds follow a sequence from past to present to future. The first or Sincere Mind repents of past sins; the second, the Mind of Faith, puts all its present trust in Amida; the third, the Mind of Aspiring for Birth by Merit-transference, works for future birth in Pure Land. Together they represent the familiar pattern of contrition, faith, and hope. Tanabe recognizes that the mind laden with karma from the past could never by itself be sincere enough to generate the pure faith in the present which is necessary to aspire for future birth in the Pure Land. Only a sudden turn, a metanoesis, in the Mind of Faith can bind the two opposites of the given-ness (thrown-ness) of the past (the *is*) and the openness (pro-ject) of the future (the *ought*). This is accomplished in the present through faith.

As it happens, the traditional commentary on the (present) Mind of Faith divided it into two aspects: objective Dharma (法 *hō*) subjective proclivity (機 *ki*). For Tanabe this vindicates his reading that when one sincerely recognizes the limits of self-power, one triggers the mechanism *(ki)* for the power of Dharmākara's vow *(hō)* to take effect. In this mutual mediation of I and Thou, the human condition is made to comply with the will of the Unconditioned. The resultant unity, 機法一体 *kihō ittai*, thus means

---

[32] PM, ch. 7.

the true compliance of freedom with the good, *jinen hōni*. This is how Tanabe's dialectics of mediation is made to work for human salvation.

A realist — all *shikaku* thinkers are realists — Tanabe harbors no illusions about the fallibility of the human condition. The absolution of past evil (karma) does not do away with relative being as relative and culpable. Nor does the promise of future perfection (Pure Land) dissolve our human, all-too-human history into an eternal now (Nishitani), a datable eschaton (biblical fundamentalism), or a Pure Land beyond (Jōdo other-worldliness). For Tanabe the meaningful advance of history is more like a series of vectors, similar but not identical, pressing forward toward the good. His view of history shares all the ambiguities of the "already" and the "not yet" familiar to Pauline scholars.

Moreover, inasmuch as *shikaku* thinkers tend to be more moral, being all too conscious of the distinction at the level of the "ethical stage" between immoral people and a loving God or compassionate Amida, we find Tanabe speaking of Amida and of God in personal terms, the vocabulary of morality.[33] *Hongaku* thinkers like Nishida, Nishitani, and Abe Masao can indulge themselves in speculations on Absolute Nothingness as the God above God, as *ekkenosis* to the divine *kenosis*, or as the *Ungrund* of the

---

[33] For example, *anātman* sounds like the opposite of the person, yet in one sense, each in its respective tradition represents the highest self-understanding of the human. It is individual person at its most authentic. Christians who regard themselves as persons cannot understand how Pure Land pietists could believe in a fictitious Amitābha. But Pure Land pietists have never considered themselves saved by the "person" Amitābha. One is always saved by the "power of the vow." The vow is what "created" Amitābha in the first place. The vow is not a person, but there is nothing impersonal about the vow which addresses itself to people. The Buddhist sees no self in himself because the self is just a bundle of karma, a coming-together of conditions. But that does not mean the bundle is unreal or all of its components are of the same value — no more than Christians regard everything about their persons as sacred. When Shin Buddhists talk about the power of the vow, they are talking about those positive bundles — the aspiration for enlightenment, the commitment to compassion — that represent and are the good and the true; in short, the forces of benevolence in the universe. Seen in this light, Christians who harp on the absence of a creator in the Buddhist faith are mistaken. For the power of the vow has in effect created *ex nihilo* a New Heaven and a New Earth, i.e. the Pure Land, the destiny of every selfless *anātman* who believes in its ultimate reality.

Urgrund — all luxuries of mystics and aestheticists — in a way that the Tanabe of *Philosophy as Metanoetics* could not. It is little wonder that Tanabe strikes such a familiar chord with Christian confessional theologies, however foreign and inaccessible much of his Buddhist language.

Nishitani and Tanabe each responded to Heidegger his way. But there is at least another way of reading Heidegger without the corrective of a "*topos* of Absolute Nothingness." In the human world, Being is not something "other" to the human. On the contrary, as Dasein, the human individual as such is the "*topos* of Being," the *Da* of *Sein*. The human world is the only world in which Being can be disclosed to us. This does not mean that our world is the same as the objective world of nature that it is for science, the mere *Umwelt* of living beings. It is always and ever the lived world, the intimate *Lebenswelt* of meaningful faces and places that we all build around ourselves. And where does Being disclose itself within this life-space of ours? In things, *seiendes*, the being of Being. It is as wrong to characterize Heidegger's Being as something set over against the human as it is to accuse him of a residual Cartesian dichotomy between subject and object, the divine and the human, phenomena and Being. Indeed the whole point in laying out the structure of our being as Dasein is to rewrite the Cartesian model, the cold world of modern science that few of us really live in but which many of us suppose we actually live in.

Our everyday lives no more belong to a subject-object world than to its opposite, those rare moments of subject-object unity that mystics and anti-Cartesians dream of. Both worlds are "unreal" to our normal experience. My world is not full of "objects," things totally other to me. My lived world is made up of things *zuhanden* and *vorhanden*, things more or less intimate and friends I neither can nor wish to objectify; it is made up of fears and enemies that refuse to be pushed aside. Science sees a world of objects within which living beings move by instinct or choice. But our world is a world of faces and places in which everything can be a messenger of the Divine — even if it usually "hides as much as it reveals."

The hiding of Being is more visible in the early Heidegger, where the finiteness of freedom and transcendence is stressed. The self-disclosure of Being is more present, though little expressed, in the later Heidegger. For all his similarity to Zen in this regard, Heidegger remains the prophet and shepherd of Being, not of Absolute Nothingness. His world is not the world of *saṃsāra*-vs.-*nirvāṇa* or of *saṃsāra-sive-nirvāṇa*. It is forever a penumbra where Being and Nothingness cohabitate like *yang* and *yin* to yield this world of mixed blessings we call home. We live in Plato's cave, facing the shadows dancing on the wall, but, says Heidegger, we should be thankful for the light that streams through the opening. That light of Being which otherwise blinds now makes visible the shadow of its being *(seiendes)* in our field of vision. From the shadow of things at hand we catch a glimpse of that which "hides even as it reveals, reveals even as it hides." For those of us content with watching the penumbra on the wall, it makes no sense to "empty the cave" (à la Nishida) or to wish that the light (of Amida) might "snatch us from the darkness" (à la Tanabe). In the end, Bodhidharma found what he found—if you pardon the mix of metaphors—gazing at the wall.

The "Self That is Not a Self": Tanabe's Dialectics of Self-Awareness

James W. HEISIG

IN a 1951 essay entitled "The Philosophies of Nishida and Tanabe," Nishitani Keiji, who had studied under both philosophers, writes:

> While Tanabe's philosophy pivots around action or praxis . . . Nishida's philosophy pivots around self-awareness. . . . Now these two standpoints are by and large the same in that they represent a standpoint of a *self that is not a self* turning on the same axis of absolute nothingness. . . . For the one, the *action* of the self that is not a self is not to be separated from its *witness*. For the other, self-awareness means that in terms of the "historical body," working is seeing.[1]

From this position, Nishitani takes up the argument of *Philosophy as Metanoetics*, points to some of its precedents in Tanabe's earlier thought, pulls out its implicit criticism of Nishida, and highlights what he sees as Tanabe's misreadings of his teacher's thought. The result is perhaps the most informed and careful critique of Tanabe's book to come out of the Kyoto circle. Tanabe did not respond to it in print. I should like here to follow up on some of the ideas found there, fully aware that what I have to say is scarcely worthy of lacing the sandals of Nishitani's footnotes.

To begin with, the term "self that is not a self" is Nishida's. As far as I know, it does not appear in Tanabe,[2] though it sounds very much like something Tanabe might have said. Nishitani's

---

[1] Reprinted in 西田幾多郎 ―その人と思想 [*Nishida Kitarō: The Man and His Thought*] (Tokyo, 1985), 222, 226-27. An English translation of this work, prepared jointly by Yamamoto Seisaku and myself, is slated for publication within the coming months.

[2] Takeuchi Yoshinori has confirmed my suspicions on this point.

choice of the term as a common ground is not without a certain irony if one recalls that Tanabe had spoken positively of his own "metanoetics" as "a philosophy that is not a philosophy"[3] while earlier he had dismissed Nishida's logic of place as the attempt to pass off "a logic that is not a logic."[4]

In any case, the idea of philosophy as the cultivation of a "self that is not a self" is a fitting crystallization of Tanabe's late thought and gives us a foothold from which to look back and trace the course of development that led to his final view of the dialectics of religious existence.

That Tanabe was not the best judge of the differences between his philosophy and that of his predecessor in the Chair of Philosophy at Kyoto University seems clear enough. It is not entirely surprising that a person as uncompromisingly rational as Tanabe would allow deep emotional interferences in the rational process to go unreflected. After having discussed this matter with some of his former students and colleagues, however, and having read what I can of the available literature, I have determined it the wiser course to leave the psychological side of the question to others and restrict myself to the texts.

From Nishida, the young Tanabe learned to think of philosophy as a self-awareness grounded in absolute nothingness, a view he never abandoned though it took time for the idea to mature in him to the level it had in his teacher. Immediately after returning from studies abroad, he acquiesced to Nishida's request and prepared a memorial essay in 1924 for the 200th anniversary of Kant's birth. The result, entitled "Kant's Teleology," was basically a critique of the formalism of Kant's third critique in the light of Scheler's ethics of concrete values. In its concluding sections Tanabe brought his neo-Kantian studies to bear on his own attempt to fill up what is lacking in "content" in Kant's third critique by combining practical reason and enlightenment. He called his idea "the finality of self-awareness" and he offered it as "a common principle weaving history, religion, and morality into an indivisible relationship with one another."[5]

---

[3] See PM, 1.
[4] Cited in Nishitani, *Nishida Kitarō*, 275.
[5] See TCW 3:72.

On his understanding, it is not a universal "moral law within" that grounds practical judgment but absolute nothingness, the self-awareness of which gives a kind of ultimate telos to moral judgment. On the surface, this is fully consistent with Nishida's thought, and yet there is a subtle subjectivism here at cross-purposes to Nishida. In the attempt to shift the universal of practical judgment from a *datum* to a *captum*, and hence to maintain absolute nothingness as the ultimate fact of reality, both the consciousness that creates meaning and the self-awareness of a necessary finality in the creative process that drives it to its deeper ground beyond being, seem to set the knowing subject up as a relative being that confronts the world and absolute nothingness as its objects. Consequently, the true self works primarily as a moral *ideal* to be brought into being and not as a "deep reality" that need only be awakened to.

Tanabe himself was aware of the latent subject-object dichotomy in his thinking, and in a 1931 collection entitled *Hegel's Philosophy and the Absolute Dialectic* (a portion of which was published in a collection commemorating the centennial of Hegel's death), he tried to make adjustments. Dissatisfied with the crudeness of his former "dialectic"[6] and feeling that his idea of moral judgment was still too formalistic and lacking in content, Tanabe had cast himself for five years headlong into the study of Hegel. Through this study he found his way out of the "vacuity" of the Kantian universal of judgment and into the enchantment of Hegel's view of history. Under the influence of colleagues like Tosaka Jun and Miki Kiyoshi, he quickly came to replace what he saw as the equally vacuous notion of absolute knowledge that crowned Hegel's system with "a self-awareness of praxis," again grounded in an absolute nothingness beyond being. Under the influence of Heidegger, whom he knew personally from his studies abroad, he dubbed his reinterpretation of Hegel an "ethico-religious existential dialectic" wherein the enlightened state of self-awareness works an absolute negation on both matter and ideas.[7]

Relative to the absolute nothingness beyond being, Tanabe's idea of the self was no longer that of a knowing subject facing

---

[6] He refers to his "finality of self-awareness" as a "dialectic of will" that combines elements Kant had left unrelated. TCW 3:4, 64.

[7] A brief account of this process can be found in TCW 3:78-81.

a world of objects but of a self of praxis *in* the world and yet enlightened to the ultimacy of absolute nothingness. The shift from the moral subject he had forged in his critique of Kant was considerable but still inadequate. Compared with Nishida's "logic of place," which was framed during the very years that Tanabe was immersed in his reading of Hegel, Tanabe's dialectics seemed to lean in the same direction of defining the self in terms of creative seeing (or praxis) rather than passive knowing; but it was still the object of the praxis, the historical world, and not absolute nothingness that gave the self the concreteness he demanded of it. In a word, the idea of affirming the self by negating the *individuality* of the self vis-à-vis a larger historical whole is clear; the idea of affirming a true self by negating the *being* of the self vis-à-vis the nothingness of the absolute is not. Absolute nothingness remained an asymptotic ideal towards which the historical self aims.

(By this time, incidentally, Tanabe's reputation as an abstract, rationalist thinker was solidly fixed. In his introduction to the collection of essays on Hegel, Tanabe admitted that "my past bias towards abstraction stems from a flaw in my speculative powers," but begged indulgence for the abstractions of the dialectic since they were not of his own doing but showed "the general form and stages of human thought."[8] If my summary of Tanabe's ideas makes him sound like a *doctus spectare lacunar* without sufficient attention to his uncommonly rigorous demand for clarity of expression, I assure you, it is not for want of sympathy.)

In any event, it was during the fifteen years that Tanabe lectured on Hegel's thought (1929-1943) that he worked hardest to appropriate Nishida's ideas into his own growing attachment to the affirmation-in-negation of the dialectic. It was also during this time that his critique of Nishida's idea of self-awareness as too far removed from historical praxis took shape. As Nishitani notes:

> Curiously, it almost seems as if the principle of negation that thoroughly opposes and rejects the tendency of the self-awareness of absolute nothingness to embrace all things gives

---

[8] TCW 3:76-77.

us a mirror-image of Tanabe himself desperately struggling
to escape the embrace of Nishida's philosophy.[9]

The results of Tanabe's critique crystallized in his theory of the
logic of species. The purpose of the logic of species was not only
to see concrete cultures as an indispensable but nonrational force
that mediates the dialectical relationship between the individual
and history, but also to include the ideas of "absolute nothingness" and "self-awareness" in the realms of the historically con-
ditioned. In addition to widening the gap between his dialectics
and Nishida's logic of place, the logic of species had two immediate effects on Tanabe's appropriation of the idea of the "true
self of self-awareness" as he had inherited it from Nishida.

First, whereas Nishida had taken the idea of a "true self" in
the wider sense to include the true essence of things in nature,
Tanabe restricted his attentions to the realm of the human. On
the one hand, he felt that Nishida had oversimplified the way
from the ordinary self to the true self, reckoning it to be a matter
for *privatized* self-awareness. On the other, he felt the lack of
sufficient attention to the moral element through overemphasis
on a trans-subjective self.[10] Tanabe's counter-tendency to relativize
absolute nothingness to historical praxis and to define the true
self as a goal to be strived for rather than as a reality to be
awakened to was, of course, already present in germ in his earlier
studies of Kant and Hegel. But it was his notion of the logic of
species that provided the pivot on which all of his later work
would turn, including his continued judgment that all Nishida's
attempts at historical concreteness were ultimately misguided.

Second, the logic of species introduced a two-edged critical
principle for judging cultures: vis-à-vis their relationship to the
wider aims of the world community and vis-à-vis their relationship
to the cultivation of self-awareness in the individual. The further
Tanabe retreated from the realms of the abstract dialectic, however, to the actual stage of historical events where totalitarian
ideals were being forged for a nation on the brink of total war,
the more he showed the weakness of his philosophy's critical powers. Since it is this disastrous venture into the concrete that oc-

[9] *Nishida Kitarō*, 217.
[10] See his "Inquiring of Nishida," TCW 4:305-28.

casioned the turning point to his metanoetics, it cannot be passed over in silence.[11]

On hearing that Heidegger had joined hands with the Nazis, Tanabe penned a short article entitled "The Philosophy of Crisis or a Crisis for Philosophy" in which he roundly criticized his former friend:

> Even as Heidegger aims at championing the racial signifi-cance of German academia, it is odd that it should look like an emphasizing of the uniqueness of German philosophy vis-à-vis Greek philosophy. Philosophy cannot, as he thinks, simply dedicate itself to the nation by means of a simple resignation to destiny.[12]

For some reason, the piece was not published, but only discovered later among his papers, bearing the date September 5, 1933. Whether or not he communicated these sentiments directly to Heidegger is not clear. (What we do know of his direct contact with Nazi Germany is that in 1941, upon hearing that Jaspers and his wife were in danger from the Nazi persecution, he inter-vened with others to secure their safety, an event for which Jaspers expressed his eternal gratitude in a letter later to Takeuchi Yoshi-nori.[13])

Despite this early reaction against the subservience of philos-ophy to national interests, in no time Tanabe was caught up in the government's problem of "inquiring into grounds for the com-pulsion of the nation's individuals and seeking rational foundations for this compulsion." He obliged the official concern in a 1936 essay entitled "The Logic of Social Existence," where he argued that "religion does not simply negate war, but clearly ought to excite humanitarians to national questions."[14] In a series of articles written in 1939 under the title "The Logic of National Existence," he melded a critique of Nishida's idea of "the self-identity of absolute contradictories" with the following kinds of statement:

---

[11] In taking up this question, I mean to redress the exaggeration of earlier comments made in my Foreword to the English translation of *Philosophy as Meta-noetics*, xvii.

[12] TCW 8:8.

[13] For references to the event, see Ienaga Saburō 家永三郎 , 田辺元の思想史 的研究 [*A Study of the History of Tanabe's Thought*], 64-66; see also above, 10-11.

[14] TCW 6:163.

The act of self-denial in which individuals sacrifice themselves for the sake of the nation turns out to be an affirmation of existence. Because the nation to which the individual has been sacrificed bears within itself the source of life of the individual, it is not merely a matter of sacrificing oneself for the other. Quite the contrary, *it is a restoration of the self to the true self.* This is why self-negation is turned to self-affirmation and the whole unites with the individual. The free autonomy of ethics is not extinguished in service to the nation and in submission to its orders, but rather made possible thereby.[15]

This tone continues all the way up until 1943. Almost immediately before his turn to metanoetics, we find him writing in an essay entitled "Life and Death":

In time of crisis country and individual are one; the people dedicate themselves out of necessity to the country. To distance oneself from one's country means at the same time to destroy the self itself. . . . On this standpoint, the self does not live and die, but is put to death and restored to life through God or the absolute.[16]

One should not suppose that these positions were part of Tanabe's break with Nishida, but neither were they entirely consistent with the latter's ideas. Indeed, in 1940 Nishida is reported to have snapped to a common friend, "This Tanabe's stuff is completely fascist!"[17] By the same token, Tanabe's eventual repudiation of these nationalistic views had nothing to do with Nishida's political views, even though his statements are encased in the language of an ongoing battle with Nishida.

Tanabe's turn to metanoetics looks, on the face of it, to be a retreat from the concrete to the safety of the abstract. If one reads the texts without too much attention to how they were received or what purpose they served, one finds that the style

---

[15] TCW 7:41. Emphasis added.

[16] TCW 8:260. Ienaga strings together an impressive array of quotes to show the pattern that has emerged in Tanabe's thinking at this time. See *A Study of the History of Tanabe's Thought*, 68-71.

[17] The statement was made to Aihara Shinsaku 相原信作 , later Minister of Education, as he reports in a brief "Remembrance" affixed to vol. 12 of Tanabe's Collected Works.

remains fairly even throughout his work. Even his own "metanoia" is carried on in the same generalized terms as his arguments for the supremacy of the nation had been—as a repentance and conversion of philosophy which is best managed by the *bombu* or "ignorant fools" in whose broad class he includes himself.

Only much later do we find in print a statement as clear and unambiguous as we could expect about his feelings regarding his former position. After the Manchurian Incident in 1931, he tells us in a 1951 essay, he began to feel indirect pressures as a professor of philosophy in a state university monitored by the government. Given his "constitutional dislike for reactionary irrationalism" of this sort, he avoided the issues the government was throwing up and devoted his energies to expounding on existentialist thought. He continues:

> But as the tensions of World War II grew ever more fierce and with it the regulation of thinking, weak-willed as I was, I found myself unable to resist and could not but yield to some degree to the prevalent mood, which is a shame deeper than I can bear. The already blind militarism had led so many of our graduates precipitously to the battlefields; among the fallen were more than ten from philosophy, for which I feel the height of personal responsibility and remorse. I can only lower my head and earnestly lament my sin.[18]

If the spirit of personal repentance works a powerful effect on the arguments of *Philosophy as Metanoetics*, they do not seem significantly to have altered the structure of his dialectical understanding of the self. What *has* changed is the focus: concrete history, which had once provided the central locus for the praxis whereby the self dies to itself to be reborn and where the ideal of the true self takes shape, is displaced to the periphery to make room for self-awareness of the finitude of all historical praxis.

In the context of Tanabe's idea of metanoetics, the "self" of "self that is not a self" is the particular individual that has broken free of everyday actions to attain to insight into the fundamental human condition of finiteness and to engage in repentance for its deluded moral behavior. Given his failure to develop the notion

---

[18] TCW 14:439. Here again, a fine list of supplementary statements is provided by Ienaga, *A Study of the History of Tanabe's Thought*, 75-82.

of the true self beyond the point of a moral ideal, this self-negating dimension of the dialectic of self-awareness (the self-power of the relative being) calls out for an equally autonomous "other" to invert this negation and affirm a new self, a "self that is not a self" (the Other-power of absolute nothingness). As Nishitani notes, this is different from Nishida's idea of self-awareness, wherein the self does not become something else from its everyday self but only becomes aware of a different mode of being. "*Ontically*, so to speak, it remains the same even though its *ontological* ground has shifted."[19] In his last essay, Nishida himself makes the point still more clearly, his references to Tanabe by this time being as indirect as Tanabe's to him:

> The question of religion lies not in what our self *should be* as an acting being, but in the question of *what kind of existence* the self has. . . .
>
> People have frequently attempted to ground the religious demand merely from the standpoint of the imperfection of the self which wanders into error. But merely from such a perspective of error the religious consciousness does not emerge. . . . Moreover, to err religiously is not to err in the purposes of the self, but concerning the place where the self truly exists. Even in regard to morality, the true religious mind does not emerge merely from the powerlessness of the self in regard to the moral good objectively conceived, no matter how acute the feeling is, as long as there lies at the bottom of this moral sentiment the self-confidence of moral power. Though it is generally called repentance [*zange*], it is merely remorse over the evil of the self, but self-power still remains.[20]

Not surprisingly, Tanabe rejected Nishida's paradoxical formation of a "continuity of discontinuity" to solve the problem of the continuance through time of a true self within the ever-changing everyday self. And he did so precisely because it seems to him

---

[19] Nishitani, *Nishida Kitarō*, 228.

[20] Trans. by David Dilworth as "Religious Consciousness and the Logic of the *Prajñāpāramitā Sūtra*," MN 25 (1970):212-12. I have adjusted the translation slightly, but still prefer this older rendition of the passage to Dilworth's later reworking of it *Nishida Kitarō, Last Writings* (Honolulu: University of Hawaii Press, 1987).

to eliminate the radical forfeiture of the actual self which he saw as the beginning of self-awareness:

> Self-awareness is not the introversion into itself of a self continuing in existence. There can be no turn inward for a self that continues identical with itself. Self-awareness is brought about when the self takes leave of this position and destroys and erases itself. . . .[21]

With Tanabe, then, it is the deluded self, the sinner filled with *avidyā* and passion, that is the self's true countenance, both ontically and ontologically. The ineluctable finiteness of human autonomy can only lead to an experience of the self as *not a self*—that is, as a self that can no longer rely on the self-power that defines it as self. To realize the ideal of a *self* that is not a self requires an Other-power, the awakening to which does not dispose of the self's finiteness and yet somehow reaffirms its existence and its relation to other relative beings.

Where Nishida's "true self" pointed to an original state of awareness that can be cultivated by transcending the work of discriminating consciousness and the realm of being it constitutes, Tanabe's ideal self is cultivated through an awareness of a radical relativity and the futility of reliance on its own powers. For each, the "self that is not a self" rests on absolute nothingness. For Nishida, nothingness is experienced as a seeing in which world and subject are one—defining each other, creating each other, erasing each other. For Tanabe, it is experienced as an absolute mediation in which all relationships between the subject and the world, between one subject and another, are seen to belong to a history whose rhythms transcend those of our own willful praxis.

After his first full-fledged experiment with Shin Buddhist categories in *Philosophy as Metanoetics*, Tanabe's thought seemed to turn more and more in the direction erasing the very borderlines between philosophy and religion that he had earlier accused Nishida's logic of place of ignoring.[22] In other words, his understanding of the implications for philosophy of the idea of the self-awareness of absolute nothingness had at last broadened to

---

[21] *Existenz, Love, and Praxis*, 11.

[22] See TCW 4:311.

[23] While I cannot speak for Shinran scholarship as a whole, it does seem to

the full reach of Nishida's understanding, different though the results were. Leaving aside questions of the validity of Tanabe's reading of Shin Buddhism,[23] the main contours of the difference are apparent in the structure of his next book, *Existenz, Love, and Praxis.*

For Tanabe, Existenz, love, and practice each point to a necessary condition for religious self-awareness. *Existenz* represents an awakening to the element of human finiteness that characterizes the self as it is (i.e., the self in-itself). *Love* represents an awakening to the mediating work of the power of absolute nothingness which affirms the self in its freedom to be other than it is (the self for-itself). *Praxis* represents the enlightened action of the self that has let go of itself and hence begun to realize its potential (the self in-itself and for-itself).[24] Together these three ingredients make up the final telos of the philosophical task. In that sense, the "philosophy that is not a philosophy" is so called because it is a *deliberately religious* philosophy.

If this same pattern of finitude, mediation, life-in-death is

---

me that Tanabe has confused one rather elemental part of the doctrine in his understanding of "self-power-*in*-Other-power" as representing a synthesis of opposites. The problem is that the two "powers" are not of the same logical type. Whereas Other-power is understood to be the real, acting power that moves all things, self-power is a misunderstanding of that power, a deluded perception of its working in the individual as one's own powers. Thus it is not a synthesis of the two but a total overcoming of the one by the other that Shinran calls for. The problem may be that Tanabe has read *ōsō* as the self-power *sō* (aspect) of reality and *gensō* as the Other-power aspect, which led him to identify "self-power-*in*-Other-power" with "*ōsō*-in-*gensō*" (see, for example, PM, 167). No less an authority on Shinran's work than Terakawa Shunshō 寺川俊昭 has confirmed my reading of the apparent contradiction of self-power and Other-power, as also that *ōsō* and *gensō* refer only to aspects of Other-power. That is, one can only speak of *ōsō-ekō* and *gensō-ekō* (the terms are present already in Donran). Finally, while I think it is within Tanabe's right as a philosopher to reinterpret the *ōsō-gensō* model as the path of self-awareness, it should be made clear that this is not the teaching of Shinran, for whom actual death and passage into the Pure Land were requisite for the conversion from one to the other.

[24] Tanabe himself so defines the purpose of his book in the preface to *The Dialectics of Christianity* (TCW 10:14). This preface, incidentally, contains probably Tanabe's clearest published statement on his own religious background, his interest in Christianity, and his search for a religion of self-awareness. Combined with his reflections on being a "Christian in the making" (TCW 10:258-61), they give an equally clear image of his own relationship to organized

repeated again and again in Tanabe's late work, in a variety of paraphrases, it is not merely because it was widely applicable. Beneath the surface of his thought flowed a deeper concern that suggests a basic shift from his earlier position: the question of death. The turning point for this concern was clearly the death of his wife in 1951. The fact that Tanabe continues to frame his comments by distinguishing his views from those of Nishida should not overshadow the importance of this final major turn of his thinking.

Up to the very end, Nishida insisted on the primacy of life for philosophy. In a 1944 essay on Descartes we read:

> The problems of philosophy arise from our self-awareness of a deep life. Even Greek philosophy, which it said to have arisen in wonder, in fact came from the intelligent Greeks' own self-awareness of life . . . Philosophy is nothing other than a self-aware expression of life.[25]

That this had long been Tanabe's own view is reflected in a 1925 essay on "The Logic of Species and the World Scheme":

> Life and logic do not exist apart from one another. It is only their correlative identity that exists concretely. When we focus on the aspect of immediacy, we speak of life, and when we focus on the aspect of mediation, we call it logic. Just as there is no logic apart from life, there can be no life of philosophical self-awareness apart from logic. Logic is the logic of life, and the self-awareness of life is the self-awareness of logic.[26]

But in the final section of *Existenz, Love, and Praxis*, Tanabe takes direct issue with this view, converting philosophy to the Socratic ideal of "practicing death."[27] The influence of Heidegger here is, of course, important; but he went on to relate it to the story of Jesus and the Zen samurai ideal in a way Heidegger

---

religion.

[25] Nishida Kitarō, TCW 11:186-87. Nishida's stress on "life" stems as much from his early interest in vitalist metaphysics as from an early personal conviction. This concern is reflected strongly in his diaries, where Nishida pledges frequently that he will put scholarship at the service of life and not turn it in on itself. See Lothar Knauth's "Life is Tragic: The Diary of Nishida Kitarō," MN 20 (1965):334-58.

[26] TCW 6:185.

could not have. In any case, the death — or negation — of the self in which one "lets go" of the self or removes it from the world of life and being to "make it nothing" turns out to be a mediation (a skillful means, *hōben*) for coming to the affirmation of a new life. In this way he brings together strands from his earlier writing to develop a dialectic of death-in-life and life-in-death that becomes the final touchstone of religious self-awareness.

In an essay written about this same time under the title, "Christianity, Marxism, and Japanese Buddhism," Tanabe describes his understanding of the content of religious self-awareness as a Love-in-Nothingness that mediates the whole of our relative existence. It is only from a commitment to the real power of this basic fact of life that one can "turn to logic what there is of myth" in religion. This includes not only the *ōsō-gensō* Pure Land myth of the bodhisattva Dharmākara, but also the Christian myth of the *kenōsis* or self-emptying of God in Christ. The dialectic common to both of them is one of self-descent (annihilating the self) and self-ascent (reaffirming the self), or of death-in-life and life-in-death. In each case, the religious person, "the subject of sin," dies the death of despair over its own finiteness and is restored to life through an absolute conversion to the infinite power of absolute nothingness, God or Other-power.[28]

Even so cursory a reading of Tanabe's work as the foregoing suffices to raise the question of how far his project of a philosophical metanoetics makes sense apart from his own repentance over the abuse of philosophy for nationalistic ends. The fact that it was clearly his intention that it should do so, introduces the further question of whether a metanoetical theory would in fact have sufficed to protect him from that abuse had he developed it twenty years earlier.

The framing of the question — as Tanabe himself would have understood immediately — already contains the answer. The function of conceptual schemes is not to replace moral judgments but to relativize them. At best our schemes work therapeutically to insure that certain questions do not go unasked by imagining (or remembering) what happens when they do. Whatever sense we

---

[27] TCW 9:190ff.

make of the moral options that history places before us, it is not a question of solidly "grounding" them in knowledge but of making biases transparent, of bringing light to bear on our certitudes. In this regard, there is no purely philosophic prophylaxis for the sort of misguided effort Tanabe made in the war years—not even one that aims at disrupting reason by reason and making a "philosophy that is not a philosophy." Ultimately, there is no way rationally to systematize the kind of metanoia he went through.

Paradoxically, then, the lesson of his metanoetics is that even rationalizations of the limits of reason only make sense in the context of concrete moral decisions. This was the *idea* from which Tanabe's work began. The story of its long path to *appropriation*, however abstract the terms in which it was couched, belongs very much to the story of modern Japan and his participation in that story.

At the same time, if the enduring value of Tanabe's contribution does not seem to rest in his critique of Nishida, neither can it be restricted to a chapter in the intellectual history of Japan. There is much more in Tanabe's view of the "self that is not a self" that excites the imagination of Western intellectual history than he himself could have known. Like Nishida, Tanabe wrote for an exclusively Japanese audience and it never seems to have occurred to him to solicit the translation of his work for foreign readership and evaluation. And yet it is precisely by taking his experiment with the idea of the self-awareness of absolute nothingness *out of its native environment* and transplanting it in Western soil, that the question of its place in world intellectual history can be asked. Happily, everything in Tanabe—even at his most nationalistic—begs for just this kind of critical study.

Tanabe's Contribution to East-West Dialogue

Carol ZALESKI

A few years ago, through the kind mediation of Professor Unno's son Mark, my husband and I had the good fortune to interview Professor Nishitani at his home in Kyoto. My first introduction to the Kyoto School thus came in a living and vibrant form (indeed, when Professor Nishitani concluded our interview by taking us on a walking tour of the shrines in his hilly neighborhood, we could barely keep up with him).

Our symposium has been a similarly live encounter, and a welcome opportunity to learn from those who have been struggling with the questions which are central to this school of thought. The four presentations on "Metanoetics and Philosophy" not only shed light on several aspects of Tanabe's work, but also offer insight into the prospects of philosophy in the present age. I especially appreciated Professor Heisig's discussion of the complex interactions between metanoetics and concrete moral decision-making, and his call (in spoken comments) for philosophy to return to its poetic and mythic roots; Professor Kawamura's clarification of the relation between the logic of place and the logic of species; Professor Lai's elucidation of the reciprocity between self-power and Other-power in Mahāyāna schools of thought; and Professor Maraldo's observations on the connections between Tanabe and more recent philosophical responses to the crisis of reason.

Since I have only recently become acquainted with Tanabe's thought, my response will identify what seem to me to be the shared concerns and questions emerging from the four papers. I begin, however, with a few remarks on the features of *Philosophy as Metanoetics* which I have found most promising and most troubling. My initial impression of Tanabe—when I first cracked the binding of *Philosophy as Metanoetics*—was one of sympathy and admiration. Tanabe struck me as an embodiment of the tradition which in the West has been called *philosophia*, the love of wisdom, and the dedication to search for wisdom—a dedication which has evoked in its devotees as deep a commitment as any religious quest. *Philosophia* as love of wisdom is not just a vague sentiment, but a concrete form of faith and discipline, handed down from teacher to disciple in the Greek philosophical tradition. As Wilfred Cantwell Smith has argued, the *philosophia* tradition is still with us today, although it may be difficult to recognize as such. The very institution in which we are holding our conversations on Tanabe is a temple to our inherited faith in reason and in the liberating power of an autonomous pursuit of truth.

Although faith in reason is the enduring legacy of the *philosophia* tradition, reason shows a different face to every generation. To Tanabe, it seemed urgently necessary to dethrone reason in order to make room for a more Socratic philosophical faith, a faith in wisdom that is at once practical in its orientation and limited in its metaphysical pretensions.

From this Socratic viewpoint, *philosophia* is not so much a contemplative flight of the alone to the Alone, as an open-ended and dialectical wayfaring; one is drawn along this way by the irresistible attraction of the ever-receding goal of wisdom. To be on this way, one must begin as Socrates did, with a purifying confession of one's own ignorance.

Hence, when Tanabe speaks of "my incompetence as a philosopher" he establishes his credentials to carry on the tradition of *philosophia*. And thus he wins our sympathy—for we are all secretly, if not openly, aware of our incompetence as philosophers. When Tanabe confesses his incompetence as a philosopher, he seems to break that mutual conspiracy by which everyone pretends to be competent, and to be efficiently building on the achievements of earlier generations.

If we begin with an acknowledgement of our ignorance, and if we think of *philosophia* as wayfaring, we are not so likely to suppose that any systematic edifice will be our final resting place. We may recognize the need to build systems, but we will also be free not to make them our fixed abodes. We will steer clear of literalness in philosophy just as vigilantly as we steer clear of fundamentalism in religion.

If, on the other hand, we begin with an absolute confidence in reason (understood in the more narrow sense bestowed upon it by the Modern West), then we must feel that our mission at all costs is to establish the grounds for certainty and overcome the circularity of our arguments. The great fear, for this kind of philosophy, is that if we acknowledge the circularity and historicity of reason, we will succumb to paralyzing skepticism.

Tanabe sees how shortsighted this fear is: the logic of skepticism is as circular as the logic of rationalism; indeed skepticism trails along behind dogmatic rationalism in the very same neverending circle. Once we realize this, we can stop "trying to jump over our own knees" — to use a proverbial analogy.

When Tanabe expresses this insight, I hear him as one of the most promising voices in the "after philosophy" or "end of philosophy" movement. This is a point Professor Maraldo makes in his paper, associating Tanabe with Heidegger, Rorty, Derrida, Foucault and others who embrace the historicity and social shaping of reason. What I find especially exciting about Tanabe's contribution is that he links this insight to a an experience of awakening and conversion in which one's whole being is involved. Finally, he makes me hope, *philosophia* might recover some of its tarnished luster and regain its effectiveness as a vehicle of spiritual transformation.

It is just at this point, however, that I become frustrated as a novice reader of Tanabe. Perhaps I have misunderstood his aims. I thought I heard him suggest that the ground rules for doing philosophy have been radically changed; but I am not sure I see this actually happening.

The papers by Professors Heisig, Kawamura, Lai, and Maraldo help us to understand both the contribution Tanabe has made and the problems he has created for reconstructing *philosophia* after the death of philosophy. Among the questions these papers raise for us, I would like to focus on the following:

1. What happens when "conversion" is treated as a category of philosophical discourse?
2. Is it possible to appropriate the polarities which are basic to Tanabe's thought (self-power and Other-Power, the logic of place and the logic of species) without oversimplifying the philosophical and soteriological traditions he represents?

3. Does the Absolute really function as a non-ontological category in Tanabe's thought?
4. Is a consensus emerging about where philosophy should be heading in these "after philosophy" times?

CONVERSION

Earlier in this symposium, Professor Kawamura raised the question of whether it is intelligible to speak about conversion as a philosophical category without filling it in with religious content.

Some insight into this question might be derived from a consideration of historical analogues. In Greek, Hellenistic, and Roman literature (as demonstrated by Arthur Darby Nock, Werner Jaeger and others), accounts of philosophical conversion abound. Conversion takes the form of turning from shadows to light, remembering forgotten truths, recovering one's true nature, or returning from the realm of multiplicity to one's home in the changeless. The imagery is varied, but all of it suggests that philosophical conversion is preeminently a self-power experience: one need only turn inward in order to rediscover the lost knowledge that has saving power.

It hardly needs to be pointed out that Tanabe's conversion is of a different kind. For Tanabe, conversion is less like self-recovery and more like being plucked from the jaws of Leviathan. It is extraordinary—and gives one pause—to find philosophical conversion described with the kind of language and imagery that is usually reserved for revelation-based and prophetic religious experience. One cannot help but wonder whether Tanabe's conversion language has burst the bounds of philosophical truth-seeking and broken forth into concrete religious confession.

A comparison to Augustine might be instructive; Augustine's conversion to *philosophia*, although an ardent one, was overwhelmed by and subsumed into his more radically Other-powered conversion to Christianity. Tanabe's account of his philosophical metanoia seems more compatible with Augustine's religious conversion than with Augustine's discovery of philosophy. All that is lacking to make the parallel more exact is overt commitment to a particular religious tradition. Yet I wonder whether we could understand or appreciate Tanabe's account of his conversion if we were unaware of his links to the Shin Buddhist tradition? If these links are essential, then why should we accept the claim that the whole salvation drama has unfolded within the horizons of philosophy?

Another illuminating comparison can be found in Nishitani's treatment of the conversion from egoity to nihility to emptiness. The conversion Nishitani evokes has a heroic quality to it. When I read Nishitani, I am reminded of the Epic of Gilgamesh, the Mesopotamian king whose failed quest for an antidote to death finally leads him (after the collapse of his false values and impossible dreams) to attain the wisdom of acceptance.

Tanabe's conversion, on the other hand, does not lend itself to depiction in the epic or heroic mode; rather, he reminds one of prophetic figures such as Jonah, Job, Augustine, Luther, Bunyan, Tolstoy, and Muhammad, who were made and remade by a holy power beyond them. These are by no means passive souls, but rather exceptionally dynamic personalities, whose dynamism is attributed to receptivity rather than to self-will. It is difficult to imagine an epic or heroic myth which could effectively portray this special religious genius for receptivity.

One question, then, is whether Tanabe is consciously using a religious and prophetic mode of discourse, but emptying it of content. And if so, why? To say that it is because he is a philosopher and not a theologian somehow fails to satisfy me. Such an answer assumes too neat a division of labor to be true either to Buddhism or to the contemporary philosophical situation.

Strangely enough, although Tanabe's conversion is not tied to a specific religion, it is nonetheless quite concretely situated in his response to the national crisis of his time. Our panelists have therefore justly asked us to consider whether Tanabe's vision of metanoetics is essentially private and untransferable. Can Tanabe's metanoetics take its place in the open public forum where philosophical ideas are normally debated; or must one believe him first, in order to understand? There are dangers here, Professor Maraldo warns us—especially in the attempt to translate Tanabe's conception of surrender to other situations of crisis or social change. As Professor Heisig puts it, "there is no purely philosophic prophylaxis" to ensure against making wrong choices in times of moral crisis.

POLARITIES

When I first approached this literature, I had the impression that there was some kind of quarrel, with Nishida and Nishitani on one side representing Zen Buddhism and self-power, and Tanabe representing Shin Buddhism (perhaps tinged with Christianity) and Other-power. I now see what an oversimplification this is. It turns out, rather, that if Tanabe is justified in his criticism of Nishida's logic of place (as a destruction of paradox and an objectification of Absolute Nothing), then he is correcting as much on behalf of Zen as on behalf of Shin Buddhism.

The four papers in this session help us to move away from facile use of self-power/Other-power and similar polarities. As John Maraldo points out, to characterize Zen exclusively as a "self-power" path is to caricature it. That may be useful for the purposes of prophetic writing — every prophet needs idolaters to denounce. But to miss what Professor Maraldo calls the metanoetic aspect of Zen would be especially unfortunate, since such misunderstandings are often self-fulfilling.

As we all know, Zen has been widely packaged, in North American culture, as one of the many self-help techniques available on the spiritual marketplace. If Zen is presented as a self-power tradition, it will all the more certainly be embraced as such. Evidently what is needed is clearer recognition that a sense of Other-power is at the heart of the entire Buddhist tradition.

Professor Lai's paper helps us attain a more balanced perspective by alerting us to Tanabe's compatibility with Mādhyamika and Tendai schools, which emphasize the reciprocity between relative being and Other-power. As if to complement this corrective offered by Whalen Lai, James Heisig makes it clear that it is unfair to Nishida to treat him as the equivalent of a Plotinian mystic.

In short, Nishida, Nishitani, and Tanabe all seem to be after the same thing, I hear our panelists saying. All are engaging in a characteristically Buddhist effort to vanquish false absolutes and to avoid settling down in either monistic or dualistic assertions. Even in the realm of philosophical discourse, the only prescription against dogmatic *stasis* is a healthy combination of both vigilance and receptivity (self-power, and openness to Other-power).

THE PROBLEM OF THE ABSOLUTE

We have heard it said that Absolute Nothingness is not an ontological category. But I do not think that solves all our problems. After all, there is a sense in which even Absolute Being no longer functions as an ontological category; the *analogia entis* — a door that used to swing both ways — has come unhinged.

A long tradition in Western philosophical theology, articulated most forcefully and programmatically by Kant and his successors, positively forbids us to understand Absolute Being (or God) as an object of possible experience. Despite the many advantages of this veto, it has had the unfortunate effect of seeming to discount the sense of direct intimacy with God that is a hallmark of intense religious and mystical experience. Moreover, the taboo against speaking about experiencing God has been intensified by our modern and post-modern consciousness of being culturally shaped; no longer can we draw innocently upon an inherited repertoire of traditional imagery which describes the relationship between individual and absolute in experiential terms. Tanabe is similarly concerned to emphasize the mediated character of this relationship, and sharply criticizes Nishida for seeming to characterize Absolute Nothing as a totality which can be intuited.

There are good reasons for such philosophical scruples; but I wonder if they really serve the religious needs of the ignorant and the common people with whom Tanabe says he is concerned. For the sake of religious relevancy, it seems, we need to find a middle path between vetoing all recognition of direct encounter with God and describing that encounter with the language of naive realism and subject/object dichotomy. Myths and stories will always, and quite properly, use the language of naive realism. Philosophy cannot do so without forsaking its special mission. But does this mean that philosophy must be cut off from any fruitful inquiry into the world of myth and story, which is also the world of popular religious experience? If so, it quickly becomes sterile and of interest only to academics.

The problem of the Absolute, at least in the West, is that deeply ingrained philosophical principles have come to interfere with our engaging with this concept in a religiously meaningful way. Further examination of Tanabe's use of the concept is needed before we can decide whether the grace of Nothingness and the logic of species have protected him from falling victim to the problems that the Absolute has created for Western religious consciousness.

PHILOSOPHY AFTER PHILOSOPHY

I could not resist asking our panelists directly, at the close of our session, where they would like to see philosophy heading.

A lively conversation ensued, in which Professor Heisig made the point that for Tanabe "conversion" meant not only change of religion, or change of heart, or returning to one's true abode—but also "overturning" of one's accustomed habits of thought. Herein lies a striking contrast between Nishitani's and Tanabe's understanding of transformation. As Professor Heisig put it, for Nishitani "all transformation is a transformation of perspective"; Tanabe, on the other hand, saw it as involving real ontic change, and later in life (according to Heisig), drew upon Christian symbols to express this.

Professor Kawamura emphasized that for Tanabe philosophical conversion is something that must take place daily, and must be situated "in the dimension of phenomena and in the dimension of the coincidence of phenomena and theory." By making this point she reminded us that practical and ethical insight is a vital part of the *philosophia* tradition. After all, the *sophia* Socrates loved was not just a matter of contemplating eternal verities; it was also a capacity for practical skill and discernment. Cicero tells us Socrates was "the first to call philosophy down from heaven," making its subject matter the ethics of human conduct, and thereby focusing attention on the horizontal dimension of which Professor Kawamura spoke.

Professor Maraldo related Tanabe's idea of conversion to analogues in Nishitani and Hakuin, and also in Socrates, Augustine, Descartes, Pascal, and Kierkegaard, who embody "a forgotten tradition of conversion as a philosophical category in the West"—a tradition for which doubt remains a vital ingredient. Conversion involves the whole self, Professor Maraldo pointed out; the category of conversion must therefore entail a "conversion of categories," transforming our conceptual mode of thinking. On the religious relevance of philosophies of the Absolute, Professor Maraldo commented that the touchstone for authenticity should be sought in everyday life, in "concrete problems that totally engage human beings." It is a hopeful sign, according to Professor Maraldo, that "philosophy is beginning to face its other"—to take into account women's experience, Asian traditions, the role of the body, and the possibilities for renewal of metaphorical language.

Professor Lai also called for philosophy, as it becomes a more global enterprise, to consider alternative ways of posing the ultimate questions. He cited the example of Chinese philosophical traditions, in which the key question of "whether the universe is benevolent" need not be answered in personalist—nor in strictly impersonalist—terms. Reciprocity is found in the three-way relationship between man, nature, and transcendence; this provides possibilities which might be overlooked if we focus exclusively on such polarities as individual/absolute or *saṃsāra/nirvāṇa*. In concert with the other panelists, Professor Lai also voiced his hope that philosophy is beginning to renew its links to storytelling, parable, and myth.

Throughout our conversations about Tanabe, conversion, the Absolute, and the future of philosophy, a common thread was appreciation for what Tanabe has shown us about the distinctively therapeutic function of philosophical discourse. The new philosophies which are—inevitably—emerging after the death of philosophy cannot afford to ignore the conditions that limit philosophical truth-seeking; but they need not be paralyzed by this awareness, nor be forced into contortions to defend reason against it. The vitality of philosophy today depends on willingness to acknowledge its therapeutic role, rediscover its mythic, symbolic, and narrative roots, and reawaken concern for the practical dimension, of which Professor Kawamura spoke so earnestly. Perhaps Tanabe does not answer every one of those needs for us today—but he does perform the inestimable service of making us feel those needs acutely.

PART FOUR

Society

Tanabe's Theory of the State

HIMI Kiyoshi

AS a philosopher who thought it important to apply his theories to the real world, Tanabe expressed his views on matters of state and public polity with greater vigor than most of his colleagues in Japan. He was full professor at the Kyoto University from 1927 to 1945, which means that he was in his post during the very period that Japan carried out its war of aggression in Asia and finally ended in defeat. In the aftermath of World War II, there were those who drew attention to a certain nationalistic tendency in his wartime statements and subjected him to criticism on that account. There were even those who regarded him as an outright advocate of imperialistic policies. This kind of hasty criticism, however, all too readily dispenses itself from the obligation of considering carefully what was the essence of his philosophical thought. For the fact is, Tanabe was at bottom neither imperialistic nor militaristic. Through his study of Western philosophy, he had acquired modes of thought that he wished to apply to the Japanese state in order to give it more solid rational and democratic footings. In so doing he set himself up against the irrationalist modes of thought that were fueling a warring ideology at the time. Obviously, his efforts failed. Not only did he not succeed in preventing ultranationalism from rearing its head; but also, and still more discouraging, he saw his own words twisted by the nationalists to purposes other than his own: to justify military aggressions. Conscience-struck at this turn of events, his thinking came to a standstill. After December of 1941, he was unable to publish any philosophical work. It was only at the end of the war, with *Philosophy as Metanoetics*, that his struggles would bear fruit and release his thinking from its deadlock.

In order to provide the discussion with fuller material, I would like to consider Tanabe's theory of the state in the light of statements made between 1934 and 1947. After examining the logical structure of his idea of the state, I will try to point out its positive significance in Japanese modern history and then single out those of its defects which seem responsible for its failure to check the rising tide of ultra-nationalism and which landed him in an intellectual *cul-de-sac*. Finally, I will consider the impact of his experience of metanoesis on his political theory, which in turn should put us in a position to judge whether in the end Tanabe succeeded in breaking off his unfortunate relationship with Japanese nationalism.

THE SIGNIFICANCE OF THE LOGIC OF SPECIES

Beginning in the year 1934, Tanabe introduced a new notion into his philosophy, something he called the "logic of species." To illuminate this idea, whose novelty earned him a reputation as an original thinker, we should begin by locating the notion of species in its traditional logical framework. As he understood it, the triad of genus-species-individual was simply a variant of the triad of propositional logic, universal-particular-singular, applied to human existence. In his logic of species, then, Tanabe was concerned with giving a new priority to the particular in human existence.

Seen from the standpoint of formal logic, human existence yields a universal concept like "humanity" or "human nature," the distinguishing mark of which is usually given as rationality. This universal is then specified step by step until it brings us to a single instance of human existence. This process of determination or specification is thought to take place without any qualitative leap. In other words, the two extremes of the universal and the single are joined together by way of the particular as a middle term which is itself lacking in positive content. Individuals are generated propositionally as essentially homogeneous atoms. And society, insofar as it is made up of such individuals, has in principle no qualitative determinations that would inhibit it from being extended ad libitum until it incorporates the whole of the human race. According to Tanabe, it was just this view of human existence and society that has dominated the Western intellectual tradition.

For his part, however, Tanabe was insistent that this way of thinking could only produce at best an inadequate understanding of the social character of human existence. The real world, prior to logic, is made up of numerous partial, particular societies, each of which has its own concreteness and can never be reduced without remainder to a mere neutral "middle term." Every particular society is possessed of its own internal unifying force which gives it the strength to organize and hold sway over its members, and to sustain the tension of confronting as an equal other internally unified societies. Now to understand these particular societies for what they are, we need to posit at their base a kind of fundamental unity of life, a real substratum for human existence. This is precisely what Tanabe has in mind by the term *species*. Accordingly, he refers to the particular society as a "specific society," that is, a society grounded in species. From this standpoint it is not possible to regard human individuals as homogeneous atoms. Each individual owes the special concreteness of its life *a priori* to the species. Any consideration of human being in its social mode has to begin from this fact. Hence the need for a "logic of species."

For the pedigree of Tanabe's notion of species, we may turn in the first place to Bergson. In his 1932 work, *The Two Sources of Morality and Religion*, he had proposed the distinction between "closed" and "open" societies. This was a mere two years before Tanabe was to advance his logic of species, which should tell us something of his familiarity with Western thought and his readiness to learn from it. Bergson himself had based his ideas on the researches of French sociologists, particularly into the area of totemism. Following his lead, Tanabe saw the totemic group as the prototype of the closed society and regarded it as typical of the species. This in turn enabled him to define species as the unity of consanguinity and locality. Of itself, of course, the simple idea of totemism could not suffice to explain developed and complex modern societies. In order to round out his concept of the species, therefore, he drew for help on Hegel's idea of objective Spirit, Tönnies's idea of *Gemeinschaft*, and so on.

Despite his efforts, however, Tanabe never succeeded in providing the notion of species with a definition clear enough to make it serviceable for precise sociological research. As easy as it is for us to criticize him in hindsight for this failure, it is far more interesting and important to consider that what was taking shape in his mind was in fact emerging from the substratum of the ethnic self-consciousness of the modern Japanese. The whole logic of species was part and parcel of the historical process of the modernization of Japan and therein lies its great significance.

As is well known, modernization in Japan not only wrought marvelous results in the way of constructing a national state, but also implanted in the consciousness of the Japanese people a certain stubborn exclusiveness. This turn of events stems from the fact that modernization began as a reform from above and did not grow naturally out of the birth of the idea of citizenship in the individual self-consciousness of individuals. Feeling the threat of the great Western powers, the "ruling class" acted on its own initiative to create a centralized state.[1] Their interests were focused almost exclusively on the power of Western nations and hence they saw it necessary to impose on the people the task of erecting a powerful "modern" state to stand as an equal among other nations. To this end they promulgated the notion that each individual shares by birth in a single ethnic unity which destines them to work in the service of national construction. This idea took symbolic form in the *tennōsei* 天皇制 or emperor system. So it was that the dominant fiction of a racially homogeneous nation came to be fabricated in modern Japan. Indeed, it proved so decisive in shaping the consciousness of the average Japanese that the idea that one is determined in the first place by human nature in general rather than by one's ethnic particularity was left no ground in which to grow.

Insofar as modern Japanese philosophy had passed over the question of cultural specificity, it was powerless to address the vital questions of nation, state, and politics. Not even the creative thought of Nishida had succeeded in this regard. Tanabe was the first professional philosopher to objectify the living consciousness of modern Japanese people. In saying this, we must of course distinguish him from the nationalists, since it was not his intention simply to accept the ethnic substratum without qualification or criticism, but rather to uncover its irrationality and show a way

---

[1] I use the term *ruling class* here in a broad sense. Strictly speaking, the leading role in the Restoration was taken by the lower echelons of the ruling class such as low-ranking samurai and landowners in the agricultural sector. After the establishment of the Meiji government, however, modernization proceeded mainly under mandate from above.

to rationalize it. Let us look more closely at just how he explained the logical relation of the species to the individual and the genus.

THE LOGIC OF SPECIES AS DIALECTIC

The individual is determined decisively by the species, but this does not mean that the relation between the two is a one-sided affair. As the subject of free will, the individual also seeks to determine the species. The two face each other as opposites in tension. Each is irrational and selfish in that each immediately wishes to affirm its own being. But through mutual interpenetration they can be purified of their irrational quality and raised to the level of rationality. The resultant synthesis is the genus. In this sense the logic of species conforms to the model of the dialectic. Some time before launching his notion of the logic of species Tanabe had already declared himself in favor of dialectic method; the logic of species was simply the attempt to apply that method to the real world.

One obstacle stood in the way of the completion of the logic of species as a dialectic—the "immediate being" of the species. The dialectic in general postulates that all things are mediated by something else. In principle nothing is permitted to exist immediately and for itself. Now since Tanabe had described species as something immediate, did this not imply a violation of that basic principle?

In fact, dialectic method also postulates that there should be something immediate, however paradoxical that might sound. For if everything has to be mediated by something else, then dialectic logic itself also needs something else to mediate it. But if that logic is already itself a mediation, then that something else must necessarily be immediate. In trying to adjust the immediate being of the species to the postulate of general mediation, Tanabe was therefore confronted with a fundamental problem that the dialectic in general was not equipped to handle. Its only way out is to explain immediate being as the "self-alienation" of the mediation itself. This was in fact the route Tanabe himself took. Identifying the mediating or synthesizing action with the genus, his formulation read: "The species is the self-alienation of the genus." We have now to consider just what this could possibly mean.

The species and the individual, which stand opposed as contradictories, are synthesized in the genus. A "particular" society or "specific" unity is "generalized." In other words, a closed society is transformed into an open one. This transformation results then in culture, morality, law, social justice and so on, all of which are essentially universal in character and which Tanabe lumps together in the notion of the "state." This means that the state is the realization of the genus or the universal, and that when that mediation ceases to function, the state can only degenerate back into to a particular, closed society, controlling its members with its whole array of specific conventions and institutions. This is when we may speak of species as a "self-alienation of the genus." This in fact is the state in which the individual finds itself in its initial consciousness as something that has been determined by the species. In short, species is not immediate being in the complete sense of the word but already bears within itself the marks of an accomplished mediation. Only when the mediation ceases to function does it become manifest as immediate being and does the individual of necessity contradict it.

In this way we can see the full coincidence of the logic of species with the fundamental schema of the dialectic. The triad "species-individual-genus" corresponds to the triad "thesis-antithesis-synthesis," and the synthesis (genus) becomes alienated and transformed into a new thesis (species). Thus the logical process of the mediation can and must be repeated again and again. In this sense, the logic of species represents an infinite dialectical process.

THE LOGIC OF SPECIES AND THE ONTOLOGY OF THE STATE

In its early stages. Tanabe's notion of the logic of species developed smoothly. By 1937 it had taken the strictly dialectical form we have seen. But at once he began to have doubts about characterizing it as a "logic of social being." Clearly, it involved an ongoing, indeed infinite, process which in turn corresponded to history or historical reality.[2] In order to stress its dynamic and evolutionary character, Tanabe thought it fit to begin speaking of the logic of species as "the logic of historical reality." And with this change of terminology the state was given a decidedly

---

[2] PM, 193-254.

great importance in his thought. The historical process represented by the logic of species was thus seen to be nothing other than the repetition of the organization and self-alienation or degradation of the state, that is, to be the perpetual self-renewal of the state. In this sense the state is the ultimate substance of history. And so it was that Tanabe took the next step and transformed the logic of species into a "logic of national existence" or an "ontology of the state."

Indeed, in 1939 he published an essay entitled "The Logic of National Existence,"[3] wherein he refers to the genus as "the Absolute" because of its unlimited universality, and to the species and individual as "the relative," with the historical world constituting the field on which the relationship between the two is worked out. In line with this schema, the state is defined as "the absolute relative" or "the relative absolute." On the one hand, it is absolute in that it includes the results of the synthesis of the genus. On the other, it is relative in that it is grounded in the unity of the species. Tanabe himself is not so eager to use such logically defective expressions but prefers to speak of the state as the *ōgensonzai* 応現存在 or actual manifestation of the genus or Absolute.

Clearly the term derives from Mahāyāna Buddhist "ontology," according to which the true nature of the Buddha—the Absolute in itself—is empty or formless, but makes itself manifest as occasion demands, like the moon reflecting itself on the surface of the water. Following this Buddhist tradition, Tanabe regards the Absolute as emptiness or nothingness, allowing it to appear in the real world only as a manifestation appropriate to a particular occasion. The state is just such a manifestation, mediating between the Absolute and the relative.

This positioning of the state leads to the conclusion that the state contains within itself the whole of the religious dimension of human existence as well. This would mean that all the forms of relationship found in the various religions of the world could be reduced without exception to the worship of the state. Tanabe tries to illustrate this in the cases of the two world religions to which he attaches most importance, Christianity and Mahāyāna Buddhism.

---

[3] PM, 255-96.

With regard to Christianity, Tanabe draws an analogy between Christ and the state by reason of the similar positions they occupy as mediators between the Absolute and the relative. He translates the dogma of Trinity into a triad of "Absolute Nothingness—the state—philosophy of the state." (By interpreting the Holy Spirit as the self-consciousness of the mutual mediation between the Absolute and the relative, it becomes analogous to a philosophy of the state.) For Tanabe, the worship of the state has the decisive merit of purifying dogma from the limitations imposed on it by the historic documents and mythology in which it is couched. Thus, by putting the state in the place of Jesus Christ, one is able to ground one's rationalistic faith on one's actual existence. In this way the *imitatio Christi* is reduced to mere service to the state.

With regard to Mahāyāna Buddhism, Tanabe recommends the Bodhisattva ideal as a corrective to Buddhist non-action. The Bodhisattva should always strive to aid others to honor the Buddha and pursue the path of spiritual enlightenment or Buddhahood. As the actual manifestation of the Absolute, the state is thus the Buddha making himself manifest as the situation demands in order to help those in need and thus giving an example to bodhisattvas. In this sense, the state is to be respected as the prototype of the bodhisattva ideal, and belief in the Buddha is reduced to service to the state.

THE FAILURE OF THE ONTOLOGY OF THE STATE

While there is no denying that in the end Tanabe fell into a position of nationalism, it bears repeating that he was not an impulsive thinker so enamored of his own ideas that he would not submit them to criticism. The basic structure of his logic of species shows just how rationalistic he was, for it pivots on a dynamic in which ethnic unity is "generalized" or sublimated into rationality through the activity of free individuals. As a logic, it offers an adequate explanation of national states and leads only to a recognition of their plurality and relativity. On the one hand, all states are "generalized" by nature; on the other, they are grounded on a "specific" unity and thus maintain their peculiar characteristics. It follows that there will be a variety of states on the earth, and that their co-existence should constitute a single world. The logic of species can and must recognize that fact. As such, it has nothing to do with the deification or absolutizing of one state above all others.

Despite the structures of his logic, Tanabe did in fact end up deifying the Japanese state, with bizarre results that betrayed his original rationalistic intentions. His inconsistency was, I believe, rooted in his falling prey to a narrowing of consciousness that is not uncommon among the Japanese, pushing sound reason to one side and putting logic at the service of unquestioned bias. In a word, he took only one species, only one state, into consideration. I would even go so far as to say that for Tanabe *species* was really no more than a euphemism for Japanese ethnic unity, and *ōgensonzai* for the Japanese state. As we saw, he began by objectifying the ethnic self-consciousness of the Japanese as a "specific" substratum, but at that point he seems to have gotten stuck. Rather than locate the Japanese nation as one species among others, he began to insist on its irreplaceable significance, unable to pull himself out of the ideological walls that closed off the consciousness of the modern Japanese.

Justice to his theories would demand that he analyze the Japanese species in an objective and thoroughgoing manner in order to determine its constitutive elements. In so doing, he would have seen through the fictional function of the emperor system and would have been in a position to argue for a pluralistic organization of the modern Japanese state. Had Tanabe taken this route, he would no doubt have contributed greatly to the establishment of Japanese democracy. Instead, he was unable to question the solidity of the arguments for Japanese ethnic unity and fell in with the dominant idea of a racially homogeneous state ruled over by the emperor. This means that he could only "generalize" the Japanese state, applauding its unique and at the same time universal character. As a result, the logic of species degenerated into a sophistry that sought to justify a nation at war on the grounds of its universality. (Johannes Laube rightly describes this result as Tanabe's confusion of the ideal state with the real Japanese state.[4])

---

[4] *History* here does not refer to chronological records but to the actual events that make up human existence. In German, these two meanings are often distinguished as *Historie* and *Geschichte* respectively.

The limitations that Tanabe's subjectivity suffered as a modern Japanese brought his philosophical reflection to a stalemate. Only by negating and eradicating these limitations would he be in a position to philosophize again. When this took place, he felt as if raised from the dead to a new life by a transcendent "Other-power." This, I would argue, is why he referred to his fresh start in philosophy as a "metanoetics."

THE METANOETIC VIEW OF SOCIETY

What change did the experience of metanoesis work on Tanabe's theory of the state? Formerly he had regarded moral action, which mediates between the species and the individual in order to promote the synthesis of the genus, as performed by one's own power. But his metanoesis meant a collapse of all such self-power and an awareness that one could return to life only through the compassionate action of a transcendent Other-power—Absolute Nothingness. In this way Other-power took the position of dominance and his own power was relegated to a merely subordinate position.

The development of philosophy as a metanoetics based on this experience of conversion led to a new theory of society, politics, and the state. Once every human action is seen not to derive ultimately from its own power but to derive from Other-power, one can no longer speak of human beings *acting* but only of *being made to act*. This view of action necessarily leads to the construction of a society different from the one Tanabe had previously envisioned in his logic of species. In considering this new view of the state, we have to ask whether it in fact eradicated his former nationalistic tendencies.

Tanabe was convinced that he had had an experience of metanoetic salvation under the guidance of Shinran. To demonstrate this definitively, he undertook a spirited interpretation of some of the principal teachings of Shinran, including the doctrine of the three vows, the theory of three minds, and the theory of two-phase *pariṇāma*.[5] This last is the most important for our considerations here.

Pariṇāma (ekō 廻向 *)* originally referred to the human activity

---

[5] 国家的存在の論理 , in THZ 7:25-99.

of transferring one's own accumulated merits so that they might serve for the salvation of oneself and others. But from a standpoint of complete obedience to Other-power, human beings are disqualified from accumulating merits for themselves. Thus Tanabe insists with Shinran that only the Absolute has the essential power to perform *pariṇāma*; its compassionate act of salvation is *pariṇāma* in the most fundamental sense of the word. One can only acknowledge one's incompetence in a spirit of obedience and accept with gratitude the *pariṇāma* of Other-power. In so doing one lets one's activity be absorbed into an absolute activity and thereby takes part in it.

Tanabe refers to this attitude as a "*pariṇāma* of no-*pariṇāma*" or a "transferring of no-transferring," and claims that this is the only way open to the human individual. This derivative *pariṇāma* as it were has two phases. On the one hand, one attains salvation through the ultimate *pariṇāma* of Other-power. This is the phase of "going-to" or *ōsō* 往相. On the other hand, one seeks to help others to attain salvation, cooperating gratefully with the ultimate *pariṇāma* of Other-power. This is the phase of "returning-from" or *gensō* 還相. Together the two phases form a single, inseparable whole. In attaining one's own salvation in the phase of *ōsō*, one must also guide and instruct others in the phase of *gensō*. Only thus does one confirm one's own salvation; without the activity of *gensō*, the salvation of *ōsō* would be annulled.

Through *pariṇāma*, relationships among human beings are given a new form.[6] The one who guides and instructs in cooperation with Other-power is a "precursor," while the one who is guided and instructed is a kind of "postcursor." This before-and-after relationship unfolds and expands endlessly throughout the course of history. In his own case, for example, Tanabe's experience of metanoesis and his attainment of salvation in the *ōsō* phase relies on the teaching and guidance of Shinran, who is his precursor. But in publishing *Philosophy as Metanoetics*, he seeks to teach and guide us, which represents the *gensō* phase. In this sense, we are his postcursors. Of course, all human beings as such are equally qualified to collaborate with the ultimate *pariṇāma* of Other-power. And yet at the same time, the order of before-and-

---

[6] See Johannes Laube, *Dialektik der Absoluten Vermittlung* (Freiburg: Herder, 1984), 274-88.

after is of the utmost importance, and is typified in the mutual relationship of brotherhood and sisterhood. This is why Tanabe proposes the general relationship of fraternity among human beings as foundation of the ideal society from the standpoint of metanoetics.

TANABE'S NEW THEORY OF THE STATE

Tanabe felt the need for a real base or substratum on which to construct the relationship between precursor and postcursor, and sought to redefine species to answer the need. To illustrate what he means by *substratum*, we may return to his own relationship with Shinran.

Tanabe is able to encounter Shinran through the mediation of the practice of the *nembutsu* (invocation of the name of Amida Buddha) and the doctrine of the Pure Land, both of which form part of the literary tradition of Japanese society. In other words, Japanese society preserves definite cultural traditions like these primarily through language, and because of these traditions Tanabe is able to accept the guidance and instruction of Shinran. Insofar as it is a preserver of cultural traditions, Japanese society qualifies as a "species" or "specific society."

Here species reveals a new aspect. Whereas it was previously understood as a primitive unity of life in its immediate, irrational, and material character, it is now grasped in its spiritual and cultural dimensions. To relate these two senses rationally to one another, we have to look to the element of "conversion" contained in the notion of species.

Because metanoesis means absolute conversion, the logic of species viewed from the perspective of metanoetics must also contain the element of conversion. The genus—the universal of Absolute Nothingness—at first appears to be an absolutely merciless negation of all relative beings, but in time it makes itself manifest as a compassionate love that saves them. Thus its aspect of conversion may be characterized as a "nothingness-*qua*-love" or a "Great Nay-*qua*-Great Compassion." The individual is broken down to the point of "death," only then to be brought back to a new and higher life. The element of conversion is in this sense a kind of movement "from death to resurrection" or (in more logical terms) a "nothingness-*qua*-being."

As for the element of conversion at the level of species, Tanabe is not as clear. A careful reading of his texts, however, suggests the following process: The species is at first a primitive unity of life, and hence refers to concrete, immediate being. But when the metanoesis takes place, species loses its determining power over the individual and is thoroughly "annihilated" or "emptied." At that point it is grounded on Absolute Nothingness and made to serve for promoting the latter's salvific work. Thus species provides a base or substratum for human relationship to develop in the *gensō* phase of *pariṇāma*. In this sense, the species may be said to serve Absolute Nothingness (the genus) as an "expedient means" *(upāya* or *hōben-sonzai* 方便存在). Its aspect of conversion is to be characterized as a movement from "immediate being to expedient means" (or in logical terms, a "being-*qua*-nothingness").

It follows as a matter of course that Tanabe's thought would come to center on the species in this converted sense. Indeed, on this basis he sought to develop a new theory of the state. As expedient means, the species has somehow to be organized into a distinct unity. This work of organization constitutes what we call "politics," whose product is the state. Hence, for Tanabe the state ceases to be an actual manifestation *(ōgensonzai)* and becomes an expedient entity *(hōben-sonzai)* of the genus. It would appear that what he understands here by "state" is a kind of community administered on the basis of a fraternal relationship among its inhabitants in the *ōsō* and *gensō* phases of *pariṇāma*. This leads him in fact to speak of the Japanese state as a "republic," even though this notion suffers from a certain time-worn conventionality that remained in his philosophical thought to the end.

The Way of Metanoia
and the Way of the Bodhisattva

Johannes LAUBE

THE present essay focuses on the eighth and final chapter of Tanabe Hajime's *Philosophy as Metanoetics*, "Metanoetics as a Religious View of Society." As important as the preceding seven chapters are to the thought presented there, I shall restrict myself to a brief account of ten points that seem to me to bear most directly on the relationship between metanoia and the Bodhisattva ideal.

PRELIMINARY REMARKS

1. Philosophy as metanoetics—the systematic elaboration of the self-consciousness of metanoia—regards itself as the only approach to philosophy that remains after autonomous human reason, torn asunder by the antinomies of theoretical and practical reason first pointed out by Kant, has died.

2. Philosophy as metanoetics is likened to an approach to philosophy by way of the self-consciousness of ethical experience and claims the sort of universality that is traditionally granted ethical philosophy. Nevertheless, metanoetics is not a philosophy based on autonomous ethical reason.

3. The *prius quoad nos* in philosophy as metanoetics is the experience of metanoia, which at first is perceived as the passive conversion of one's total Existenz that affects all activities, especially those of theoretical and practical reason. As an experience of turning from one's former way to embrace a new path, metanoia is realized as the effect of another power (*tariki* 他力) different from our own power (自力 *jiriki*). Metanoia is understood as the effect of an absolute Other-power (*zettai tariki* 絶対他力). Metanoia

in this sense is action of the absolute Other-power (*zettai tariki no gyō* 絶対他力の行) and therefore called "great action" (*taigyō* 大行). At first sight, metanoia looks like heteronomous action and its self-consciousness seems to be a self-consciousness of heteronomy — that is, a "faith" in absolute Other-power (*shin* 信) based on a metanoia that is the "action" (*gyō* 行) and "witness" (*shō* 証) of being turned from death to new life.[1] Tanabe calls it "circular dialectical mediation" of *gyō-shin-shō*. Hence philosophy as metanoetics shows itself to be a heteronomous philosophy, a philosophy mediated by absolute Other-power (*tariki-tetsugaku* 他力哲学). In this sense, philosophy as metanoetics may be classified more generally as a form of "religious philosophy," because it is not based on autonomous reason (although it begins there) but on converted reason, on metanoetical reason, i.e., on Other-power faith.

Although Tanabe, like Hegel, regards "absolute knowledge" as the ultimate goal of philosophy, he pursues another path to that end. His new way is influenced by Christian theology, in particular by a theology that proceeds by way of Kierkegaard and the Buddhist Amidalogy of Shinran. Attention must therefore be given throughout to the way in which Tanabe himself uses the term *philosophy*.

4. The ontological structure of metanoia is described by Tanabe as the same dialectics of absolute mediation that rules the world (or reality) as a whole. In the dialectics of absolute mediation, each and every element is mediated by negation (reciprocal negation or self-negation). Nothing remains unmediated in its *an sich* reality. In the dialectics of absolute mediation even the absolute is understood as mediated by an absolute self-negation for the sake of the relative elements. Indeed, this is why Tanabe can speak of it as "absolute nothingness."

In the dialectics of absolute mediation the absolute realizes itself in the reality of the relatives, which in turn is described as a network of reciprocal negations (self-negations) of relatives, as a community of reciprocal mediation. Both for the absolute and for the relatives, this reciprocal mediation is necessary for each to *realize itself* — in both senses of the word. Ultimately, categories

---

[1] The term *based on* needs to be understood in Tanabe's dialectics of absolute mediation to mean *mediated by*.

like "self" and "other, "active" and "passive," "autonomous" and "heteronomous" are no longer applicable in the dialectics of absolute mediation. The selfsame action, the Great Action, is at once the action of absolute Other-power and the action of the relatives. In this sense, every action is absolutely mediated action. That this action is perceived by us as metanoetical action is due to the fact that metanoia is the *prius quoad nos*.[2]

5. For Tanabe metanoia is not to be identified with any particular emotional phenomenon of repentance, since such states are spontaneous, transitory, and self-centered. Of course, the meaning of metanoia evolved in the course of Tanabe's lecturing and writing on his experience of metanoia, but his *mature* notion of metanoia was not bound to any *one* state of mind. Rather, metanoia was for him as universal an element in human existence as its reverse: the radical evil that he recognized to be an integral part of human existence, Kant before him had demonstrated persuasively.

Tanabe saw that there is no one who is not corrupted by the radical tendency to evil at the heart of all human activity, a tendency that he spoke of as "egoity" (*gasei* 我性). In some contexts he even considers finiteness or contingency as such to be radical evil, though more commonly he describes it as a tendency to absolutize the self, putting it in the place of the absolute.

Everything human is prey to the workings of radical evil, and for Tanabe this applies first and foremost to the individual person. In a revised version of his essay on "The Logic of Species,"[3] however, he extends the notion to include society in general, both the state and other specific groups. In both cases, radical evil and metanoia are two strands of the same thread, and it is the self that entwines self-affirmation (radical evil) and self-negation (metanoia) into one. All is evil—all is metanoia.

6. Tanabe confesses in the foreword to his work that the first

---

[2] Thus Tanabe's description of his new philosophy as an "Other-power philosophy" has to be amended to an "Other-power/self-power philosophy." This is referred to variously as "absolutely mediated philosophy," "philosophy as absolute mediation," and "philosophy as dialectics of absolute mediation."

[3] The original essay was published in 1946 as "Dialectics of Logic of Species" (THZ 7:251-372). For a partial English translation, see David Dilworth and Satō Taira, "The Logic of the Species as Dialectics," MN 24 (1969): 273-88.

time he experienced metanoia consciously he tried to analyze the phenomenon through recourse to philosophical, theological and general religious literature, East and West. Aside from a few meta-noetical elements in the Old and New Testaments, in Augustine, Luther, Pascal, Kierkegaard and a handful of others, he was not able to come up with enough to constitute a complete and universal metanoetical philosophy. Nor did Eastern literature—in particular, Buddhist sources—yield up what he was looking for. It was only in the texts of Shinran (1173-1262), the founder of the Amida Buddhist community of Jōdoshinshū, that he discovered expressions of *zange* 懺悔 which he interpreted as his metanoia.

In both his main work, the *Kyōgyōshinshō* 教行信証 (Collection of Passages revealing the true "Teaching, Practice, Faith and Enlightenment" of the Pure Land), and in his *Jōdo-wasan* 浄土和讃 ("Hymns on the Pure Land" of Amida-Buddha),[4] Shinran expresses his profound grief and sorrow over the fact that as an old man who had come to faith in Amida Buddha a long time previously, he was still unable to sever the bonds that enslave him to this corrupt world of the Final Age of the Dharma (*mappō* 末法), bonds that work within him as blind passions (*bonnō* 煩悩), preventing him from ascending the path of the Bodhisattva (*bosatsu* 菩薩) step by step through ethical discipline (Skt., *śīla*), meditation (Skt., *samādhi, dhyāna*), and enlightenment (Skt., *prajñā*, wisdom). For Shinran, no one in the Final Age of the Dharma can take this Bodhisattva path. Only Amida Buddha, who in the far distant past as Dharmākara Bodhisattva vowed to realize this way both for himself and, through the transfer of his spiritual merits, for all other sentient beings, only this Amida Buddha who now abides in his heavenly "Pure Land" (*jōdo* 浄土) can extend a hand to help Shinran the foolish sinner (*bompu-akunin* 凡夫悪人). In expressions of *zange* like these, Tanabe was able to discover meta-noetical thinking in Shinran, albeit a thinking that had not yet

---

[4] There are a number of English translations of the *Kyōgyōshinshō*, the most recent of which was prepared under the general editorship of Ueda Yoshifumi as *The True Teaching, Practice, and Realization of the Pure Land Way* (Kyoto: Shin Buddhism Translation Series, 1983-1987), 3 volumes. For a translation of the *Jōdo Wasan*, see the volume in the Ryūkoku Translation Series, *Jōdo Wasan: The Hymns on the Pure Land*, translated and annotated by R. Fujimoto, H. Inagaki, and Leslie S. Kawamura (Kyoto: Ryūkoku Translation Center, 1965).

been developed dialectically into the synthesis of Amidalogy (particular theology) and universal philosophy.

7. After criticizing philosophies of autonomous reason from Kant to Heidegger (and including the philosophy of Nishida Kitarō, though the latter is not mentioned by name) in the first five chapters of *Philosophy as Metanoetics*, Tanabe devotes two chapters to what he considers the primordial metanoetical philosophy, namely Shinran's *Kyōgyōshinshō* and in particular Shinran's idea of faith in Amida Buddha.

At the core of the *Kyōgyōshinshō* lies the relation between Amida Buddha as savior and the faithful foolish sinner, which is described as a relation of merit-transference in Amida's phase of returning to this world (*gensō-ekō* 還相回向). There is nothing that sentient beings, as fools and sinners of this Last Age of the Dharma, can do for their own salvation. Even faith in Amida's promise and practice of salvation is bestowed by Amida's merit-transference. Amida's *gensō-ekō* ("returning" or "descent") to the world is at the same time the foolish sinner's *ōsō* (往相 , "going" or "ascent") to the Pure Land. Ascent to the Pure Land of Amida Buddha does not mean an immediate attainment of Buddhahood and entry into *nirvāṇa*. It means that by being born in the Pure Land of Amida Buddha through the fatherhood and motherhood of Amida Buddha—his wisdom and his compassion—the sentient beings of the Last Age of the Dharma are empowered to perform the disciplines of the Bodhisattva path with the aid of Amida Buddha, to attain to Buddhahood at the end of that path, and then to enter *nirvāṇa* or return to the world of their fellow sentient beings. According to the twenty-second vow of Dharmākara Bodhisattva, sentient beings born in the Pure Land are able to perform Bodhisattva acts of merit transference with the help of Amida Buddha. Hence Amida's *gensō* is at one and the same time the phase of ascent (*ōsō*) and the phase of descent (*gensō*) to the faithful foolish sinners.

Tanabe interprets this relationship between Dharmākara Bodhisattva and sentient beings as a relationship of absolute mediation. In the *Kyōgyōshinshō* itself, absolute Other-power, Amida Buddha, is the only cause of salvation, and sentient beings in the Last Age of the Dharma are absolutely incapable of effecting their own salvation in any way; in other words, sentient beings are completely and absolutely mediated beings while the working of Amida Buddha is completely unmediated. But what Tanabe tries to do is to uncover in the *Kyōgyōshinshō* a dialectics of absolute mediation.

8. Tanabe opens the eighth chapter of *Philosophy as Metanoetics* with a résumé of the contents of the previous seven chapters and then takes a decisive step away from the metanoia of the individual person to the metanoia of the state and society as a realization of the dialectical moment of species. In so doing, he sets out on a course of rethinking and reformulating the theory of the "Logic of Species" that he had forged in the pre-war years. Tanabe's point of departure is now the social character of radical evil and of metanoia, which are seen as two elements that make up the relative selves who in turn make up the network of reciprocity that we call "reality" or "world." There is solidarity *(rentai-sekinin* 連帯責任) in sin and solidarity in salvation. Each and every one of us share in the responsibility for all sin throughout the world, especially for sin particular to our species in its confrontation with other species. And if there is shared responsibility in sin, so must there be shared responsibility in a metanoia that turns away from self-assertion or self-absolutizing, namely, the turning away from self by being negated from other relatives that affirm themselves absolutely. On the one hand, the *self-affirmation* of relative beings annihilates the network of mutual negation and does away with the individual relative beings that make it up. This is seen as the effect of a solidarity in radical evil. On the other, the *turning away from the self* to accept the other manifests the network as one of reciprocal self-negation or shared metanoia. Only then does the network of relative beings constitute a community of Existenz *(Existenzgemeinschaft)*, an idea which Tanabe later developed as the culmination of his logic of species.[5]

9. Just as he had made use of Shinran's primordial metanoetical philosophy of the relation between Amida Buddha and the faithful

---

[5] See the commemorative collection, *Martin Heidegger zum siebzigsten Geburtstag*, ed. by Günther Neske (Pfullingen: Neske Verlag, 1959), 93-133. There the ideal of the Mahāyāna Bodhisattva is related to the community of Existenz. The German text is an abridgement of the original, which can be found in THZ 13:525-641.

individual person as a model for his own dialectics of the univer-
sal-and-individual as absolute mediation in chapters 6 and 7, in
chapter 8 Tanabe draws on the Amidalogy of the *Kyōgyōshinshō*
for his dialectical view of society, and at the same time demythologizes Shinran's model.

10. In the following pages I would like to examine chapter 8 to
show how Tanabe makes use of the general Buddhist notion of
the Bodhisattva and Shinran's notion of the *ōsō* and *gensō* of Amida
Buddha. Having done so, I would then like to indicate those
points at which it seems to me Tanabe has contradicted Shinran's
Amidalogy, as well as some self-contradictions against his own
dialectics of absolute mediation.

THE GENERAL BUDDHIST NOTION OF THE BODHISATTVA IDEAL

The word *Bodhisattva* (Chin., *púsà*, Jap., *bosatsu*) is not found in
Sanskrit Vedic literature or in early Hindu or Jaina literature. It
is only in early Buddhist literature written in Sanskrit and Pāli
that the term shows up. At the latest, the Bodhisattva ideal was
known and accepted in Buddhist communities in India by the
second century BCE.[6]

If we may take the Pāli canon as the oldest source of Buddhist
literature that has come down to us in relatively complete form
(whatever earlier versions may have existed in the eastern Indian
dialect that was spoken by the historical Siddhārtha Gautama Buddha, they are lost), let us consider first the Pāli variants of the
term *Bodhisattva* and the Sanskrit variants which seem to be translations from the Pāli or other Indian dialects.

The meaning of the original Pāli word *Bodhisatta* is not clear.
The Sanskrit equivalents of the Pāli term are these:

> Bodhi*sattva* a being, whose essence is *bodhi* (perfect enlighten-
> ment). Hence, "*bodhi*-being" or "Buddha-being."

---

[6] On the various ideas of "Bodhisattva" in Buddhism in general, see Leslie
S. Kawamura, "The Bodhisattva Doctrine in Buddhism," in *Collected Papers of
the Calgary Buddhism Conference, 1978* (Waterloo, Ontario: Wilfrid Laurier University Press, 1981). I have drawn on material from this book for the historical
explanations in the text of my essay.

Bodhi*sakta*   a being who is attached or devoted to *bodhi*. Hence, "future *bodhi*-being" or "Buddha-to-be."

Bodhi*satvam*   a *bodhi*-hero or warrior fighting for *bodhi*. Hence, "future *bodhi*-being/Buddha-to-be."

The second and third variants are distinct from the first in that they put the stress on the future attainment of *bodhi* (the ascent to *bodhi*), whereas the first stresses the present *bodhi* (or even the descent from the present *bodhi*). Historically, however, it was the element of ascent to *bodhi* that we find emphasized in the earliest extant Buddhist texts. Generally speaking, early Buddhism[7] regarded the Bodhisattva as a being who had attained a high (superhuman) level of spiritual knowledge and power, and hence was close to the achievement of perfect wisdom (*bodhi*) that brings Buddhahood and entry into *nirvāṇa*.

According to the later Theravāda (or Hīnayāna) and Mahāyāna Buddhology, the chain of *saṃsāra* or birth-death-rebirth that finally led to Siddhārtha Gautama Buddha is highlighted by the conversion and spiritual ascent of a young ascetic named Sumedha, who lived at the time of the Dharma-preaching Dīpamkara Buddha, aeons before the historical Siddhārtha. Sumedha made a vow to strive for Buddhahood and proceed to ascend the Bodhisattva path stage by stage. In his evolution as a Bodhisattva, Sumedha was reborn 547 times on earth in the form of various sentient beings. In the intervals between rebirths, he remained in heaven as a Bodhisattva. Finally, he was reborn as Siddhārtha Gautama, who left home and family, secluded himself in the forests, studied under the guidance of various masters of the spiritual life, and eventually, through his own effort, attained enlightenment and became the Buddha. After forty years of wandering throughout India preaching the Dharma, he entered *parinirvāṇa* (perfect *nirvāṇa*). Hence for early Buddhism, as well as for Hīnayāna and Mahāyāna in their early years, the "Bodhisattva path" meant first of all the ascent to Buddhahood of Siddhārtha Gautama.

Following the model set by Siddhārtha Gautama Buddha, Buddhists undertake the eightfold path of the Buddha, pronounce

---

[7] "Early Buddhism" here refers to Buddhism from the third to the first century BCE; it should be distinguished from "original Buddhism," which is prior to the third century BCE.

vows, practice the disciplines and meditations, pass through the 51 stages of the Bodhisattva course, and strive for enlightenment (gradual or sudden) and *nirvāṇa*, the extinction of the individual, passion-ridden self.

For both Hīnayāna and Mahāyāna, the ultimate goal is *annuttara-samyak-saṃbodhi* (unsurpassed perfect wisdom), one of whose effects is *nirvāṇa*. But the Mahāyāna conception of the Bodhisattva differs from that of the Hīnayāna. As long as there are sentient beings not yet saved from the darkness and bondage of this life, the Mahāyāna Bodhisattva refuses the fruition of perfect wisdom for himself, and out of compassionate love turns to others to help bring about their liberation by way of particular salvific means (*upāya*). These means may even include a new incarnation of the Bodhisattva in some form of sentient being or other, according to the needs of those to be saved. This return to the world of sentient beings is what Shinran was later to analyze systematically as *gensō*.

The Hīnayāna Bodhisattva or *arhat*, in contrast, always advances upwards. If he manages to attain perfect *bodhi* and *nirvāṇa*, he does not come back. He is not reborn or reincarnated; there is no miracle of merit-transferring by which he can turn around and transfer his merits to others. Each one has to struggle for one's own liberation. No one can fight that battle for anyone else.

For Mahāyāna Buddhism, which is the chief concern of Tanabe and Shinran, the use of the word *Bodhisattva* is not univocal in the literature. Still, we can extract four types of Mahāyāna Bodhisattvas from Indian, Chinese, Tibetan, Japanese, and other Mahāyāna sources:

     1. Bodhisattvas of the "Rebirth-Stories" (*Jātakas*)
     2. heavenly Bodhisattvas
     3. meditation Bodhisattvas
     4. Bodhisattvas living on earth

Let us look more closely at the second type, the heavenly Bodhisattva, which is where we may classify Amida Buddha, who strived on earth for Buddhahood as Dharmākara Bodhisattva, and who is the central figure for Shinran.

Unlike the Jātaka Bodhisattvas, the heavenly Bodhisattvas no longer need to be saved. The former, even though they dwell in some particular heaven between rebirths, must be reborn after a certain time in order to continue striving for Buddhahood. The heavenly Bodhisattvas, in contrast, have already been liberated from the chain of rebirth, having cut themselves off from the blind passions that bind one to earth. They enjoy *bodhi* for themselves and turn its effects to sentient beings as yet unsaved. The heavenly Bodhisattvas are possessed of all compassionate love and wisdom as well as of the miraculous powers needed to expedite the salvation of the slaves of this evil world. In Buddhist terms, the heavenly Bodhisattvas are personal manifestations of the trans-personal Dharma-as-such, the *dharma-kāya* or "Dharma-Body", and hence are only salvific tools of the Dharma-as-such.

THE NOTION OF THE BODHISATTVA IN TANABE

As we noted above, Tanabe opens chapter 8 with a recapitulation of the origins and essence of his philosophy as metanoetics, to which he felt himself obliged to turn after the collapse of the philosophy grounded in autonomous reason that he had formerly espoused. In other words, he summarizes the turn from self-power philosophy to Other-power philosophy (i.e., a philosophy mediated by religion). There he argues that in our day "Eastern and Western thought, in mutual dependence, seem to be developing in the direction of metanoetics." This development, he goes on, is brought about by "the grace of the Tathāgata's Great Compassion" and that his own efforts in this direction "are nothing other than an act of gratitude for that grace."

In developing his own philosophy as metanoetics as a philosophy of Other-power he feels himself guided by Shinran and the *Kyōgyōshinshō*. Indeed, Tanabe speaks of Shinran as "the master and the teacher of my philosophy."[8]

These pious confessions incline one to interpret Tanabe's texts in general, and chapter 8 in particular, as a faithful rethinking and reformulation of Mahāyāna Buddhist ideas, especially of Shinran's idea of faith in Amida. But, as I intend to show below, even though Tanabe presents his philosophy as metanoetics as a philosophy mediated by religion, it does not represent a faithful re-interpretation of historical Mahāyāna or of Shinran's Amidalogy. Tanabe's philosophy as metanoetics has rather to be understood

---

[8] PM, 260-61.

as a new and independent universal philosophy mediated by Tanabe's own religious experience of "metanoia." To be sure, the
influence of Buddhism and Shinran, of Christianity and Kierkegaard, and of nearly all the important Eastern and Western philosophical and theological traditions, is at work. If we may borrow
the Buddhist term, however, these traditions are no more than
"expedient means" for Tanabe, who used them as tools for reflection and formulation. His dialectics of absolute mediation, even
in its corrected version of philosophy as metanoetics, does not
logically depend on historical religions like Christianity or Buddhism, and that includes Shinran's Amida Buddhism.

After having reviewed and criticized the Western philosophies
of society from Plato to Hegel Tanabe turns to Buddhist concep-
tions of society:

> Buddhism, which began simply as an intellectual doctrine
> about the human condition aimed at delivering the individual
> from the cycle of birth and death, moved beyond primitive
> Buddhism's standpoint of solitary enlightenment to a commu-
> nitarian approach according to which the Dharma is transmit-
> ted from master to disciple. A parallel evolution took place on
> the doctrinal level. With the development of the Bodhisattva-
> ideal in the Mahāyāna-tradition, Buddhism developed the
> ideal of "benefiting oneself-*qua*-benefiting others." This evo-
> lution culminates in the Shin doctrine of *gensō*. Strange as it
> may seem, this process is but the natural unfolding of the es-
> sential Buddhist teaching of *muga* — that there is no self or ego
> in all of reality — which is the principle of absolute nothing-
> ness. This paradox is the very hallmark of Buddhist truth.
> Under the guidance of Shinran's attitude of total *zange*, meta-
> noetics is thus able to develop a social doctrine inaccessible by
> way of Western philosophy alone. I have tried to touch on this
> as one of the promising aspects of metanoetics.[9]

The English translation of *Philosophy as Metanoetics* is not in general
reliable,[10] and here is no exception. In what follows I shall amend
what I consider the most important errors. Reading the above

---

[9] PM, 270.

[10] I have pointed out some problems with the English translation as a whole
in a critical review which appeared in *Oriens Extremus*, 32 (1989): 265-288.

quotation we can clearly recognize how Tanabe understands the history and essence of Buddhism in relation to his own philosophy. He interprets the history of Buddhism as a dialectics of its self-understanding that necessarily passes through several stages of evolution. Tanabe distinguishes the stage of primordial Buddhism with its early ideal and its later ideal. The early ideal is represented by the "self-awakened" eremite (the original Japanese uses the Buddhist term *dokkaku* 独覚, *pratyekabuddha*). The later ideal was the communitarian life of monks, in which the Dharma is handed down from master to master (this is the literal translation of *shihō-sōshō* 師法相承, and not "from master to disciple"). The communitarian life of monks or nuns gradually came to be regarded as the normal way of Buddhists to salvation. If one had not the opportunity to enter a community of monks or nuns in this life, that chance would certainly be provided in a future life—or so the Buddhists hoped. According to Tanabe the next necessary step, dialectically speaking, was the appearance of the Mahāyāna Bodhisattva ideal as a further development of the communitarian moment of Buddhist life.

The expression "benefiting oneself-*qua*-benefiting others" (*jiri-soku-rita* 自利即利他) can easily be misunderstood to mean that the Mahāyāna Bodhisattva seeks *his own* benefit *through* benefiting others. In fact *jiri-soku-rita* must be understood to mean that the Mahāyāna Bodhisattva turns the merits of his spiritual exercises to the advantage of others. In other words: "The benefits of oneself are (made to) the benefits of the others." For Buddhology, this merit-transference is effected by superhuman, miraculous powers.

According to Tanabe the dialectical development of Buddhist self-understanding culminated in Shinran's conception of *gensō*, which Shinran originally referred to as *gensō-ekō*, the "transference (of Bodhisattva-merits) by returning." Shinran always supposes that the only one who can transfer merits is Amida Buddha. But Tanabe does not use the word *ekō* here, nor does he speak of "merits." His only concern is with the exemplary Buddhist life of the Bodhisattva. The term *gensō* ("returning") Tanabe takes only as "return from the absolute" or "descent from the absolute," without reference to Shinran's idea that only Amida Buddha can accomplish such a return.

Consequent upon his understanding of the development of Buddhist self-understanding as a dialectics, Tanabe refers to the community life of monks, with its transmission of the Dharma from master to master, as the "*an sich* stage," Buddhism's dialectics of the social. Shinran's notion of *gensō* he calls the "*für sich* stage" of this dialectics. (The English translation glosses over this distinction.) We need to pay close attention to Tanabe's dialectical view of the self-understanding of Buddhism precisely because he relates his own philosophy to this dialectic. In his view, Shinran's idea of *gensō* is the culmination of the dialectical evolution of the social element in Buddhism. This culminating point *within* historical Buddhism Tanabe called the "*für sich* stage." But one stage in the dialectic remains to be spelled out, the "*an und für sich* stage." This is the stage of synthesis, of universality, of the liberation of Buddhism from its traditional, historical limitations.

According to Tanabe, however, Buddhism can only reach this universal stage if it is mediated by the Christian notion of a "trinity of love." It is this mediation that he works out himself in amending his philosophy of the dialectics of absolute mediation in the form of a philosophy as metanoetics. What traditional, historical Buddhism—including the Buddhism of Shinran—has lacked heretofore is the element of the social *an und für sich* as universal law that applies to societies throughout the world. This is the dialectical element that Tanabe's philosophy as metanoetics supplies.

Psychologically speaking, philosophy as metanoetics was inspired by Buddhism in general (the absolute as absolute nothingness), by Christianity (the ideal of community as a trinity of love), and by Shinran (the notion of *gensō*). Taken as a whole, the philosophy as metanoetics regards itself as dialectically *above* all of these, as a universal religious philosophy transcending all Western and Eastern traditions up to the present.

Elsewhere in chapter 8 Tanabe describes the functions of Dharmākara Bodhisattva/Amida Buddha in relation to the human being in greater detail:

> To express the same thing in symbolic terms: Tathāgata, who is the absolute, does not rest peacefully on some distant summit of absolute perfection, but is forever on a journey of descent to relative beings below. Tathāgata is not poised sedately within the inner sanctum of his home, but is ever ready to set off, at the first sign of alarm, to save relative

beings. Tathāgata cannot exercise his absoluteness apart from his descent to save relative sentient beings. It is for this reason that the essence of Tathāgata is taken to be absolute *gensō*. Meanwhile, as the subject of absolute mediation, Tathāgata makes room for the independence of relative beings, thereby restricting his own work in an act of self-negation in order to collaborate with the spontaneity of relative sentient beings as his mediators. Thus he instructs all sentient beings by providing an example of action which sentient beings can learn from him and imitate. This is his salvific work, aimed at elevating all sentient beings and directing them into the realm of the Buddha.

In fact, as I shall explain later, the absolute *gensō* performed by the Bodhisattva Dharmākara is embodied in the relative *gensō* of the relationship between relative beings in which the more advanced on the way of *ōsō* guide the less advanced, quite apart from the order of seniority that would characterize them as members of a society of "species." The work of the absolute Tathāgata begins as a work of mediation between one relative being and another. To simplify this twofold relative mediation for a moment and treat it as one, the meaning of the doctrine comes down to this: Amida Buddha, as Dharmākara, performs absolute *gensō* as the more advanced who provides a model of the action that less advanced sentient beings must perform to be saved, and he does so at the stage of Dharmākara—that is, prior to his enlightenment or while he is at the stage of disciplined preparation for enlightenment (*inni*). All sentient beings who enter upon the path of salvation are promised Buddhahood and participation in *nirvāṇa* if they take the discipline of Dharmākara as their guide and model, and of their own accord make their action conform to his through absolute negation. This is *ōsō-ekō*, merit-transference on the way toward the Pure Land. It is understood to mean that, mediated by the absolute *gensō* of Tathāgata, stimulated and supported by his transforming power, one offers up one's self-power to mediate the Great Action of Tathāgata.[11]

The passage is a complex one. Let me begin by correcting the following important part of the English translation:

---

[11] PM, 273-74.

In fact, as I shall explain later, the absolute *gensō* performed by the Bodhisattva Dharmākara is embodied in the relative *gensō* of the relationship between relative beings in which the more advanced on the way of *ōsō* guide the less advanced, quite apart from the order of seniority that would characterize them as members of a society of "species."

I would rather translate:

Nay, in fact, as I shall explain later, the absolute descent of Dharmākara Bodhisattva again is mediated and substituted by the relative descent of those relatives, who are forerunners (already) saved through (their) ascent, and the sentient beings — the forerunners and the following beings together — belong to one common society characterized as species.

While the former version seems to *deny* that the forerunners and their followers build a common species, the latter sees the element that Tanabe meant to explain by way of the Amida/Dharmākara symbol to lie *precisely* in this common species, characterized by the distinction between forerunners and followers (or characterized by the Bodhisattva-function of the forerunners in relation to their followers).

Both in the above passage, and in Tanabe's dialectics of absolute mediation in general, the absolute as absolute nothingness only acts through the mediation of the activity of relative beings. Thus, Amida's absolute *gensō* is mediated by the absolute *gensō* of Dharmākara Bodhisattva. The point of my rendition is to stress, then, that the absolute *gensō* of Dharmākara Bodhisattva *is again mediated* by relative beings, who are more advanced on the way of *ōsō* — or more generally speaking, in the spiritual life — and hence can guide the less advanced. They give a good example of ethico-religious life for the less advanced to imitate. The advanced *substitute* Amida Buddha and the Dharmākara Bodhisattva (rather than simply "embody" it). Ultimately, according to Tanabe relative beings, in their relation of reciprocal mediation as forerunners and followers in the ethico-religious life, form a common society which is characterized as a species *distinct from* other species. For Tanabe these latter are not marked by an abstract equality of its members but rather by the historical and concrete difference of *seniority* in the ethico-religious life, in other words by the concrete difference of the *Bodhisattva function* of the forerunners to the followers. This is Tanabe's religious view of society as species. In this view, there is no place for a mythological figure like Amida Buddha/Dharmākara Bodhisattva, only for a species-community of relative beings and for the absolute as absolute nothingness (both of which are related in absolute mediation).

The following quotation, taken from the original Japanese, gives us a clear picture of the scheme of absolute mediation, without mentioning the names of Amida or Dharmākara:

> The salvation-(activity) of the absolute in favor of the relative is performed with the mediation of two kinds of relatives with the relative, which is the object of salvation, and with the relative, which is the advanced (forerunner) in relation to the (first) relative. The fact that till now I have spoken of it as if the absolute would stand immediately vis-à-vis the relative and would cooperate with (the relative), is the result of abstraction to express the relation analytically. In reality, also the fact that the absolute makes the two kinds of relatives to its mediation and comes into relation with the relatives, is realized by running through the relations between the relatives themselves. This is the reason why the absolute descent is the base for the relative descent. Further: the performer of the (above-mentioned) actions, which conform to (the actions of) the relatives, which are the objects of salvation, is not the absolute itself; because its mediation is the relative, which is on the relative descent, the two (relatives) are mediated through (their) opposition on (their) common base, that is: the species, which the two relatives embrace. In such a way the absolute is nothing else than absolute mediation, which makes the reciprocal relation between the relatives to (its) mediation.[12]

Here we see how Tanabe regards Amida and Dharmākara as merely symbolic figures. For philosophy as metanoetics, as a dialectics of absolute mediation, there is no room for one-sided causalities, especially when they are regarded as a *deus ex machina* who saves relative beings by superhuman miraculous power. But for a dialectics of absolute mediation, the functions of Amida and Dharmākara are taken over by other dialectical elements, namely, relative beings themselves. By providing other relative beings with

---

[12] Translated from THZ 9:251.

a model of life, the particular relative assumes the function of a relative *gensō* to promote the salvation of the others. Providing a model of life for others presupposes that one has gone through one's own relative *ōsō*, which in turn is made possible by the relative *gensō* of another forerunner further back in history.

In this way, the reciprocal relation of mediation among relative beings (again mediated by the absolute *gensō* of the absolute as absolute nothingness or as absolute self-negation/absolute love) realizes all moments of a species-society as a community of reciprocal salvation or a community of mutual love. But this species-society should not be misunderstood as meaning the universal community of humanity which, in Tanabe's view, is an abstraction. Concretely speaking, there are several species-societies, each of which is ruled by a manifold of dialectical relations that affect its internal and external relationships. These relations are characterized as negation (mutual strife) and self-negation (the praxis of love in one form or another). Each species-society is determined by its own specific history and tradition, by its own chain of forerunners and followers, who themselves in turn become forerunners for those that follow. Each species-society has a specific *linear* direction in history at the same time that it is mediated by the *circular* presence of the absolute as absolute nothingness.

Accordingly, Tanabe stresses the mediation of relative *ōsō* and *gensō* through the absolute *gensō* of the absolute. The absolute is forever moving outwards for salvation; it is absolute *gensō*. This going out of itself means a negation of itself. Salvation of relative beings means affirming relative beings as such, and this assumes that the absolute negates itself as absolute. Thus Tanabe points out again and again that it is only by affirming relative beings while negating itself that the absolute can realize its absoluteness.

It is of course impossible to present here all the different aspects of Tanabe's religious view of society as viewed from philosophy as metanoetics, which he enumerates in chapter 8 rather unsystematically. In particular, we cannot here go into his political statements and his symbol of the pompon-dahlia to illustrate the idea of "history as a dialectics of linear time and circular eternity." Let us rather concentrate on the Bodhisattva role of the members of the species.

In describing the mutual relation between relative beings as a relation of spiritual forerunners and followers, Tanabe stresses the spiritual seniority of the forerunner as a Bodhisattva and uses the Buddhist term *kyōke* 教化 — "teaching the doctrine (Dharma)" — to characterize it. Through the exercise of this Bodhisattva function, the relation of mutual equality within a species is accorded a certain order, which Tanabe regards as indispensable for societies of our time. He states:

> In this regard I would argue that the three ideas that form the slogan of the French revolution, *liberté*, *egalité*, and *fraternité*, are not independent but mutually mediating notions. Left on its own, freedom ends up in inequality. There can be no doubt that democracy and liberalism are producing the inequality of today's capitalistic societies. Socialism, meanwhile, sets up equality as its goal, but there is no disputing the fact that the socialist system invariably limits freedom and in that sense negates it. Freedom and equality are not concepts that can easily be linked together into a formal identity, but are contradictory concepts that oppose each other. The only thing that can unify them is the transforming action of those who make up the membership of a society, but this is no easy task. The standard for such unification would seem to be a kind of fraternity that retains the literal meaning of "brotherhood." It is conceivable that the social order that freedom provides can be preserved in this way and at the same time the demand for equality be realized, thus disclosing a concrete unity that would actually synthesize the two.
>
> Ordinarily when we speak of fraternity, the emphasis is put on equality, as is the case with brotherly love, and this makes it hard to distinguish it clearly from friendship. But if we insist on the true meaning of brotherhood, priority joins equality as an essential element, or rather as *the* main aspect of fraternity. In the case of brothers the guidance that the elder brother gives the younger affects the latter's entire personality; it is literally a learning and an imitation. The instruction that goes on between them can be compared to that of the master-disciple-relationship. As Kierkegaard remarked, a true master exists only in religion. In other words, there is no absolute master who does not allow for equality except for the absolute as such, as is the case when God — or Christ — is said to be the master. As relative beings, teachers, however eminent they be,

334 • JOHANNES LAUBE

retain an aspect of equality with their disciples as fellow trav-
elers. The fact that the absolute *gensō* of Amida Buddha takes
as its mediator the discipline and practice of Dharmākara
means that the absolute humbles and restrains itself to take on
relativity for the sake of mediating the way for relative beings.
This is the Great Compassion of Other-power.[13]

Or again:

Unlike Aristotle's idea of friendship and the Christian idea of
love, which are exclusively based on equality, this relationship
is based on the twofold dynamic of *ōsō* and *gensō*—an extremely odd but concrete idea. At the same time, just as the
brothers and sisters, who maintain an order of seniority
among themselves, maintain their equality as children of the
same parents, relative beings are of a kind and equal to one
another vis-à-vis the absolute.[14]

To sum up Tanabe's religious view of society, we may adopt
some of his own formulations: Logically speaking, the individual
and the universal (in other words, the human self and God) must
meet each other through the mediation of the species (i.e., the
historical society to which the individual belongs). The species in
question is the salvific means (*hōben, upāya*) which the absolute as
absolute nothingness uses for the salvation of relative beings in
question. But the absolute, too, is mediated by the species in order
to realize its absoluteness. Finally, the species itself is mediated by
the mutual negation (and self-negation) of relative beings, which
are members of the species in question, and mediated by mutual
negation (and self-negation) among different species. We can call
this kind of manifold mediation by negation the "middle way" or
"way of mediation."

Referring to the relations between the relative beings who
constitute a species by their reciprocal negation (and self-negation),
Tanabe speaks of "the way of brotherhood" (here again, stressing
the aspect of self-negation). But he interprets this brotherhood
not as a "friendship" after the manner of Aristotle, nor as a
"brotherly love" (*agape*) after the manner of Christianity, nor as
a "*fraternité*" after the manner of the French bourgeois. For Ta-

---

[13] PM, 278-79.
[14] PM, 276-77.

nabe brotherhood is not a *yū-ai* 友愛 but a *kyōdaisei* 兄弟性 or *kyōdai-ai* 兄弟愛 , by which he means the relation of love between elder and younger siblings. He calls it the principle of seniority, which is based not on domination but on instruction. Tanabe compares the elder brothers and sisters with the Mahāyāna Bodhisattva after the model of Shinran's Dharmākara Bodhisattva, and in that same vein refers to the relation within the species as the "way of the Bodhisattvas."

Generally speaking, the Mahāyāna Bodhisattva may be a Bodhisattva in ascent (*ōsō*) or in descent (*gensō*). But because in Shinran the only Bodhisattva is the savior Amida Buddha who is always on the path of descent, Tanabe demythologizes the singularity of Amida to argue that the way of the species is the way of the *gensō* Bodhisattvas as a *plurality*!

CONTRADICTIONS AND SELF-CONTRADICTIONS

CONTRADICTIONS IN SHINRAN

For Shinran there is only one *gensō* Bodhisattva, Dharmākara Bodhisattva. There is no plurality of Bodhisattvas on earth in this Last Age of the Dharma. Sentient beings born in the Pure Land can be called Bodhisattvas, but there they lack contact with the corrupt *mappō* world and with the reality of sin. What is more, they can be called Bodhisattvas only because they have been assumed into the one great Bodhisattvaship of Amida Buddha, who is the sole cause of their salvation and elevation to Bodhisattvaship.

Shinran does not distinguish between "relative *gensō*" and "absolute *gensō*." There was no systematic need for such a distinction in his thought. Amida Buddha is the only *gensō*. This does not mean that we can simply identify Amida Buddha with the absolute (the absolute *dharma-kāya*). Even for Shinran Amida Buddha is no more than a salvific means for the absolute. Ultimately, Amida Buddha is subsumed into the absolute Dharma. For Shinran, the salvation of the sentient beings is not the result of an internal necessity of the absolute itself but of the compassion and wisdom of the Amida Buddha as its agent vis-à-vis sentient beings. Salvation is wrought through the merits of Amida Buddha as Dharmākara Bodhisattva and their transference to sentient beings. This transference is made possible only by miraculous power. Hence for Shinran it is not the model life on earth of the Dharmākara or the idea of a Dharmākara-like human forerunner that brings about the salvation of sentient beings, nor is it their own imitation of such a forerunner. There is no self-power cause of their salvation whatsoever.

To be sure, there the dialectics of self-power and Other-power is found in Shinran's thought, but not in the sense of Tanabe's dialectics of absolute mediation, which can speak of "placing too much emphasis on Other-power." Such language is entirely foreign to Shinran, who could not stress the grace of Other-power enough, and whose dominating sentiment was not that there was something he could do for himself but that everything has already been accomplished by Amida Buddha. (We may note, however, that for Shinran this is true only for the age of *mappō* in which he lived.)

The passage from which Tanabe's statement was abstracted reads as follows:

> By placing too much emphasis here on the Other-power, we end up in the usual position of claiming that whatever action sentient beings perform is done *qua* the Great Action of Tathāgata. But this "*qua*" refers to mediation, not to a mere causal relationship. If this latter were the case, we would be forced to conclude that the Great Action is itself the action of Tathāgata, or at least its effect, so that the meaning of action by sentient beings would be completely lost. By the same token, persistence in this position lands us in a sort of mysticism that places the action of the Tathāgata and the action of the sentient beings in a relationship of contradictory self-identity. Obviously neither of these solutions is suited to the spirit of metanoetical transformation. In my view Shinran's *zange* has nothing at all to do with such ideas, but is rather concerned with absolute mediation.[15]

Finally, according to Shinran the salvation of the individual self is only and of necessity mediated by the species. There are indeed certain elements of the social present in Shinran's consciousness of himself as a foolish sinner in the time of *mappō*, especially with regard to his relation to his master Hōnen. But this relation belongs to the category of the "conditions" (*en* 縁) of salvation, not of its "causes" (*in* 因). To Shinran's way of seeing,

---

[15] PM, 274-75.

it is not the relation between one self and another that is the cause of salvation but rather the relation between the human self and Amida Buddha in his Pure Land. This is why he can claim, "As for myself, Shinran, I do not have a single disciple."[16]

CONTRADICTIONS IN TANABE

First of all, I should like to make it clear that I grant Tanabe the perfect right to use Shinran's texts as tools for his own thought and even to use formulations that go against Shinran's own intentions. This is, after all, part of the freedom of philosophical reflection.

Secondly, one has to see that there are many ways to philosophy. Among them, the approach to philosophy by way of ethical experience ("What should I do?"), while always a possibility, is coming to look more and more like a matter of necessity. Although Tanabe's basic ethical experience may not suggest so much the question, "What should I do?" as "Oh God, what have I done!" his approach clearly belongs to the ethical way of philosophy. It was through the (sudden) experience of being confronted by "God" (or "absolute Other-power"), and turned around by that power to the way of *gensō*, that his new philosophy on the *gensō* path took its start as a religious philosophy in the sense of a philosophy "mediated by religious experience amidst the death of theoretical and practical autonomous human reason."

In combining this new philosophical approach with his former dialectics of absolute mediation, Tanabe was able to bring into relief for the first time what was hidden in his earlier thought: its metanoetical character as a dialectics of negation and self-negation. According to this dialectics of absolute mediation reality always contains *two* elements of negation and self-negation. More concretely speaking, reality always discloses a manifold of opposing elements such as absolute and relative, Other-power and self-power, self and other, active and passive, death and resurrection, nothingness and love, radical evil and continual metanoia, foolish sinner and Bodhisattva, species as power that negates the individual and species as a means of salvation, and so on.

Now at the outset of *Philosophy as Metanoetics*, Tanabe is at

---

[16] *Tannisho: A Shin Buddhist Classic*, trans. by Taitetsu Unno (Honolulu: Buddhist Study Center Press, 1984), 11.

pains to put the stress on the *negating* elements, and only near
the end does he stress the *salvific* elements. But once he has made
the shift, he stops pointing out the duality that characterizes the
nature of absolute mediation. In dubbing his philosophy a *tariki-
tetsugaku* 他力哲学 (Other-power philosophy), he seems to have forgotten that according to his own dialectics of absolute mediation,
he should really call it a *jiriki-tariki-tetsugaku* (self-power/Other-
power philosophy), or perhaps better a *tariki-jiriki tetsugaku* (Other-
power/ self-power philosophy). This is but one example of the
consequences that Tanabe fails to draw from his dialectics of absolute mediation. Personally, I am fascinated by this dialectics of
absolute mediation, but I cannot help thinking that it should be
carried through to the end and that the consequences that are
latent in Tanabe should be brought out into the open.

For the same reason, I feel Tanabe's interpretation of the
way of species as a "way of *gensō* Bodhisattvas" does not suit the
logical consequences to which a dialectics of absolute mediation
leads. In any case, the relationship of these *gensō* Bodhisattvas to
radical evil and sin need to be made more explicit. The *gensō*
Bodhisattva, for Shinran, is an absolute pure being. We have
already seen how for him the only individual that qualifies as a
gensō Bodhisattva is Amida Buddha.

But the *gensō* Bodhisattva that Tanabe has in mind is none
other than the individual relative being that makes up the species-society. Both the individuals and their species-society, according to Tanabe, are corrupted by radical evil and personal sin.
Even the religious forerunners whom Tanabe regards as the spiritual leaders, religious "elder brothers," or *gensō* Bodhisattvas, even
these pioneers of salvation need to be understood as sin-ridden
and slaves of radical evil if we are to bring the dialectics of absolute
mediation and its metanoetical character to term. In fact, nowhere
in chapter 8 does Tanabe speak of the corruption of *gensō* Bodhisattvas, but only looks to their self-negation and salvific role.
But, we have to ask, is self-negation even a possibility in this
world of radical evil to which even the human *gensō* Bodhisattvas
belong? How could such individuals ever come to salvific wisdom
in such a world as ours? If a pure *gensō* Bodhisattva were to
appear in a certain sin-ridden species-society, it would not be
because of that evil society but *in spite of*. The species-society and
its corrupt members would scarcely be able to recognize him as

a pure Bodhisattva, since "only a Buddha knows a Buddha," as the scriptures are wont to say. Nor would there be any imitation of the pure example he sets on the part of fellow human beings within the common species.

If a pure *gensō* Bodhisattva were to appear in this corrupt world, it would result either (a) from his own individual and singular power (not the power of other corrupt relative beings or their corrupt species-society as a whole); or (b) from an absolute Other-power that would effect his salvation and purity by some transcendent miracle. Purification and salvation on the first model would follow the way of autonomous ethics; on the second, the way of heteronomous religion. But what Tanabe was trying to explain was the appearance of the *pure* in the midst of the *impure* — and to do so precisely by *not* having recourse to either of those two options. His was a search for a third way.

It seems to me that in his dialectics as absolute mediation, Tanabe has the makings of a possible solution, but a solution whose logical and textual consequences he did not elaborate or pursue adequately. I regard his dialectics of absolute mediation as posing a necessary challenge to all theologies and philosophies of today: to rethink their concept of the absolute and of the relation between the absolute and the relative *mediated by the species-society*. In this regard, Tanabe Hajime has given us an epoch-making philosophy for the East *and for the West!*[17]

---

[17] See Johannes Laube, *Dialektik der absoluten Vermittlung: Hajime Tanabes Religionsphilosophie als Beitrag zum "Wettstreit der Liebe" zwischen Buddhismus und Christentum* (Freiburg: Herder, 1984).

Dialectic and Religious Experience
in *Philosophy as Metanoetics*

Jeffrey WATTLES

TANABE Hajime's *Philosophy as Metanoetics* treats religious experience dialectically and aims to lay a groundwork for a philosophy of living for scholars and non-scholars alike. From this complex book one may reconstruct a sequence of stages. (1) In the first stage, complacent confidence in reason and in the independent self abounds. (2) Then reason exhausts itself in the effort to resolve insuperable theoretical and / or practical problems, "antinomies." (3) Then comes the religious breakthrough: one confesses one's weakness and repents of one's sins and pride and receives "resurrection" through the saving grace of Other-power (*tariki*). (4) Thinking, newly revived, expounds the contradictions of life and thought using the dialectics of absolute *mu*, nothingness. In particular, philosophy reflects upon Other-power and criticizes a naive concept of the otherness of Other-power. (5) Then a reconstructive way of thought is found which affirms a mediated unity of the absolute and the relative. (6) Finally, all activities of truth and goodness and beauty (PM, 199) are transformed.[1] People are "restored to life as co-workers of God or the Buddha" (190).

In fairness, it must be emphasized that Tanabe does not offer such a sequence of stages but at times presents the essential process as a ceaseless, circular, two-stage movement of consciousness

---

[1] I cite Tanabe's order — truth, goodness, and beauty — here, while following the sequence truth, beauty, and goodness in the closing exposition. Tanabe's sequence suggests the spontaneity with which goodness (*gensō*) emerges from the realization of truth (nothingness). The exposition here aims for a symmetry in which the danger of neglecting beauty is reduced and the dominance of goodness is highlighted. Indeed, Tanabe portrays so radically the unity of thought and action that it is difficult to separate truth and goodness as realms of value for him.

oriented now toward relative (finite, intuitable) being, now toward absolute nothingness; and some expositions would condense some of my stages. Two problems motivate the separation of these stages. First, how can we sustain three moments, all of which belong to *Philosophy as Metanoetics:* the religious orientation to Other-power; the dialectical critique of the otherness of the Other; and the Hegelian identity of the absolute and the relative? And second, how can religious philosophy produce a philosophy of living for the broad category in which Tanabe includes himself—"ordinary, ignorant people" (lx, 16, 85, 187)?

STAGE 1: NAIVE SELF-CONFIDENCE

The evil tendency intrinsic to finite beings is to take their relative independence (both as individuals and as a group) to be absolute. This evil is reflected in pride, in the materialism of the present age, and in the inability of existing political arrangements to achieve both liberty and equality.

STAGE 2: REASON CRASHES ON THE ROCKS OF ANTINOMY

Tanabe adapts the pattern of Hegel's *Phenomenology of Mind* and insists that everyone must go through the breakdown of practical, scientific, and philosophic reason. Tanabe insists that the critique of reason must go beyond Kant to criticize the reasoning subject as well as the objective discourses of reason (38). The model of Tanabe's own experience suggests to him that without radically acknowledging the impotence of reason to reconcile its contradictions, one will never perform thoroughgoing *zange*, repentance, which opens the way fully for the invasion of grace.

Tanabe explains that scientific theory has often been misleading, and philosophy cannot accept science as an unquestioned starting point. Science needs to be understood not only in terms of its announced results but also historically and in terms of its philosophical components and their difficulties (34, 97, 226). The most basic problem in the scientific method (noted more than a decade before Thomas Kuhn's *The Structure of Scientific Revolutions*) is this: one cannot be too optimistic about the heuristic value of the experimental method, since any scientific hypothesis projects an interpretation that hinders revolutionary discoveries (62, 108).

Indeed, scientific theory may "fall into absolute disruption in its opposition to and estrangement from the irrationality of actuality" (97). Revising previous notions of rationality, relativity and quantum physics have restricted the application of the concept of causation, formerly regarded as univocally and universally applicable to physical phenomena (60). Tanabe's critique of science stands in tension with the role of science in the resurrected life (stage six).

STAGE 3: REPENTANCE AND CONVERSION AND RESURRECTION THROUGH THE GRACE OF OTHER-POWER

After the breakdown of reason comes repentance and saving grace. Metanoetics in effect begins in and remains in a fundamental either/or: either one has repented and submitted to Other-power, or one has not. One of Tanabe's contributions is to reaffirm spiritual experience as the center of philosophy. The modern temper prefers to domesticate spiritual experience, to treat it as a hypothesis, to assign it a marginal role, or to present it as a report of something extraordinary which is immediately thematized and treated objectively.

A reductionist critique is waiting in the wings for Tanabe's claims about Other-power. A Freudian and historicist analysis might read like this: Tanabe's sustained and intense mental crisis during the war led to psychic exhaustion. This exhaustion he acknowledged as he abandoned his previous philosophical orientation. Upon releasing his hold upon the subjective factors that had led to his exhaustion, Tanabe experienced an influx of power from the unconscious. He interpreted that influx in terms of the only live alternative available to him—Shinran's religious philosophy. Though he had not been consciously thinking of adopting this alternative religious teaching, he had been aware of it; and the reorganization of his psychic life was being prepared in his unconscious during the time of his mounting crisis. Thus he mistook his psychic influx for a gift from "Other-power." Steven T. Katz, for example, has emphasized that religious experience is mediated through tradition.[2] But Tanabe's critical relationship to

---

[2] "The 'Conservative' Character of Mystical Experience," in *Mysticism and Religious Traditions* (Oxford: Oxford University Press, 1983), 3-60.

Shinran begins to address this concern. And James Robertson Price III has challenged the assumption that claims to religious experience can only be claims to a form of immediate knowledge.[3] Tanabe gives us the information that would permit a reductionist critique to be mounted while maintaining superb allegiance to the ground upon which alone that critique could be defeated: the quality inherent in the very insurge of Other-power which "sweeps aside all doubt about itself" (2). He refuses to descend to the level of trying to prove the validity of his own metanoesis or the reality (non-illusoriness) of Other-power. It is rather his strength to affirm and unceasingly to reaffirm Other-power in undoubting faith, whether expressed in the moment of the immediacy of indubitable power (2), in the dialectics of mediation, or in symbol (294-95).

What qualities of the religious Other are manifest in spiritual experience? Other-power saves the sinner; it is the Great Compassion (24), whose activity inspires gratitude. Other-power engages the total personality (88). It acts through relative beings whom it chooses to function as axes of transformation (24). Other-power is to be obeyed (81), and it may be discerned as the deepest part of the self.[4] Nor could one repent without the grace of Other-power.

Tanabe refuses theistic accounts because he sees in them a static, dogmatic tendency to view God as *another being*. Static concepts are fatal to progress in thought; philosophy articulates what Hegel called the fluidity of the concept. Theism represses freedom of thought (thereby reflecting the arbitrary and selective "divine" will) and insists on a fixed starting point in myths and revelations which do not permit reciprocal transformation of faith and reason. But God, as Tanabe recognizes, need not be limited to this caricature. "Of course, if we identify the will of God with the love of God, and divine grace with the working of divine love, then

---

[3] "The Objectivity of Mystical Truth Claims," *The Thomist* 49 (1985): 81-98. But note Katz's distance from the position Price attacks, clarified in "On Mysticism," *Journal of the American Academy of Religion* 66/4 (Winter 1988): 751-57.

[4] According to Johannes Laube, Tanabe continued to develop the Christian terminology of love and God, though redefined philosophically; and he regarded Jesus as the paradigm of liberated existence. *Dialektik der absoluten Vermittlung: Hajime Tanabes Religionsphilosophie als Beitrag zum "Wettstreit der Liebe" zwischen Buddhismus und Christentum* (Freiburg: Herder, 1984), 158-65.

grace, far from destroying human freedom, only draws it out" (82).

Tanabe explores transcendence primarily as transcendence-in-immanence. He records "the transferring activity of Other-power working within and flowing forth from the bottomless depth of one's mind" (205). He finds the "center of the self" located in decision (10). "In metanoesis the Original Vow of the transcendent Amida Buddha becomes active in a direct manner, entering immanently into the consciousness of sentient beings" (227). The "higher and deeper self" is identified as "the spontaneous ideal element of self-consciousness" (175), as the authentic existence implied in self-consciousness of inauthentic existence (152) and simply as self-consciousness of the higher self as realized in action (72).

The phrases just cited illustrate a problematic continuum that joins two distinct factors: (1) Other-power operative as an uncanny kind of other, a non-intuitable presence *within* the depth of the mind and (2) one's own higher self, accessible in self-consciousness. The point that is essential to Tanabe is that Other-power cannot be intuited as an immanent, eternal now (113, 75). If "the Buddha-nature within" or "the Kingdom of Heaven within" are taken as terms indicating some datum for introspection, then, he says, they are nothing more nor less than symbols of "the realization of eternal nothingness in one's individual existence brought to action-witness" (292). But if Tanabe wants to avoid the danger of too easily ascribing every movement of repentant mind to the guidance of Other-power, does he not need something like a distinction between self-consciousness (even consciousness of a higher self) and indwelling spirit, however obscure the distinction may be phenomenologically?[5]

---

[5] This concern may perhaps be answered by some way of interpreting the Mahāyāna thought that *nirvāṇa* is non-different from *saṃsāra*, but Tanabe does not take this route. A similar problem occurs in Hegel's *Lectures on the Philosophy of Religion*, when Hegel identifies soul with concept (186), spirit with reason (206, 396n), and spirit with knowledge (110); see Peter C. Hodgson, ed., *The Lectures of 1827* (the one-volume edition) (Berkeley and Los Angeles: University of California Press, 1988).

On repentance see *Lectures on the Philosophy of Religion*, vol. 1: *Introduction and The Concept of Religion*, Peter C. Hodgson, ed., (Berkeley and Los Angeles, University of California Press, 1988), 220:

STAGE 4: DIALECTICAL CRITIQUE

But how is the Other-power encountered in repentance to be conceived? Tanabe speaks of *mu*, nothingness, whose meaning derives partly from Mahāyāna tradition and partly from Western philosophy; following the latter, nothingness is simply that which is not any one of the relative beings, but their context. The concept of nothingness operates to radicalize the philosophic drive to overcome the human tendency to conceive of transcendence as something or someone on the model of relative things and persons. The concept of nothingness also honors mystery and launches an unceasing effort to articulate the most remote subtleties of consciousness and action, as attention continually moves between the finite which it can conceive and nothingness which is finally unfathomable.

What is the motivation for regarding Other-power as an *other*?

> Since that which the self obeys in faith must transcend the self as an "Other," and since the Great Nay of absolute critique transcends the relative self by virtue of its being absolute, the Great Nay of the transcendent power of negation, even though it is nothingness, is believed in as that over against which the self is posited and through which the self is mediated (88).

Relating to nothingness, or the absolute, as an other is both necessary and not quite right. On the one hand, "the relative is relative in virtue of its opposition to other relatives, and can confront the absolute only by way of this relative-to-relative relationship" (236). On the other hand, such a relationship cannot

---

Religious sensibility swings back and forth between the determinacy of their antithesis and their unity and satisfaction. . . . Being aware of one's own inner existence and conviction as of no account, along with self-consciousness on the side of the universal condemning the former, results in the sensation of *repentance*, of *anguish* about oneself, etc. Being aware that one's empirical existence, furthered on the whole or in one or another of its aspects — and indeed not so much through one's own self-activity [as through] a connective power external to one's strength and prudence, which [is] represented as and attributed to the universal's having being in and for itself — results in the sensation of *thankfulness*, etc.

go unchallenged by philosophy: "Between being and nothingness there can be no such relative relationship" (234, 213).[6] Tanabe concludes that the relative and the absolute are neither simply identical nor exactly different, neither simply one nor exactly two (176, 257).

The legitimate conclusion of this critique is that thinking about Other-power on the basis of analogy with otherness between relative beings does not yield an adequate cognition. But a problem remains. This critique addresses the most fundamental concept in religion, the concept of Other-power, or, put more generally, the conviction that there is some *other* person, reality, or level beyond the relative or mundane. There has been controversy (for example, in Hegel scholarship) about whether genuine religion can survive such an incursion into its essential concept. But as Tanabe goes into the cave of thought to do battle with the Minotaur of static concepts, the one thread that he carries with him is a concept of nothingness which is no cold and distant abstraction. It is not a postulate of reason, though reason can explain that *mu* cannot be one of the relative beings. Tanabe tacitly associates the notion of being with the notion of thing, and so it is clear that Other-power cannot be a thing but rather no-thing— *mu*. Nothingness is an ab-sent (nonperceived) reality whose significance is mediated by the life and rigor and warmth of Mahāyāna Buddhism, especially the Pure Land tradition, as well as by other Eastern and Western philosophers.

If Tanabe's concept of nothingness were a mere abstraction of rational negation, his critique of the alterity of Other-power in the name of nothingness would leave a dilemma: either (1) gratitude to Other-power loses all focus and reference, and merges into aesthetic bliss (which Tanabe consistently rejects); or else (2) a stalemate results between a naive affirmation of Other-power and a flat, thoroughgoing, logical denial of the alterity of Other-power—an antinomy characteristic of stage two. This second horn of the dilemma is a non-progressive circling between religion and secularism from which there is no exit. In such conflict, both intellectual and spiritual levels would become falsified. The concept of Other-power would ossify, and intellectual dialectic would pre-empt the spiritual significance of nothingness. From the intellec-

---

[6] See Hegel, *Lectures on the Philosophy of Religion*, vol. 1, 396-406.

tual standpoint, gratitude to Other-power would be demoted to the status of a mere antechamber to truth. Affirmation would be seen merely as a moment in an overarching negation. Artistry in action would mean skating over that thin and now transparent ice that portends doom for the slow and over-heavy tread of naive consciousness: it is transparent to the bottomless movement that hastens to negate every taking or rejecting of a position. A new religion of philosophy would result that the non-scholar could not share. One could no longer say, "How great Thou art!" but only, "The greatness is so transfinite that it cannot be a Thou."

Wisps of tension between the primacy of the spiritual and the adventure of dialectic do linger in *Philosophy as Metanoetics*. If that circle were the best that we could do without compromising our integrity, then we would learn to rejoice in it and find nobility in resolutely following its turns. But the conflict would confuse and exhaust the spiritual impulse. Nor does it point to the goal: "A religion of the people must offer peace of soul and inspire trust in action" (284). Therefore, to move forward, Tanabe appeals to a further phase of dialectic.

STAGE 5: PHILOSOPHICAL UNITY

Contradiction is suspect in formal thought because it permits chaos. In dialectic, talk of contradiction must take care to avoid confusion. At one point Tanabe defines negation as "the simultaneous presence of annihilation and preservation. These two meanings, or two aspects of one and the same dynamic, interpenetrate with the accent shifting now to one, now to the other as the situation changes" (218). Everything depends on how that accent is placed. If the first phase of philosophy is "contradictory and negative" development, the second phase is "affirmative and unifying" return (74). Philosophy strives to "break through to a point where the contradictories can be brought into dialectical unity by the transforming mediation of absolute nothingness" (232). Once we admit the negation of negation, it is possible to resurrect versions of concepts that were previously rejected as onesided.

A striking example of dialectical unification appears late in the book, where Tanabe takes up the contradiction between the religious orientation to Other-power and philosophic negation of the alterity of nothingness. He revives what from any previous perspective can only appear to be the enemy (174) — the Hegelian identity of the absolute and the relative. Any absolute worth its salt will be a knowing absolute which also *encompasses the relative, includes human consciousness.*

> Basically, absolute knowledge means a wisdom that knows the absolute. If this were understood in the sense of making the absolute an object of one's knowing, all knowledge of the absolute would have to remain relative, and there could be no attaining to absolute knowledge. Absolute knowledge can only mean that knowledge as such belongs to the absolute, that it is the self-consciousness of the absolute. That on the one hand. On the other, philosophy is something that takes place in us relative beings, so that if absolute knowledge is limited to the self-consciousness of an absolute apart from us, it has to be relative as something opposed to our consciousness. Hence absolute knowledge must be the self-consciousness of the absolute and at the same time our knowledge. And if it is not to be knowledge of an absolute that stands opposed to us, the self-consciousness of the absolute must at the same time signify our self-consciousness (270).[7]

A true Infinite must somehow include the finite; a true absolute must include the relative. Not wishing to affect a standpoint outside of and superior to the human situation, Tanabe makes his point here through conditional statements and explications of meanings. But his conclusion situates the relative in the framework of the absolute. Resurrection through Other-power gives the basis for realizing this mediated identity of the absolute and the relative. Tanabe criticizes Hegel for not seeing that the concept of "the identity of absolute contradictories" could only be grasped by resurrected self-consciousness (lvi).

In the unifying phase of dialectic we see an emerging real-

---

[7] Tanabe follows Hegel in asserting that only in human consciousness does the absolute achieve self-consciousness (*The Lectures of 1827*, 118). These philosophers did not utilize the resources of Christianity and Buddhism for affirming the self-consciousness of the absolute on a superhuman level of perfection. A cosmology that accepts multiple levels of mind can better harmonize humility and dialectic: human mind is merely a humble level, but one whereon may occur not only error but also the revelation of the Infinite to itself.

ization that an adequate concept of the absolute (or God or *mu*) must perform at least two tasks. (1) It must validate the heterological religious orientation to transcendence insofar as one is saved by, feels gratitude to, and obeys the Focus (and note that the Focus is not simply a phenomenological correlate of subjective intending, since that intending is now understood as enabled and empowered by the absolute).[8] (2) Such a concept must also sustain the philosophical dialectic that teaches, among other things, that the absolute is not properly conceived as simply *a different being*. An adequate concept, like a living cell, must have stability as well as flexibility. It should be possible to enhance the stabilization of this movement without ossification of the dialectic.

There is a spectrum of alternatives here between the extremes of a static theism and a corrosive nihilism. Tanabe's solution assigns priority to negation, but there is an alternative that assigns priority to affirmation. This is to conceive of God as *the self-focalization of Infinity*.[9] (God is here conceived as spirit, transcendent with respect to consciousness, anterior to actuality and to potentiality and in that sense beyond being.) It then becomes possible in a *sequence* of thoughts to do justice both to the religious orientation to Other-power and to philosophical reflection: First, God is. Next, God is in us. Finally, in God we live and act and have our being.[10] The first of these affirmations is consistent with a direct heterological, even theistic orientation; it validates gratitude and obedience. The next one finds transcendence in immanence, modifies the heterological implications by its inward turn, but does

---

[8] Heterology is the discourse on the other (Greek: *heteron*).

[9] Regarding the use of "infinity" rather than "the absolute," Tanabe sometimes names *mu* with the term infinity—in juxtaposition with finitude (PM, 38) and in a cosmological context (111). He is willing to speak of the "infinity and eternity of *zange*" (lii). Despite his affirmation of the infinity of space and time (110) he warns of taking time as a "bad infinity" of mere unlimited extension (73), and also of Augustine's symmetrical infinity of time (130) and of the mysticism of infinite transcendence in abstraction from immanence (174).

[10] Hegel says that "God gives himself this ultimate singularization of thisness," and becomes "the object for a cognizing activity," "gives himself the relationship of God to the feeling subject" (*Lectures on the Philosophy of Religion*, 1, 140). This concept is not immediately bound up with that of incarnation; what is essential is a trans-subjective Focus which sustains itself through the progressive moments of thought.

not remove all sense of otherness; it can acknowledge guidance, and God is still named. The last one validates brotherhood, diffuses the heterological focus, but continues to refer in thought and word, thus making possible continuity with the two previous phases of faith-witness.

STAGE 6: THE NEW LIFE IN NATURALNESS

"In this resurrected life, philosophical thought and other cultural activities of a moral nature that were once abandoned in despair are now reinstated . . . performed in naturalness" (248). The resurrected life is not immune from antinomy, but it is experienced in antinomy, a veteran of the trenches of contradiction, and is not continually occupied in explicating every possible mediation when confronted by the appearance of immediacy.[11] It is the achievement of *Philosophy as Metanoetics* to have labored so nobly to set foot in this promised land; yet much work remains to be done in giving accounts of the activities in the realms of truth, beauty, and goodness as these activities are resurrected in the new life. On some topics Tanabe did stage 4 critical work but did not complete the unifying return of stages 5 and 6.

TRUTH

SCIENCE

Along the way of reintegration, Tanabe now honors science for bringing us face to face with the brute facts of actuality, thus countering the prejudices of a moralistic approach to reality (263). Facts may dis-illusion us, occasioning repentance. In any case, facts are not to be taken as atomic, obvious tools for self-power, but viewed in the light of mediation. On the scientific level of truth, Tanabe hardly casts a glance at what might be called the grammaticality of circumstance ("propositional truth"). And clearly a coherence theory will not work, since each of our theories is

---

[11] Hegel (like Tanabe) generally uses "immediacy" to name naive resistance to the recognition of mediation; but he also acknowledges that both immediacy and mediation are complementary and mutually necessary (*Lectures on the Philosophy of Religion*, 1, 407ff). Without this relaxation of dialectic, daily life cannot be lived.

contradicted, sooner or later. In addition, the task of philosophical mediation between science and religion comes into view as a priority (264).

Tanabe's demarcation between what he rejects of science and what he accepts largely follows the distinction between fact and theory. But on two points he shows positivist tendencies in the ease with which he classifies certain religious teachings as myth. He appears to regard the question of the continuation of the soul apart from the body as an empirical question. And without attempting to provide a cosmological framework for human existence, he lets the current state of cosmology decide about the existence of the Pure Land or Heaven. "Given my high regard for science, I can find no basis for belief in either the Pure Land or the Kingdom of Heaven, nor can I believe in the continuation of a disembodied soul after death" (157, 295 — but note the hope for survival at 148). While criticizing Kant's enterprise of religion within the limits of reason (50), Tanabe praises Pure Land Buddhism for the ease with which it can be demythologized such that "its doctrine makes no appeal to miracles or anything that contradicts the scientific mind" (225). But Tanabe also uses infinity as a factor in cosmology (34) and speaks of "the strongly resistant functioning of karma in the present enters into the pulsation of infinity as the transforming stuff of creation that gives birth to the stars" (111).

PHILOSOPHY

Truth is possible because philosophy participates in the inner dynamics of the process — the mutual mediation of nothingness and finite beings — which occurs throughout the universe and within the mind. Metanoetics, philosophy in the resurrected life, is no longer a pastime or a profession of self-power reason, but a capacity rooted in repentance to range over stages two through five as the situation requires. Tanabe insists on the inclusion of theoretical work into the transformed life of action. The new philosophy is always already praxis. The fundamental praxis is casting oneself into repentance. All transformed action is rooted in repentance.

Tanabe's refusal of a robust sense of personal identity is profoundly argued, yet finally unsatisfying. The difference between the sinful past and the future of resurrected freedom is so substantive that Tanabe refuses to acknowledge any identity of the personality that persists throughout these changes (74, 109). But it is difficult to see how one could continue to feel sorry for sins prior to one's conversion without presupposing one's identity through time. How can we make sense of our ability to recognize one another and to anticipate a future that is ours? Indeed in many ways Tanabe softens his denial of personal identity, though never renounces it. His language implies personal identity when he uses the first-person pronoun to talk about his experiences prior to his conversion and when he says that "the self is resurrected" (88). True, the selfishness of the ego clinging to life must be abandoned (197, 243); but how does "ethical" abandonment relate to "metaphysical" abandonment? Tanabe's main point appears to be that a rigid notion of the self as a kind of substance or quasi-thing will not facilitate resurrection (18). And no action can proceed on the basis of (clinging to or consciousness of) self-identity (75).

I interpret this point as an instance of the larger point that action transcends contemplation and, *a fortiori*, self-contemplation. Tanabe acknowledges the need for a ground or unity underlying the temporal process: "Freedom is in need of the ground of transcendent nothingness in order that the self may break through itself without destroying its spontaneity in the process (86)."[12] Can responsible individuality be located on a chart that has only nothingness and temporal discontinuities? The closest thing to personal identity that Tanabe does acknowledge is continuous repentance, "unshakable or irreversible faith" (5, 189). So long as one persists

---

[12] For this point I am indebted to Langdon Gilkey's review article on *Philosophy as Metanoetics* in the *Journal of Religion* 68/3 (July, 1988): 30.

[13] Tanabe's exposition is distinguished by abstaining from the traditional categories of philosophical anthropology and from the language of "inner" and "outer" and even "experience" with its potentially dualistic implications. I can only propose here that heterology consider such a rich concept of personality as Nicolas Berdyaev provides in the opening chapter of *Slavery and Freedom* (New York: Charles Scribner's Sons, 1944). His concept of personality includes the following features: Personality is that which is identical throughout all change, all growth. Personality is a mystery. Personality is unique. Personality includes physical, mental, and spiritual factors which move toward mature unity as spirit strives for the mastery.

in repentance, any future sin "would not add further negativity to the nature of its new being" (5).[13]

RELIGION

"Religion" no longer names a set of devotional activities insulated from the operation of nothingness in thought; it now becomes a name for the whole of resurrected life. Spiritual truth is available only through repentance, which reveals simultaneously our wretched sinfulness and our gracious acceptance. Note that when religion is defined in terms of authority, revelation, doctrine, historical beliefs, spreading the faith (31, 226, 247-48; 91, contra), then philosophy rather than religion is the domain of genuine experience (248). By characterizing philosophy and religion as I have done, I have sought to preserve metanoetics from a fate which is a tendency evident in *Philosophy as Metanoetics*: the creation of a religion in which philosophers alone can participate. What we have on the whole in the book, I would suggest, is a religion whose consciousness is philosophical. Renewed religion might loosen positions that were tightly held in previous stages without betraying the spirit of metanoetics. I will suggest three revisions, beginning with the one that I think Tanabe could most easily accommodate, and moving to the one that might be hardest for him to accommodate.

First, Tanabe regards the concept of revelation as pre-empting the initiative of philosophy, yet he writes of Shinran's returning to teach him personally (30) and of disciplining himself to the guidance of Shinran's writings (224). But Tanabe preserves a critical and creative distance from Shinran. Why not take Tanabe's practice as contributing to a de-absolutized notion of revelation and a critical relationship to revelation?

Second, it might not be necessary for metanoetics to regard all religious contemplation as the sacrifice of praxis and an opiate of the people (283), the illusion of immediate aesthetic unity with absolute nothingness. The gratitude that Tanabe celebrates rises to worship. He challenges spiritual relaxation with the insight that a given moment of mediation in nothingness "quickly recedes into the past as an established fact, which then needs to be mediated again" (96); but this insight may be used to assist contemplation rather than to reject it. Nor does sustained devotion entail that its Other is displayed for inspection as an object present at hand.

Finally, it is possible to ask about the predominance of repentance as a religious technique. Tanabe has great insight into the need for continuous adjustment in living. And every adjustment may be characterized as a negation of what went before. But not every such negation need be undertaken as repentance. Many of Tanabe's negations are intellectual, not encounters with evil and sin. And even in relating to one's lesser past, repentance is sometimes required by the situation, sometimes not. There are tacit and cheerful ways of letting go of the old by welcoming the new. Not that one's sins merit anything less than shame and bitter regret. Nor does one's radical evil cease in its capacity to become actual evil. Tanabe sees the ethical perspective of repentance and the metanoetic perspective of forgiveness as both valid and mutually contradictory. But forgiveness is the larger concept, incorporating ethical consciousness as a presupposition within itself and freeing the self from crippling memories. Those memories are valuable safeguards against pride. But just as we want to avoid static concepts, we also want to avoid crystallization of emotions. Is this last suggestion consistent with the core of metanoetics? Probably no, if *Philosophy as Metanoetics* is taken as canonical and stages 5 and 6 are tightly constrained by stage 3. Otherwise, perhaps, yes.

BEAUTY

The "wondrous" grace of Other-power is our introduction to beauty. But how far may beauty be said to extend into human life? Continuing Kierkegaard's radical distinction between aesthetic and religious modes of life, Tanabe sustains a radical critique of aestheticism as a hedonistic, upper-class, ethnocentric, indulgence of immediacy whether in artistic creation (self-expression) or contemplation, a serene betrayal of the dialectic of nothingness into the hands of a naive intuition that can only provide the illusion of basking in pantheistic union with the absolute.[14] But neither will Tanabe identify with the moralistic rejection of pleasure. Against each mistaken alternative he heralds

the joy and fullfillment of love in human social existence. . . .

[14] See PM, 168, 47, 98, 167, 262, 265, 283.

In the negativity of the Great Nay, love has something in common with moralistic austerity; and in the gratitude and joy of the Great Compassion, it can also partake of the aesthetic enjoyment of culture. Love synthesizes both as aspects of itself and transforms negation into a mediator of affirmation (265).

The key to metanoetical *aesthetics* is the concept of symbol. A symbol, e.g., "the lotus in the fire" (191), transcends expression and cultural formation (*Bildung*) and incorporates absolute mediation within it (42). A symbol is also defined by the action-response required to comprehend it:

> The material existence and spiritual meaning of the symbol do not coincide immediately and inseparably here as they do in expression, but are . . . united relatively through action (263).

Symbolic speech conveys that behind every intuition lies nothingness; indeed, everything is a symbol of nothingness (183). Since symbol is defined by its mediating function, Kant's concepts of God, freedom, and immortality are included (43); so is Amida Buddha (212). But that functional definition also enables Tanabe to use "shining darkness" as a metanoetical symbol (189) while rejecting Heidegger's "bright night of the dread of nothingness" (84) as latent ontologism.

The tension of Tanabe's struggle to integrate dialectic and religious experience is dissipated when poetry shines forth, such as when Tanabe quotes Zen poets or Shinran, when his own luminosity radiates in the prose, and when he expresses himself symbolically. Thus it is no accident that Tanabe uses poetry to convey central truths about the resurrected life in *mu* (49, 153, 157, 172).[15] And his supremely dramatic conclusion to the book is an elaboration of the image of spiritual reality as an ellipse with the Dharmākara as the visible son of the unseen Father,

---

[15] Three of these, drawn from Zen, identify the stage of resurrected living with stage four negation. The stages of frustration in antinomy and the invasion of Other-power fall away. Stage five unification persists simply in the identification of negation and freedom.

[16] One can find in both Buddhism and Christianity the concept of humankind as the children of a divine Father. Cf. from Nichiren's Dedication to the Lotus, "Our hearts ache and our sleeves are wet (with tears), until we see face to

surrounded by the finite beings in a communion of mutuality ordered by spiritual teachings (294-95).[16]

What about the *beauties of nature?* Nature and history fall outside one another in *Philosophy as Metanoetics*. Tanabe's intellectual-moral rigor almost wholly dominates his response to nature. He is repelled by the notion, which he attributes to Kant, of identifying God and nature, since it "brings religion perilously close to art" (267). Tanabe speaks of the Taoist hermit falling into a subethical "state of nature" (171); "naturalism" names a constricted philosophy; and a "natural" view of religion connotes reductionism (268). The desire for deliverance from *saṃsāra* is a "demand of nature" (289). Nature is delivered up to natural science, whose business is "to replace myths with laws" (295). Indeed, Tanabe, strictly speaking, writes not so much about resurrection to new life as about resurrection to a state which is neither death nor life (55). He does assert that "there are no grounds for preferring artistic pleasures over material ones" (265). But, except for resurrected wonder and gratitude and the pangs of repentance, he generally deprecates feelings (174, 180).[17] He tends toward a dualism between the realm of freedom and the realm of determinism within the self, a dualism which arguably impedes the liberty of resurrected living.

How shall metanoetics develop a rich appreciation of the beauties of nature? While acknowledging the mystery that things are and that things are the way they are (295), Tanabe rejects the concept of a Creator on account of the mutual implication of absolute and relative and the beginninglessness of the relative (23; 242).[18] Can Tanabe regard the beauties of nature as the gift (*gensō*, the return from the Pure Land) of nothingness (291, 292)?

---

face the tender figure of the One, who says to us, 'I am thy Father.'" Quoted in William Theodore de Bary, ed. *The Buddhist Tradition in India, China, and Japan* (New York: Random House, 1972), 349. This concept preserves the relative independence of brothers and sisters and affirms at the same time a relatedness which removes atomistic individualism. Any substantive affirmation of humankind as a family, however, comes into tension with Tanabe's high claims about the role of the nation (species, politically articulated culture) which can be called "sacred" inasmuch as it mediates the absolute (284, 28,88).

[17] See Hegel, *Lectures on the Philosophy of Religion*, 121, 138, 143.

[18] Tanabe does not exploit this insight for its potential to resolve Kant's first antinomy, that the world must and cannot have a beginning in space and time.

Mu, after all, is artistic, uses *upāya*, skillful means, whereby absolute mediation transpires (22, 42). The need for a more replete meta-noetical aesthetic is not trivial, since it affects how far love, art, and authentic temporality involve our perceptual and bodily life.

GOODNESS

Among the values of truth, beauty, and goodness, Tanabe's emphasis on action effectively assigns priority to goodness. Tanabe rejects Hegel's identical reason in favor of Kant's practical faith, in order to "mediate knowledge and faith by action" (57). We have traced his critique of aestheticism. He has a similar critique of what we could call "aletheism." He criticizes a merely hermeneutic standpoint (82, 78, 86). And he levels the charge of merely contemplative mysticism at the tendency to interrogate praxis only for its contribution to theory (89). He writes that the "realization of a higher and deeper self is based on a breakthrough, an overcoming of the self in action. This is why action becomes the mediator of self-consciousness" (72). Therefore he treats religious and philosophical consciousness as action, not contemplation. The action of actions is interaction with the absolute as "one casts oneself into absolute mediation" (257).[19]

Authentic goodness is to participate in the *ōsō-gensō* process of the Dharmākara, whose discipline of self-perfection (*ōsō*) culminated in the manifold vow to save all beings (*gensō*). We (except for "sages and saints") cannot manage the arduous ascent of *ōsō*, but in repentance we can open ourselves immediately to the influx of Other-power. Tanabe's metanoesis thus solves a problem widely faced in religion—how to maintain a vital unity between the inner orientation to transcendence and outward service to others. What if striving for God consumes one's major energies? What if one must first master a philosophic labyrinth before emerging into the light of natural living? Or what if service projects so monopolize

---

[19] Tanabe does not attempt to integrate modern ethical theories in the light of a religious theory of action. For that project, see Jean Nabert, *Elements for an Ethic* (Evanston: Northwestern University Press, 1969). Tanabe's repentance is comparable to Nabert's three-fold negation—the experience of fault, the meaning of failure, and the deepening of solitude. This negation of self prepares the way for an absolute affirmation, the beginning of a spiritual ethic.

one's attention that primal spiritual contact is neglected? When these two sides of the spiritual life fall apart, the result is a monastic asceticism which loses its social conscience or a social activism which loses its spiritual fragrance. Tanabe's philosophy achieves a striking integration of these two sides. The practice of repentance short-circuits the potentially endless human effort to climb towards the Absolute. Rather, *zange* is simply an opening to Other-power whose grace is already there. But secondly, Other-power is understood as Compassion itself, so that the natural outworking of spiritual restoration is service: ". . . gratitude issues in an enthusiasm to act on behalf of others" (48). Metanoetical thinking is located within these two vectors of spiritual action—(1) repentant opening to Other-power and (2) the resurrected life that follows.

One of Tanabe's key concepts is the axis of transformation, the fulcrum against which Other-power can apply its lever of power. At times Tanabe speaks as though we can only find salvation through the mediation of other beings (22), but it is not clear how to identify the axis of transformation. If the point is that the Absolute does not work directly on a given relative being, R_1, but only through another relative being, R_2, then the question remains how the Absolute gets R_2 to work on R_1, except, perhaps, by persuading R_3 to get involved. At some point a more direct influence must occur if this way of talking is to be sustained. And this is what we find. Faith in the present can become an axis of transformation of the past (241). And ". . . the center of the self, which is at the same time the axis of absolute transformation, is located in the decision of each religious existence . . ." (10). I interpret this to mean that the center of the self is the transcendence-in-immanence which requires decision as its axis of transformation.

Tanabe grounds participation in history in the deepest layer of self-consciousness, our temporal structure of past, future, and present. We are "thrown" into a situation in which we must simply accept the contingency of historical facts. They are what they are; we cannot ground them in reason. The past "determines our existence in such a way that our existence has to avail itself of its mediation in order to achieve authenticity" (65). But we are not the prisoners of the past. It is our freedom to project into the future. Indeed "negation and transformation of the past" are involved in any action (211). Authentic existence, moreover, highlights a most intimate aspect of the past—its own misdeeds. Repentance now determines what will be taken from the past (161). The past accepts "the continual renewal of its meaning," while the future renews the past "from its own deeper sources," and without the tradition of the past the future "cannot produce any creative content" (241).

Tanabe rehearses Shinran's teaching that "the future-oriented desire for rebirth is transformed by metanoesis for the past into the sincere mind of action of no-action" (221, 218). Eternal nothingness is present in the mutual mediation of past and future (277). In Tanabe's culminating metaphysical symbol of the ellipse, the two foci of past and future generate cycles of activity (292).

What hope for *character achievement* does Tanabe hold forth? He appreciates Hegel's critique of the confident and exclusive "beautiful soul" that presumes itself to be supreme and good (266). By insisting on the "radical evil" that remains after conversion, the continued capacity for or tendency toward sin, Tanabe discourages optimistic expectations of growth. He tends to regard saints and sages as almost a different variety of the human species. Moreover, the joy of the Great Compassion is eternity in time; one does not think of growth in that delight. But Tanabe does offer one goal to hope for—naturalness that stems from sustained fidelity to nothingness as Other-power. That naturalness not only reflects the soul peace and trust in action of unified, affirmative living; it also leads one, as the situation requires, into and through the contradiction and pain and humiliation of repeated repentance.

Tanabe's Metanoetics:
The Failure of Absolutism

Jamie HUBBARD

THE ideas of the so-called Kyoto School have caused a great flurry of excitement in the West, particularly among theologians and philosophers of religion. I must preface my comments with the disclaimer that these ideas belong no more to my usual field of study than does Tanabe *tetsugaku*. Furthermore, I am limited by a lack of access to the Japanese originals of their collected works. However, I do recognize the tenor of the Buddhist tradition from which they speak, and I would go so far as to say that despite their massive use and critique of the concepts of the Western tradition, and regardless of the route of study and reflection by which they arrived at their conclusions, the categories, concerns, and problem areas dealt with in Nishida, Tanabe, and Nishitani (the major thinkers of this school known to the West) are precisely those of the East Asian Buddhist tradition. My comments, then, will attempt to contextualize the three papers presented on this panel in light of that tradition.

PHILOSOPHY AS METANOETICS AND TANABE'S METANOIA

It is fitting that we finish up our symposium on Tanabe Hajime's thought with a discussion of its implications for society, for, as all three papers point out, Tanabe was centrally concerned with the specifics of the real world; his philosophy is said to be born of those specifics.[1] It is somewhat difficult, however, to reconcile this

---

[1] Takeuchi, in his introduction to *Philosophy as Metanoetics*, writes that "the dialectics of the logic of species represent a system of thought that demands a perspective on the real world" (PM, xliii). In his paper Himi echoes this, writing that Tanabe was "a philosopher who thought it important to apply his theories to the real world" (303). Ultimately, concludes Professor Laube, "his approach

intense personal and philosophical concern for historical reality and social justice with the consistent charges raised against Tanabe (and the Kyoto school in general) for not merely having fanned the fires of wartime fanaticism but actively stoked them. The charges of racism and militarism leveled against Nishida and Nishitani, but especially brought against Tanabe, have not faded with the years. As early as the mid-1930's writers in Japan (Tosaka Jun and Nanbara Shigeru, among others) warned of the absolutist or totalitarian tendencies of the philosophers of Kyoto Imperial University, and these charges are still made today.[2] John Dower, for example, widely acknowledged as one of the foremost scholars of wartime Japan and author of *War Without Mercy: Race & Power in the Pacific War*, writes:

> For all their abstract theorizing [about such broad and amorphous concepts as "perpetual war" and "total war"; "life space" and "historical space"] . . . the Kyoto School also made it clear that the current conflict represented Japan's ascension as the leading world-historical race.[3]

Some wish to describe the role played by the philosophy of Nishida, Tanabe, and their students as something beyond their control, an unfortunate twisting of their ideas by unscrupulous militarists in a way that was unrelated to the original aims of the philosophers.[4] Himi, for example, writes that Tanabe was "at bottom neither imperialistic nor militaristic," and that "he saw his own words twisted by the nationalists to purposes other than his own" (303). Although we can sympathize with the difficulty of

---

clearly belongs to the ethical way of philosophy" (337); Wattles concurs that Tanabe's main contribution to ethics is his philosophy of action, that his philosophy is thus action-oriented, dominated by goodness. In the preface to *Philosophy as Metanoetics*, Tanabe himself writes that his metanoia was brought about by a wrenching awareness of the dismal failure of his thought to adequately respond to the historical reality, the thorough failure of the Japanese war effort; this realization in turn led to the birth of his philosophy as metanoetics (PM, 1).

[2] See Heisig, 13-14; Peter N. Dale, *The Myth of Japanese Uniqueness* (St. Martins Press, 1986), 196.

[3] John Dower, *War Without Mercy: Race & Power in the Pacific War* (Pantheon, 1986), 227.

[4] Heisig, PM, xvii. Note that in his contribution to this collection, he has again taken up this question to "redress the exaggerations of earlier comments."

standing against the tide, this view of a scholar's responsibility for the impact of his or her intellectual stance is dangerous, to say the least. In the case of Tanabe and other Japanese intellectuals it seems especially disingenuous: Nishida, Tanabe, Kōosaka, and others all contributed their ideas to the war effort in much more positive fashion than we are often led to believe. Their wartime writings on such topics as the "Philosophy of Total War" and "The Logical and Historical Nature of the Greater East Asian Co-prosperity Sphere" hardly seem to indicate a passive stance on these matters.[5] One writer has said that while the Kyoto philosophers' ideas in general were co-opted to support a racist form of militarism, in the case of "Tanabe Hajime's articles on the 'logic' of social and national existence—the question was not one of cooptation so much as virtual, albeit unintended, prostitution."[6] Perhaps unintended, yet Tanabe himself assumes full responsibility when he writes of the "collective responsibility for every event that takes place in our society" and his refusal to find any room for "excusing the standpoint of the innocent bystander so often adopted by members of the intelligentsia" (PM, liv).

It seems to me clear that he did lend his considerable talents to the war effort;[7] it seems equally clear, as he wrote in *Philosophy as Metanoetics*, that he felt deeply that he had betrayed society as well as self for having done so. Yet, the logic of species continued to serve as the dialectical model for his philosophy as metanoetics. What has changed?

RÉSUMÉ OF THE PAPERS

The three papers of this panel have all, in one way or another, addressed the question of the place of society and the world in Tanabe's thought. Granting that Tanabe's goal was to criticize the blind nationalism of his time rather than aid its development,

---

[5] Cited in Dower, 351, n. 46. See also Heisig, 13-14.

[6] Andrew Barshay, *State and Intellectual in Imperial Japan* (University of California Press, 1988), 30.

[7] Considering the equally racist and imperialist morality of the Allies at this point in time, I have no intention of throwing stones; perhaps the difference is that the victorious Allies were never forced to experience repentance and thus their attitude continues unchecked to this day.

Professor Himi's paper seeks to understand where his critique went astray. Jeffrey Wattles seeks to abstract a philosophy of living from Tanabe's *Philosophy as Metanoetics*, and Johannes Laube relates Tanabe's thought to general Buddhist notions of Bodhisattva practice. All three papers, then, attempt to delineate the place of the real world, real people, or real practice in the thought of Tanabe. Although all three papers have clarified important points in Tanabe's work, it seems to me that they miss a fatal flaw at the most basic level of his philosophy, a flaw that precluded any real implementation of a social or religious philosophy of Buddhist compassion such as one might expect from a Shinran-inspired philosopher. Ironically, the same flaw allowed Tanabe and others to twist his thought to serve the ends of wartime totalitarianism. The flaw is absolutism.

ABSOLUTISM

ABSOLUTISM AS A THEME IN THE KYOTO SCHOOL

If there is one term that marks Tanabe's discourse (and that of the Kyoto school in general) it is absolutism: *absolute* mediation, *absolute* repentance, *absolute* nothingness, *absolute* disruption, *absolute* transformation, *absolute* critique, *absolute* Other-power, and so on. Dictionaries define *absolute* to mean free, unrelated, unmediated, unconditioned; this derives from the Latin root of the word, *absolvere*, which means to set free or absolve. The basic meaning, then, is something that is set apart from, self-sufficient, not qualified in any way, as in the absolute power of a monarch, or, in grammatical usage, a part of speech that is independent or able to stand on its own. *Zettai*, the Japanese rendering of absolute, is a recent term (used mostly in Chinese and Japanese for Western mathematical and philosophical ideas), composed of the characters for "to cut off" and "facing, opposed, *related*." Thus the Japanese also carries the sense of "without relation, independent, unmediated."

WESTERN ROOTS OF TANABE'S ABSOLUTISM

The three papers under consideration all document the influence of Western categories in Tanabe's work, and it is worthwhile to keep this influence in mind. In the German idealist tradition from which Tanabe draws, for example, the absolute has usually referred to that which is unconditioned, or without cause, as in Kant's "absolutely necessary being," Bradley's "harmonious non-relational whole," or Hegel's "Absolute as the Whole" (God).[8] It is fair to say that most of these thinkers were striving to understand an ontology that admitted of a logically universal yet non-contingent reality (read God) existing in relation with a contingent world. Through all of this there runs a concern for a transcendent reality as the ground of contingent appearance, a harmonious and unrelated (unmediated) Being, consistent and unified in nature, yet somehow validating or grounding relative, finite, plural existence.

The way this Absolute mediates the existence of contingent being varied greatly, of course, from losing the merely apparent separateness of individuality in a blur of monism to the absolute existence of individuals within a non-real phenomenal world—indicative, I believe, of the difficulty of establishing a relationship between the phenomenal world of relatives and a logical, ontological, and epistomological other (the otherness of which stems primarily from its homogeneous and non-contingent nature). It seems to me that Tanabe and others of the Kyoto school are wrestling with exactly these same issues, those of relation vs. independence, universal vs. particular existence, etc., though their own *episteme* includes Buddhist developments in the Zen and Pure Land traditions as well as the Western problematic.

Tanabe's contribution to this tradition is a sophisticated expression of the mediation of the absolute by the relative itself along the lines of Buddhist non-duality, expressed in terms of *tariki* and *jiriki* (PM, 8). As Laube states:

> In dubbing his philosophy a *tariki-tetsugaku* (Other-power philosophy), he seems to have forgotten that according to his own dialectics of absolute mediation, he should really call it a *jiriki-tariki-tetsugaku* (self-power/Other-power philosophy), or perhaps better a *tariki-jiriki tetsugaku* (Other-power/ self-power philosophy) (338).

---

[8] It might have been instructive had Nishida, Tanabe, and others brought their comparative skills to bear on the work of G. E. Moore, Wittgenstein, William James, and others who not only rejected the idealist and absolutist philosophies but also are often compared more favorably to the philosophical and soteriological tenor of the Buddhist tradition.

BUDDHIST ROOTS OF TANABE'S ABSOLUTISM

Tanabe's metanoesis centered around his conversion-and-resurrection, which he describes as a "regeneration to a new life . . . granted to me from the transcendent realm of the absolute . . . defined as absolute nothingness" (PM, li). "Absolute nothingness" refers to the Buddhist notion of emptiness, *śūnyatā*; emptiness, of course, refers to a lack of permanent and independent existence and thereby the simultaneous affirmation of impermanent, related existence. Tanabe, fully in keeping with the Mahāyāna Buddhist tradition, affirms this: the experience of absolute nothingness is none other than nothingness-*qua*-love or, in traditional Buddhist terms, the wisdom of emptiness and the implementation of that wisdom in compassionate action. Yet we must exercise caution at this point, lest we lose sight of Tanabe's contributions in a muddle of Buddhological reductionism. We still need to consider carefully the structure of Tanabe's absolute and its relationship to the relative, and, indeed, that is where he poured most of his considerable talents and religious fervor.

Recognizing the importance of this relationship, Jeffrey Wattles organizes his paper around "six stages in transformed living" abstracted from Tanabe's thought. This higher-level ordering he feels necessary in order to account for a) the relationship between the relative and the absolute (self and Other) and b) how religious philosophy can produce a "philosophy of living for the broad category in which Tanabe includes himself: 'ordinary, ignorant people'" (341).

Wattles has surely gone to the heart of the matter; but rather than attempt to resolve these problems through a higher-level ordering (a kindness which renders his paper a sort of apologetic), I would ask if they do not rather point to a defect in Tanabe's approach rendered by the incessant references to the absolute. Absolutes, of course, are usually considered anathema to the Buddhist tradition, and the critique of absolutism is found in almost all strata of Buddhist thought, usually translated as the critique of "eternalism."

In the early Buddhist thought of the *Nikāyas* the target is the notion of *sat*, or existence defined as self-caused, i.e., a unity that logically precludes differentiating between cause and effect. (Later this came to be known as the *satkāryavāda* theory of the

Sāṃkhya).[9] This understanding of an absolute was rejected primarily because it contradicted the Buddha's experience of a causally determined world, a world that admitted of no unchanging existence (such as an effect which was the same as its cause). Further, the notion of such an absolute was seen to lead to a denial of the plurality of the phenomenal world as appearance, illusion, merely "adventitious," and thereby encompassing a moral nihility in the bargain.[10] The point relevant to our discussion is that an absolute, *by definition* as well as general usage, is seen to have the same attributes as the target of the Buddhist critique of eternalism, i.e., homogeneity, non-contingency, permanence, non-relation, etc. Still, the difficulties of personal and material identity through time and the human proclivity for completeness, continuity, and stability led to a variety of forms of absolutism creeping into the Buddhist tradition.[11] Among these may be counted the *svabhāva* theory[12] and the notion of *asaṃskṛta* (unconditioned) dharmas in the non-Mahāyāna, perhaps the *ālayavijñāna*,[13] and especially the idea of *tathāgatagarbha* as both cause and result in the Mahāyāna. Although the tradition vigorously debates all of these ideas on their philosophical and religious merits, in contemporary times it seems as though the uncritical use of the Western notion of an absolute to describe Buddhist highest goals and realizations has allowed absolutism to again creep into the tradition.[14]

---

[9] This continued to be a central thrust of the Buddhist critique of Being; cf. Chapter XX of Nāgārjuna's *Mūlamadhyamakārikā*, which explicitly takes up the question of the identity or difference of cause and effect.

[10] Cf. David Kalupahana, *Causality: The Central Philosophy of Buddhism*, 6-15.

[11] For a contemporary and engrossing exposition of some of the difficulties in the Buddhist critique of the notion of enduring substance see Paul Griffiths, *On Being Mindless* (Open Court, 1986).

[12] Inasmuch as the notion of *svabhāva* may fairly be considered an attempt to answer the question of identity of a thing through time it is interesting that Wattles, reviewing Tanabe's view of personal identity, concludes that "Tanabe acknowledges the need for a ground or unity underlying the temporal process" (352).

[13] Cf. L. Schmithausen's suggestion that the notion of the *ālaya* is borrowed from the Sāṃkhya in order to account for the problem of the continuity of the person; L. Schmithausen, *Ālayavijñāna: On the Origin and the Early Development of a Central Concept of Yogācāra Philosophy* (Tokyo: The International Institute for Buddhist Studies, 1987), 28ff. Cf. Griffiths, *On Being Mindless*, 91ff.

[14] This has not gone unnoticed: David Kalupahana has gone far in arguing

ORIGINAL ENLIGHTENMENT

One of the more problematic areas in this regard is the wide-spread Japanese acceptance of the doctrine of original enlighten-ment (*hongaku*). Related to the *tathāgatagarbha* and Buddha-nature theories, this teaches that our original nature is that of enlight-enment, thus guaranteeing access to, or, in the case of the dom-inant Japanese reading, asserting the continuous existence of, the state of perfected Buddhahood. Laube has written that Shinran does not subscribe to the prevailing original enlightenment theo-ries of his day (319), primarily because of Shinran's radically pes-simistic assessment of sentient beings' capacity for practice and attainment. I am not so sure that such an assessment of our lived reality has anything to do with the theory of original enlighten-ment, and in fact it is usually held to be precisely the existence of our originally enlightened nature that allows deluded beings to respond to the compassion of Amida: without this original pu-rity there could be no recognition of or response to Amida. Shin-ran, for example, wrote:

> Buddha-nature is none other than Tathāgata. This Tathāgata pervades the countless worlds; it fills the hearts and minds of the ocean of all beings. Thus, plants, trees, and land all attain Buddhahood. Since it is with these hearts and minds of all sen-tient beings that they entrust themselves to the Vow of the dharma-body as compassionate means (*hōben hosshin no sei-gan*), this *Shinjin* is none other than Buddha-nature. This Bud-dha-nature is dharma-nature. Dharma-nature is the dharma-body.[15]

---

against any form of absolutism in early Buddhism, especially the uncritical as-sumption of such by T. R. V. Murti, Stcherbatsky, and others. More recently, scholars in Japan have vigorously attacked the notion of *tathāgatagarbha* as struc-turally identical to the monism of the *ātman-brahman* tradition. Cf. Hakamaya Noriaki 袴谷憲昭 , 本覚思想批判 *[A Critique of Original Enlightenment Theory]* (Tokyo: Daizō, 1989). For a brief résumé of this work, as yet untranslated, see the review by Paul Swanson in *Japanese Journal of Religious Studies* 17/1 (1990): 89-91. See also N. Hakamaya, "A Critique of the Kyoto School," in *Critical Bud-dhism* (Tokyo: Daizō, 1990).

[15] *Yuishinshō mon'i*, in Y. Ueda and D. Hirota, *Shinran: An Introduction to His Thought* (Kyoto: Hongwanji International Center, 1989), 265; Cf. *Jōdo wasan*,

Tamura Yoshirō, one of the foremost scholars of the Japanese development of *hongaku*, identifies it as the basic structure of Shinran's thought,

> an affirmation mediated by negation, absoluteness in relativity. . . a synthesis by sublation (*Aufhebung*) of both the absolute monism and affirmation of factual reality of Tendai's Original Awakening thought and the relative dualism and negation of factual reality of Hōnen's Pure Land Nembutsu conception.[16]

Still, Professor Laube makes the important point that Tanabe's philosophy "does not represent a faithful reinterpretation of historical Mahāyāna or of Shinran's Amidalogy" (325). Indeed, Tanabe tends to castigate Buddha-nature thought as typical of a Zen circularity of self-identity in which there has not yet been a "self-negating transformation" (PM, 169). In place of an original purity, Tanabe avers evil as a "negative determination of our being itself that lies at the foundation of human existence in general" (PM, 4) and explains this evil as "the tenacity of egoity [which] can never be avoided in any act brought about directly by will. This is our radical evil" (PM, 188). This would seem to substantiate the position that Tanabe does not subscribe to Buddha-nature ideas, in which salvation is a matter of removing the accidental dross (*āgantukakleśa*), an "arithmetical subtraction" which reveals that which has always existed, pure and untainted (*tathāgatagarbha*). Unless, that is, our constitutive "metaphysical self" is defined as originally enlightened while our accidental ("ethical") self is defined as foolish and evil. In this case, though, we are back to a model of no essential change. This is not a transformational model of religious experience, in which a deluded or sinful person undergoes fundamental change and is reborn into wisdom or grace.

The issues surrounding this teaching in the Buddhist tradition

---

hymn #94, partially quoted in PM, 215; see also the many passages on Buddha-nature quoted in the *Kyōgyōshinshō*. This of course begs the question of the differences between Buddha-nature and Original Enlightenment, a distinction made, for example, by Dōgen.

[16] Tamura Yoshirō, "Critique of Original Awakening Thought in Shōshin and Dōgen," *Japanese Journal of Religious Studies*, 11/2-3 (1984), 254. Similarly, although Laube has included the "Zen school" as proponents of *hongaku* thought, most research stresses Dōgen's vehement opposition to the idea (cf. Hakamaya, *A Critique of Original Enlightenment Theory*).

are manifold, but they include (again) the question of whether the cause and result are the same (*satkāryavāda*), and if so, how the inherently pure nature and the accidental defilements came to be related in the first place, etc. Generally and with many caveats it can be said that this understanding dominated the East Asian Buddhist sphere, while a transformational model prevailed in the Indo-Tibetan and Theravādan traditions.

That having been said, the importance of Tanabe's resurrection of self-power is not to be underestimated. Both Laube and Wattles recognize this. Wattles states, "Tanabe wants to avoid the danger of too easily ascribing every movement of repentant mind to the guidance of Other-power" (344). Laube cites Tanabe:

> By placing too much emphasis here on the Other-power, we end up in the usual position of claiming that whatever action sentient beings perform is done *qua* the Great Action of Tathā-gata. . . . By the same token, persistence in this position lands us in a sort of mysticism that places the action of the Tathāgata and the action of the sentient beings in a relationship of contradictory self-identity (PM, 274-275).

Hence the transformation involved in the death and resurrection of the subject in Tanabe's thought seems to speak more directly to a transformational model of spirituality than to a model of arithmetical subtraction. It seems to me that in his opposition to Nishida's Zen-styled identity of opposites Tanabe wanted first and foremost to retain Shinran's profound understanding of the existential depths of human frailty, and so refused a simple identity of absolute and relative. Yet, the structure of existentially constitutive evil also logically demands an Other to begin the process of transformation. Tanabe still could not push far enough to a completely *jiriki* model of transformational religious practice because of this and his acceptance of the deeply embedded notion of the Absolute as an existent, empowering *force* in the process of transformation.[17] Thus he could not take the most important

---

[17] Cf. Stephen H. Phillips, "Nishitani's Buddhist Response to 'Nihilism'," *Journal of the American Academy of Religion* 55/1, in which the author discusses Nishitani's notion of emptiness as "a unitary field and force." The notion that emptiness functions more positively than simply as the lack of permanence (which thereby allows change) is another issue of long-standing debate.

step and simply throw out the notion of the Absolute; and, in the case of transformation, we are still left with the question of the origin of the repentant attitude: is it self, or is it Other?[18]

SELF-POWER OR OTHER-POWER?

This relates to another issue raised by Laube (as well as Professors Ueda and Unno), that is, there appears to be self-power lurking in Tanabe's Other-power, which would clearly separate his stance from the more radical insistence on Other-power found in Shinran. It also speaks to the most basic problem in Buddhist forms of absolutism (present in the Christian doctrine of grace as well), namely, how is movement toward salvation effected from the standpoint of ignorant living beings if the structure of the Other is, in fact, *logically* other? "Between being and nothingness," writes Tanabe, "there can be no such relative relationship" (PM, 234). Wattles speaks of this as the "fundamental concept in religion, the concept of Other-power, or, put more generally, the conviction that there is some *other* person, reality, or level beyond the relative or mundane," and remarks that Tanabe responds to this question with the "the life and rigor and warmth of Mahāyāna Buddhism" (346), a warmth which Wattles deigns to elaborate.

As noted above, Tanabe means by Other no more nor less than emptiness. Emptiness, however, is simply a lack of something, a lack of any inherent or ultimately existing nature, and to signify it as Other is, I believe, a religious move to deny the psychology of self-centered grasping; it does not posit an alterity, ontic or otherwise, which must be mystically fused with self. I believe that Tanabe's significant contribution lies in the clear recognition of this within the context of Shin faith (hence the *jiriki*), yet because of the Western influences on his thought, the pervading East Asian affirmation of the positive virtues of emptiness, Buddha-nature, and the like, and a lack of attention to the long debate in the Buddhist analytic tradition regarding the dangers of such affirmation, he persists in talk of the Absolute Other, landing him

---

[18] Professor Unno highlights this contradiction in Tanabe's thought (there can be no self-power in a doctrine of constitutive evil and absolute reliance on Other-power) when he concludes that Tanabe's *zange* is, after all, a path for sages and saints (Unno, 127).

in precisely the dilemma of relation alluded to by Wattles and criticized in the Buddhist tradition from its inception. This is why in the 5th stage, "philosophical unity," Wattles is concerned that:

> A true Infinite must somehow include the finite; a true absolute must include the relative. . . . It must validate the heterological religious orientation to transcendence insofar as one is saved by, feels gratitude to, and obeys the Focus (348-49).

While it seems plausible that a monistic Absolute or perhaps the God of contemporary Christian discourse might feel itself weighed down by such an imperative, I think that Buddhist ultimacy (either as the doctrines of causality and emptiness or the experience of Buddhahood) has precisely negated such a focus. If we try to understand how "the Absolute is mediated by the relative" in the context of Nāgārjuna, for example, it would mean simply that there are no emptinesses apart from the things empty, emptinesses are dependently established in relation to the conventional existences, and when those conventional existences pass away so does the emptiness dependent upon them—there is no infinite, functioning emptiness swooshing around the universe, relating to dependent beings and thereby validating its own existence. Apart from the particular (the empty), there is no universal (emptiness), established from its own side, independent of what is negated.[19]

REASON AND METANOIA: THE RADICAL DISJUNCTION OF SUDDEN ENLIGHTENMENT?

Another aspect of Tanabe's thought that I believe betrays the influence of Buddhist absolutism is his oft-heralded notion of the "death of theoretical and practical autonomous human reason," the "impotence of reason to reconcile its contradictions" (Wattles, 341). This position is characteristic of the teaching of sudden enlightenment (see below), an anti-intellectual stance common to both Ch'an and Pure Land traditions and popular in Western interpretations of Buddhism generally. Such a position, however, renders his entire philosophical edifice, post-metanoia as it is, au-

---

[19] Cf. Jeffrey Hopkins, "Ultimate Reality in Tibetan Buddhism," *Buddhist-Christian Studies* 8 (1988): 118-121; David Kalupahana, *Nāgārjuna: The Philosophy of the Middle Way* (Albany: State University of New York Press, 1986), 85-86.

tonomous and non-mediated for those of us who have not experienced *zange* — it logically has value only for Tanabe. Similarly, Wattles claims that Tanabe stands firmly on "the ground upon which alone that [psychological or historicist] critique could be defeated," (343) i.e., on the ground of his metanoetic experience, a clearly self-validating experience of repentance and resurrection. Laube also remarks that "the philosophy as metanoetics regards itself as dialectically *above* all of these, as a universal religious philosophy transcending all Western and Eastern traditions up to the present" (328). The philosophical difficulties of self-validating experiences are legion *and* notorious, including the arrogance of the triumphalist seen here. Such a position certainly has dubious utility for furthering interesting discussions![20]

On the other hand, to paraphrase Mark Twain, the reports of the death of autonomous human reason are greatly exaggerated. William Wainwright, for example, has made the point that we cannot simply shift our focus to religious experience and dismiss the propositions that people make about their religious beliefs as unimportant to religious life.[21] From the earliest times the Buddhist tradition also has related the path of rigorous, conceptual, critical analysis to the ultimate fruit of enlightenment. In fact, that it were not so would mean that the experience of things as they are would be an accident with no cause, akin to peach trees growing from acorns![22] Given that Tanabe himself not only used reasoning in his post-metanoetic works, but presumably used theoretical and practical autonomous human reason to get him to the brink of that experience, we need more carefully to describe the place of *pre-metanoetic* reason and practice in his thought.

---

[20] Paul Griffiths has unpacked some of the criticisms of such a position in the philosophy of Nishitani Keiji; see "On the Possible Future of the Buddhist-Christian Interaction," in Minoru Kiyota, ed., *Japanese Buddhism: Its Tradition, New Religions, and Interaction with Christianity* (Tokyo: Buddhist Books International, 1985), 145-61.

[21] William Wainwright, "Wilfred Cantwell Smith on Faith and Belief" in *Religious Studies* 20, (1984): 353-66.

[22] For the early Buddhist attitude towards reason and the experience of truth see K. N. Jayatilleke, *Early Buddhist Theory of Knowledge* (George Allen & Unwin, Ltd., 1963), 418ff.

RELIGIOUS AND MORAL LIFE FOR THE TRULY IGNORANT

The second difficulty raised by Wattles questions how a "religious philosophy can produce a philosophy of living for the broad category in which Tanabe includes himself—'ordinary, ignorant people.'" I take it that this philosophically informed "living" refers to the entire process of the six stages, culminating in the 6th stage, "new life in naturalness," in which philosophy, morality, science, and other activities are again allowed, the "promised land of truth, beauty, and goodness" (350). Yet it would seem to be the case that the vast majority of *truly* ordinary and ignorant people live their lives solely in the 1st stage, "naive self-confidence," though the whole tenor of Tanabe's thought is such as to deny any validity whatsoever to the human enterprise *before* metanoia. This is clearly brought out in Wattles' schema of stages in transformed living, to which *transformed* is the key—these stages of living speak precious little to "ordinary, ignorant people" before the transforming experience of *zange*. Thus it is appropriate that the stage of the truly ignorant, i.e., the first stage, receives a scant two sentences in Wattles treatment. In this I would judge that for ordinary, ignorant folk, Wattles' stages are true to the tenor of Tanabe's thought, i.e., equally irrelevant. They, too, imply a great conceit or facade of false modesty in continuing to call the resurrected person "ordinary and ignorant."

In the Pure Land tradition generally, but especially in Shinran's thought, there is an explicitly stated disjunction between our acts and the salvation of *shinjin*, solely a function of *tariki*. Shinran's thought, like that of the Zen traditions, is a teaching of sudden enlightenment. The sudden teachings stem naturally from the absolutist position, in that the gulf between an absolute and anything else is, by definition, complete—there is no logical possibility of relation between practice (the conventional, ethical self) and enlightenment (the absolute, metaphysical self).[23] In the Zen tradition this is often phrased in terms of an attack on the conceptual process as not able to lead "beyond" to the non-conceptual, e.g.,

---

[23] See the essays in Peter Gregory, *Sudden and Gradual: Approaches to Enlightenment in Chinese Thought* (Honolulu: University of Hawaii Press, 1987) for discussions of the disjunction between practice and realization in this context.

374 · JAMIE HUBBARD

"If you are trying to attain enlightenment, you are creating and being driven by karma, and you are wasting your time on your black cushion."[24] Tanabe's position on radical evil, cited above, is a good representation of the dilemma necessitating absolute reliance on something outside of one's own constitutive evil (Other-power) typical of the Pure Land tradition. Again, this is the kind of religious and moral paralysis that was criticized by the Buddha as a natural outcome of absolutism.[25] Akin to the extreme of nihilism, it is seen as a form of fundamentalism or essentialism that does not conduce to a moral and (ultimately) religious life.

BODHISATTVA PRACTICE

This leads to the main point of Professor Laube's paper, Tanabe's idea of the "relative *gensō*," i.e., the relative beings who "give a good example of ethico-religious life for the less advanced to imitate" (330). He identifies this as the path of the Mahāyāna bodhisattva.[26] This ethico-religious life of the relative is possible

---

[24] Shunryu Suzuki, *Zen Mind, Beginner's Mind* (Tokyo: Weatherhill, 1970), 99.

[25] The disjunction between relative and absolute leads to the doctrine of action so forcefully and elegantly presented in the *Bhagavadgītā*: the True Self is eternal and unchanging and the phenomenal world of change is illusion; hence, Reality is neither slayer nor slain, so go forth and do your duty on the battlefield (chapter 2). This is precisely the moral vacuity that the Buddhist critique of absolutism attacks.

[26] This part of Laube's paper, though undocumented (one would really would like to have the reference for Śākyamuni's "547 earthly rebirths," (323) is problematic in many respects. One of the most egregious difficulties is the uncritical adoption of the dogma of the Mahāyāna polemic as the basis of his discussion. Simply put, the Hīnayāna practitioner is oriented towards "*nirvāṇa*, the extinction of the individual, passion-ridden self. . . . Each one has to struggle for one's own liberation." The Mahāyāna bodhisattva, Laube contrasts, "refuses the fruition of perfect wisdom for himself, and out of compassionate love turns to others to help bring about their liberation by way of particular salvific means (*upāya*). These means may even include a new incarnation of the Bodhisattva in some form of sentient being or other, according to the needs of those to be saved. This return to the world of sentient beings is what Shinran was later to analyze systematically as *gensō*." The facile move from polemic to actual Buddhist movements, e.g., Theravāda (which he identifies as "Hīnayāna," 323), is not grounded in historical fact, cult, or theory. Laube's suggestion that this distinction of the bodhisattva path was one reason for the emergence of the Mahā-

because the absolute negates itself as the absolute, thereby affirming the relative. This is, of course, the traditional Buddhist teaching that it is precisely the lack of permanent, independent existence that allows the existence of the impermanent, the related. Laube has pointed out that this mutual mediation of the relative in which the relative serves to teach or benefit the relative itself is alien to Shinran's thought, in which the only benefitting of living beings is done by Amida, the absolute *per se* (or others born into the Pure Land and thence returning).

Professors Ueda and Unno have also pointed to this discrepancy in Tanabe's thought, i.e., for Tanabe, the experience of *zange* includes resurrection and hence the possibility of action on the part of the relative. In other words, there is *jiriki* in Tanabe's *tariki*, in this case after the experience of metanoia, whereas in Shinran there can never be any possibility of *jiriki*. As noted above, I feel that this is one of Tanabe's most significant contributions, yet the problem of the absolute persists.

Towards the end of his paper Laube faults Tanabe for not fully explicating this relationship:

> But, we have to ask, is self-negation even a possibility in this world of radical evil to which even the human *gensō* Bodhisattvas belong? How could such individuals ever come to salvific wisdom in such a world as ours? (338)

Again, this is the traditional problem of Absolutist philosophies:

---

yāna does not reflect current understandings of the origins of the institutional Mahāyāna; it doesn't reflect the central role of compassion in Theravāda doctrine and the correspondingly important role of the *bhikkhu* in virtually all aspects of community life; it also does not reflect the fact that the Mahāyāna follower *does* strive for the full enlightenment of Buddhahood so as to be most effective in her or his compassionate activity of *upāya* (Dharmākara being one example that readily jumps to mind). The idea of all beings mutually postponing Buddhahood until everybody else is enlightened is obviously incoherent (nobody could ever attain enlightenment); it would also render the Buddha selfish for actually having attained enlightenment instead of waiting! It is the idea of Buddhahood that changed, and with the denial of Śākyamuni's final nirvana the *Buddha's* continued compassionate activity is ensured. See, for example, Nancy Lethco, "The Bodhisattva Ideal in the *Aṣṭa* and *Pañca Prajñāpāramitā Sūtras*," in *Prajñāpāramitā and Related Systems*, Lewis Lancaster, ed. (Berkeley Buddhist Studies Series, 1977). Gregory Shopen's studies on the origins of the Mahāyāna also indicate the need to correct past assessments.

how can there be movement of any sort between the Absolute and the relative? To simply say that the Absolute is mediated by the relative either changes the nature of the Absolute (as Tanabe recognizes, PM, 234) or leads to self-referential incoherence. What can the contingent being ever do, either individually or as a mutually mediated species, that would approach the non-contingent?

Another question that arises is what do the relative beings teach? Given the absolutely disjunctive "relationship" that prevails between Amida and foolish living beings, what is the purpose of mutual relative mediation? Where could it possibly lead? In the final analysis, how can *jiriki* function in any meaningful sense among the relative if the absolute inequality vis-à-vis the absolute persists? Related to this question is the uncertainty of the status of the relative beings, after *zange*, who are performing relative *gensō*. Is it the sinful teaching sin to the sinful? Or is it a life of "becoming so of itself," *jinen*, a life spontaneously and irrepressibly in accord with the wisdom of Amida?

POLITICAL AND SOCIAL CONSIDERATIONS

This brings us back again to the question of the possibility of a religious philosophy concerned with historical reality and social justice emerging from Tanabe's philosophy as metanoetics. Professor Himi's paper tells us that when all is said and done Tanabe's logic of species is a reflection of the myth of ethnic and racial homogeneity created to help Japanese state-building in the late 19th and early 20th centuries. "We must here distinguish him [Tanabe] clearly from nationalists," Himi writes, for "it was not his intention simply to accept the ethnic substratum without qualification or criticism, but rather to uncover its irrationality and show a way to rationalize it" (306-307). In other words it was not militarism but philosophic concerns that motivated his logic of species, and the fact that it was used to justify a racial view of historical necessity was unintentional.

Nonetheless, Himi notes that Tanabe's philosophy logically recognizes a plurality of species, and closes his paper wondering why he could have fallen into the deification of the Japanese state. "In a word," he contends, "he took only one species, only one state, into consideration. I would even go so far as to say that for Tanabe *species* was really no more than a euphemism for Japanese ethnic unity, and *ōgensonzai* for the Japanese state" (311).

Himi also points to Laube's suggestion that Tanabe confused the ideal National state with the actual Japanese state (311), concluding that his inconsistency was "rooted in a narrowing of consciousness that is not uncommon among the Japanese." Although no doubt this "narrowing of consciousness" played a part in keeping the focus of Tanabe's interest on a particular species (Japan), the existence of a State conceived as the unifying ground of the plurality (citizens) or as the relative Absolute (the "appropriate manifestation of genus or the Absolute") betrays the same tendency to lose the plurality, the messy facts of the relative, *in favor of* the logical other-ness of the unifying ground, the Absolute. This is instructive, inasmuch as this same structure characterizes his metanoetics in spite of the attempt at religious and philosophical affirmation of the relative. The nature of his dialectic has stayed the same. We need to remember that the use of dialectic by Nāgārjuna was not an attempt to display the structure of truth as dialectic, but rather to eliminate the errors that result from such dualism.

CONCLUSION

To sum up, it seems clear to me that, as all three papers claim, Tanabe was quite concerned with the real world, the world of conventional, related existence. He wanted to avoid any reification of emptiness that would render related existence meaningless; he seems to provide a view of the religious person (foolish but repentant beings) that suggests a transformational model of religious cultivation; and he clearly preserves the action-role of the relative, both as *gensō* bodhisattva and as functioning to mediate the Absolute. But this is the hitch: Tanabe's thought is thoroughly colored by the Absolute — the Western notion of an Absolute as well as a Buddhist notion of an active, unified, consistent original purity. Related to this is the radically disjunctive relationship between this purity (Absolute Other-power, etc.) and the relative — the teaching of sudden enlightenment — that makes an Absolute the necessary starting point of repentance at the same time as it forever prevents the relative from reaching it. Thus, in spite of heroic efforts and the intellectual strengths that he brings to his task, he does not adequately address the relationship between Absolute and relative (given that Absolutes are by definition non-related this should not seem surprising) nor can he really provide any philosophy of living for the beings in the pre-*zange* stage; his thought could not lead Tanabe himself beyond his limited subjectivity as a Japanese, nor, apparently, could it give him in life that measure of peace known in Shin circles as "assurance." Tanabe's focus on "truth, and it alone" was a search for the Absolute, a quest, in spite of his professed interest in the relative, for perfected Euclidean constellations of meaning.

Is this just a question of language? Can we simply throw out the term *absolute* and retain the structure of his thought? Is this one word a red herring that has led me to miss the point of Tanabe's thought completely? I think not. It seems to me that all three papers have addressed anomalies in Tanabe's thought that arise precisely in the notion of a related (mediated) absolute and I have tried to indicate that these problems are just those that have fueled Buddhist doctrinal debates for millennia. Langdon Gilkey notes the importance of word choice in this discussion and writes that although the Nothingness of the Kyoto school is clearly an analogical concept which includes being, Buddhists refrain from including Being analogically in their conceptual structure. He also suggests that if they think through Tanabe's arguments they would have to do so (Gilkey, 84).

It seems to me that Tanabe has already done so. Yet he, like many others in the Buddhist tradition, have consistently refused to entertain Being in their discourse because they realized that it packed so very much baggage in terms of the stance we take in the world, our practice, our ethical selves. That is, it conduces to affirm living beings in their belief in and attachment to static entities, independent *things*, selves, and the like. It is well known that Śākyamuni asserted that the Buddhas make use of current forms of speech without being led astray by them; at the same time he was always very careful about clarifying his use of terms like *I* or *self* in his conversations with others, lest they infer the existence of absolutely existing entities from his conventional usage. As sensed by Gilkey, Tanabe's consistent use of terms like *Absolute* and *God* as synonyms for emptiness betray the existence of Being in his Nothingness, in spite of Tanabe's protestations to the contrary.

Although displays of hermeneutical high-wire prowess are the stock in trade of those who would dialogue at Tanabe's level, I think that before a notion of Being is exported from the Buddhist tradition (or imported into it) we should call to mind the Buddha's famous dictum:

> The world rests on the two doctrines Being and Non-Being, but he who rightly sees the *arising* of the world as it really is, does not hold that there is Non-Being in the world and he who rightly sees the *cessation* of things, as it really is, does not hold that there is Being in the world.[27]

For the Buddhist tradition, the notion of Being is structurally equivalent to contemporary ideas of the Absolute. Not merely an intellectual mis-presentation of the way things really are, it is also seen as the psychology of attachment and the attendant inability to deal with simple related existence. The individual as well as the social ethic of Buddhism is based on this realization, a realization that figures in the activities of the enlightened, but is especially important for the truly ignorant and suffering. The failure to realize this, the failure of Absolutism, is similarly understood as not merely personal failure, but failure that enfolds all of society as well. This is also the failure of Tanabe's absolutism.

---

[27] *Saṃyutta Nikāya* II.17, quoted in K. N. Jayatilleke, *Early Buddhist Theory of Knowledge* (Delhi: Motilal Banarsidass, 1963), 317.

Index

INDEX